CHURCHILL'S
PHONEY
WAR

Titles in the series

Studies in Naval History and Sea Power

Studies in Naval History and Sea Power advances our understanding of sea power and its role in global security by publishing significant new scholarship on navies and naval affairs. The series presents specialists in naval history, as well as students of sea power, with works that cover the role of the world's naval powers, from the ancient world to the navies and coast guards of today. The works in *Studies in Naval History and Sea Power* examine all aspects of navies and conflict at sea, including naval operations, strategy, and tactics, as well as the intersections of sea power and diplomacy, navies and technology, sea services and civilian societies, and the financing and administration of seagoing military forces.

CHURCHILL'S
PHONEY
WAR

A Study in Folly
and Frustration

GRAHAM T. CLEWS

Naval Institute Press
Annapolis, Maryland

Naval Institute Press
291 Wood Road
Annapolis, MD 21402

Library of Congress Cataloging-in-Publication Data
Names: Clews, Graham T., author.
Title: Churchill's Phoney War : a study in folly and frustration /
    Graham Thomas Clews.
Description: Annapolis : Naval Institute Press, [2019] | Series: Studies in
    naval history and sea power | Includes bibliographical references and
    index.
Identifiers: LCCN 2019017398 (print) | LCCN 2019981500 (ebook) | ISBN
    9781682472798 (hardcover : alk. paper) | ISBN 9781682472804 (ebook)
Subjects: LCSH: Churchill, Winston, 1874–1965—Military leadership. | World
    War, 1939–1945—Great Britain.
Classification: LCC DA566.9.C5 C553 2019 (print) | LCC DA566.9.C5 (ebook)
    | DDC 940.54/1241—dc23
LC record available at https://lccn.loc.gov/2019017398
LC ebook record available at https://lccn.loc.gov/2019981500

♾ Print editions meet the requirements of ANSI/NISO z39.48-1992 (Permanence of Paper).
Printed in the United States of America.

27 26 25 24 23 22 21 20 19   9 8 7 6 5 4 3 2 1

First printing

Maps drawn by Chris Robinson.

To Juliet,
Marlene, and Tom

Contents

Maps

Acknowledgments

It is impossible to complete any substantial piece of academic research without the assistance and support of many. The risk in acknowledging those who have contributed, supported, or suffered while I have completed this task is that I might overlook or omit. I, therefore, apologize in advance for any omission. First and foremost, I must express my thanks to my family, in particular my wife, Juliet; my son, Amery; and my daughter, Imogen. They have experienced too often my distraction, my frustration, my absence, and my occasional neglect but always remained positive and supportive. I would also like to thank my extended family for their interest and support.

I consider myself especially blessed to have had as my primary supervisor Debbie Lackerstein of the Australian Defence Force Academy (ADFA) School of Humanities and Social Sciences. In every respect her contribution to the completion of this thesis has been above and beyond the call of duty. Her patience and wisdom have been appreciated enormously. There is no doubt this work is the better for her contribution. My thanks, too, to my secondary supervisor, Robin Prior, who was able to find time in a busy schedule to offer important feedback and advice.

I would also like to express more broadly my appreciation to the staff of the ADFA School of Humanities and Social Sciences and the wonderful staff of the ADFA Library for the support given me. In particular I must thank Bernadette McDermott, who came to my rescue on a number of occasions. Additionally, and in no particular order, I would like to thank Craig Stocking, David Lovell, Peter Dennis, Vera Bera, Marilyn Anderson-Smith, and Jennifer Carmody.

This study has benefited greatly from access to primary resources retained at several archives in England. These include the British National Archives; Churchill Archive Centre, Churchill College, Cambridge; National Maritime Museum Archives, Greenwich; Cadbury Research Library (CRL), University of Birmingham; and Nuffield College Archives (NCA), University of Oxford. One of the great joys of historical research is, of course, the "treasure hunt" in the archives. My experience in these archives was made all the more enjoyable by the professional staff who, without exception, offered their time generously to smooth the path of my investigations.

Finally, I wish to acknowledge the assistance of the following at various stages during the completion of this work: Grace and Geoff Kempster, who offered, at various times, extraordinary assistance in accommodation and document searching; also, Chris Bell, David Morgan-Owen, James Levy, Julian Jackson, Hans Houterman (unithistories.com), Sarah Whale (Hatfield House), Natalie Adams (Churchill Archives Centre), and the staff at Deutsches U-Boot Museum.

Abbreviations

ACIGS	assistant chief, Imperial General Staff
ADGB	Air Defence of Great Britain
ASF	Advanced Striking Force
A/SWD	Anti-Submarine Warfare Division
BEF	British Expeditionary Force
BNA	British National Archives, Kew
CAS	chief of the air staff
CIGS	chief of the Imperial General Staff
CNS	chief of naval staff
COS	Chiefs of Staff (Committee)
CS1	First Cruiser Squadron
CS2	Second Cruiser Squadron
DA/SWD	director of the Anti-Submarine Warfare Division
DCNS	deputy chief of naval staff
FAA	Fleet Air Arm
JPS	Joint Planning Staff
KGV	*King George V*–class battleships
LFC	Land Forces Committee
MCC	Military Co-ordination Committee
MEW	Ministry for Economic Warfare
MP	member of Parliament
MSF	Main Striking Force
NID	Naval Intelligence Division
RAF	Royal Air Force
SWC	Supreme War Council
UP	upward projectile weapon
WO	War Office
WRU	*Weekly Return U-Boats*

Introduction

Winston S. Churchill is one of the most studied figures of the twentieth century. Historians have scrutinized his entire life, although his involvement in the two great conflagrations of that century, World Wars I and II, has gained most attention. In these conflicts lie his greatest successes and his most significant failures. However, studies of Churchill in war are uneven in their focus. In assessments of his role in World War I, most attention is unsurprisingly given to his performance as first lord of the Admiralty. For World War II the period after Churchill became prime minister in May 1940 is, also unsurprisingly, most studied. Yet the Phoney War, from September 1939 to May 1940, represents the most extraordinary transformation in his fortunes. The period is bracketed by the end of his "wilderness" years and, nine months later, his assumption of the premiership. With the only work dedicated to Churchill and the Phoney War now over forty years old, this study is a timely reassessment of this important period in Churchill's life.[1]

The aim of this book is to reassess Churchill's contribution to the British war effort during the Phoney War. It explores how Churchill proposed to fight the war and, in particular, how he attempted to animate the Royal Navy, the British War Cabinet, and sometimes the French toward a more aggressive prosecution of the conflict. An important objective will be to understand why, despite his efforts, inaction and inertia prevailed. This study will address the strengths and weaknesses of Churchill's strategic vision and explore the various obstacles that beset this vision as the war progressed.

The core of this work has two parts. Part one considers Churchill's performance as first lord of the Admiralty, with particular attention to his contribution to the anti-U-boat war, his search for a naval offensive, and his attitude toward, and the strategic rationale behind, the wartime naval construction program of 1939–40. Also considered is Churchill's view of aircraft's threat offered to Britain's traditional naval supremacy. Part two considers Churchill's contribution to the wider war effort: his efforts to encourage the War Cabinet to adopt a more aggressive prosecution of the war; his attitude toward Allied air policy; his role in the development and ultimate failure of his two key offensive plans, the Narvik scheme and Operation Royal Marine; and finally, his involvement in and influence on the one great land battle of the Phoney War, the Norwegian campaign.

In the last chapter Churchill's ascendancy to the premiership is explored. Although many of the issues discussed in the body of this work have little direct bearing on this momentous event, the broader conclusions of this study—that, for Churchill, the Phoney War was a period marked by folly, frustration, and too often, failure—demand a consideration of why he found himself prime minister on 10 May 1940.

Several important themes develop within and across both parts of this study. The most important of these is Churchill and strategy, that is, the nature and caliber of his strategic thinking and the risks—strategic, operational, and political—he was prepared to accept in its implementation. This exploration provides insight into several attendant issues. His relationships with his naval staff and, most important, his first sea lord, Sir Dudley Pound, are particular considerations. Churchill and Pound did not necessarily see eye to eye on how, when, and where the substantial might of Britain's fleet should be used. Nor was there much agreement on how best to address Britain's imperial obligations while meeting the German threat. Understanding the extent to which Churchill was able, and willing, to impose his vision and priorities on his naval staff and the extent to which this staff contained and constrained their first lord is important to any assessment of Churchill as a potential war leader.

Another important theme is Churchill's interaction with members of the War Cabinet and, most important, his relationship with Neville Chamberlain and Lord Halifax. From the beginning, Churchill had definite views on how the war should be prepared for and fought, but so too did Chamberlain. For the most part Chamberlain's view prevailed and Churchill's did not. At its most polarized, this division has been explained as a conflict between a pugnacious first lord denied a more aggressive prosecution of the war by a timorous prime minister. The relationship is also oftentimes viewed in a political context as a conflict between a man determined to ascend to the premiership and the man clinging to it.

This study gives attention to the shared views of Churchill and Chamberlain, as well as their differences, and argues that their agreement represents and reflects more accurately the wartime relationship of the two.[2] Even at the beginning of the war, the differences in the strategic views of each were less marked than is often believed, and these lessened over time. Churchill's "bulldog" spirit had its limitations, as did Chamberlain's passivity.[3] Points of difference between them are better understood in the context of the challenges inherent in taking effective offensive action against Germany in this period rather than fundamental differences in personality or strategic outlook.

Churchill generally accepted Britain's "sit tight and rearm" approach to the war, a policy, it must be emphasized, endorsed fully by Britain's Chiefs of Staff (COS). It was never Chamberlain's policy alone. It was founded on the proposition that time was on the Allied side and that any hiatus offered by the enemy should be welcomed as an opportunity to prepare for the offensive. Churchill's objection to the "sit tight and rearm" policy was primarily at the margins. All plans for offensive action had to run the War Cabinet gauntlet of real action that would make a real difference versus palliative measures that would be of limited efficacy, potentially hurt the Allies more than the enemy, and invite retaliation and escalation. Churchill's two primary offensive initiatives, the Narvik plan and Royal Marine, failed to pass this scrutiny, whether imposed by the War Cabinet or by the French, and this was a source of frustration for him.

The development of war strategy was never only about Churchill, Chamberlain, the COS, and the British War Cabinet. Strategy was an Allied affair that at all times involved the French. They increasingly showed an interest in the offensive, but their priority was to promote action as far from their borders as possible. French strategy included proposals that invited war with Russia; this was a risk they were prepared to take if it would deny Germany the resources necessary to fight an aggressive war in the West. This desire to redirect, at almost any cost, the war away from France became increasingly problematic for the British as the Phoney War progressed. A significant divergence in view developed over air bombing policy and, more particularly, the circumstances in which Britain would unleash its much-vaunted strategic air weapon against Germany. The French determination to keep the war away from France for fear of retaliation and escalation became a serious obstacle for Churchill when he sought to garner support for Operation Royal Marine. It created a personal dilemma for him because his support for Britain's conservative bombing policy was driven by the same apprehensions over escalation and retaliation that caused the French to resist his plan. A study of this episode and its implications for Churchill's bulldog image will be an important element in this work.

For the Allies, and especially for Churchill, who led the service that would implement it, strategy was all about the periphery of Europe during this period. This perspective brought with it many problems that ultimately proved intractable. On the matter of French proposals for peripheral action, especially in southern Europe, Churchill was oftentimes no more enamored than Chamberlain and the wider War Cabinet. He was keen to keep Benito Mussolini and Italy as nonbelligerents and was fully aware of the potential problems if they were not. He accepted there would be no fighting in the west and was cautious about southern Europe. Given his support for existing bombing policy, this left only northern Europe as a theater for offensive operations, and this is where much of the focus of this study will be. A northern strategy chimed with Churchill's personal inclinations, and he began investigations into a naval offensive immediately upon becoming first lord. From December 1939 War Cabinet interest in Swedish iron ore placed Scandinavia at the center of strategic planning. Churchill's Narvik palliative to stop Germany's winter supply of ore was replaced by the COS and Foreign Office's initiative, the Finnish option, a wish-filled plan to stop the flow of all Swedish ore to Germany.[4] The Finnish option failed, and the Narvik plan was implemented very much too late to make a difference. Churchill attributed this failure and delay to a War Cabinet determined to take the "line of least resistance." The merit of this explanation will be considered.

Another important focus of this study is how Churchill operated as leader and colleague in the Admiralty, the War Cabinet, and the cabinet's committees and how successful he was in achieving his aims. A lasting criticism of Churchill as first lord is that he browbeat his staff into submission to achieve what he wanted and that he was aided in this by a compliant first sea lord.[5] Similar criticism is leveled at his performance within the Military Coordination Committee (MCC), most particularly when he became chairman in April 1940. Churchill's own views of the decision-making process and the problems that developed within the MCC were quite different. Churchill believed the three-way War Cabinet–MCC–COS structure established by Chamberlain to be slow, cumbersome, and ineffectual, and he attributed to this structure much of the phoniness—or inaction—of this time. Power to act, he argued after the war, should have been placed in the hands of one man—and he was that man.[6] The extent to which Churchill's performance in the Phoney War justified such self-confidence is assessed here through an analysis of his contribution to the War Cabinet and two of its ministerial committees: the Land Forces Committee (LFC) and the MCC. The LFC was the body that determined the size of the British Army that would fight World War II; the MCC was, from November 1939, primarily responsible for the development of strategy and the supervision of operations.

The questions of Churchill's skills as strategist and the potential he showed as a war leader are further explored through his performance in the Norwegian campaign, the single great land and sea conflict between Germany and the Allies during the Phoney War. During this conflict Churchill was both first lord of the Admiralty and chairman of the MCC, the body, along with the COS, primarily responsible for the conduct of the campaign. Churchill's dual role imposed a hefty burden of responsibility. His successes and failures, and his strengths and weaknesses, during this campaign must be balanced here against extraneous factors to determine if he proved the warrior and war leader he believed himself to be and if the considerable criticism of his performance is justified.

Another recurring theme in this study will be the influence Churchill's World War I experiences had on the proposals and policies he pressed in this new war. His past experiences as first lord bore heavily on matters of strategy and issues of ship construction, while his role as minister for munitions later in that war were reflected in his approach to Britain's war effort and his somewhat too optimistic hopes for the rapid escalation of this effort at the start of World War II.

In existing work Churchill is often assessed or condemned by a single utterance or phrase cited to illustrate his point of view on complex issues or his culpability in a particular matter.[7] For example, Churchill's attitude toward convoy—"We should secretly loosen up the convoy system"—has been represented as proof positive of the "First Lord's prejudice against the convoy system." Churchill's comments in a letter to Franklin Roosevelt on 16 October 1939—"We have not been at all impressed with the accuracy of the German air bombing of our warships"—have been used as evidence that Churchill "blithely assumed that the Fleet, unprotected by fighter cover, could cope with German dive bombers." Churchill's assertion in a March 1939 memorandum that "an air attack upon British warships, armed and protected as they now are, will not prevent full exercise of their superior sea power" has been inaccurately used to represent his wartime view on the air threat to British capital ships. Within weeks of the outbreak of war, Churchill was displaying considerable anxiety over the ships' capacity to defend themselves: "It certainly is a very disquieting fact with which we cannot possibly rest content that the multiple pom-pom and AA guns failed to hit any of these aircraft. We must regard this as a major weakness to be repaired at the earliest possible moment." A final objective of this work is, therefore, to look beyond these summary judgments to determine more accurately Churchill's views on several important issues, including the air-sea debate, and restore their complex context.

The consideration of Churchill and the Norwegian campaign will bring together the central themes of this work and anticipate many of the conclusions contained therein. Churchill did some things well and some things poorly. He often did not have the influence attributed to him, nor was he responsible for certain policies and decisions as supposed. He could be profoundly persistent in pursuing his objectives in some instances and open to persuasion and sound argument in others. He was often not the key arbiter of a policy or program but made decisions through consultation; he oftentimes listened to advice but did not always choose wise counsel; he was greatly influenced by the past, especially his experiences of World War I, but had insufficient knowledge and awareness of the present; he displayed occasional strategic insight but more often encouraged and pressed strategic and operational folly; he had a taste for risk that was not shared by his naval staff or War Cabinet colleagues but found himself more in tune than is admitted with the chief of the Imperial General Staff (CIGS), General Edmund Ironside. He knew that risks had to be taken in war but not necessarily which risks to be taken. Perhaps most important of all, this study will show that Churchill and Chamberlain, two men purportedly in constant rivalry, worked much more closely and successfully than imagined, and on important issues such as air policy, there was little difference between them.

Part One

CHURCHILL
AS FIRST LORD

U-BOATS AND THE
PROTECTION OF TRADE

In World War I the German assault on Britain's maritime trade brought with it great fears of defeat. British shipping suffered grievously under the assault of the U-boat and Germany's policy of unrestricted naval warfare. It was not until 1917 that convoy, in combination with the extensive arming of merchant vessels, stemmed the immense tide of British losses. Until this time Britain's enormous fleet of small craft had been primarily employed in largely fruitless offensive patrolling and sweeps designed to hunt down and destroy the U-boats. This had done little to sink them and even less to reduce losses in merchant shipping.

Despite this near-death experience Britain failed to learn fully the lessons of this war, and in World War II the U-boat again proved itself a potentially decisive weapon. A great deal of the dynamics of the war at sea in World War I remained obscure and inadequately understood, and because of the interwar development of asdic (sonar), there even developed an element of complacency. In the interwar period Winston Churchill was among a number who believed that in a future conflict, the U-boat threat would not be repeated on anything like the scale of the previous war; yet he subsequently characterized the Battle of the Atlantic as his greatest anxiety of World War II.

A lesson incompletely learned was the full merit of convoy. At the start of World War II, this weapon of defense was the cornerstone of Admiralty planning, but ambivalence existed as to the timing and extent of its implementation. Similarly, there was disagreement and uncertainty over the degree to which the convoy system slowed trade and the circumstances uznder which convoy could, or should, be forgone to maintain the necessary level of imports and exports.

This chapter examines Churchill's contribution to the anti-U-boat war and the defense of trade during his term as first lord. A primary objective

is to understand why he allowed the great folly and failure of World War
I—offensive patrolling—to function alongside, and sometimes at the expense
of, a convoy system that had proved the salvation of Britain a quarter century
before. While the early adoption of convoy in World War II suggested that
the Royal Navy had learned the key lessons of the past, the continued pursuit
of offensive patrolling at a time when there was a great shortage of escort
vessels suggested it had not. Churchill was at the center of these issues, and
he has been viewed as anything from ambivalent to hostile toward convoy.[1]
Often in company with Pound, Churchill is considered an irresponsible
and misguided advocate of offensive patrolling, and he is often viewed as
complicit in delaying the full implementation of the convoy system. This
assessment requires clarification and qualification.

Protecting Britain's Lifeline: The Admiralty View

Despite the resounding success of convoy in the closing months of World
War I, the lessons learned by the Admiralty were far from complete at the
start of World War II. By 1939 Admiralty policy was to ensure preparations
were made during peacetime to put "the convoy system into force, wholly or
in part, immediately on the outbreak of war." This did not mean that convoy
would be implemented at the start of war but only that the Admiralty be
ready to do so if this were needed.[2] A final decision as to the implementation
of convoy would be based on the "conditions prevailing, or likely to prevail
in the trade routes."[3] More specifically, convoy would be instituted "in any
area or on any route as soon as there is reason to believe that attacks will be
made on British shipping on that area or route in sufficient strength to cause
serious losses comparable to the loss of carrying capacity to be anticipated."[4]

It was assumed these conditions would occur only during unrestricted
U-boat warfare. Anything short of this could be satisfactorily dealt with by
traditional methods of defense, such as the patrolling of focal areas and the
arming of merchant vessels.[5]

The foundations of this policy were seriously flawed. The time lost to
convoy was not significantly greater than the time lost to the evasive rout-
ing of independent vessels. Conversely, the risk of independent sailing was
considerably understated, especially for faster merchant vessels. The patrolling
of focal areas could not do what was expected of it. Nevertheless, these

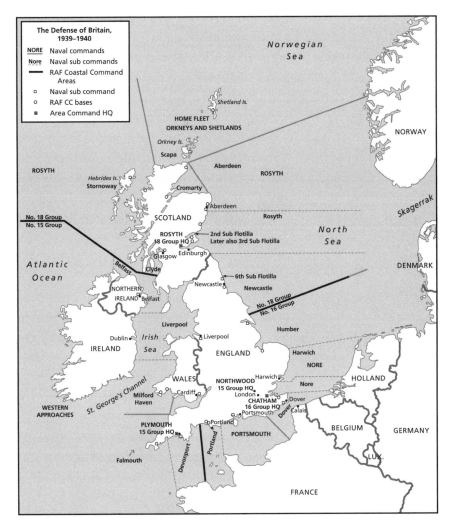

The Defense of Britain,
1939–1940

NORE   Naval commands
Nore   Naval sub commands
━━━   RAF Coastal Command
        Areas
□   Naval sub command
○   RAF CC bases
■   Area Command HQ

Map 1.1. The Defense of Britain, 1939–40

misapprehensions, and their unfortunate consequences, lingered throughout the Phoney War and for some time thereafter.

In the last days of peace, the Admiralty confirmed that in the event of war, a limited program of convoy would be implemented. What happened thereafter would await the action of the Germans. However, a decision regarding the extension of the convoy system was forced on the Admiralty on the first day of war, when, against the strict rules of engagement outlined by

Adolf Hitler, a U-boat sank the liner *Athenia*. This suggested the Germans had begun "unrestricted" U-boat warfare, and the Admiralty authorized a broad implementation of convoy, save for the slowest and fastest of merchant vessels. By the end of September much of British shipping moved in convoy, albeit oftentimes with limited escort.

While convoy was being instituted, offensive patrolling and sweeps claimed numerous successful attacks against U-boats in what appeared to be a ringing endorsement of asdic-enhanced offensive action. However, as the month progressed and more and more vessels were committed to convoy, the number available for patrolling diminished. This led to friction between the proponents of convoy and those who continued to believe offensive hunting operations were the best way to protect Allied shipping. By the end of September, Admiral Martin Dunbar-Nasmith, commander in chief, Western Approaches, and champion of offensive patrolling, found his command short of vessels for offensive sweeps and patrols. He had anticipated having a substantial force available for the hunting and killing of U-boats, but the early introduction of convoy had robbed him of this. Frustrated, he wrote to the Admiralty seeking to use twelve of his destroyer force of fifty-seven for "purely offensive operations" and as a dedicated antisubmarine strike force. This request received a wide circulation, including Churchill and Sir Dudley Pound. In response to Dunbar-Nasmith's request, the deputy chief of the naval staff (DCNS), Admiral Tom Phillips, wrote that success against the U-boat would be achieved only when "any submarine that attacks a convoy has say a 60% chance of being destroyed" and that this could be achieved only by having more escorts with convoys. Once all trade was in convoy, U-boats could do harm only by attacking the convoys, and this would expose the submarines to escorts. This tactic, Phillips believed, would achieve much more success than "if they [antisubmarine craft] are wandering about the ocean as striking forces."[6] Phillips thought Dunbar-Nasmith's request identified an important matter of principle that ought to be decided. All respondents, including Pound, agreed with Phillips, and Dunbar-Nasmith was informed that the Admiralty would consider the formation of antisubmarine hunting groups only after the number of escorts with each convoy had been brought up to four.[7]

The Admiralty had powerfully reinforced the navy's commitment to convoy and had thus begun the war by making the very best of decisions.

The first sea lord and his deputy evidently understood one of the core virtues of the convoy system: that to sink ships under escort, a U-boat must place itself in harm's way. Moreover, it is evident that each appreciated the only way to ensure the safety of the convoy, and provide an opportunity for offensive operations by the escorts, was to ensure convoys were accompanied in force. Additionally, the policy appeared to be an acknowledgment that, as far as the Admiralty was concerned, the protection of trade was more important than killing U-boats via offensive patrolling.

Despite this seemingly emphatic pronouncement of policy, many craft, including destroyers operating in the vital Western Approaches, were routinely involved in largely fruitless offensive patrols and sweeps even while convoys were inadequately protected. Destroyers were also available to respond to distress calls and U-boat sightings, but this only rarely resulted in a U-boat find. This division of resources between patrolling and escort most likely began in the naval stations themselves and was sustained by their respective commanders in chief, including Dunbar-Nasmith. That Pound and Phillips did nothing to arrest this development, despite the September correspondence with Dunbar-Nasmith, can perhaps be explained by three factors. First, the Germans pulled back from unrestricted U-boat warfare, therefore giving the Admiralty reason to rethink its policy. Second, not all shipping was under convoy by the end of September. Ships capable of sailing at fifteen knots or more sailed independently, and a great number of neutral ships trading with Britain and France refused to join convoys. All these vessels required some kind of support. Third, and very probably the most important, before the first two months of war were over, the Admiralty had accepted that offensive patrolling was working wonders in the finding, hurting, and killing of U-boats.

Protecting Britain's Lifeline: Churchill's View

It is difficult to judge how Churchill would have chosen to implement the Admiralty's trade protection policy had he assumed the position of first lord before the outbreak of war. The sinking of *Athenia* prompted the Admiralty to implement a much broader program of convoy than planned and to do so more quickly. Thus, this tragedy was also a blessing for Britain. Churchill found himself presented with a fait accompli, but there is no evidence that he disagreed with these decisions. Despite the continued uncertainty over Italy, he immediately acceded to the recommendation that destroyers be withdrawn from the eastern and Mediterranean theaters "with the object of adding if possible twelve to the escorts for convoys" in the Western Approaches.[8] Moreover, from the beginning of war, he made clear that he fully supported convoy as a vital part of the anti-U-boat solution.

Nevertheless, Churchill soon showed he did not view convoy as the complete answer to the U-boat problem and the protection of trade. In his first major speech to the House of Commons on 26 September, he presented his three-pronged approach to the U-boat threat. His first prong was implementing the convoy system, which "is a good and well-tried defense against U-boat attack," but he added, "No one can pretend that it is a complete defense. Some degree of risk and a steady proportion of losses must be expected." The second prong, as per the guidelines in "Protection of Shipping at Sea," was defensively arming all merchant ships and fast liners against the U-boat and the airplane. The third prong was "British attack upon the U-boats" using a rapidly expanding force of hunting craft.[9]

This third prong was not part of the Admiralty policy guidelines, but Churchill was undoubtedly impressed by the evidence that offensive patrolling, combined with the new asdic weapon, was achieving remarkable success. Churchill's prewar faith in asdic was as absolute as his understanding of it was incomplete. He, more than most, was captivated by this new tool and had succumbed too readily and too uncritically to the potential it offered to solve the U-boat problem. In June 1936 he had visited Portland with the then first sea lord, Sir Ernle Chatfield, to see a demonstration of asdic. He was taken with what he saw and never thereafter questioned its value as a decisive anti-U-boat weapon. In March 1939 he ventured this bold assertion regarding the development of this weapon: "The submarine has been mastered, thanks very largely to Lord Chatfield's long efforts at the Admiralty. It should be quite controllable in the outer seas, and certainly in the Mediterranean. There will be losses, but nothing to affect the scale of events."[10]

Here, then, was the expectation that with the assistance of asdic, the U-boat would not pose the threat it had in World War I. By the end of September 1939 this expectation had met results that suggested these hopes were fully justified. From the beginning of war Churchill was inundated with a veritable barrage of positive news on anti-U-boat operations. The first lord's daily update provided numerous reports of attacks on U-boats and, oftentimes, estimates as to damage or destruction.

In his statement to the House on 26 September, Churchill spoke with great enthusiasm about asdic and the success it was reaping: whereas once, he declared, it had taken a flotilla of fifteen or twenty vessels a whole day to track down a U-boat, the same task could now be achieved by two destroyers; it was "no exaggeration to say that the attacks upon the German U-boats [had] been five or six times as numerous as in any equal period in the Great War, in which, after all, they did not beat us."[11] As for the numbers of U-boats destroyed, he estimated these at six or seven; "that is one tenth of the total enemy submarine fleet as it existed at the declaration of war destroyed."[12] This was just one of many positive messages Churchill gave over the following months to a variety of forums: in his speeches to the House of Commons and to the nation, in his letters to President Franklin Roosevelt, and in his correspondence with the French navy.

Churchill spoke even more effusively of the anti-U-boat war to the House of Commons in October: "Nothing like this rate of destruction was attained at any moment in the last war. During the last week for which I can give figures . . . seven U-boats were sunk. If we look back over the whole period of six weeks since the war began we may estimate that 13 U-boats have been sunk, that five have been seriously damaged, and possibly sunk, and several others damaged. These figures are probably an understatement. Besides this, two-thirds of the U-boats which have been raiding have suffered attack from depth-charges."[13]

All these facts and figures grossly exaggerated the true state of the anti-U-boat war. Historical analysis attributes this exaggeration to wishfulness and, at worst, a willfulness by Churchill intended to sustain morale and boost his standing with the British public.[14] However, it is likely Churchill's overstatements, at least in the first two months of war, were much less calculated and more inadvertent than such views allow. For the greater part, the figures quoted by Churchill in these various forums were the all too optimistic official figures provided by the Naval Intelligence Division (NID) under Admiral John Godfrey and, from the beginning of October, by the Anti-Submarine Warfare Division (A/SWD) under its new director, Captain Douglas Adams Budgen.[15]

Admiral Godfrey subsequently became the most earnest critic of Churchill's exaggeration of the harm being done to the U-boat. It is surprising, therefore, that one of the earliest and most significant overstatements was drawn from an assessment made by Godfrey himself. On 29 September Godfrey circulated a tabulation titled *German Submarines: Estimated Numbers, Building Program and Losses*, in which he estimated seven U-boats had been sunk up to 26 September. Within days this estimate was reduced to two, a figure that was correct. Unfortunately, this correction occurred too late to avoid embarrassment for Churchill and Chamberlain, both of whom had referred to the figure of six or seven in the House of Commons.[16] Godfrey's tabulation included a warning that the figures should be treated with caution and that they would be subject to amendment. This advice was provided too late for Churchill and Chamberlain, although whether either would have exercised the requisite caution is a moot point, especially given the enormous volume of other positive news on the anti-U-boat war. In October NID provided the following figures for September in its first *Monthly Anti-submarine Report*. These suggested the U-boats were receiving a severe battering and would, for the most part, have justified Churchill's exuberance:

Attacks by ships on U-boats		124
Attacks by aircraft on U-boats		14
U-boats:	Known sunk	2
	Probably sunk	6
	Probably seriously damaged	5
	Probably slightly damaged	3[17]

This positive news diminished but did not abate, and by mid-December the A/SWD's *Weekly Return U-Boats* (*WRU*), the first of which had been published in mid-October, recorded the success against U-boats as follows:

U-boats:	Known sunk	8
	Probably sunk	18
	Probably seriously damaged	5
	Probably slightly damaged	10
	Not yet classified	4

Meanwhile, the widely circulated *Monthly Anti-submarine Report* recorded the total number of attacks on U-boats in October, November, and December as fifty-two, thirty-one, and thirty-five, respectively. These figures, one must emphasize, were those of the A/SWD Assessment Committee after it had sifted attacks deemed to have been obviously on non-U-boat targets.

Such were Admiralty estimates. The reality was quite different. While Admiralty staff had estimated the number of attacks on U-boats at the end of September 1939 to have been 124, the U-boat captains recorded a mere seven attacks against their vessels.[18] Rather than receiving severe punishment from asdic-assisted patrol craft, U-boats were rarely being found and rarely being attacked, and this despite the fact that far more U-boats were at sea in September than at any other time during Churchill's tenure (and for some considerable time thereafter).

By the time Churchill became prime minister in May 1940, the U-boats had recorded fewer than thirty-five attacks on their craft from any source, and of these only a few had caused harm to the U-boat.[19] At the end of 1939 the official "known sunk" figure was eight, and the true figure was nine. Churchill had been estimating thirteen sunk as early as October. By January his estimate had risen to over thirty, and he was even bold enough to suggest a figure higher than this.

There was probably little dispute among those concerned with anti-U-boat warfare that gilding the lily was to be eschewed. Giving false estimates could invite complacency and cause the misallocation or reallocation of resources, and these anxieties animated Godfrey and caused him to start challenging the process. A disagreement developed primarily because while NID believed lack of rigor was causing an overestimation of U-boat kills, A/SWD, Churchill, and Pound did not. Rather, for some considerable time, Churchill believed NID was obtusely determined to underestimate success against the U-boat.

The Origins of Doubt

The explanation for the great disparity between NID's official and more accurate figures of U-boat kills and Churchill's high estimates lies in issues of definition and computation. The confusion caused by these problems—and subsequently reinforced by A/SWD and advice offered by the first lord's personal adviser, Professor Frederick Lindemann—led Churchill to a stubborn conviction that his assessments of success against the U-boats were more accurate than those being pressed on him by NID.

The problems very likely began with NID's decision at some point in late September to be more demanding in the evidence required to declare a U-boat sunk. This manifested in the readjustment of September losses from six to two. The other four of the six U-boats estimated to have been sunk were then recorded as "probably sunk." NID's view was that to record a U-boats as "known sunk," there had to be incontrovertible evidence, such as wreckage, survivors, or bodies, or evidence gleaned from German sources, including death notices and radio announcements. The "probably sunk" category was described as "incontrovertible evidence is not forthcoming but, after full investigation, the Committee believe that the U-boat has been destroyed."[20]

Evidence shows that for the first six to eight weeks of the war, Churchill was not aware a distinction had developed between "known sunk" and "probably sunk"; another explanation for the confusion is that the distinction itself was not being consistently maintained by those providing the first lord information. NID and A/SWD certainly viewed the distinction between "known sunk" and "probably sunk" differently; the latter division believed that the "probables" were sunk, while the former was decidedly more cautious. There may also have been confusion over the status of U-boats considered "seriously damaged." On 1 November Churchill wrote to the director of A/SWD, Arthur G. Talbot, that he was

> concerned at the variations in figures given from time to time for the submarines we have sunk. On the 17th October I was told, and announced to the House, that we then estimated 13 U-boats had been sunk and 5 other seriously damaged and probably sunk. I am now told that 11 days later the estimated number sunk is 5 certain, plus 9 probable, ie., 14. . . .
>
> It is necessary that these disagreements should be finally cleared up. It would not be correct to give the impression that the sinking of submarines has virtually ceased since the 17th October—which is the effect of the answer proposed on this paper.[21]

Churchill's claim, made to the House of Commons in mid-October, of thirteen U-boats sunk was evidently a combination of "known sunk" and "probably sunk" estimated around that time. Churchill referred to the figure as an "estimate." Whether he was cognizant that this was a combined figure is unclear; nevertheless, it is reasonable to assume, given the definition of "probably sunk," that he would have felt comfortable presenting this high figure as an estimate. His comments here also suggest an assumption that U-boats estimated as seriously damaged could be accepted as probably sunk.

The question of whether Churchill's statements about U-boat losses reflected a conviction based on information supplied to him or were willful and calculated expressions of unjustified optimism will likely remain moot. However, in any effort to determine his true mind-set regarding this and subsequent public estimates of U-boat losses, it must be noted he was not alone in believing the combined known and probable categories more accurately represented the number of U-boats sunk. Pound was just as willing to bundle "known sunk" and "probably sunk." On 28 October the COS told a gathering of dominion ministers that to date fourteen U-boats had been sunk, an estimate, one might add, that appeared to reflect Churchill's assumptions about more U-boat losses in the second half of October.[22] During January 1940 Pound's estimate of U-boat losses, although lower than Churchill's, considerably exceeded the number accepted by Godfrey. Perhaps most important in understanding Churchill's attitude to U-boat losses is that the A/SWD and, in particular, its new director, Captain Talbot, accepted that the considerable number of "probably sunk" had been sunk.[23]

If Churchill did not know before November that NID and A/SWD disagreed on the number of U-boats sunk, he did thereafter. This made him more cautious, but only marginally and only briefly, in his public statements on the anti-U-boat war. In the War Cabinet and at the Admiralty, there was little caution to be found. At the War Cabinet of 13 November, Churchill informed his colleagues of intelligence that indicated a total of thirty U-boats had been lost, were overdue, or had been badly damaged. By an unfortunate coincidence this figure of thirty U-boats approximated the existing estimate of "known sunk," "probably sunk," and "probably seriously damaged." Churchill therefore concluded the U-boats in the "probably seriously damaged" category should be bundled with known and probable figures to provide an accurate representation of U-boat losses.[24]

This conclusion fractured further an already uncomfortable relationship with Godfrey, who believed the intelligence in question to be obscure and unreliable and who maintained that evidence of U-boat kills must be unimpeachable. In his postwar writing Godfrey attributed Churchill's hopelessly optimistic assessment of harm being done to U-boats to "very senior officer veneration," which, to quote Patrick Beesly's biography of Godfrey, was "the tendency to accept that not only is the Senior Officer always right but that only the Senior Officer is right."[25] This criticism was probably a reference to the optimism surrounding U-boat kills from officers like Dunbar-Nasmith, who by February 1940 believed ships in his command had destroyed twenty-seven U-boats.[26]

Godfrey's criticism seems a little unfair, for it ignores the fact that Churchill's own estimates were based on information supplied by A/SWD, which vigorously assessed each claim and rejected many. If Churchill's behavior over this matter can be deemed willful, and if his attitude to "seriously damaged" U-boats can be viewed as stretching credulity too far, it seems reasonable to argue it was a willful determination to accept figures he considered largely correct against the advice of NID and not a willful refusal to reject figures he knew were wrong; this is a small but important distinction to make.

It is important to note that despite Churchill's apparent keenness to view the November intelligence as corroboration of Admiralty estimates of harm done to the U-boats, the War Cabinet had been, since mid-October, provided information via the COS *Weekly Résumé of the Naval, Military and Air Situation* that clearly distinguished the different categories of known and probable losses and serious and minor damage. It seems likely, however, that Churchill and Pound encouraged the War Cabinet to believe, as they did themselves, that the combined number of known and probable more accurately represented U-boat losses. In late November, as the dispute between Churchill and NID escalated, the COS weekly résumés ceased providing details of U-boat losses. There is no evidence the War Cabinet members noticed this change, knew the reason for it, or asked why if they did not.

In March the discovery of documents on board U-49 indicated the Allies had been much less successful in killing U-boats than Churchill supposed, and this entirely justified NID's insistence on concrete evidence.[27] Churchill rejected even this information, and it is here one might first begin to question the integrity of his position. However, even on this point doubt must remain over Churchill's motivation. When he became prime minister, he remained emphatic that the accepted estimates of U-boat kills were wrong, and he sought a formal inquiry into the matter. This inquiry, conducted under the auspices of Admiral Frederick Dreyer, was completed by November and concluded that the NID's assessments were correct. The records of the investigation and the interviews of Churchill's principal scientific adviser, Professor Lindemann, suggest Churchill's views, although based on seriously flawed deduction, cannot easily be described as willful or wishful or as a product of very senior officer veneration. Lindemann's interviews also make clear the extent to which the professor, rather than senior officers, helped sustain Churchill's convictions regarding U-boat losses.

Several factors appear to have contributed to Churchill's inaccurate estimates and conviction that NID and, after April, A/SWD figures were wrong. These included the suggestion of a "safe side" mind-set within the assessment committees; the belief the Germans used subterfuge and deception to conceal the number of U-boats sunk; and the existence of evidence and examples that hinted at, or which he believed could only be explained by, greater U-boat losses. During his interviews Lindemann contended that NID and A/SWD were excessively, but not unnaturally, conservative in their assessment procedure and inevitably underestimated the number of U-boats sunk.[28] This view was influenced by misapprehensions surrounding NID figures indicating that despite having neither asdic nor as many patrol craft for antisubmarine work, the Germans had suffered no more U-boat losses than Britain had experienced in its own submarine fleet. A particular influence on Churchill's and Lindemann's deductions was that official figures of U-boats sunk did not include any allowance for accidents or unknown events, which they believed must have afflicted the Germans in the same way they had affected the British submarine fleet. Yet another influence was the aforementioned Danish-sourced intelligence of late 1939, which provided an estimate of the German U-boat fleet to that time. By coincidence, this figure had matched almost precisely the then-A/SWD assessment of "known sunk," "probably sunk," and "probably damaged"

U-boats. This information prompted Churchill's huge estimates of U-boat losses in February.

Of particular interest to Churchill and Lindemann was the mysterious curve in graphs of U-boat activity and success against Allied shipping the professor had produced. This curve had led them to conclude that U-boats were operating in great ebbs and flows; there were times when the majority of U-boats were at sea and then times when they were in port to rest.[29] Lindemann estimated that during the flow periods some ten to twelve were operating at any one time. If this number remained fairly constant over time and represented the strongest force Germany routinely put to sea, and if the construction of U-boats had grown as NID had projected, it must be deduced that more U-boats had been sunk.[30] Finally, Lindemann presented his conviction, held also by Churchill, that the Germans had been successfully concealing the greater number of losses through a process of substitution. That is, they would reuse a sunken U-boat's number on hidden German construction or on submarines acquired from the Russians, Norwegians, Danes, or Poles. That a U-boat with a given number was operating did not necessarily mean that a U-boat with this number had not already been sunk.

In short measure nearly all Lindemann's assumptions, and those of Churchill, were challenged and then compromised. Admiral Dreyer questioned the proposition that the A/SWD assessment committees were acting conservatively. He had not heard of the committees making decisions "on the safe side," and he contended that the only safety was in accuracy.[31] He also doubted the efficacy of a policy of underestimation, noting that this might lead to an unnecessary diversion of resources "which might otherwise be better occupied."[32] Moreover, he pointed out that if a bias existed, it was more likely to be on the plus side with the A/SWD endeavoring to show they were "producing the goods."

Discussion led to the comparative losses of the U-boats and British submarines, and it was concluded that this could be adequately explained by the restricted and dangerous areas (such as the Heligoland Bight) within which British submarines worked. Moreover, the disparity in loss rate could not be offset by the advantages offered to the Allies through asdic and a greater number of patrol craft. Against the Danish-sourced intelligence, the committee was able to draw attention to the information gained from U-49, of which, remarkably, Lindemann indicated he had no knowledge. Lindemann was less willing to accept arguments against substitution despite the absence of evidence to support it. Dreyer made a small impression on him when he asked whether it would be to the Germans' advantage to understate or overstate the size of their U-boat fleet or to make any effort to conceal its numbers. Lindemann thought the Germans would prefer the enemy believed they were sinking fewer U-boats but then conceded that the opposite might have been just as possible.[33]

The discussion became quite extraordinary when the issue of the mysterious curve was raised. Lindemann was disabused of several keenly held assumptions. First, with the exception of September 1939, nothing like ten or twelve U-boats had operated together in the Western Approaches. It was typically only a third or so of this, and the number did not ebb and flow to anywhere near the extent Lindemann believed but was fairly constant. The professor appeared not to understand that the maintenance of even four U-boats in the Western Approaches required there be four on the way to the operation zone and four returning from it.[34] Additionally, it was explained, a considerable portion of the existing German fleet was unsuited to operate in this theater. Finally, in addition to those U-boats in the operational zone or going to or returning from this zone, there must always be a portion at rest or under repair and refit. Thus was Lindemann required to recognize that even a modest number of four or five U-boats operating continuously in the Western Approaches signaled the existence of a much larger number to sustain them. If this were the case, however, and the Germans were not conducting an all-out all-back campaign, how did one explain the ebb and flow of losses? To his credit, Lindemann proposed an answer to this question that was not without merit: the periods of great German success reflected the activity at sea of the "star-turn captains." The ebb and flow of merchant losses was less a result of regular surges of U-boats at sea than of the presence of the aces of the German U-boat fleet at a particular time.[35]

Lindemann's interview revealed a key adviser's remarkable ignorance of important—indeed basic—elements of the U-boat campaign. While Churchill had a wide understanding of a great number of things, his uncritical acceptance of Lindemann's reasoning shows a disturbingly and surprisingly shallow grasp of the facts. Similarly, it shows that Churchill sometimes placed

Lindemann in a role in which he was very much out of his depth. Although Churchill had not been merely obtuse in his convictions, since he had relied on advice and analysis, he had to take some responsibility for accepting it so uncritically. From the beginning of war, he had taken upon himself to seek external and independent advice through Lindemann and his own statistical section (the Admiralty Statistical Branch). This reflected his awareness of the great power of specialized information and statistics, especially when he alone was privy to it—or at least when he was the first to have access—and he applied this knowledge routinely within the War Cabinet to drive his own agenda. It also reflected a certain lack of trust in existing structures, including the NID, and an unwillingness to engage them. Throughout the war Lindemann provided considerable, but not always reliable or accurate, service to Churchill. During the Phoney War his fledgling statistical section was occupied with all manner of business and was evidently incapable of providing Churchill adequate guidance on anti-U-boat policy. The Dreyer committee quickly demolished many of the matters that confounded Lindemann and Churchill and showed how quickly such important issues might have been resolved many months before on Churchill's initiative.

Nevertheless, despite the success of the Dreyer committee in finally resolving the issue of U-boat kills, it failed to resolve what was arguably the more significant issue surrounding the anti-U-boat campaign: the assumption that whether or not U-boats had been destroyed, the Allies had been remarkably successful in finding and seriously hurting them. Although it was now more readily accepted that many of those U-boats deemed "probably sunk" in the first year of the war had almost certainly not been, those U-boats were simply moved to the "seriously damaged" or "slightly damaged" categories; a great many of the attacks themselves remained unchallenged.

From the beginning of the war, the question of why the large estimate of contacts had failed to result in more kills had raised eyebrows. Many attacks were accepted as false, including by Churchill, but a large number continued to be accepted as real. Churchill was among those who attributed the lack of fortune to the failings of the depth charge and the method of attack. As early as September 1939, he had explained the disparity between contacts and kills as unfamiliarity with depth-charging. This misapprehension was shared by others in high places, including Pound.[36]

There is another important aspect to this overstatement of success against the U-boats. Up to December 22, 1939, Coastal Command pilots believed they had destroyed or damaged twenty U-boats. Early in 1940 Talbot informed Coastal Command that no U-boats could be confirmed as sunk. No doubt, however, the pilots continued to believe they had caused damage to quite a few U-boats when this was also untrue. The explanation offered for aircraft's failure to sink U-boats was the inadequacy of the bombs they used. Again, failure in the anti-U-boat war was being found in the killing and not in the finding. However, from September 1939 to the end of May 1940, the U-boats themselves recorded few attacks from the air, and there is little reason to doubt this reflects the true state of affairs at this point in the war. This information had considerable ramifications for the policy of offensive patrolling, in which destroyer craft responded to U-boat sightings from the air. If pilots thought they were attacking U-boats when they were not, it seems reasonable to assume they were just as often directing hunting craft to U-boats that were not there to be found. Until aircraft secured equipment for the detection of surfaced U-boats later in the war, it was more likely a U-boat would sight an aircraft before the aircraft sighted a U-boat.

Thus, although it was concluded by the end of 1940 that fewer U-boats had been sunk than once believed, this did not mean a more clinical assessment of asdic-assisted (or air-assisted) offensive patrolling and the finding of U-boats was needed at this juncture in the war. Admiral Dreyer wrote a letter to the new first lord, A. V. Alexander, in October 1940: "We should have sunk 100 more U-boats by now if we had also developed depth finding tactics."[37] Thus, even after Churchill had become prime minister, the Admiralty had still to learn that their apprehensions about the killing of U-boats were being inflated by an overestimation of their success in finding and attacking them.[38] Despite the valuable corrective offered to the Admiralty via the U-49 documents in April 1940, the A/SWD continued to overestimate successful attacks on U-boats and real attacks on U-boats whether or not they did damage. While a large number of attacks were recognized as occurring against non-U-boat targets, too many continued to be thought of as 'real' and too many were recorded as doing harm—whether that harm was sinking or damaging—when no harm was done.[39]

Had the extremely limited success of incidental anti-U-boat activity (that is, activity other than escorts' reacting to an attack on a convoy or surface craft responses that happen to be in close proximity to a U-boat attack on merchant shipping) been known and understood, such knowledge would have provided a strong justification for a complete focus on convoy. Only while attacking escorted convoys were U-boats forced to place themselves in harm's way, and this maximized the potential for a successful attack. However, such false trails help explain why Churchill maintained his enthusiasm for offensive patrolling and destroyer sweeps; they appeared to produce successes when they were not. In the circumstances it is unreasonable to hold Churchill too severely to account. Nevertheless, that he should have done more and acted earlier to arrive at a better understanding of the U-boat war is a reasonable criticism.

The Consequences of Offensive Patrolling

The foregoing has established that Churchill and elements within the Admiralty misread the virtue of offensive patrolling during the Phoney War period, and it has presented a number of reasons why this was so. This section will discuss the actual consequences in terms of lost ships, matériel, and personnel. For the war as a whole, the historical record stands out decidedly in favor of the convoy-escort school over the offensive patrolling–independent sailing school, and there can really be no dispute about this; the best place for anti-U-boat forces was with convoys, and the more present the better. Another principle ignored, or forgotten, or not yet learned from World War I was that there was no strong correlation between the number of U-boats at sea and the number of merchant ships sunk; killing U-boats was, therefore, not essential for the protection of trade.

Critics of offensive patrolling, of course, argued that by encouraging or permitting the siphoning of resources to offensive patrolling, Churchill and others denied convoys adequate protection, and this led to unnecessary losses. However, it is probable that the negative consequences of Churchill's ongoing support for offensive patrolling were much less than has been suggested. While it is possible that the energy applied to offensive patrolling occasionally denied convoys a full escort, it is questionable this led to significant losses in merchant shipping. Further, although offensive patrolling led to few U-boats being destroyed, it is also likely that patrolling contributed more positively to the anti-U-boat effort than is generally accepted. Finally, and most important, it is probable that the decision to permit independent sailing of merchant ships—a practice that did cause unnecessary losses—had little to do with a shortage of escorts caused by an ongoing practice of offensive patrolling. Rather, this decision was subject to other influences. Each of these issues will be considered in turn.

It is open to question if applying all resources to convoy, as Pound and Phillips were determined to do in September, would have saved ships, especially on the Western Approaches. As escorts became available, Pound and Phillips intended to add to the number of escorts per convoy, not necessarily to add to the number of convoys, nor to escort convoys for longer periods—something that might have proved efficacious—nor even to insist on all shipping being placed in convoy. However, if convoys were rarely being found and rarely being attacked during the Phoney War period—and they were almost entirely unscathed during this time—would there have been advantage in adding more escorts to a convoy? Extra escorts became a critical issue from the second half of 1940 onward because the German U-boats, working from France and in growing numbers—and often in packs (called wolf packs) with the assistance of air reconnaissance—had great success in finding convoys, while Britain, post-Dunkirk and fearful of invasion, had many fewer escorts. Once the convoys were found, the wolf packs could sink multiple ships in a short time. However, during the Phoney War it was not primarily the number of escorts that was saving ships in convoy but the empty ocean effect of convoy and the small number of U-boats available to find convoys and then attack them.[40] Serendipitously for Churchill, therefore, any shortage of escorts due to offensive patrolling or the existence of striking forces was not likely to have caused great loss. Conversely, the ongoing presence of independently sailed vessels—primarily neutral—required the Admiralty do something to defend this shipping within the focal areas around Britain. After all, these ships were suffering most at the hand of the U-boats, and their cargo was also important to Britain. They could not be left without protection.

It is also open to question if offensive patrolling, aggressive responses to U-boat sightings, and the sinking of merchant vessels were quite as useless as assumed. Although Admiral Dunbar-Nasmith, Captain Talbot, and

others exaggerated the success of offensive patrolling during the Phoney
War, postwar historical analysis has likely understated it and, in so doing,
has contributed unfairly to criticism of Churchill's interest in these operations. The sinking of two U-boats in the first two months of the war has
been inaccurately, or at least, inappropriately, attributed to escorts in some
postwar assessments when they ought more appropriately to have been
attributed to destroyers in offensive patrolling mode. Offensive patrolling did
occasionally have its successes, and more of these could have been expected
as long as Hitler shied from unconditional U-boat warfare; for as long as he
did so, his U-boats were oftentimes forced to dangerously expose themselves
during their attacks.

Additionally, an assessment of the value of offensive patrolling must not
be based entirely on the number of U-boats sunk by patrolling craft. It must
also be assessed in terms of its capacity to disrupt or disturb the activities
of the U-boats whether or not a U-boat was found, attacked, damaged, or
destroyed. It might oftentimes be sufficient for a U-boat to see a patrol craft
for the patrol to have a direct impact on the U-boat's efficiency and subsequent
opportunity to catch and sink merchant ships.[41] The presence of a patrol, or
the probability or possibility of a patrol, caused submariners considerable
anxiety in meeting a variety of needs, including the recharging of batteries
and the moving of stored torpedoes to firing compartments. A similar anxiety
could be induced if U-boats learned to expect the arrival of patrol craft after
sighting by aircraft. Without the constant and real threat of patrol craft in
focal areas, convoy routes, and the routes traveled by U-boats (to the extent
these could be determined), these anxieties and risks would have likely
disappeared. It is probable, therefore, that offensive patrolling, judiciously
planned and undertaken, closely linked to intelligence, supported from the
air, and operated in conjunction with convoy, had virtue. The extent of this
was and is, necessarily, difficult to quantify.

Such issues highlight the unreasonable and inaccurate criticism leveled
at Churchill over the use of the carriers *Courageous* and *Ark Royal* in the
opening weeks of the war. The use of these valuable vessels in the fruitless
pursuit of U-boats is typically viewed as dangerous and profligate. Tragically, *Courageous* was lost during the operations, and *Ark Royal* almost
shared the same fate. Malcolm Llewellyn-Jones has correctly addressed

the unjust criticism of Churchill over this matter.[42] It made sense to use the aircraft from these ships in the early weeks of war to shepherd the large number of unconvoyed ships present at the time, and the carriers' activities were never only hunting and killing U-boats but also keeping the U-boats beneath the waves and denying them their surface mobility. They need not have sunk, nor have seen, a single U-boat to have fulfilled a significant role in disrupting U-boat activities over a large area if they themselves were seen by a U-boat. The folly of the carrier operations lay in not maintaining an adequate destroyer screen at all times, but Churchill cannot be blamed for this.[43]

More important is the supposed link between the use of potential escorts for offensive patrolling and the extent to which this forced ships into independent sailing. It is doubtful that a direct or close link ever existed between the ongoing support of offensive patrolling in the Western Approaches and several practices adopted during this time. The most relevant of these practices was the decision to permit the independent sailing of ships that could journey at fifteen knots and over. This was not a decision based primarily on a shortage of escorts but on an ongoing uncertainty surrounding the risk-versus-time-saved equation of independent sailing of fast vessels versus the delays believed to be inherent in convoy. Ships continued to be sailed independently because it was thought this would be better for the national war effort in the longer term.

Time Saved over Ships Lost

It is to this vital question of the risk-versus-time-saved equation that one can trace the claims of Churchill's ambivalence to convoy and the suggestion he disliked convoy because it was too defensive. Such claims rest almost entirely on two minutes written to Pound and Phillips on 9 and 20 November 1939. In the first Churchill wrote of "secretly loosen[ing] the convoy system (while boasting about it publicly), especially on the outer routes." In both minutes he referred to the idea of supporting this change with an independent flotilla force "sweeping the Western Approaches," making this area untenable for U-boats, and providing the Navy with "more freedom."[44] However, while these minutes reflect Churchill's misguided confidence in asdic-assisted patrolling, they do not sustain the claims about Churchill and convoy.

Churchill's suggestions were grounded almost entirely in the practical matter of how best to maintain an adequate level of wartime trade. A reduction in the rate of trade had always been expected with the introduction of convoy, and from the beginning of war, Churchill had gone out of his way to explain to the War Cabinet and to Parliament that this would occur but would not be a major problem. Further, this problem would diminish as the convoy system established its routine and became more efficient. However, by November the rate of trade had dropped well below Churchill's own expectations, and he now had doubts as to the risks and rewards surrounding convoy. He thought it possible the problem could be ameliorated by the "loosening" of the system. He explained to the War Cabinet that "delays resulting from the convoy system were, in a sense, equivalent in their effects on the flow of trade to the sinking of ships," and he thought the government should "overhaul the system and accept greater risks."[45] Thereafter, Churchill organized a meeting with Admiralty staff at which he argued that "we shall have failed in our task if we merely substitute delays for sinkings," and he suggested an "intricate study of the restrictions now imposed."[46] Although Churchill's reasoning was flawed, it had an entirely rational basis to it. It would be a mistake to assume his recommendations were evidence he did not understand that convoy saved ships. He was fully aware of this. From very early in the war, it was clear that independently sailed vessels suffered the depredations of the U-boats much more heavily than those in convoy, and Churchill knew that what he was proposing would likely result in the loss of more ships—hence his reference to increased risk.[47] What Churchill was seeking from his chief of naval staff (CNS) and DCNS was a cold-blooded assessment of whether the additional losses to be expected from the loosening of convoy would be offset by an increase in trade. The meeting of Admiralty staff, including Professor Lindemann, concluded that not all shipping delays or much of the decline in trade were attributable to the convoy system. Other problems included the requisitioning of merchant vessels for Admiralty purposes and the need to arm merchant ships. Several recommendations were put forward to ameliorate the situation, including the division of convoy into fast and slow groups, a reduction in port restrictions, the introduction of daily convoys along the east coast, and the giving of permission to ships up to 2,500 or 3,000 tons to use the east coast unescorted.[48]

Churchill's so-called ambivalence surrounding convoy had little or nothing to do with offensive mindedness or a fundamental dislike for the system. His views, and those of the naval staff, had their origin in the lack of statistical certainty surrounding one simple equation: Would time saved over ships lost result in an increased rate of trade? The Admiralty had already made this decision for ships that could sail at fifteen knots and over. It is difficult to find anyone who gainsaid this policy, and it continued for much of the war. In early November Pound asked if the minimum speed for independent sailing should be reduced below fifteen knots.[49] In doing so he, like Churchill, was weighing the risks and rewards of this issue. His suggestion was rejected. Unfortunately, despite Churchill's request for a broad investigation into trade, there appears to have been no concerted effort to initiate a statistical analysis of the risks and rewards of the fifteen knot benchmark itself or to gather statistics of shipping losses at lesser speeds.[50] One year later, in even more desperate times, these issues were revisited by the Admiralty and War Cabinet and a change was acceded to, much to the considerable future misfortune of many captains and crews. Only then were investigations begun by the Trade and Plans Divisions of the Admiralty. Not until mid-1941 was it finally and definitively concluded that the risks and rewards of reducing the speed of independently sailed vessels to thirteen knots did not stack up, and a decision was made to return to the fifteen knot and over policy. Unfortunately, in part because of the intervention of Lindemann, who insisted that convoy statistics include stragglers and ships sunk post-convoy, the risks of independent sailing for vessels traveling fifteen knots and over vis-à-vis the risks for ships in convoy remained understated; thus did fifteen knot independent sailings continue.[51] There is little doubt that the failure to insist on an early analysis of the risks and rewards of independent sailings at high speeds represented another great missed opportunity and an extraordinary oversight. Churchill must take his share of responsibility for this.

The Magnetic Mine

Unfortunately, the failure in November 1939 to fully explore the ramifications of independent sailing was simultaneously compounded by the Admiralty's reaction to the German magnetic mine, and this threatened to compromise further the existing faith in convoy. Churchill's particular culpability in this is more obscure. It is evident in much of the foregoing that a core contention of this chapter is an assessment of Churchill's contribution to the resolution of the convoy–offensive patrolling debate—and to the successful prosecution of the anti-U-boat war—must be tempered by the degree to which his own staff struggled with such matters. He was not an ardent and independent arbiter of Admiralty policy, routinely rejecting the good advice of his advisers, but like his staff, he sometimes groped in the dark, a victim of a wider systemic ignorance. The question is whether he did enough as first lord to alleviate the ignorance. The way Churchill and the Admiralty dealt with the German magnetic mine helps answer this question. For a period the magnetic mine threatened to turn upside down the Admiralty's faith in convoy as the primary solution to the U-boat problem. It also provided a boost to the proponents of offensive patrolling, but Churchill did not drive this agenda.[52] Magnetic mines were laid by aircraft, surface vessels, and on the west coast, U-boats. By the end of November 1939, the losses caused by mines began to dominate the statistics and briefly surpassed losses due to the torpedo and the gun. This threw the Admiralty and Churchill into something of a panic. The Admiralty ought to have been prepared to deal with this problem, but it was not. A "perplexed" DCNS, Phillips, found himself asking in desperation, "How had we dealt with unsweepable mines in the 1914–18 war?"[53] No answer could be supplied beyond presenting him with large volumes of the minesweeping records. Thus, until the matter was analyzed by the Royal Navy Historical Section, which was rapidly re-formed as a result of this problem, Churchill and the Admiralty were required to fly blind.

To his credit Churchill aggressively sought the means to defeat the mining threat. The greater part of his effort focused on sweeping the mines or exploding them before they could do harm. The navy had to undertake damage control, that is, to find the ways and means to minimize the impact of these weapons until a permanent solution was found. Unfortunately, some of the measures adopted, all of which were endorsed by Churchill at board meetings, proved unwise and had the potential to make the problem worse. They also threatened to substantially delay shipping. The core decisions were several.[54] Given that the Germans sought to lay mines in channels and along known shipping routes, a decision was made to extinguish lit buoys and require ships to anchor at night. This resulted in a significant delay in trade.

Potentially the most disastrous proposal, however, was to suspend convoys along the east coast and begin independent sailing. This, of course, went against all the lessons of the last war, but such were the losses to mines, this proposal, briefly, seemed the best solution to the problem. Churchill expected that the delay caused by not sailing at night would be offset by time saved in not waiting for convoys. For a time, the whole dynamics of convoy were challenged and compromised.

The rather panicked reaction to the mining threat had even more far-reaching consequences than these immediate measures. It provided a renewed emphasis on hunting and patrolling and intensified the focus on "killing" U-boats rather than protecting convoys. It was expected the escorts released from convoys would hunt the mining craft, but this proved an almost fruitless task. Captain Talbot, who had just become the director of the A/SWD, was quickly convinced that this would be the new face of submarine warfare: "Mine-laying from U-boats . . . can be carried out unseen and the U-boat can be well clear of the area before a ship is blown up; moreover, convoy escorts can provide no protection against mines. It therefore appears probable that the U-boat operations round the BRITISH ISLES will be devoted more and more to mine-laying."[55]

Talbot believed there were two solutions to this problem: more local patrolling and an intensive campaign to stop the U-boats breaking out of the North Sea. This meant a new emphasis on offensive patrolling and offensive mining and a policy of containment, the latter of which sat well with Churchill's own inclinations. However, there remained the matter of finding the necessary patrol craft. Talbot proposed temporarily sourcing ten or twelve destroyers from the Western Approaches Command. This, he contended, could be achieved by reducing to one the number of escorts per convoy in the outer approaches.[56]

Talbot's anxiety over the mining threat continued into 1940 and was at the center of his lengthy report *Review of Methods of Dealing with the U-Boat Menace*, in which he declared, "There was one way, and one way only [to] overcome the U-boat menace, and that is to kill U-boats." To this end he wanted more minefields, more antisubmarine vessels, and fast-striking forces to hurl at the U-boats.[57] The plan was to block the exits to the Atlantic from the North Sea by mines. Surface craft would patrol these fields and destroy any U-boat attempting to find a path through them. The proposals were always of doubtful efficacy but were acceded to. However, the fields would require time to prepare and huge numbers of mines. The northern mine barrage (discussed later) was particularly problematic. Talbot's efforts to promote an increased focus on offensive patrolling and a policy of containment were met with limited interest by those concerned with the protection of trade. They were loathe to see escorts drawn from convoys to achieve this, especially before minefields had been sufficiently developed to make such a policy remotely viable.

Churchill contributed to two important decisions influenced by the panic surrounding the magnetic mining threat. He signed off on a substantial new program of patrol and escort craft. In his draft submission to Pound, Captain Victor Danckwerts, director of plans, proposed, in addition to 336 escort vessels, the construction of 100 whale catchers to be used strictly as striking forces. Among the reasons he gave for this new force was the enemy campaign of mine laying by submarines off British harbors. "Experience has shown that only a vast number of asdic fitted vessels will ever be able to cope with this menace."[58] Churchill accepted a reduced, but nevertheless substantial, number of vessels intended for this purpose. Thus were the nation's slipways filled with ships that proved to be unsuited to future needs: a battle with the U-boat on the wide expanse of the Atlantic Ocean.[59] Of course, the construction of these vessels would prove serendipitous in the future war on trade when the U-boat threat developed far beyond Churchill's expectations, but it is an inescapable fact that they were first conceived for operations that would likely have served little constructive purpose.

The escalation of the magnetic mining problem also coincided with, and was a significant influence on, Churchill's decision to support the North Sea mining barrage.[60] Pound had been pressing the idea of this barrage since the beginning of the war, but Churchill had been greatly disturbed by the projected cost of the scheme. He finally acceded to the request and presented the idea to the War Cabinet on 19 November. He explained the drain on resources, actual and potential, caused by raiders, U-boats, and U-boat minelayers operating outside the North Sea. The mine barrage was intended to contain these threats and problems. Additionally, Churchill believed it would assist contraband control, provide added protection to

Scandinavian convoys, and reduce the loss by attrition of capital ships from U-boat activity.[61] The efficacy of the entire project was doubtful in the extreme and was based, in part, on flimsy evidence from World War I produced on short notice by the Admiralty Historical Section. The whole concept became redundant when the Germans acquired bases on France's Atlantic coast.

Extraordinarily, the real answer to the magnetic mining problem was already under Churchill's nose and was to be found in the direction he and some elements within the navy were taking. In a speech to the country in December, Churchill noted that the war at sea appeared to be targeting the more vulnerable neutrals.[62] Not only had they, relatively, borne the brunt of losses caused by the torpedo and gun, but they were also suffering grievously from the mine. Unfortunately, he took the observation no further, and neither he nor anyone else appeared to ask why this was so. The answer was just as it was for the wider war at sea: the neutrals were denying themselves the advantages of convoy, and convoy was saving British and French shipping. For both conventional and magnetic mines, the administrative advantages of a convoy were enormous. Postwar analysis showed that had all trade been placed in convoy, especially on the east coast, the losses due to mines would have remained within manageable levels.[63] Certainly, the German mining campaign would not have caused the panic it did during the last months of 1939 and the first months of 1940. Perhaps most influential in the significant decline in losses in early 1940 was that the U-boats and surface craft disposed fewer and fewer magnetic mines as time went on. Despite Talbot's expectations, Karl Doenitz always wished to return to the Western Approaches, especially when a further relaxation of prize conditions by Hitler provided even more opportunities. The magnetic mining operation was suspended briefly on the west coast when Hitler recalled the U-boats to prepare for Norway. Thereafter, the focus was the Western Approaches and, after the fall of France, the even safer waters of the wider Atlantic.[64]

Churchill and his naval staff worked in earnest to solve the mining problem, and many meetings were dedicated to this issue. Although he had unwittingly endorsed a rather counterproductive solution—the suspension of convoy—Churchill ultimately gained a not entirely justifiable kudos for the decline in losses to mines as a result of the degaussing procedure. Degaussing eventually made an important contribution, but in the immediate term losses to mines diminished more quickly than the number of degaussed vessels grew. Churchill and the Admiralty were fortunate that the decision to suspend convoy on the east coast did not proceed. It would have made matters very much worse, not better. Again, however, it is difficult to apportion blame to Churchill for the folly of these proposals. The recommendations were evidently a result of a system-wide ignorance, and no evidence indicates that Churchill did anything other than support a consensus view.

Conclusions

Churchill's role in the offensive patrolling folly is much less than is generally supposed. Much of what occurred during the Phoney War period accorded with Churchill's own inclinations, but these were not a driving force in, or a significant influence on, policy and practice. The dual policy of convoy and offensive patrolling developed because it appeared to work and because it appeared to serve well the circumstances.

For all the criticism of Churchill, he was a strong and vigorous supporter of convoy. That he subsequently questioned its universal application and got caught up in the killing of U-boats has been shown to be a rational and reasonable response to the challenges of the time. Moreover, he was not alone in asking the questions he did of convoy. He was a contributor to the errors subsequently made, not the primary cause of them. Decisions surrounding the loosening of the convoy system and the misinformation that sustained offensive patrolling had much more to do with interwar parsimony—which stifled historical inquiry—and a failure to learn the lessons of the previous war than with Churchill's strong character and personal preferences during this new one. Conversely, the early successes against the U-boat appeared to show there was real advantage in offensive operations, and the statistical record sustained this misperception for a long time. There was never any doubt that convoy protected ships, and the system did a remarkable job during the Phoney War; however, offensive patrolling appeared to be making its own significant contribution to the protection of trade, especially given the many independently sailed vessels that otherwise would have been left undefended. Moreover, offensive patrolling conducted appropriately and wisely was not without virtue.

The most serious criticism that might be leveled at Churchill and other supporters of offensive patrolling was that this practice denied convoys protection they might otherwise have received. This is doubtful, as is the link between offensive patrolling and the number of ships forced to sail independently. The primary influence on the decision to convoy or not was the assumptions surrounding two erroneous calculations: that the risk to faster vessels sailing independently would be offset by quicker turnaround in trade and that the separation of slower vessels—which constituted only a small percentage of overseas trade—from the main convoys would do the same. These were entirely rational influences. The uncertainty surrounding these calculations tended to sustain the view that killing U-boats was an essential element in the safe and timely arrival of cargo. Churchill recognized the importance of convoy to the safe arrival of ships; he was somewhat confused over the questions of timeliness, the risks and rewards of independent sailing, and the virtue of offensive operations to keep U-boat numbers down. The issue of U-boat mining operations and the fact that U-boats need not go anywhere near escorts to destroy shipping added another dimension to the confusion over the best course of action. However, in making errors of judgment, Churchill was always in good company. In criticizing Churchill's inclinations toward the offensive, it is also important to recognize that long after he left the Admiralty, disagreement continued over the importance of killing U-boats to the safe and timely arrival of a convoy. In any given situation the extent to which a convoy should be put at risk to facilitate the pursuit and destruction of an attacking U-boat was difficult to determine.

Nevertheless, a legacy of Churchill's time as first lord was the limited effort applied to achieving a more scientific understanding of the most efficient use of patrol and escort craft against the U-boat threat. An aspect of his tenure that stands out is how rarely, if at all, Churchill actively sought to learn the lessons of World War I. He had always been a great lover of statistics; the Admiralty Statistical Branch under Lindemann produced all manner of vital statistics of World War II, and it was expected lessons would be learned from them. Yet Churchill seemed very much less animated to seek out answers from the evidence of the earlier conflict. He sought statistics from 1917, a time when Britain was struggling mightily against the U-boat, but these inquiries seemed primarily intended to demonstrate how well, comparatively, the navy was doing in 1939. The limited initiative regarding the lessons of World War I came primarily from DCNS Phillips, and it was not enough.

Although Churchill's offensive spirit was not a significant influence in the convoy-patrolling debate, matters misread and misunderstood might have been better understood or more accurately interpreted by someone less offensively minded than he. Evidence that hinted at other and better paths was there to be found. For example, the attacks on and defense of *Courageous* and *Ark Royal*, which resulted in the destruction of one U-boat and damage to another, showed that U-boats could draw close to asdic craft without detection and were not easily found until and unless they first exposed themselves—a recommendation for convoy and escort. Yet the lesson learned from this episode, apart from the need for more caution in the use of carriers, was that offensive patrolling by destroyers, even over great distances, worked. An analysis of most other confirmed kills would have reaffirmed that asdic helped kill U-boats but did little to find them, except in situations where a U-boat had recently identified itself. A close analysis of the statistics kept by A/SWD would have shown that the greater part of the harm done to the U-boats was recorded as occurring in the frenetic opening weeks of the war and that the numbers of killed and damaged U-boats grew only modestly over time, thus hinting that the successes proclaimed were just a little too hopeful. Also, a more inquiring mind might have grasped why it was that neutrals were suffering so uniquely in the German mine campaign. However, this criticism must be viewed in the context of a time when Churchill, as first lord, was exposed to much more evidence showing that his admirals were doing well just as they were and that the U-boat had resorted to mining for that reason.

For all the apparent success Churchill believed he had in combating the U-boat menace, it is unlikely the anti-U-boat campaign lived up to his expectations. He had begun the war with the belief that the U-boat would not prove a major factor in the war at sea and that this would free naval forces for other activities, including plans to use Britain's surplus sea power in major offensive operations. These hopes likely ebbed and flowed throughout the Phoney War. At the end of October 1939, they were high, only to be dragged down over the next several months by the mining threat, the dispute over U-boat kills, and then, in January and February, Doenitz's renewed assault in the

Western Approaches. They were buoyed again in March when Churchill and others misread the hiatus in U-boat activity as a sign of German capitulation rather than as preparation for Norway, and they were then shattered when the real reason for this quiet time was realized. This disappointment was quickly followed by evidence via U-49 that suggested the navy had not been as successful in combating the U-boat as Churchill had thought. Although there were periods of high optimism, he could not claim the threat had been defeated, and he readily acknowledged that there would, in time, be a recrudescence of the problem as Germany prepared itself for a substantial U-boat construction program. Thus was Churchill's wider strategic agenda compromised; for so long as the U-boat was undefeated or not contained, the surplus flotilla forces needed to fulfill his offensive aspirations were not available. We must now turn to Churchill's wider plans for the use of the surplus forces of the navy.

CATHERINE

Operation Catherine was a plan proposed by Churchill in the opening fortnight of war to place a large British naval force in, and then to take command of, the Baltic Sea. The aggressive use of sea power was particularly attractive at the start of World War II, when it became quickly apparent that Britain and France were ill-prepared and unwilling to take action in the air or on land and Churchill already had a strategy to hand. Of the three services, the navy alone had a preponderance of forces over Germany, and the first lord wished to use some of this surplus force to take the war to the enemy. However, given existing strategic threats in Europe and Asia, the notion of surplus sea power for high-risk operations was dubious at best, and Churchill's naval staff did not welcome his proposal. Nevertheless, Churchill was deeply wedded to the idea of an incursion into the Baltic. It had been with him since World War I, and his history of that war, *The World Crisis*, had characterized it as the great missed opportunity.[1] Thus the stage was set for a vituperative conflict between naval staff and their new first lord.

Despite being known to students of the period, Operation Catherine has not been studied in any detail and generally remains inadequately understood. A close study of Catherine's origins and development can inform our understanding of Churchill's strategic vision and, more particularly, provide insight into the risks he was prepared to take to see his vision fulfilled. In support of Catherine, Churchill displayed a disturbing stubbornness despite mounting evidence of the operation's unviability. It is important to understand why this was so. Additionally, a study of Catherine supports an understanding of Churchill's relationship with Admiralty staff and identifies the challenges this staff had in managing him and his more aberrant plans for offensive action against the Germans.

The Origins of Catherine and Churchill's Strategic Blueprint

Within three days of becoming first lord, Churchill instructed his Plans Division to prepare an appreciation on the forcing of a passage into the Baltic by a British naval force. He had placed the Baltic at the center of his strategic thinking as far back as 1914–15, when he had also been the first lord. In 1936 he had suggested such an operation to curtail Germany's aggressive resurgence; he did so again in his "Memorandum on Seapower," written in March 1939 and forwarded to Chamberlain. The strategy outlined in this memorandum was a plan to use Britain's surplus naval strength in the Baltic for offensive inshore operations against Germany. Churchill believed command of the Baltic was a vital German interest. The loss of this command would threaten access to Scandinavian supplies, including Swedish ore, and would allow potential allies such as the Soviets to attack Germany along its undefended northern coastline "in one place little more than 100 miles from Berlin."[2]

For Churchill, entering and taking command of the Baltic was the "sole great offensive against Germany of British sea-power."[3] However, despite the Royal Navy's considerable preponderance over the German navy, the notion of a surplus of ships for high-risk operations was not an idea easily entertained by anyone other than Churchill. Although Britain had the support of the French marine in the event of war with Germany, the formidable threat of the Italian and Japanese fleets and the possibility that war with one of these powers might involve war with all three seemed to have discounted altogether the proposition the Royal Navy had ships surplus to potential needs. Britain's existing policy was, in time of war, to send a substantial naval force to Singapore to protect Australia and New Zealand and to discourage Japan from taking advantage of any tensions in Europe. Actual war with Japan would possibly require Britain to send an even larger force to the East. The addition of either threat to that of Germany would be more than enough to consume the surplus forces Churchill needed for the Baltic, and it would be difficult to determine when these threats would develop; they were always more likely to occur if Britain was embroiled in a war with Germany. Beyond the issue of surplus capital ships, there was the question of a potential U-boat campaign and the existing shortage of small craft, especially destroyers, needed to deal adequately with this threat. Finally, there was the question of German airpower, which would undoubtedly pose a serious challenge to any forces attempting to enter the Baltic and remain there.

Churchill believed he could see a way through all these difficulties. He argued that in the event of war with Italy and Germany, the former could be dealt with in the Mediterranean within two months. As for the Japanese threat, he was, almost uniquely, sanguine. It would, he declared, be neither necessary nor desirable to send a fleet to East Asia in the early stages of conflict with Japan. As heavily occupied as it was in China, Japan was unlikely to do more than attack Britain's "interests and possessions in the Yellow Sea."[4] Churchill proposed that these possessions be surrendered and retrieved in Britain's own good time after the defeat of Italy. Until then naval forces should not be sent to the East unless the United States entered the conflict. "On no account must anything which threatens in the Far East divert us" from "the main struggle with Germany. . . . In war . . . one only has to compare one evil with another, and the lesser evil ranks as a blessing." As for a wider threat to Australia and New Zealand, to the aid of which Britain had long promised to come, Churchill dismissed this absolutely. Japan would have to take Singapore, and he put this in the realm of the impossible, but if "per impossible, they were to attempt it, a British victory in the Mediterranean might be followed a few months later by a decisive naval relief of Singapore."[5]

Churchill was similarly dismissive toward the U-boat and air threats. He believed that the U-boat had been mastered. As far as the potential air threat to a fleet inside the Baltic, he expressed the view, "given with great humility (because things are very difficult to judge), an air attack upon British warships, armed and protected as they now are, will not prevent full exercise of their superior sea power."[6] This view of the air threat changed once war broke out, but for the time being the underestimation helped sustain Churchill's Baltic vision.

If the Royal Navy, with the support of the French navy, found itself in command of the Mediterranean and at peace with Japan in the opening months of the war, it would have a surfeit of forces for offensive operations against Germany. These could be directed to the Baltic, and Churchill recommended that "ardent officers" be set to work resolving the problem of "entering the Baltic and living there in indefinite ascendancy."[7] Left unaddressed in Churchill's memorandum was what his plan would be if Italy, along with Japan, were not at war, but merely hostile or "indeterminate." Would he be content to await the unfolding of events before he began pressing for an operation in the Baltic that would quickly consume his surplus forces and inevitably compromise the navy's ability to fight Italy or Japan or both at any point in the future? The outbreak of war would show that he would not.

Filled as it was with hypotheticals, Churchill's March memorandum evinced little interest with either Chamberlain or the minister for coordination of defense, Ernle Chatfield, the two men to whom it was sent.[8] Churchill nevertheless remained resolutely committed to his plan, and two days after he had been appointed first lord of the Admiralty by Chamberlain, he set his "ardent" officers to work to explore the possibility of a naval incursion into the Baltic.

On 12 September Churchill produced a new memorandum titled "Catherine," the ostensible purpose of which was to address the need for a special force that he and the director of naval construction, Stanley Goodall, had agreed a few days earlier would be needed to deal with the Luftwaffe if the operation took place. In this memorandum Churchill acknowledged that the air threat demanded special preparations. He suggested the core of his naval force should be two or, preferably, three of the old R-class battleships raised and protected by caissons against the mine and torpedo and strengthened by thick steel decking to "give exceptional protection against air bombing, which must be expected."[9] He also addressed the strategic objectives of the operation; these were much as they had been in his March memorandum, but most notably they included the isolation of Germany from Scandinavian supplies of ore and food and other trade. He now added, in response to (or anticipation of) concerns over locking up a large force in the Baltic, that the presence of such a force would hold "all enemy forces on the spot." Also added was the assertion that success would cause the Germans to "arm the whole northern shore against bombardment" or, with bases in Scandinavia, "military descents."[10] This latter suggestion reflected precisely his Baltic plans of World War I.

Significantly, unlike in his March proposal, Churchill did not mention Italy or Japan, presumably because neither was at war with the Allies. He proposed beginning the operation the moment the ice began to melt in the Baltic at the beginning of March, a time frame much too early for any certainty to have developed regarding these countries. The new Soviet threat was acknowledged only in the sense that this country might be positively influenced by the operation, although he noted, "We cannot count on this."[11] Unlike many within the government who viewed the Soviet Union as acting collusively with Germany, Churchill, at this point in the war, viewed its activity as primarily self-serving and defensive in nature and a potential boon to the Allied cause. He did not view the Soviets' nonaggression pact as a veto for operations in the Baltic, and this view did not change when they occupied eastern Poland in the middle of September.[12]

Overall, Churchill's effort at a strategic and operational outline of Catherine belonged to the cigar-butt strategy of which he is often accused.[13] Given the certainty of overwhelming German airpower, his reference to bombardments of and military descents on Germany's Baltic coastline was fantasy. His plan also ignored the massive advantage the Germans would have via their internal lines of communications in countering such an assault. Just as fantastic as the notion of military descents was his casual acceptance that his force would enter the Baltic and operate for up to three months without the certainty of a secure base. Planning for this possibility was necessary because it was impossible to divulge plans to enter the Baltic to any country until the attempt was made for fear of the loss of secrecy. Thereafter, it might take time before Sweden—the most likely place of refuge—was prepared to offer a fleet a safe harbor, if the offer was made at all. Thus, Churchill's intentions were to enter the Baltic and hope for the best, and he blithely contended that if after three months a base had not been found, the fleet could return the way it had come. A more naive and hope-filled prospect surely was not conceived throughout the entire war.

The Admiralty Response

The first formal Admiralty response to Churchill's Baltic plans was completed by the director of plans, Captain Danckwerts. The response was submitted the day Churchill circulated his Catherine memorandum, but it is unlikely Danckwerts saw the memorandum before he had completed his response. His assessment, nevertheless, addressed some of the more absurd proposals made by Churchill, and this suggests they had already been canvassed in discussion. Danckwerts contended that the only "sound" object of the operation would be the stopping of Germany's summer supply of iron ore via Sweden. He believed this would make an operation worthwhile so long as Britain's ability to maintain its worldwide sea communications was not prejudiced. He also considered it essential that Britain was not at war with Italy and Japan and that there was no prospect it would be.[14] The operation's viability thereafter would depend on two key issues: The first was access to a base, probably in Sweden or Finland. Danckwerts warned that to secure a base would be highly problematic because neither country would welcome becoming embroiled in war with Germany. The second issue was the German air threat (estimated at 1,400 bombers in the region), which he thought made the operation impracticable; however, he conceded this view might be amended by experience. As for the force needed, he believed this must be built around three modernized battleships and not the old R class, which were too slow to meet German ships in battle.[15] Furthermore, because the operation would need to take place in the early spring, it would not be possible, in the time available, to make the necessary improvements to the R class.[16]

Two days later the DCNS, Admiral Phillips, who by this time had seen Churchill's paper and Danckwerts', wrote his appreciation.[17] He thought that the operation, if successful, "should have a major effect on the war" and that the Plans Division assessment showed, save for the air threat, which was an "unknown quantity," a fleet could enter the Baltic. As for the air threat, Phillips agreed with Danckwerts that, by the time the operation could take place, they would have "a good deal more information" as to how dangerous this might be.[18] However, Phillips still assumed the R-class battleships would be used in the operation and insisted these be given exceptional protection to the upper deck and the "entire exposed superstructure." This would take at least six months, and therefore, preparation would have to begin immediately if "the operation is to be undertaken next spring." Phillips wondered whether it would be possible to "spare even the three R's to be fitted out" and shared his opinion that they could not "unless we can be sure that we shall not at a later date have Italy and Japan against us." Like Danckwerts, Phillips had two major concerns. The first was the need for a secure base inside the Baltic. He doubted any temporary base could be used for more than a week, and he suggested the government would have to accept that if Finland or Sweden declined to provide a safe base, the fleet should be given permission to seize one. Phillips' second concern was that Russia must not enter the war.

Phillips' appreciation prompted a supplementary assessment from Danckwerts and the Plans Division. Its salient point was the rejection of any proposal to use a "specially protected fleet of old battleships. . . . A well-balanced force of modern ships, including 3 capital ships, appears essential." Beyond this the appreciation returned to the vital importance of Swedish cooperation, without which the operation would not be viable. Danckwerts repeated a cautionary note, also present in Phillips' assessment, regarding the Soviet Union, which had only just invaded eastern Poland. If the Allies were at war with the Soviet Union, the latter's naval and air forces would increase the risks of the operation to "unacceptable levels."[19]

Apart from the disagreement over the use of R-class battleships, the appreciations by the Plans Division and Phillips shared much in common. Both considered a naval excursion into the Baltic as possible, but each had nominated preconditions that did not seem readily resolved. However, Churchill had to secure the support of his first sea lord to have any hope of advancing the scheme. During the evening of 18 September, Churchill and Pound met and discussed Catherine. We do not know what transpired at this meeting, but the following day Churchill proposed to Pound that all further investigation on Catherine be conducted by a "high officer," and he nominated the fiery, offensively minded admiral of the fleet, the Earl of Cork and Orrery (hereafter referred to as Lord Cork or Cork), for the role. This ex officio and somewhat anomalous role for Cork replicated the role Churchill had given the former first sea lord, A. K. Wilson, in the early months of World War I, when he was seeking to implement a similar operation.[20] Churchill suggested Cork could "work quietly in the Plans Division for some time until ready to make a report."[21] On 20 September, in response to this correspondence, Pound forwarded a note to Churchill that was essentially a barebones summary of the conclusions drawn in Danckwerts' and Phillips' papers, with two observations of his own thrown in regarding the objectives of Catherine: he considered its purpose to cut Germany's sea communications with Russia and influence the neutrals. His comments reflected little or no enthusiasm for the project and appeared to deliberately play down the single, albeit significant, virtue Danckwerts was able to find in it: the severance of Swedish ore trade to Germany through Lulea. Pound considered this "only of value from April to November owing to the Northern part of the Baltic being frozen up" and "likely to be of less value now that Germany and Russia have direct contact through Poland."[22] Nevertheless, he acknowledged that holding the Baltic for a considerable period would greatly enhance Britain's prestige. He emphasized, however, that the fleet must be "assured of the active support of Sweden and the force sent into the Baltic *must* be such that we can with our Allies at that time win the war without it in spite of any probable combination against us."[23]

Thus Pound left the door ajar for Catherine, while doing enough to dampen Churchill's enthusiasm for the operation. More privately, he had already passed definite judgment on the project in a letter to Admiral Charles Forbes, the commander in chief, Home Fleet, in which Pound had declared, "I do not feel that we are justified in risking our whole sea supremacy on what must after all be somewhat of a gamble."[24] Pound must have been fairly confident that given his political and operational preconditions, the plan would advance no further. Churchill replied to Pound that he entirely agreed with his assessment: "At present the decision is only for exploration; and no question for action arises. But the search for a naval offensive must be incessant."[25]

If Pound had concluded that Catherine was now a most unlikely prospect, it was because he had yet to grasp the full nature of Churchill's strategic vision and his determination to see it fulfilled.

Lord Cork: His Assessment and His Plan

Despite Churchill's expectation that Lord Cork would work quietly in the background for some time on Catherine, he took less than a week to complete a preliminary report.[26] Cork thought the operation was "perfectly feasible, hazardous no doubt but, for that very reason, containing the germ of a great triumph."[27] He believed the most serious potential problem of the operation was not getting into the Baltic, but the maintenance of the force thereafter, and he therefore urged that all effort be made "to procure [through diplomatic measures] a sheltered anchorage in the very near future." Cork also agreed that modernized battleships already in an efficient state be used, in part because the need to begin the operation early in 1940 would not permit any significant work on the Rs.[28]

Thus, in the blink of an eye, Churchill's rather ad hoc prewar plan to put to work the redundant and "surplus to need" R-class battleships of the Royal Navy in a bold offensive operation had taken on entirely new dimensions. Cork's conception demanded the use of the best of the available "recon-structed" battleships in what was likely to be a near-term operation. Over the next two months Catherine, under Cork, achieved enormous proportions. In addition to his Baltic force, he anticipated having a substantial portion of the Home Fleet in support and the assistance of three aircraft carriers, which, in addition to their contingent of Fleet Air Arm aircraft, would carry up to 150 Spitfires to protect the Baltic Fleet through its passage to the Baltic. Nor did his plan stop there. He also recommended the greater part of Britain's bomber force in the UK and France conduct continuous raids on airfields and other objectives in northern Germany during the operation. Finally, he expected Allied forces in France to carry out an offensive on the western front to coincide with the entrance of the fleet into the Baltic.[29]

Cork and his team were meticulous in their investigation and covered every potential aspect of the Baltic plan. The four large volumes of documents in the British National Archives reflect the enormous time and effort put into building a viable naval operation. However, an operation of the magnitude conceived by Cork had all sorts of ramifications. While the resources Cork wanted to commit to Catherine provided Churchill's conception with a modicum of operational viability, it made it much less likely it would ever take place, whatever Churchill and the navy might recommend. This level of aggression against Germany during the Phoney War would have been the very antithesis of War Cabinet policy, much of it endorsed by Churchill. The Allies' conservative bombing policy, a mixture of humanitarianism and self-preservation, would have had to change, as would the view that the less fighting the better while they prepared and rearmed. Cork's plan also demanded discussion with and the cooperation of the other two services. It is difficult to imagine the Royal Air Force (RAF) supporting a plan that would see 150 Spitfires operating in the Skagerrak and then flying on to bases in Sweden; all this while simultaneously inviting a substantial backlash from the Luftwaffe in France and England. It is probably for this latter reason that, throughout the planning of Catherine, Churchill maintained a cloak of secrecy, and only three or four people were officially aware of it.[30] No discussions were ever had with the army or air force. Until and unless Churchill secured Pound's full endorsement of the operation, he was not prepared to present Catherine to a wider forum. Try as he might in the following months, he was not able to gain the support he needed.

Churchill's Insistence and Pound's Resistance

Although Pound might reasonably have believed he had done enough to stop Catherine, he instead found himself at the beginning of October in a much more serious predicament than he had faced a fortnight before. Catherine had been endorsed by an admiral of the fleet, and because of the need to take advantage of optimum weather conditions, the operation had become very near term. The proposal to use modernized battleships meant it was also much more high risk. At a meeting of 3 October, Pound sought to regain lost ground by explaining to Churchill and Cork that, although he had agreed the passage into the Baltic was a practicable military operation, his remarks had not covered the political situation that he obviously thought was prohibitive. This declaration fell on stony ground and was another rather unwise tactical move. After all Cork had acknowledged certain political preconditions had to be met, most notably the support of Sweden, while Churchill had maintained he wished nothing more than to "prepare the gun for firing." Each, therefore, wished only to be ready for circumstances in which the right political situation developed.

The problem for Pound in this new line of argument was that Churchill considered Catherine itself might be the solution to the political impediments Pound had put before it. In his March memorandum Churchill had written, "In war . . . one only has to compare one evil with another, and the lesser evil ranks as a blessing."[31] Nine months later he wrote, "We have to select from a host of dangers the one which can best be dealt with, and which, if dealt with, causes all others to fall away."[32] At the start of World War II, Britain's enemy was Germany alone. Churchill held that if Britain could take the fight to Germany and defeat or compromise the enemy, all other threats would fall away. He also thought it was the navy's responsibility to address the operational issues of Catherine; political matters were beyond its remit.

The minutes of the 3 October Admiralty board meeting suggested that Pound was aware that by giving qualified support for the operation, he had made things difficult for himself. He therefore resorted to what would eventually be his most successful weapon against Catherine; he claimed that "it was not possible for any ships to be withdrawn from service in order to be prepared for the operation." He declined to agree to a deadline for the operation, and he rejected a formal program of preparation. However, unwilling to tackle his first lord head on, he agreed to permit work on vessels as they came in for general maintenance and repair, but only if the improvements assisted in the prosecution of normal duties and only if they did not produce undue delay.

Pound's deliberate stalling tactics were a double-edged sword. Believing he had secured Pound's, albeit reluctant, acquiescence, Churchill set about securing the many millions of sterling necessary to advance the preparation for Catherine, and this led to a great deal of wasted time, money, and resources. Further, Cork was so committed to an early start that he was willing to forgo a great deal of the structural preparations needed for his ships, and he believed that if the risk to the fleet was thereby increased, this could be compensated by an increase in the number of vessels used. In short, Pound's obstruction threatened only to lead to a larger and less well-prepared force attempting to enter the Baltic in early spring.

Such a scenario became more real as the final months of 1939 progressed. By December the idea of separating Germany from Swedish iron ore had developed war-winning dimensions for Churchill and the British War Cabinet. Although Churchill had mentioned early that cutting off Germany's supply of Swedish ore was a significant benefit of Operation Catherine, it was only in December that he began to view this as having "decisive" potential. For Churchill this enhanced considerably the risk-reward dynamics of Catherine and would cast Pound's preconditions for the operation in a completely different light. Here was a trophy worth great risk: "If dealt with [it would cause] all the others to fall away."[33]

Churchill continued to count on Italian neutrality, and he continued to discount a serious threat from Japan. He was also keenly motivated during this time to minimize tensions with these countries and to make these threats even more remote.[34] Unfortunately for his plan, the issue of the USSR had become more problematic with its threatening behavior toward, and subsequent invasion of, Finland at the end of November. In Pound's mind this aggressive behavior was an insurmountable obstacle for Catherine. Churchill and Cork viewed the Soviet threat as creating opportunity. Each believed (and this would become the War Cabinet view also) that fear of the Soviet Union made it more likely Sweden would become involved in the war on the Allied side. Each also believed such a prospect would be considerably enhanced if Britain could tell the Swedes that the Royal Navy was ready to come to its aid.[35] Cork, who was increasingly frustrated at the slow progress of preparation, wrote another memo to Churchill and Pound on 17 November seeking a deadline for Catherine and reminding them why it was desirable to conduct the operation earlier rather than later. Moreover, Cork argued, "if we cannot promise her [Sweden] instant support by the presence of a strong British or Allied naval force in that sea, we shall miss our chance, and lose the alliance of a virile and determined people."[36]

Churchill's response to Cork's request for a deadline was to suggest an ill-considered compromise. He deferred the date of Catherine to 30 April but insisted that "every preparation must be made to work with certainty" to this new time frame. He was remarkably unfazed by the potential military consequences of delay, including appreciably diminished hours of darkness through which to make a passage into the Baltic. Just as remarkably, Cork, who had repeatedly emphasized the need for concealment and surprise for the success of the enterprise, accepted the postponement.[37] Churchill's solution to the increased risks of operating in "short darkness hours" was breathtakingly inadequate. He thought the problem, which markedly increased the risk of air attack, might be ameliorated by equipping the naval force with the upward projectile (UP) device.[38] The UP weapon was a device of doubtful efficacy in which Churchill had developed, for no readily apparent reason, great faith. It would prove a complete failure when it was finally used. That Churchill imagined this weapon could prove, in such a short time, the answer to the air threat to Catherine, represents folly not easily explicated.

Pound's views of the implications of the Soviet threat were considerably more rational than Churchill's or Cork's, and on 3 December his criticism of Catherine became considerably more aggressive. He argued that after its invasion of Finland, Russia was now the "determining factor" in Catherine.

He rejected Churchill's new request to draw up a program of preparation, declaring, "Until the trade route has been cleared of raiders, and the U-boat menace, whether from torpedoes or mines, has been destroyed, it will be quite impossible to spare the force which will be required for 'C.'" He thought the resolution of all these problems—none of which would disappear over-night—would give adequate warning for the reconsideration of Catherine, and he proposed that in the interim, Cork's committee be disbanded.[39]

Churchill maintained quite the opposite view and was far from ready to surrender Catherine. The plan's growing risks were being offset by Churchill's developing awareness of the importance of Swedish ore to the German war machine, a subject for a subsequent chapter. Success in Scandinavia could secure Germany's defeat, and war with Russia was not an inevitable adjunct to this. Cork was of an even more aggressive mind-set. On 5 December he recommended that the Allies use the Soviet invasion of Finland to mobilize the anti-Bolshevik forces of the world, including Italy and Japan. In short, he foresaw an exchange of belligerents: Russia for Italy and Japan. Churchill subsequently noted in response that he hoped "that war with Russia may be avoided."[40] Nevertheless, he was willing to contemplate the possibility with a degree of equanimity. In the aftermath of the Russian invasion of Finland, he advised, "It would be premature to anticipate a solid alliance between Germany and the USSR."[41] However, if this alliance developed, he thought that whatever material aid the Soviet Union might offer to Germany would "no doubt" be compensated for by a change in attitude from Italy, Japan, and other countries.[42] With such extraordinary thoughts in mind, on 11 December Churchill rejected Pound's argument that Soviet aggression against Finland was a veto on Catherine: "No opinion can be formed on this at present. . . . We may find ourselves at war with Russia, and Allies of Sweden, Norway, Finland and Italy. In this case the Baltic would assume capital importance. Bases would be forthcoming, and Air protection from England might be available. . . . I should wish that both preparations for stores and ammunition for 'C' should be pressed in so far as they do not impede daily operations."[43]

Churchill was discovering all sorts of possibilities in the new political situation. Such accumulated wishful thinking made the risk-reward scenario of Catherine much more attractive. Thus, despite Pound's concerns Churchill refused to relinquish his plan. Rather, as December progressed, Churchill's views hardened on the subject. By mid-December the War Cabinet had conceived the Finnish option. This plan is a subject for a subsequent chapter. It suffices here to say that the objective of this plan was to secure the cooperation of Sweden and, thereby, to secure the Gallivare ore fields. As far as Churchill was concerned, the shortest route to Swedish cooperation was Catherine.

By coincidence, on 25 December Churchill and Pound sent each other their strategic appreciations in personal and private letters. It is probable that neither read the correspondence of the other before sending his own, but Catherine figured prominently in both. Pound did his best to discourage further pursuit of the operation by promoting the Finnish option, for which he believed a high-risk naval operation was unnecessary. He returned to the navy's extensive responsibilities, which were now expected to grow; in the circumstances he could not envisage the forces needed being available in 1940. Moreover, he maintained the risk would be too great unless the fleet entered at the invitation of the Russians, and as a sop, he offered an incursion into the Baltic by a submarine force, although he did his best to dampen this idea.[44]

Churchill, in contrast, thought Catherine now had "a far greater measure of strategic relevance and urgency." He wrote that recent political developments and War Cabinet initiatives might soon place Britain in a position of close friendship or alliance with Sweden and Norway, with all the attendant advantages for Catherine. However, Churchill's continued emphasis on using surplus naval force for Catherine was surely disingenuous. Given Britain's actual and potential commitments and the number and the nature of the ships Cork intended to use in his operation, Churchill must have known that Catherine had moved far beyond his original conception. But if the risks of Catherine had grown, so too had the potential reward. Indeed, Catherine, political developments, and War Cabinet strategy were dovetailing like never before. Through one decisive move and the use of a superior, if by no means surplus, force, Germany's capacity to wage war might be severely compromised; thereafter, the lesser threats, the Soviet Union, Italy, and Japan, would pose no serious concern. "The supreme strategy is to carry the war into a theatre where we can bring superior forces to bear, and where a decision can be obtained which rules all other theatres."[45]

The great decision, of course, was Swedish ore. So enamored was Churchill with the prospects of separating Germany from its ore supply, he was now prepared to accept war with Russia. Any threat from Russia, he argued, would be dwarfed by success in the Scandinavia. "If Germany is starved by want of iron ore, Russia could be no serious menace to the victorious Western Allies. All would stand or fall upon success in Scandinavia."[46] Thus, Churchill casually put to one side all the obligations made by Britain at this time. Over the previous several months, he and the War Cabinet had been touting Britain's naval power with considerable largesse. A naval force was offered to Turkey in the event it was threatened by the Soviet Union. The early departure of the Second Australian Imperial Force (AIF) from Australia had been secured by Churchill's reaffirmation of a commitment to seal up the Mediterranean and send a fleet to Singapore if Australia were threatened by Japan. France had been offered significant naval support in the Mediterranean in the event of war with Italy. None of these potential commitments was compatible with the maintenance of a significant force within the Baltic, but if Catherine succeeded in all its objectives, it was unlikely Britain would be called on to fulfill them. It was an extraordinarily all-or-nothing approach to strategy. Catherine was not only a risk at an operational level but, if it failed, a great gamble at a grand strategic level because it would compromise Britain's capacity to meet other commitments in the Mediterranean and the Far East.

Despite his continued promotion of Catherine in his 25 December letter, there was, for the first time, evidence of hesitation from Churchill. This had more to do with an alternative presenting itself rather than a diminished view of Catherine's efficacy. Like Pound, he saw promise in the War Cabinet's Finnish option, and he did not wish to see this plan compromised by a dependence on an operation that might not prove possible.[47] Nevertheless, he pressed on Pound the advantage offered by Catherine to the burgeoning plans for action in Scandinavia. A willingness to enter the Baltic in March or April or later might be decisive in determining Norway's and Sweden's attitudes. Conversely, should support from Sweden be forthcoming, many of the problems surrounding Catherine would disappear.

The fortnight between Christmas and the end of the first week of January was the most intense period of disagreement between Churchill and Pound over Catherine. For Churchill, by this time the gravest threat to Catherine was Soviet and German airpower. Although he acknowledged it would be wrong to go forward unless we can "see our way to maintaining [the fleet] under air attack," on 29 December he sent Cork a list of hypotheticals, copied to Pound, that he hoped might ameliorate this and other problems.[48] Among them were that the Soviet Union was hostile but "pretty rotten" and "not actually at war with Britain and France and that Sweden and Norway were allies."[49] Even if Churchill's hypotheticals had received a positive response—and they did not—his ongoing interest in Catherine beggared belief. He was no longer asking about a fully prepared inshore squadron ready to enter the Baltic during the longer nights of late winter and early spring; he wished now to know if Cork would support an incompletely prepared force, with reduced destroyer support, attempting this extraordinary challenge as late as May, at a time when Scandinavia and the Baltic was expected to be a major war zone.[50]

Pound's reply challenged Churchill's propositions one by one. In presenting his argument, he sought to use the preparations needed for the COS's Finnish option as a block to Catherine.[51] He pointed out that the Germans could use Russian airfields to attack the fleet in the Gulf of Bothnia; the railway could not supply the fleet because it would be needed to supply the expeditionary force (which was then being mooted with the War Cabinet as part of the Finnish option); only three air squadrons could be maintained near Lulea, well short of the numbers required to protect the fleet; and not even the two destroyer flotillas Churchill now proposed would be available for the operation, for these would be needed to support amphibious landings elsewhere. "Catherine," he concluded, was "a great gamble" that was "courting disaster."[52]

Nevertheless, Churchill refused to concede the arguments against Catherine and responded with a repudiation of many of the obstacles Pound had put before him. Some, however, he accepted were, for now at least, beyond contesting. He was particularly concerned by the number of destroyers required for the plan, whether it be two or three flotillas, an enormous commitment given the status of the U-boat war and the magnetic mining threat. However, if it were not possible to use two British flotillas in April or May, "perhaps at the end of 1940." Thus, Churchill argued, there was "no reason why the study of the question should not continue," and he reminded Pound of one of the core virtues of his original proposal: "It must be remembered . . . that if a British Fleet were placed in the Baltic, it would act as a magnet to draw in German vessels from the outer seas and that very great relief would come thereby."[53]

It was, belatedly, Cork who made the most significant contribution to the demise of Catherine. His appreciation of 3 January generally supported Pound, although in a display of moral fortitude and continuing operational insanity, Cork still thought the plan worthy of consideration in certain circumstances. On 5 January he argued that Russian forces "are not so formidable as previously represented" and that "if the object to be attained is of such great importance as to justify the possible loss of a considerable portion of the Fleet, then I consider that risk should be taken." This prompted Pound's last and most powerful response. He wrote that he "would be in agreement with this last statement, if I thought it was conceivable that a surface force, such as proposed, could attain its object." He then outlined, step by step, the obstacles and challenges that would be faced by the fleet before concluding in a manner that clearly marked the distinction between his own strategic view and that of Churchill and Cork: "Our first object must be to win *this* war, but it is important that we should, if possible, end the war with our sea supremacy unchallenged."[54] Finally, Churchill capitulated, but only conditionally: "I have come reluctantly but quite definitely to the conclusion that the operation we outlined in the autumn will be not practicable this year."[55] Catherine was gone, but only for the year 1940. Despite all that had taken place, Churchill maintained his Baltic vision and insisted all provisions accumulated for the operation be stored for the future. Thoughts of using the modernized Warspites were given up; instead, he would spend much of 1940 agitating for his pet project, the reconstruction of the R class.

Conclusions

Catherine was born of Churchill's long-standing preoccupation with the Baltic and his belief that an incursion there represented the best offensive open to the Royal Navy if it were to have a decisive influence on Germany's capacity to wage war. The attraction of Catherine for him was that it was a low-risk gamble for high stakes. The battleships he proposed to use were slow, redundant, surplus-to-need vessels that nevertheless carried 15-inch guns. A successful incursion into the Baltic might secure the allegiance of Norway, Sweden, and perhaps even Soviet Russia, and it would separate Germany from vital trade with Scandinavia, most particularly Swedish ore, and make a major contribution to the economic isolation of Germany.

Churchill's naval staff viewed the operation with much greater reservation. First Sea Lord Dudley Pound considered Catherine a high-risk operation with vessels—including destroyers—he thought Britain could not afford to lose in view of the potential future threat of Italy and Japan. Although he conceded the advantages of a successful operation, he doubted that, at either a political or operational level, success would be achieved. Churchill's appreciation of the potential value of the operation, especially his attitude to the separation of Germany from its supply of Swedish ore, clouded his judgment. The operation's potential had no such effect on Pound. While in the broadest sense Churchill's preparedness to take significant risks in the pursuit of a major surprise is not without merit, Catherine must ultimately be judged on the probability of success. Operationally, Catherine was always problematic and became ever more so as time went on. Churchill showed little more political awareness and, arguably, much less than his naval staff, which recognized early that the Swedes were always likely to feel more threatened and not less by Churchill's offer of a Baltic fleet. Moreover, in its last incarnation—with Russia and Germany potential antagonists—the prospects for Catherine, whether operational or political, reduced to zero, but for a time Churchill persisted. In the circumstances, there is little for which Churchill is to be commended over Catherine. Visionary grand strategy has value only if it is centered in operational practicability.[56]

Churchill's sense of grand strategy and his risk taking goes a long way to explaining the challenges Pound and other naval staff had in deflecting him from his plan. Once the viability of the plan had been conceded—and despite the extensive codicils and preconditions put forward—Churchill's "prepare the gun for the firing" approach combined with his reluctance to permit Pound to trespass on the political arena to ensure planning and preparation would run a long course before he finally capitulated. Pound's challenge was made all the more difficult by the endorsement given the plan by Cork. In the circumstances, he did as much as he could and, arguably, as much as was wise to resist Churchill.

Pound's victory over Catherine was not the end of Churchill's pursuit of the ways and means to apply Britain's appreciable naval preponderance to the winning of the war. It merely took another guise.

THREE

NEW CONSTRUCTION AND CHURCHILL'S INSHORE SQUADRON

A New Perspective on Churchill and the Air-Sea Debate

The kind of naval war Churchill expected to fight as first lord is evident in the construction programs he supported in the early stages of World War II. The priorities he set, most particularly regarding capital ships, placed him in ongoing conflict with Pound, Phillips, and other members of his naval staff. Two core issues were at the heart of this conflict: Churchill's decision to delay the construction of the 16-inch-gunned battleships of the 1938 and 1939 programs (hereafter called the Lions) and his determination to convert several existing battleships into an inshore squadron for aggressive offensive operations. Each initiative reflected Churchill's strategic priorities and his wider strategic vision, including the priority he gave to the war with Germany over the longer-term protection of Britain's imperial interests and obligations. They also reflected the considerable influence of Churchill's previous wartime experience on the directions he chose to take at the start of World War II. The study of these matters opens an opportunity to assess Churchill's view of the threat of airpower to the function and mobility of the Royal Navy, a subject on which there exists much misunderstanding.

New Construction: The 1939 Emergency Construction Program

From his first days at the Admiralty, Churchill was determined to prepare for only the first two years of war, a time during which he believed Britain would be at its most vulnerable. Despite having no direct involvement in the Royal Navy for a quarter century, Churchill set about amending many of the construction priorities then under discussion at the Admiralty in an effort to refocus the construction program on securing warships for "this war" with Germany.[1] The needs of the "next war," perhaps with Japan, were to take a distant second place. Among the most important changes introduced by Churchill, and the most relevant to this study, was his recommendation that save the first three or four of the *King George V*-class battleships (KGVs), all capital ship construction be suspended for a full year, with the decision to be reviewed every six months.[2] On 10 September Churchill explained his rationale to Chamberlain: "It is by this change that I get the spare capacity to help the Army in the heavy stuff. On the other hand I must make a great effort to bring forward the smaller anti-U-boat fleet. Numbers are vital in this sphere."[3] Churchill's impressive altruism toward the needs of the army, not commonly found in a first lord, was based in his clearheaded pragmatism that Britain must have a strong presence in France to help sustain French morale. Although Churchill had some apprehensions to the contrary, he generally held that the western front would not easily be broken by an assault, and the Germans would be shy of attempting one, especially so late in the year. His determination to see the rapid growth of the British Army and the equally rapid transfer of divisions to France was also his insurance policy against this possibility. He was determined naval needs did not entrench unduly on these objectives.

Another important influence on his altruism was a legacy of, not only his liberal roots, but other positions he had held in government: his former role as first lord; his work as the chancellor of the exchequer; and more particularly, his duties as minister for munitions in the final year of World War I. As first lord he had emphasized from the beginning the importance of economy. In August 1914 he had announced to his personal secretary, Rear Admiral Horace Hood, his intention to suspend all construction that could not be completed before the end of 1915, adding that "thrift & scrupulous attention to detail are the mark of efficient administration in war. After all these years the Admiralty is now on its trial as an organisation, & the First Lord is vy [very] anxious that vigorous action shd be combined with strict economy."[4]

In his later wartime role as minister for munitions, he endeavored to rationalize the distribution of resources, and he faced the navy's unreasoned resistance to such efforts: "In the last war," he wrote in his letter to Chamberlain, "the Admiralty used their priority arbitrarily and selfishly, especially in the last year, when they were overwhelmingly strong, and had the American Navy added to them."[5] One can sense Churchill's annoyance that a bloated Royal Navy had sought more than was needed and his frustration that it had done so little with what it already had. His determination that this behavior would not be repeated was at the heart of his capital ship construction policy.

Churchill's proposals met with immediate resistance from the Admiralty. A preliminary appreciation warned that a delay of more than a few months would cause a deficiency in battleships over the combined forces of Germany and Japan. An Admiralty Board meeting recommended that all five of the KGVs be advanced as fast as possible and that this would require bringing forward HMS *Beatty* and *Jellicoe* (later *Howe* and *Anson*) to 1941.[6] A final decision about the last two KGVs and the Lions was put off until the 28 September board meeting, and this gave Pound time to submit a paper disputing any long-term suspension of new capital ships. "Once we have delayed these ships," he argued, "we cannot retrieve the situation."[7]

These arguments between Churchill and Pound represented another important difference in their views of the war beyond their respective tolerances for risk. Pound wanted to build for a future strength while fighting the present conflict. Churchill saw little virtue in this. Preparing for a future war, years ahead, could result in the loss of this war.[8] There was prescience in Churchill's approach, especially regarding Germany. In December Hitler suspended all work on capital ships that could not be completed by the end of 1940.[9] His objective was to apply resources to winning the war by the end of that year, or shortly thereafter; one of Churchill's objectives, in contrast, was to avoid losing it within the same time frame.

Despite Pound's concerns the question of the Lions was resolved somewhat anticlimactically. Gun mounting and other issues meant the hulls could be postponed without any practical delay in construction. Meanwhile, the controller, Admiral Bruce Fraser, had concluded that a postponement would relieve the "situation in all branches of naval shipbuilding work" and allow the laying down of eight intermediate-class destroyers.

Less than a week later, however, Churchill revisited his proposal to focus on some and not all the KGVs when he learned of the extensive delays in the completion of the battleships, aircraft carriers, and cruisers already in hand. He now took an even more vigorous stand over construction priorities and his strategic time frame: "It is far more important," he argued to Pound, "to have some ships to fight with . . . than to squander effort upon remote construction which has no relation to dangers!" He wanted all skilled labor shifted to vessels that could be completed during 1940: "Those finishing in 1941 fall into the shade, and those of 1942 into the darkness. We must keep superiority in 1940." Churchill sought two new battleships, four aircrafts carriers, and a dozen cruisers "commissioned and at work before the end of 1940."[10] His focus was on one or two modern ships to take on *Bismarck* in the not too distant future, and not on a hypothetical Japanese threat.

The Inshore Squadron

Even more controversial than his decision to delay new construction was the pressure Churchill simultaneously applied to secure resources and slipways for the reconstruction of several existing battleships for his inshore, or close action, squadron. On 18 September he wrote to Pound, "We must have all armour capacity, which can be spared, for strengthening HM ships against air attack."[11] This statement was initially made in support of Operation Catherine, but Churchill would pursue his inshore squadron independently of these requirements. On 21 September he expressed concern to Pound that ships had been reconstructed to fight in the line of battle when Germany had no line of battle with which to fight. Modernization, he thought, should be reconsidered from the point of view of air attack.[12]

One month later, in a 21 October letter to Pound, Churchill again expressed his determination to have several capital ships capable of withstanding the German air threat:

> I address this to you alone, because together we can do what is needful. We must have a certain number of capital ships that are not afraid of a chance air bomb. . . . It is quite true that it may well be a hundred to one against a hit with a heavy air-torpedo upon a ship, but the chance is always there and the disproportion is grievous. . . . I want four or five ships made into tortoises that we can put where we like and go to sleep content. There may be other types which will play their part in the outer oceans; but we cannot go on without a squadron of heavy ships that can stand up to the battery from the air.[13]

Churchill's insistence on an inshore squadron had its antecedents in his experiences of World War I.[14] In 1917 he had argued that the vast preponderance of the combined British and U.S. fleets would permit the establishment of two fleets: a blue-water fleet for maintaining the supremacy of the seas and oceans and another, rendered comparatively torpedo-proof, to discharge the functions of an "Inshore Aggressive Fleet" and to contain the enemy forces within their ports.[15]

A quarter century later Churchill had precisely the same mind-set, and he made almost precisely the same distinction. The single difference was his concern with the air threat. When writing and speaking of the battleship as the ultimate arbiter of sea power, he did so only in the context of blue-water strategy. He believed that at ranges beyond the enemy air threat, the battleship would continue to reign supreme. His view on the role of Britain's battle fleet operating within range of land-based aircraft was a different story: almost none of his capital ships were ready to face this modern threat, although he assumed his new ships would be. Only in exceptional circumstances, Catherine among them, would he risk the existing fleet of battleships within range of aircraft.[16] He was anxious to have ready several KGVs to deal with Germany's large ships during 1940–41, but what he really feared was a rerun of World War I, in which, he believed, the overwhelming power of the Royal Navy's capital ships had played so little role in Germany's final defeat. No advantage could be gained from this preponderance in naval power unless, and until, some battleships were reconstructed to resist the threat from land-based aircraft. His inshore squadron was the answer to fighting this war more aggressively.

In the existing literature Churchill is almost universally declared to be dismissive of the air threat and its capacity to influence strategy and tactics. This is untrue. He was fully alive to this threat, and at times it preoccupied him. His search for the ways and means by which to deal with this problem was at the heart of his strategic thinking. At the start of World War II, Churchill was far from the "gun and battleship sailor" preoccupied with fighting another Jutland.[17] Rather, he wanted the battle fleet—or at least part of it—put to work to help win the war on the continent: "If we allow ourselves indefinitely to be confined to an absolute defensive by weaker forces, we shall simply be worried and worn down while making huge demands upon the national resources. I could never become responsible for a naval strategy which excluded the offensive principle and relegated us to keeping open lines of communication and maintaining the blockade."[18]

Churchill, the British War Cabinet, and the French government were all looking to the periphery of Europe for opportunities to hurt Germany, to influence friends, and to deter potential enemies. This made eminently desirable the provision of extra protection for the navy's warships against land-based aircraft. Churchill hoped he had the Baltic covered by Operation Catherine. However, from the beginning of October, it was apparent that this operation would be undertaken, if at all, by the Warspites, reconstructed vessels that, nevertheless, were ill-prepared to cope with the air threat. Churchill accepted that, in the instance of Catherine, this would make the plan a major strategic gamble for high stakes, but the substitution of the Warspites for reconstructed Rs also meant he would be denied his inshore squadron unless he addressed this matter independently. If Catherine failed to develop, other operational prospects would arise that would require well-protected capital ships. His interest in an alliance with Turkey and the need to sustain Romania had already convinced him of the importance of holding the Black Sea against a German or a Soviet threat, and there was, of course, always the prospect of war in the Mediterranean against the Italians.

Churchill also thought it might become necessary to conduct inshore operations in the North Sea to contain the German naval threat.[19] As the previous quotation suggests, he was acutely aware of the enormous drain that could be made on the navy's resources by even a single raider operating in the wider oceans, and there was also the recrudescence of the U-boat problem he anticipated in 1940. One objective of Catherine was to contain German naval forces to the Baltic. It was also with containment in mind that Churchill had supported Pound's mine barrage. This policy would restrict or discourage German naval activity outside the North Sea but would increase the likelihood of naval action within range of Germany's land-based aircraft and thus required specially protected capital ships.[20] The policy of containment was also important because it was the shortest possible route to freeing capital ships for operations in the Far East.

In correspondence with Churchill, Pound conceded that "we are now entering on the contest between air power and sea power in the narrow seas," and he authorized an inquiry to determine how Britain's capital ships could be made "inexpugnable except by their own class."[21] His willingness to do this was surprising given his attitude toward Catherine, but it was possible

Pound expected that an investigation would counsel against improvements requiring the withdrawal of ships from service. He might also have believed an inquiry would reinforce the need for new capital ships.

The inquiry found that all capital ships had room for improvement in one way or another but that none then in service should undergo any significant structural change, including the addition of protection against aircraft. This included the Rs, the candidates for Churchill's inshore squadron.[22] The Rs were considered "valuable units in the event of the fleet going to the Far East, but no value as battleships if re-bulging and re-arming took place." Moreover, they were currently needed for convoy duty.[23] Curiously, no comments about deck armor were made. This suggested that Pound, despite his concession, was still not taking the inshore squadron seriously. Certainly, naval staff had difficulty in maintaining a consistent line on the value of capital ships. As justification not to reconstruct them, they were described as valuable units for operations in the Far East in time of trouble; as justification for building new battleships, these vessels were described as redundant, of little value, and incapable of facing any enemy. In the circumstances, there was no doubt Churchill would revisit the reconstruction of the Rs.

The 1940–41 Construction Program

The dimensions of Pound's capital ship new construction program emerged in early January. He wished to bring forward Churchill's time frame and begin *Lion* and *Temeraire* in July 1940 and *Conquerer* and *Thunderer* in September. Additionally, he adopted the idea, first broached with and endorsed by Churchill at the beginning of December, for a 15-inch-gunned battleship or battle cruiser type using four available spare turrets of the R class. This ship would be ordered in July 1940 and completed by December 1943.[24] Pound also wanted a second 15-inch-gunned battleship to be ordered in 1940, but this would depend on decisions regarding other construction. It was anticipated that two 16-inch-gunned battleships and two 15-inch-gunned battle cruisers would be laid down for the two years thereafter. Evidently, Pound had yet to grasp Churchill's determination to contain naval spending and secure his own strategic agenda.

There was not the slightest chance this expensive capital ship construction program would prove acceptable to Churchill, who wrote to the chancellor of the exchequer, Sir John Simon, and promised to "sedulously" examine the entire naval construction program "with a view to making sure that the Admiralty does not trench unduly upon the National War effort."[25] Pound's program was certain to do just that. Moreover, none of the proposed construction, except for the first 15-inch-gunned battleship, complied with Churchill's expectation that all energy be put into the completion of ships for this war.[26] Further, Danckwerts' recommendation that a total of five 15-inch-gunned battleships be built seemed designed to produce particular offense. These ships could be constructed only by using turrets from the existing R-class battleships, which, only a few weeks before, had been deemed too important to be withdrawn from duty and reconstructed for Churchill's inshore squadron. To add insult to injury, to achieve Pound's program, each R-class battleship would be decommissioned a full three and a half years before the completion of its replacement.[27] Churchill's own recommendations for the Rs had two or three of them out of operation for nine to eighteen months. Thus, it appeared his naval staff was willing to do without these ships to produce new vessels in the longer term but not to produce Churchill's inshore squadron in a very much shorter term. The Admiralty was focused on the possible needs of the next war. Churchill, in contrast, viewed the navy as already having a capital ship program in excess of likely needs; rather than build more for a remote threat, he wished to focus on construction for an immediate one.

On 1 February Churchill submitted his draft naval program for 1940–41 for the board's consideration. It bore little resemblance to the program Pound and Phillips had in mind. He proposed that the Admiralty not ask for any new capital ships for 1940–41. Progress would be made on *Lion* and *Temeraire* "in due course," *Conqueror* would be proceeded with, but *Thunderer* would be held over until 1941. In the interest of economy and an appreciably earlier completion date, Churchill proposed that *Conqueror* become a 15-inch-gunned battle cruiser instead of a 16-inch-gunned battleship and suggested this might be repeated with *Thunderer* the following year.[28] In other words, the last two 16-inch-gunned battleships would disappear altogether and be replaced by two 15-inch-gunned ships that would use the spare R-class turrets and another set from one existing ship. The final element of this proposal was a recommendation to "give very strong additional deck armour" to the remaining four R-class battleships to "make these old vessels effective units by the summer of 1941."[29]

Churchill's proposals represented another deft attempt to meet Pound's demand for more new construction and his own demand for economy and ships for this war. They also represented a calculated gamble that these vessels could meet the Japanese 16-inch-gunned ships successfully in battle. His proposals also reflected his conviction that if the Japanese threat developed during this war, it would be better to have 15-inch-gunned battleships sooner rather than 16-inch-gunned battleships later. Churchill's expectations regarding the Rs and his inshore squadron remained as they had been, although he accepted that fewer of these would be rearmored. Two weeks earlier, in announcing the suspension of Operation Catherine on 15 January, he had reaffirmed his determination to have a close action squadron mounting thirty-two 15-inch guns that in the spring of 1941, "could be used with much confidence in the Baltic, if we decided to go there, or in the Heligoland approaches, or in the southern part of the North Sea, or of course in the Black Sea or Marmora."[30]

The naval staffs' shocked and quick response demonstrated further how little they understood Churchill's motivation and strategic direction. Phillips unwisely made reference to the substantial building program that had taken place during World War I, and he lamented, "It is not often realised how comparatively small the demands which the Navy makes upon the country's efforts in war are compared to that of the other services."[31] Such sentiments, so naively expressed by Phillips, were the antithesis of Churchill's own views. The extra wartime construction pressed on Churchill by Fisher, which played so little part in the 1918 defeat of Germany, was the issue against which Churchill was now reacting and to which he had drawn Chamberlain's attention in the first week of war.

Churchill's determination to limit new capital ship construction and focus on preparation for this war ultimately withstood the challenge of the naval board. He had the sympathy of Admiral Fraser, who had several times warned Pound that his capital ship program was excessive, especially given the large merchant ship program required. Although Fraser worked hard to find a way to meet Pound's program with regard to Japan by dropping other vessels, he did so with little conviction: "It seems to me that if Japan is going to take action at all her only chance is to do it during this war in which case the three battleships . . . would still be of no avail."[32]

The Japanese threat continued to be pressed by Pound and Phillips, but Churchill appeared interested in Japanese construction only to the extent it allowed him to justify even the modest program he was seeking. By mid-February Churchill and his sea lords were finding more common ground. Although the rate and nature of progress on the capital ships was kept vague, the two 16-inch-gunned battleships, *Temeraire* and *Lion*, would go forward.[33] Preliminary work would proceed on *Conqueror* and *Thunderer* but would not exceed £1 million in expenditure. Only one new ship, the 15-inch-gunned battle cruiser HMS *Vanguard*, was to be sought.[34]

These proposals fell well short of the original aspirations of Pound and Phillips. That the navy secured Churchill's agreement on this program probably had much to do with the fact they had agreed to the reconstruction of two Rs, although this commitment would never be fulfilled. On 7 February Churchill again made clear he was "not prepared to agree to further programs of battleships for the next war until adequate provision of ships that can venture within range of the enemy's shore-based aircraft has been made for the needs of this one."[35]

In due course this modest capital ship program was constricted further. War Paper (40) 53 of the 1940–41 program, circulated to the War Cabinet, had several important amendments. It was decided no progress would be made on *Conqueror* and *Thunderer*, although the paper noted the board's insistence that this decision be reviewed before the end of the calendar year. *Vanguard* would proceed, as would the rearmoring of two R-class battleships. No mention was made of a second 15-inch-gunned battle cruiser.[36]

Although the program was generally welcomed by the War Cabinet, primarily for the savings it was trying to achieve, former first sea lord Chatfield expressed his earnest concern at the limited nature of the capital ship program in view of Japan. His preference, like Pound's and Phillips', was the opposite of Churchill's: larger gunned battleships completed later at greater expense to address the threat from Japan rather than 15-inch-gunned battleships or battle cruisers finished sooner and with considerably more economy.

On this count there is little doubt Churchill was taking the wiser course, although it must be recognized that Churchill's and the Admiralty's intense focus on battleships over carriers indicated blindness to how a sea war against the Japanese would develop. The 16-inch-gunned battleships would have been more expensive to build and would not likely have been completed in Churchill's "this war" time frame; moreover, they would have been a drain on the resources needed to successfully fight the war with Germany, and for Churchill, it was here the risk lay. Moreover, the utility of 16-inch-gunned battleships was really at its best only in a situation in which Britain was determined to seek a decisive battle with Japan's main fleet. Churchill was building for a more likely scenario, that is, one in which Japan entered this war and the Royal Navy avoided a main fleet conflict with Japan unless it had the support of the United States. In presenting his argument for the construction of the 15-inch-gunned *Vanguard*, Churchill referred to Japan's program of 12-inch-gunned cruisers of the super-pocket-battleship type. If Japan were building these vessels (and it was not), it would not have been for a main fleet action but for trade interdiction. Churchill viewed the fast, big-gunned *Vanguard* as the most economical way for Britain to deal with this threat.

Collectively, the various parts of Churchill's strategic outlook—his "this war" view, the construction of *Vanguard*, the delay of the Lions, and his plans for the R-class battleships—made a great deal more sense than the perspective offered by the Admiralty. The reality was that by 1940 Britain had already lost the capacity to deal unilaterally with the threat from Japan, whether or not it was at war with Germany. Even without a conflict with Germany or Italy, the Royal Navy, existing and under construction, lacked the dominance over the Japanese fleet, existing and under construction, necessary to secure a decisive naval victory. Britain's future as the dominant power in the Far East was inextricably linked to the fact that, in calculating its own strategic direction, Japan was compelled to consider the potential threat of the U.S. Navy in combination with a British fleet. Whether or not Churchill entirely grasped this himself, his "this war" approach was the best and perhaps the only way to prevent this de facto dependence on the United States from becoming de jure. Britain could not avoid the stark reality of its strategic position by trying to build its way out of trouble or by remaining averse to risk; instead, it had to do everything in its power to defeat Germany as soon as possible or, at the very least, to not appear vulnerable. Britain had to act in a way that would discourage Japan from ever chancing a war with Britain in which the United States would not be involved or chancing a war with the United States because Britain appeared too weak to offer assistance. Such aggressive and confident action would also prevent the Italian threat from developing.

Churchill's agitation for an inshore squadron did not end with the War Cabinet's acceptance of the 1940–41 program in mid-March. Before the invasion of Norway and the fall of France changed the strategic landscape in Europe, Churchill nominated the closed waters of the Baltic and Black Seas as the most likely theaters for naval offensives. On 23 March he wrote to Pound of these "two supreme strategic operations." "I am anxious to know that you are with me in regarding the Baltic and the Black Sea as the two main objectives of Naval strategy so long as our prime duty is being thoroughly discharged." To meet the needs of war in these theaters, he requested the resources set aside for Catherine to be regularly updated "and every effort compatible with our prime duty . . . made to prepare the special equipment and vessels" for the possibility of such operations in 1941 and even 1942.[37] As for the air threat, Churchill saw this might be remedied in the future by the reconstruction of the Rs or his UP weapons.

The timing of this correspondence should be linked directly to the discussions then taking place in the War Cabinet. The Finnish option had collapsed, and the British and French governments were desperately exploring their other strategic options. Scandinavia, the Baltic, and the Middle East—most especially the prospect of securing Turkish allegiance—continued to be at the center of discussion. The British remained preoccupied with northern Europe while the French sought a diversion in the southeast. Beyond such plans there was little else on offer, and this helps explain Churchill's intense focus on an inshore squadron. Most of the strategic prospects being canvassed risked placing British naval forces within easy reach of enemy aircraft. To this extent Churchill's efforts to reconstruct a number of British battleships against air attack made some sense, and similarly, it has made the reasons for Pound's rejection of this effort more obscure and difficult to assess. We do know that Pound feared improvements would make these ships too slow for normal duties. If the Rs were slowed, it would slow all ships that accompanied them, and this might prolong the period during which these vessels would be exposed to air attack. In any event, extra armor atop the Rs would not have made them proof against this threat and would have done nothing to protect them from the torpedo.[38] It might be, therefore, that Pound's reservations were based primarily on a lack of utility. It might also have been that he feared an inshore squadron, if completed, would be recklessly used.

The most likely explanation for Pound's resistance was he remained hopeful the Rs would be turned into his new force of 15-inch-gunned battleships or battle cruisers. The invasion of France in May 1940 temporarily drew such discussions to a close. Remarkably, despite the new strategic paradigm that emerged after the fall of France, the matter of new battleships versus an inshore squadron was revisited and very similar battle lines drawn. The Royal Navy was now even more fearful that Japan would take advantage of Britain's strategic dilemma while Churchill was as determined as ever to find a way to take the war to Germany and, by this time, to Italy.

Churchill and the Air Problem

It is evident from the foregoing, and in contrast to all the accepted wisdom on the subject, Churchill was very alive to the threat aircraft presented to the full function of his capital ships. In his 23 March letter to Pound, he wrote: "The danger from the air is at the present time decisive against committing any of our ships to prolonged attack from shore-based enemy aircraft. But we must not assume that this danger cannot be overcome."[39] This admission, it should be noted, occurred less than three weeks before the outbreak of the Norwegian campaign, a conflict oftentimes attributed to Churchill's underestimation of airpower.

Churchill was correct in arguing the air threat could be overcome or, at least, ameliorated. Unfortunately, the solutions he was most determined to pursue—extra armor and his "UP weapon in its many variants"—were weak and ineffectual.[40] His view of the air threat was Eurocentric; there were no enemy carriers and enemy torpedo bombers operating in European waters.[41] Largely ignored in Churchill's thinking at this time was the possibility that the best counter to the German air threat against Britain's own naval forces was the Fleet Air Arm (FAA)—this despite Britain's substantial carrier construction program. Rather than grasping the importance of the navy's own air arm and pursuing its improvement relentlessly, Churchill was responsible for virtually mothballing Britain's existing force of carriers during the Phoney War period. It was an aberrant, shortsighted, and narrowly focused effort to meet a core element of his naval policy: that the FAA would not draw unduly from the common purse.

The FAA had suffered much prewar neglect and indifference under the RAF, and Churchill began the war determined to improve its station. He would soon learn the parlous state of the naval air service was such that a large and a sustained injection of funds was needed. This disconcerted him; he had already given his support to several big ticket, extraneous proposals for substantial expenditure, including the northern barrage and Operation Catherine. Additionally, there was the continuing staff pressure regarding capital ship construction and an enormous demand for escorts and patrol craft. This additional, unexpected expense was unwelcome, and Churchill placed the FAA under scrutiny to ensure "the Fleet Air Arm makes a real contribution to the present war in killing and defeating Germans." He quickly concluded it was not doing this and would not do so any time soon. He believed the carrier-based FAA fighters were obsolescent and incapable of facing the enemy's land-based aircraft or offering adequate protection to their own carriers, let alone the fleet, in offensive operations near the enemy's coast. This, he contended, left the FAA with only "the most important duties of reconnaissance in the ocean spaces, of spotting during an action with surface ships and launching torpedo seaplane attacks upon them."[42] However, as he was so fond of saying during the Phoney War, the enemy fleet was only a small threat, and this did not justify the expense involved in maintaining an extensive carrier force in constant readiness.

Against this rather bleak assessment of the FAA's value, Churchill pitted his other anxieties: "Our Air Force has fallen far behind that of Germany and under present conditions the Air menace to this Island, its factories, its naval ports and shipping, as well as to the Fleet in harbour, must be considered as the only *potentially mortal* attack we have to fear and face." Thus, he expressed his intention to "liberate the RAF from all ordinary coastal duties in the narrow waters and the North Sea" and give the task to the FAA, "which then, and then alone, would have a task proportioned to its cost and worthy of its quality."[43] In short, the FAA aircraft were to take over the responsibility for the protection of the fleet while in harbor and on other coastal duties so that the RAF could concentrate on other matters.

To this end, Churchill requested the establishment of six to eight naval squadrons of 100 to 150 FAA pilots, many of whom were to be taken from the carriers, together with mechanics and administrative staff for land-based operations. More significant, he proposed to seek fewer carrier-borne aircraft and to "ask in return to be given a supply of fighters or medium bombers, perhaps not at first of the latest type, but good enough for short-range action."[44] Admiral Forbes, the commander in chief, Home Fleet, was a major influence in this whole process. He had little faith in the value of the FAA in winter months, and his anxieties over the U-boat risks to the fleet in harbor had already resulted in the redirection of certain FAA craft to land-based duties.[45]

Among traditional supporters of the FAA and in the Royal Navy Air Service, Churchill's proposals were met with consternation. Acclaimed champion of the FAA Sir Roger Keyes hoped "the navy would not overdo the paying off of the carriers." He defended the carriers and reminded Churchill that during the search for *Graf Spee*, *Ark Royal* had "carried out the work of a number of cruisers, which would otherwise have been required, but do not exist!" Portentously, he added, "And I am confident that the carriers will justify their existence if more German raiders come out. The *Bismarck* and the new '*Deutschland*' will probably cause you much anxiety before this war ends!"[46]

Fifth sea lord and chief of the Naval Air Service Vice Admiral Guy Royle expressed his reservation also, but Churchill responded forcefully on 26 February that the focus must be on protecting the fleet when in harbor: "Our present battleships are not built to withstand heavy bombs from the Air. . . . Meanwhile, hardly anything has been done . . . to improve the AA gunnery of the Fleet by firing at fast targets."[47] As for Royle's desire for a well-trained offensive force with which to attack the enemy's large ships, Churchill was, as he had been throughout this period in a variety of forums, dismissive: "Of course, it would be very nice for our torpedo seaplanes to attack the enemy battle-fleet. But it happens they have not got one. Should our Fleet go into the danger zone in the North Sea, they would not need the torpedo sea-planes to protect them from the attacks of the far weaker German battle-cruisers. They would, however, very much need a couple of squadrons of fighting aircraft, if these could be produced from an armoured carrier."[48] This statement hinted at a limited vision of the tactical problems that might beset naval forces in the North Sea. Churchill seemed not to have envisaged a variety of situations in which enemy ships would be more wisely attacked by carrier-borne bombers than by Britain's naval vessels or in which Royal Navy vessels would welcome, and be greatly assisted by, the existing force of FAA fighters. This lack of foresight was particularly surprising given Churchill's ongoing interest in amphibious operations in Norway and elsewhere. Should these have taken place, Britain would have had to make do with the FAA forces it had.

Churchill reaffirmed his determination to arm the two armored carriers with aircraft of the Spitfire type for the protection of the fleet when in harbor or at sea against land-based aircraft, and he made clear that they were not to "concern themselves with torpedo attacks on surface vessels or (except incidentally) with reconnaissance."[49] Pound counseled caution. In early March he wrote that while he accepted that the FAA must take a greater role in the protection of the fleet when in harbor, he thought this should not "capsize the Fleet Air Arm to such an extent that it cannot be used in a legitimate manner should opportunity occur," including the need to attack the enemy's large ships. He did not think it advisable to convert a "great offensive weapon into a purely defensive one."[50] Moreover, as desirable as was Churchill's pursuit of single-seat modern fighters in the longer term, it was not at all efficacious at this time. The FAA still needed aircraft that had greater range, could fulfill multiple tasks, and had the appropriate navigational facility for operations over water.

As a result of Churchill's proposals, by early March 1940 the FAA in home waters had been more or less mothballed. Fleet fighters had been removed from HMS *Furious* and put to work protecting the fleet in harbor and conducting antisubmarine duties. The FAA torpedo bomber forces had been marginalized as expensive to maintain and unlikely to be used in offensive operations, and they too were disembarked from *Furious*. Thus, despite being fully alert to the German air threat and its capacity to severely limit the activities of the Royal Navy, in the weeks and months before the Norwegian campaign, a conflict in which Britain's carrier forces played an often vital role, Churchill was instrumental in compromising Britain's most effective weapon for operations of an inshore nature within range of the enemy's land-based aircraft: the carrier force of fighters and torpedo bombers. A major criticism of the navy's handling of the early, critical stages of the Norwegian campaign has been that HMS *Furious* only belatedly set sail for the North Sea from the Clyde and that it did so minus its complement of fighters, which then stood at Hatston airfield at ten hours' notice. This not only delayed the Home Fleet but might have contributed to the commander in chief's subsequent reluctance to risk his forces within range of enemy aircraft at vital junctures in early operations. The proposition must be put that the explanation for many of the failings in the early stages of the Norwegian campaign is not to be found in an underestimation of the German air threat but in the underestimation of the FAA to deal with it, and Churchill must bear his share of the responsibility. The FAA fighters were obsolescent, but when pitted against aircraft other than the enemy's modern fighters, they were at much less disadvantage than assumed, and they provided a considerable service to the fleet during this campaign. The FAA Swordfish torpedo aircraft—by most definitions an obsolescent aircraft—proved a remarkably successful weapon during the war.[51]

Conclusions

Churchill's attitude to new capital ship construction at the start of World War II and his determination to build an inshore squadron were manifestations of four important influences: his disillusionment with the Royal Navy of World War I; a determination to spend the British public's funds wisely; a conviction that the Royal Navy must make a decisive contribution to winning the war in Europe beyond the traditional role of protecting Britain's lines of communication and destroying the enemy's; and a belief that aggressive naval action would help deter two potential enemies, Italy and Japan. When Pound and Phillips began to argue for a substantial program of capital ship construction, they were repeating the navy's modus operandi of World War I. Churchill believed Britain already had a considerable preponderance in capital ship strength and the construction program then in progress would more than maintain that advantage in respect to its most likely enemies, especially with support from the French. Moreover, Churchill was certain that to consume resources to prepare the navy for the next war would necessarily compromise success in this one and leave Britain vulnerable on land (via its support of France) and in the air, two areas where Churchill viewed Britain to be more exposed and vulnerable.

Churchill's construction priorities represented the practical policy edge of his "this war" and "next war" philosophy, which he had also demonstrated to some degree in his plans for Catherine. It is difficult to fault his priorities and his prescience in construction matters. Italy entered the war only when it became evident that France would be defeated. Churchill was equally correct about the impact German ascendancy in Europe would have on the Japanese. The Japanese decision to go to war with the United States and Britain in December 1941 was undoubtedly made easier by the defeat of France and the loss of its fleet, the apparently successful invasion of the USSR, and the neutralization of much of Britain's fleet in its fight with the combined forces of Germany and Italy. In calculating the threat Britain offered to Japan, Churchill could not have anticipated the extent to which the U.S. embargo on essential raw materials would motivate Japan to risk a suicidal war with the West to avoid the loss of China.

None of the limitations Churchill placed on capital ship construction had a negative impact on Britain's war with Japan, but they undoubtedly helped free resources for more vital construction for the Royal Navy and for other needs in the war against Germany. Churchill's emphasis on celerity of construction over numbers of ships and size of guns was eminently wise. Apply maximum and timely force to achieve success against Germany, and the threats of Italy and Japan would not likely arise. If the threat from Japan developed, Britain would respond in a significant way only if Australia and New Zealand were threatened with invasion or the United States was also at war with Japan. If the war with Germany was won, or ascendancy maintained, Japan would take no independent action; if it were lost, the empire was at great risk, save for U.S. intervention. It is notable that except for the 15-inch-gunned *Vanguard*, none of the battleship construction to which Churchill reluctantly agreed was completed before the defeat of Germany or Japan.[52]

Churchill was far more realistic than his staff in his assessment of Britain's ability to meet its imperial obligations. He was fully aware that while Britain was at war in Europe, its empire in Southeast Asia was entirely dependent on the combined threat of the United States and Britain and not on Britain alone. Whether or not the Admiralty liked it, Britain was already dependent on the United States' fleet. However, success in Europe was also the best way for Churchill to protect himself from the criticism that his policies had contributed to the reality Britain now faced. Should Japan go to war, it would expose how incapable Britain was of independently dealing with this threat and how dependent it was on the United States to take the fight to the Japanese. Perhaps more cuttingly, it would expose to ridicule the policies, such as the ten-year rule, that Churchill had championed in the 1920s and 1930s in the name of economy and his frequently dismissive attitude toward the threat posed by Japan.

Just as with Catherine, Churchill's grand strategic vision fell apart at the tactical and operational level. His manic preoccupation with the reconstruction of the R-class battleships—at a time when there was a pressing need for armor for British tanks—assumed that such improvements would allow him to use this surplus force in some spectacular way to influence events on the continent. Apart from Catherine these operations were never identified, although the theaters of war in which they would take place were: the Mediterranean, the Baltic, the North Sea, and the Black Sea. While the presence of capital ships still had the capacity in certain circumstances to provide comfort and a sense of security potential to friends and allies, it is hard to see a practicable military application for his inshore squadron in any situation in which it might have made a decisive difference. Whatever his aspirations the work done to these vessels would not have made them proof against air attack; in his preferred theaters, the Baltic and the Black Seas, the air weapon, if applied in earnest by an enemy, would have been devastating for being inescapable.

A core problem was that Churchill had selected the wrong tools for the job. What was really needed if Britain's superior sea power was to function within range of the enemy's airpower was the development of a strong defensive umbrella built around a modern FAA and Britain's force of armored carriers. This might at least provide temporary local air superiority for amphibious operations.

However, despite being aware of the FAA potential and cognizant of the obsolescent nature of its aircraft, Churchill was neglectful of this service, and the FAA capacities deteriorated under his stewardship as he redirected its resources to static defense on the mainland. Had Churchill put the same energy into securing modern aircraft for his FAA as he did in attempting to secure his force of unsinkable battleships, the Royal Navy and British strategy would have been the better for it and much more quickly. Instead, his vision for the FAA was obscured by what he believed to be an absence of potential targets for carrier-based aircraft and by more immediate needs: the defense from air attack of Britain's cities, harbors, and factories. His proposals for the FAA helped reduce the burden on the RAF and Coastal Command in such duties, but only marginally.

It remains difficult to understand why his aspirations for offensive naval operations in combination with his evident awareness of the shortcomings of his capital ships did not lead him more readily to the appreciation that the best way forward was to secure support of carrier-borne aircraft. Similarly, it is extraordinary he failed to consider circumstances in which an inshore military or naval target would be better dealt with by aircraft flying from a carrier out of range of enemy aircraft than by surface craft placed in the way of enemy bombers, mines, or submarines. These scenarios were eminently foreseeable in the kind of operations he desired. These matters would become issues of importance when Britain went to war with Germany in Norway, a subject for later chapters.

Part Two

CHURCHILL
AND THE
WIDER WAR

FOUR

FIGHTING THE WAR
The War Cabinet and Its Committees

When Churchill joined the British War Cabinet at the beginning of September 1939, his participation was met by much apprehension among his detractors and much satisfaction from his supporters, the latter of whom included elements of the British public, pockets of the British press, and a small group of agitators in his own party. Well before the war Churchill had made it known he wished to join Chamberlain's government and could "work amicably with the P.M. who had many admirable qualities some of which he did not have himself." However, Churchill believed he too had "great qualities and could do much to help the P.M. to bear his intolerable burden."[1] When, therefore, the invitation to join the War Cabinet finally came, Churchill accepted it with much appreciation and relief. He expressed a determination to be loyal and supportive to Chamberlain and remained so throughout the Phoney War.

Churchill brought to his new role a mixed bag of well-known strengths and well-known weaknesses, many of which were exaggerated or understated by the disposition of those passing judgment. Chamberlain had long resisted extending an offer to Churchill to join his government, primarily because he believed to do so would have destroyed whatever slim hopes existed for peace with Germany. Further, he wished not to subject himself to Churchill's idiosyncrasies and inconveniences: his loquacity, his badgering, and his constant but inevitable offers of advice.[2] Nevertheless, Chamberlain was not oblivious to Churchill's strengths, although he doubted these outweighed his weaknesses. Chamberlain was aware of Churchill's energy and knowledge of war, and Churchill had demonstrated skills of organization and leadership in previous roles. Chamberlain hoped to maximize the positive Churchill could offer and contain the excesses, and the prime minister would adopt a decision-making structure, not entirely of his own making, to achieve just that. The difficulty for the Churchill-Chamberlain relationship was that those qualities Churchill viewed as his strengths were oftentimes the characteristics Chamberlain believed to be his weaknesses. As genuine as Churchill's determination to work "amicably" with his prime minister was, it would be compromised by his determination to exercise what he believed to be his "great qualities" and to bring these to bear on fighting the war.

Within a fortnight of the war's outbreak, the role Churchill intended for himself could be readily identified. In actions and behavior he assumed the persona of a minister for war, a role he had long hoped Chamberlain would formalize (though he did not). Churchill displayed a supreme self-confidence based on a considerable, if somewhat dated, experience in a variety of roles. He also began to press an offensive agenda using the only force he believed was immediately capable of taking the war to Germany: the Royal Navy. However, from the beginning he had the wider war in mind and not only the war at sea. He adopted and maintained a big picture approach that included a clinical and nonpartisan view of the needs of his own service relative to the needs of the other two to ensure Britain was readied as quickly as possible to fight a war against Germany on all fronts. The demands of his navy were always viewed in this wider context; where needs conflicted, he asserted, and acted on, a willingness to accommodate and compromise. It was an attitude, no doubt, partly sustained by his conviction that the Royal Navy was, in many respects, already well resourced.

However, Churchill's big picture view extended well beyond merely accommodating the needs of the other service departments. He challenged the practices and tackled the (perceived) shortcomings of any and all departments and in due course used his own investigative section to do so. In short, everybody's business was his business, including that of the army, RAF, Exchequer, Foreign Office, and even prime minister. Churchill's approach was not designed to garner the support of his colleagues or necessarily his prime minister. It inevitably suggested a conviction that he knew better than most of his colleagues and that he was, predictably and in quick order, reverting to type. Churchill was set on an expansive role, but never with the usurpation of his leader in mind. It was just Churchill being Churchill. His overreach was foreseen by Chamberlain, who began the war with plans to contain Churchill; these plans would be encouraged even more strongly by the prime minister's advisers in the opening weeks of the war.

This chapter aims to assess Churchill's contribution as War Cabinet minister to the wider war effort with a focus on the success or otherwise of his big picture approach to the British war effort. Particular attention will be given to his role on two ministerial committees: the Land Forces Committee (LFC) and the Military Co-ordination Committee (MCC). In these committees the full force of Churchill's vision was felt. The LFC was established at the beginning of war to "report as quickly as possible on the size of the Land Forces at which we should aim in the present war, and the date of completion of equipment of the various contingents, as a basis for the production arrangements to be made by the Ministry of Supply."[3]

The LFC was short-lived, but the controversy it generated was prolonged and subsequently passed to the MCC to resolve. The MCC was the key advisory body to the War Cabinet in matters of strategy and the general conduct of the war. Churchill, the other two service ministers, and the COS were the core members of this committee. Ernle Chatfield was its chairman in the ongoing position of minister for coordination of defense until he was replaced as chairman by Churchill in early April 1940.

This chapter will explore the decision-making structure and process instituted by Chamberlain in order to understand why Churchill achieved so little in seeking to take the war to Germany and animate the British war effort during the Phoney War. To what extent was this a result of structure and process—Churchill's own explanation—or the inherit challenges of the period or other factors, including Churchill himself?

The LFC: What Size the Army?

Unsurprisingly, given the small size of the British Army at the start of the war, one of the first and most important tasks the War Cabinet set itself was to determine the size of the army with which Britain would fight. From the very beginning Churchill was among the most adamant of those who believed Britain must aim at a substantial army. He was even more adamant that this could and should be achieved in quick order. As desirable as these objectives now were for Britain, Churchill's interest in the British Army and the importance he placed on its capacity to sustain French morale were belated epiphanies; he now placed too much store in his conviction an army could be improvised in a manner similar to Kitchener's army in World

War I, and he expended a great deal of energy and effort—his own and others'—attempting to prove he was right.

The LFC was brought into being by the War Cabinet on 6 September with Lord Privy Seal Samuel Hoare as chairman, and it met for the first time on 10 September. It soon set a target of fifty-five divisions for the wartime army, with twenty divisions to be ready within twelve months, although it recognized these targets would not be easily achieved.[4] As recently as February 1939, Britain had been contemplating a force of only six divisions. This had been raised to thirty-two divisions in April, but even this was well shy of the new objective and the proposed rate of growth. Another important target to be set was the number of divisions to be in France before spring 1940, the likely beginning of any campaign. The CIGS, General Ironside, believed it would be possible to send overseas eleven divisions within six months, a contribution well in excess of the two mobile divisions and four infantry divisions promised to the French in prewar discussions. Churchill hoped for many more.[5]

Churchill's focus on the army was not shared by Chamberlain. The prime minister's priority was, and had long been, the air force, and he believed the fighting in Poland demonstrated the importance of the air weapon. There was, Chamberlain argued, little point in building a large army if it could be quickly neutralized or defeated by the enemy's superior air arm. Churchill's view was that a fifty-five division army was the bare minimum for which Britain and the Commonwealth should aim, and he worked hard to persuade his prime minister. He doubted if "the French would acquiesce in a division of effort which gave us the sea and air and left them to pay almost the entire blood-tax on land."[6] This was sound reasoning but did not address the problems inherent in meeting his target.

Churchill's big picture thinking, along with the benchmarks needed to sustain it, is first found in correspondence with Chamberlain. The benchmarks reflected Churchill's perception of Britain's military and industrial efforts in and his personal experiences of World War I. He believed that no service or organization should receive absolute priority, and to support his case, in a letter to Chamberlain he referred to the behavior of the Admiralty, which had used "their priority arbitrarily and selfishly, especially in the last year, when they were overwhelmingly strong." He added, "I am everyday restraining such tendencies," but he evidently believed the air force was not doing the same. He believed an army of fifty-five divisions would not compromise the air program and noted that at the end of the last war, Britain "had about ninety divisions in all theatres. . . . We were producing aircraft at the rate of 2000 a month . . . [and] maintaining a navy very much larger than was needed, and far larger than our present plans contemplate."[7]

Churchill contended if his targets for the British Army could not be met, it would not be because of the fundamentals of Britain's industrial capacity but because of the pessimistic estimates and dubious assumptions of the Exchequer and such ministries as Labour, Supply, and Shipping and the excessive requirements of the air force. This view was influenced by his conviction—rapidly formed and quickly expressed—that the War Office was making inflated and "unreal demands" and was attempting to supply the British Expeditionary Force (BEF) beyond what was reasonable or necessary and that this would delay sending divisions to France.

Within a matter of weeks of his joining the War Cabinet, it was apparent that Churchill had set for himself the overview of the entire war effort. With the assistance of his technical adviser, Professor Lindemann, he challenged just about every aspect of British war preparation.[8] Lindemann's personal papers make clear that his assessments—or those of his committee—were routinely repeated in the memoranda Churchill submitted to the War Cabinet in criticism of, and comment on, the work of other departments. The greater part of the correspondence was directed at proving that Britain could, after all, build and supply a fifty-five-division army and do so more quickly than the government was inclined to believe possible. It was Churchill's belief (and that of Lindemann and his committee) that Britain ought to be able to, as a minimum, match its war effort of World War I and the French effort in this one. At least one memorandum focused on the war effort in World War I to demonstrate the tardiness of the existing effort and the inadequacy of the targets in World War II.[9]

A major criticism of the Chamberlain government's war effort was that it was "handcuffed," or chose to be "handcuffed," by the Exchequer and matters of finance. In time, and certainly when Churchill was prime minister, this influence and attitude diminished considerably. However, during the Phoney War it is difficult to find evidence of the Exchequer refusing to sign off on any program vital to the war effort. Moreover, in reducing the obstructions that existed in this regard, Churchill showed no particular leadership. His focus was always on finding savings, and monitoring revenue and spending, rather than on challenging the need to live within means. He was not in the vanguard of those who recognized Britain must break free from the conservative view of the "fourth arm" of Britain's war effort.

A persistent problem facing Churchill and Lindemann in their efforts to animate the war effort was that while their objective was to show things could be done better within the existing financial and labor constraints, they found themselves criticizing "pessimistic" departmental projections and calculations that would, in time, prove very much too optimistic.[10] Their own assessments were particularly hopeful and were sometimes based on their own dubious assumptions. For example, in defending his conviction that the fifty-five-division army was a viable proposition, Churchill argued that the needs of the Royal Navy would not exceed, and would probably be much less than, those of the last war.[11] He would be 100 percent wrong.[12]

Perhaps the most significant example of Churchill's misplaced optimism regarding what Britain could do and how quickly it could do it was his attitude toward Britain's import program. On 23 February, and following ongoing anxieties over the decline in trade, Samuel Hoare submitted a review of the shipping situation that contended British and neutral shipping would be sufficient only for between 41.7 and 44.7 million tons in the first year of the war. Estimates since the beginning of the war had been that a target of 47 million tons could be met. Hoare, therefore, argued that action to rationalize the import program should be taken because with "the passage of every day the likelihood grows that some of the imports that are arriving are imports which in the last resort we could do without, with the result that at the end of the first year of war we may find that we have failed to obtain imports which are absolutely vital to our war effort."[13]

Hoare was certain that matters would only get worse and, moreover, that a variety of problems could make the fulfillment of his own estimates difficult to achieve. Not only should the decline in certain stocks be arrested, but an effort needed to be made to build against future calamity. In contrast Churchill and Lindemann were confident that Britain would meet its 47 million tons of imports in the first year of war. Each was loathe to impose rationing and restrictions on the British people any earlier than necessary. They acknowledged that sacrifice would be needed at some point, but it was a question of "to what extent and when."[14] Churchill was also keen to ensure the British public and the House of Commons recognized any restrictions imposed were not a result of the navy failing to do its job.[15]

In late February Churchill presented his case, a product of Lindemann's committee, that despite poor imports earlier in the war, there were no reasons why the 47 million–ton target could not be redeemed during the remainder of the year. He presented several reasons why this should be so—not least, the improved import statistics for the most recent months and some miscalculations of the lord privy seal, which he believed were a result of flawed assumptions. Churchill's paper went further than reaffirming the 47 million–ton target and contended it could even be possible to achieve 51 million tons.[16]

Evidence suggests that Churchill was justified in questioning the pessimism of the lord privy seal's assessment. While the figure of 51 million was highly improbable unless access to neutral shipping improved dramatically, it was likely that the Ministry of Shipping's original estimate of 47 million tons could have been fulfilled with the resources available had it not been for the German invasion of France.[17] In the event, imports for the first year of the war were approximately 44 million.[18] Churchill's folly—and Lindemann's too—was the failure to support adequately the caution that Hoare and the Ministry of Shipping were seeking. While the arrival of spring and summer was, as they argued, likely to boost imports in the normal course, it was equally likely to bring forth a German offensive, and this was certain to interrupt British trade and draw shipping away from it. Unlike Hoare, neither Churchill nor Lindemann had seemed particularly inclined to factor such a prospect into their calculations, and they were again proven unreasonably hopeful.[19]

Churchill's somewhat irresponsible attitude to Britain's import program was reflected further in his ongoing pursuit of a scheme to stop Germany's winter supply of ore via the port of Narvik in Norway; this scheme by coincidence was reaching a point of decision while the imports discussions were taking place. Action against Norway threatened to compromise one of the more immediate avenues by which Britain's shipping prospects might be improved: the completion of the Norwegian shipping and trade agreement. In finally coming down against the Narvik scheme, Chamberlain included among his reasons his anxieties over Britain's shipping problems and the need to protect the Anglo-Norwegian relationship.

Not only was the advice given by Lindemann, and represented by Churchill, sometimes inaccurate, it could also be gratuitous (and sometimes both) in that it failed to reflect the challenges inherent in its implementation. Labor was a particularly intractable issue during the Phoney War, in particular the need to move troops to where they were needed, a process not easily expedited. Churchill and Lindemann were generally unsympathetic to the Chamberlain government's cautious approach. During War Cabinet discussions on labor issues, Churchill proposed a version of Lindemann's idea of conscripting people up to forty or fifty years of age and "only exempt[ing] on condition they carried out approved work at an approved place."[20] Churchill acknowledged that his suggestion would "meet with great hostility on the part of Labour," a view that received the full endorsement of Minister of Labor Ernest Brown, but it was evident Brown believed much more could and should be done.[21] In due course, severe conscription measures were introduced, but this was after the fall of France at a time when the general public's view of the conflict was quite different than it had been in the early months of the war. These changes were also achieved in cooperation with the Labour Party and trade unions, and not in opposition to them. It is undoubtedly true that Chamberlain's government was never likely to have gained the full support of the trade union movement, but it did make progress, albeit slowly.

It is open to question, however, if Churchill was better disposed to resolving these issues more judiciously or successfully before he became prime minister. The best and certainly the quickest solution to labor problems was always the national government that emerged in May 1940 and that would have secured the Labour Party's full cooperation. In the name of national unity, Churchill might have proposed a coalition government early in the war, but not a word on this was spoken; as subsequent discussion will show, it was probably the last thing on his mind. Several times in speeches Churchill did his best to calm public concerns about several government measures, including the employment of women. Elsewhere there were indications he recognized labor matters needed to be addressed with an element of delicacy and patience.[22] However, within the War Cabinet Churchill was critical of the degree to which social welfare expenditure was compromising the war effort, and our earlier discussion has indicated his willingness to be heavy-handed if needed.[23] How successfully, therefore, Churchill might have performed in the matter of labor, had it been his own responsibility, will likely remain moot.

If Chamberlain was too pedestrian, then Churchill was often too zealous in seeking to drive the war effort. Labor issues were but one part of the efficiency equation. Factories had to be built, training undertaken, machine tools purchased, and raw materials accumulated for the best use of the available labor to be achieved. Moreover, the urgency Churchill displayed over ramping up the war effort coincided with a simultaneous determination to put as many men in uniform as quickly as possible. Chamberlain justifiably took a cautious approach toward conscription, limiting it to 60,000 troops per month.[24]

In pushing the growth of the army, Churchill's benchmark was to do as much as the French in this war and as much as Britain had done in the last. The French, however, had been overzealous in their mobilization and found their productive capacity decline as a result. While Churchill was pushing the growth of the armed forces, the French were reducing theirs and sending men back to the factories. Churchill remained stubborn on this issue, and upon becoming prime minister, he drew in recruits before resources were available to arm them. British production paid its own price as a consequence.[25]

Even before their assault on the general economy, Churchill and Lindemann had begun an inquisition into the perceived indulgences of the air force, army, and Air Defence of Great Britain (ADGB) to show that it was excess and profligacy rather than anything more fundamental that prevented the more rapid growth of the BEF.[26] Churchill challenged the RAF's estimates of small arms ammunition consumption and of wastage, arguing that they were unnecessarily high and did not reflect genuine wartime need or likely operational circumstances. He also challenged the army's equipment levels for the BEF, contending that since the French could do well enough with much less, the BEF could and should do the same. Elsewhere he challenged the RAF's policies on frontline squadrons, training squadrons, and reserves. He found it difficult to understand why there were so few new squadrons to show for the vast sums spent on the air force. He was reluctant to accept the issues surrounding the replacement of obsolescent aircraft with modern and also seemed unwilling to acknowledge the importance of reserves or the need to allocate substantial numbers of aircraft for training purposes.

Churchill showed a penchant for wanting to put "everything in the shop window" when he expressed his concern that despite a large number of troops in France, few British divisions were on the front line. As far as frontline soldiers were concerned, Churchill somewhat dubiously asserted that "it is upon the forces actually brought to bear upon the enemy that eyes must be fixed," an observation that suggests he was still very much fighting the previous war.[27] His concern with troop levels and the front line hinted at his apprehension that despite his confidence in the French army, the Allied forces in France might be defeated by a superior German force before Britain was able to make a substantial contribution. However, his focus on raw numbers in the air force and the army was misplaced, especially when the price paid would have been, for the air force, fewer reserves and training delays and, for the army, less mobility, lower standards of equipment (on top of current equipment shortages), and a probable drop in efficiency and support.[28]

The RAF's message to Churchill was that it was becoming more formidable every day, and this it was. Much of Churchill's anxiety was based on flawed assumptions about the strength of and growth in the Luftwaffe. Britain would match German production rates by mid-1940 and surpass them soon thereafter. The army's response was to explain that the BEF was, after all, an expeditionary force and was compelled by circumstance to take everything with it. The modern British Army was different in all respects from the one that went to war in 1914. Moreover, owing to the air threat, the army's depots and organization were dispersed over sixteen ports up to five hundred miles distant from the front lines.[29] Churchill's frustrations over the small head and enormous tail of Britain's fighting forces continued long after the Phoney War, particularly when it became apparent that the target of fifty-five fully equipped infantry and armored divisions could not be met.[30] In 1941 he was still arguing there was "too much fluff and flummery behind the front-line troops," and this complaint undoubtedly led to more problems and anxiety than were necessary.[31] Similarly, almost the moment he became prime minister, he initiated an investigation into what he perceived as an inadequate number of established squadrons for the number of aircraft being produced.[32]

Churchill's big picture view of his role and rigorous oversight of the underachievement of departments and the excesses of his sister services extended to the performance of his own service. From the beginning of the war, he highlighted the unique nonpartisan nature of his leadership of the Royal Navy and emphasized his willingness to contain naval spending for the sake of the wider war effort.[33] Although he was genuinely determined to pursue economy and was willing to upset his admirals to do so, he ultimately fell well short of achieving it. The unexpected contingencies of war, as they did everywhere, played a role in this.

Admiralty programs were never submitted to the scrutiny Churchill imposed on the programs of other services.[34] He failed to subject his big ticket expenses to the due diligence he expected of the secretaries of state for air and war. He took particular liberty on behalf of the Admiralty to meet the needs of his own strategic preferences and projects, and he was willing to circumvent appropriate procedure in doing so. It had been under a protective cloak of secrecy that Churchill had gone directly to the prime minister and then the chancellor to secure the funding for Catherine. In support of Pound he took the matter of the northern mine barrage directly to the War Cabinet, but it cannot be said that he gave adequate scrutiny to the project's efficacy before doing so. On a much smaller but nevertheless significant scale, Churchill was content to recommend spending £1 million to manufacture 100,000 of his aerial mines—ten times the number proposed by the air force—at a time when the efficacy of this weapon remained in doubt.[35] This particular defensive weapon was integral to his plans for the offensive use of the navy, and his haste and lack of caution no doubt can be attributed to this. It is, nevertheless, an example of the extent to which he was prepared to make himself an exception to his own rules of scrupulous economy and the War Cabinet's policy of openness, especially when these rules and policies conflicted with his offensive aspirations and notions of what was good for the war effort.[36]

There is no doubt Churchill justified the liberty he gave himself in terms of his wider strategic vision as it existed at the time. His spending, like his pursuit of economy elsewhere, had a purpose and was intended to lead to future savings. Broadly, for him, it was about balance. The navy was strong, and the air force would soon be; the army was lagging, and this was where the attention had to be. More specifically, Churchill could contend his spending would have a material and precisely targeted impact on the war. Catherine was a plan of potentially decisive dimensions. Not only would it constrict the Scandinavia ore trade with Germany; it would compel Germany to retain its forces in the Baltic. If the operation did not take place, the improvements made to his ships would generally be efficacious for other duties. The mine barrage, as expensive as it would be, was intended to address all manner of ills; if the German fleet and U-boats could not be contained in the Baltic, then the North Sea would do. Such a success would free resources for other potential problems, the Mediterranean and the Far East among them. Rather than trying to be strong everywhere, Britain could concentrate its resources where they were most needed. It was important, however, to secure the bulwark on the western front, and this needed a substantial British contribution as quickly as possible.

Unfortunately, the three examples identified previously, two of which involved substantial spending, were either complete failures or produced no material advantage for the war effort. There was, for example, much more spending involved in Catherine than was applied to the improvement of ships; little of this spending on Catherine would have achieved value. As far as Churchill's efforts to muscle along the British war effort were concerned, it is equally difficult to identify the value of his inquisition. As it existed at the time, Lindemann's committee was a scattergun attempt to oversee the war effort. Given Churchill's determination to analyze and criticize just about everything, it is unsurprising that on occasion his criticism made a positive contribution and drew attention to a failing or inefficiency that might have been overlooked. However, it is questionable if these successes justified the price paid in time and effort to the departments under scrutiny or compensated for his errors of judgment.

Strategy and the MCC

The MCC came into being in late October 1939 with the following brief: "To keep under constant review, on behalf of the War Cabinet, the main factors in the strategical situation and the progress of operations, and to make recommendations from time to time to the War Cabinet as to the general conduct of the war."[37] This body gave Churchill much frustration, and his role as chairman beginning April 1940 had a significant impact on his reputation as a warrior and potential war leader. Churchill had much cause to be frustrated with the decision-making apparatus employed by Chamberlain. However, Churchill himself was always part of the committee's problems and a significant impediment to the achievement of his own initiatives.

The MCC's origins shed considerable light on the Churchill-Chamberlain relationship. At the start of the war, Chamberlain considered Maurice Hankey's recommendation that he adopt a small war cabinet of ministers without portfolio to conduct the war. Churchill was to be a member but not the service ministers.[38] According to Hankey's diary, the members were to be Churchill, Chamberlain, Lord Halifax, and Hankey himself, presumably authority enough to gain the best from Churchill while keeping him in check.[39] Upon hearing this plan, two service ministers, Kingsley Wood and Leslie Hore-Belisha, threatened to resign, so Chamberlain formed a larger war cabinet of nine men, with Churchill the first lord rather than a minister without portfolio.[40]

It had been suggested—by whom is unclear—that giving Churchill a portfolio would keep him fully occupied and prevent him from interfering in the business of others.[41] The containment of Churchill was always an all too hopeful aspiration, and although Chamberlain counseled his first lord on one or two occasions, little evidence suggests that as the war progressed, he tried too hard to rein Churchill in. Rather, Chamberlain gave Churchill extraordinary leeway. This included the freedom to broadcast to the nation and to communicate directly with President Roosevelt, oftentimes on behalf of the government. No doubt Chamberlain was aware that given Churchill's popularity in some quarters, such leeway was generally to the advantage of his government. Similarly, Churchill's claim to a special relationship with Roosevelt seems to have been considered a considerable boon, and nothing was done to hinder it.

Nevertheless, it is probable that in the war's early weeks Chamberlain had the containment of Churchill in mind. Whether or not Churchill realized it, he had played a part in determining the nature of the decision-making structure that Chamberlain used to fight the war and that Churchill himself so volubly criticized in the following months. It is likely that the composition of Chamberlain's nine-man War Cabinet was intended to constrain Churchill. Lord Chatfield retained the anomalous position of minister for coordination of defense, despite having no executive authority over the service ministers. This concept did not prove especially successful. Equally anomalously, although unsurprising given his experience, Hankey was added to the War Cabinet as the lone minister without portfolio. He viewed his role as "keeping an eye on Winston," and this he attempted to do even after he had been excluded from the MCC.[42]

However, Chamberlain's decision to opt for a nine-man War Cabinet presented its own problems. The body was too large for the discussion and development of strategy, and the service ministers, in particular Churchill and Hore-Belisha, sought a forum in which war strategy could be discussed independently of nonservice ministers, the COS, and other advisers.[43] At the same time, and in view of Chamberlain's role as prime minister and, therefore, the main coordinator of defense in the War Cabinet, Chatfield considered his position as minister for coordination of defense redundant and offered his resignation.[44] Apparently unwilling to take on the personal responsibility for the "development and adjustment of strategy" and loathe to lose Chatfield's counsel, Chamberlain began exploring the establishment of a committee that would resolve both problems. He discussed the issues with his private secretary, Sir Horace Wilson, who, after consulting War Cabinet secretary Edward Bridges and Deputy Secretary General Lionel "Pug" Ismay, concluded that the COS must be included in such a committee.[45] The service ministers, however, continued to resist the inclusion of the COS. The matter was finally resolved at a 25 October 1939 meeting between the ministers and Chatfield, during which it was decided the COS would attend the MCC meetings only as expert advisers to their own ministers.[46] The most important factor in all these discussions was that Chamberlain had divorced himself from the formulation of strategy, at least in its early stages, but still retained the primary responsibility for it. This did not make for timely and efficient decision making.

The MCC began functioning formally at the beginning of November, but it proved an unsuccessful element of an unnecessarily cumbersome decision-making process that did not satisfy anyone.[47] Despite his initial interest in such a forum, Churchill became increasingly convinced that in the absence of some degree of executive guidance, strategy built around the disparate concerns and interests of three service ministers was difficult to achieve. Service ministers were inevitably influenced by the need to meet the core responsibilities of their own service—something they believed at this time they were well short of doing—and this was not necessarily compatible with the development of aggressive strategy. The inclusion in MCC deliberations of the COS as advisers to their own ministers was only likely to compound this problem and create a conflict of interest, especially where advice given conflicted with the conclusions of their own committee. Churchill, in particular, continued to be frustrated by the excessive influence of the COS in the policy process.[48] The anomaly of Chatfield's role also remained; his position and authority as chairman was dependent on the goodwill and ongoing deference of the service ministers, and this was not always forthcoming, especially from Churchill. Additionally, Chatfield's own recommendation that the MCC deliberations be limited to the service ministers and the COS proved unwise and did not last long; it soon became evident that discussion of strategic policy that extended beyond the accepted War Cabinet policy of "sitting tight and rearming" was dependent on input from other authorities, most particularly the Foreign Office. Another significant omission from the MCC and the War Cabinet was Minister for the Dominions Anthony Eden. Under the existing structure, input from the Dominions most often came at the end of the process, yet their influence was sufficient to alter or defeat policies that had been days or weeks in making. Moreover, the Dominions demanded more and more influence as the war progressed.[49] Another issue facing the committee and its effectiveness was that it quickly found itself addressing many matters other than strategy, in part because the War Cabinet was not selective in referring matters to it and the MCC brief was ill defined. The first two issues discussed by the committee on 11 November were prisoners of war and publicity for the exploits of Dominion forces, hardly within the ambit of its intended responsibilities.[50]

The MCC was never likely to be the right structure through which to conceive strategy. Always needed was a clear executive authority guiding its deliberation. Chamberlain had to delegate or participate, and he chose to do neither. At the time of the MCC's conception, the shortcomings might not have been evident. Given the almost universal acceptance of the "sit tight and rearm" strategy, there was not much strategy to discuss. However, from December onward Churchill began developing his ideas for offensive naval operations, all of which involved action against neutrals. The French too became more animated regarding strategy. It made little sense to have the prime minister a party to Supreme War Council (SWC) discussion and not directly involved in the MCC. Inevitably, the latent limitations of the decision-making structure and process came into play to create discord, delay, and frustration.

During the Norwegian campaign, the MCC proved an even more problematic vehicle for the guidance and conduct of operations. Chamberlain acceded to a request from Churchill and other members of the MCC to sit in on proceedings and take over the chair in order to resolve disagreement and speed decision making. The evidence is that on these occasions business ran much more smoothly.[51] Chamberlain and his supporters attributed this to his skills as chairman.[52] Although it is probable that he was an effective and efficient chairman, his success undoubtedly had a great deal to do with his executive authority. Of some importance for any assessment of the Churchill-Chamberlain relationship is that as chairman Chamberlain endorsed nearly all Churchill's recommendations and initiatives. Churchill was correct in believing that the service chiefs would take from Chamberlain what they would not take from him.[53] The relative ease with which Chamberlain gained support for Churchill's initiatives reflects poorly on the service chiefs and suggests Churchill's proposals were being rejected primarily because they were emanating from him rather than from the prime minister. When confronted with Chamberlain's support of Churchill, their objections typically disappeared.

Nevertheless, it is certain that in his manner, attitude, and contribution, Churchill exacerbated the failings of this body. He was the main reason why in its early days the committee became immersed in the frustrating minutiae of Britain's war effort rather than being a big picture body seeking to offer guidance to the War Cabinet on broad issues of strategy and the general conduct of the war. The greater part of its business was generated by Churchill's relentless pursuit of detail regarding the army and air force. This was cause for much annoyance from his colleagues, as was recorded by Sir Edward Bridges:

This Committee is becoming a positive menace. Everything is referred to it which the First Lord would like to discuss for further detail and this includes a great many matters affecting both the Air Ministry and the War Office.

The Secretary of State for Air remarked in a caressing tone (which did not disguise the possible existence of claws) that when the MCC had finished discussing the War Office and the Air Ministry, no doubt it would be pleasant to have a discussion in that Committee, into how the Admiralty was managing their affairs.[54]

Additionally, Churchill was less than cooperative when it came to matters of strategy. The MCC was expected to produce consensus on all matters under discussion, consensus that would be conveyed by Chatfield, as chairman, to the War Cabinet for a final decision. Chatfield was unable to fulfill this duty when discussion turned to Churchill's plans. If Churchill did not share the consensus view, neither the predigestion of COS reports nor the lengthy discussion within the MCC prevented the full reconsideration of matters at the War Cabinet. This situation arose in mid-December when Churchill's proposal to stop the flow of Norwegian ore via Narvik became the core business of both forums. It was Chatfield's responsibility to convey the consensus view of the MCC meeting of 20 December to the War Cabinet on 22 December, but he found the discussion hijacked from the beginning by Churchill. Of some considerable importance to development of the Churchill-Chamberlain theme, this hijacking occurred with Chamberlain's willing support.[55]

The series of meetings during December and January also illustrated the folly of expecting the MCC to make recommendations about strategy without a regular political input from the Foreign Office. The appearance at an MCC meeting of Northern Department official Orme Sergeant, acting on behalf of Halifax and the Foreign Office, set up the first of many political roadblocks to Churchill's Narvik scheme, which, in a strictly naval sense, would have been an easy operation to undertake. The introduction of a political dimension into MCC discussions had a decisive influence on future strategy, and this raises the question: Should the MCC have ever attempted to exist without it, especially in circumstances when proposed offensive action involved friends and neutrals?

Although the structural issues surrounding the MCC were considerable, and surely prolonged the decision-making process, they were not the
main reasons why Churchill's plans failed to bear fruit. The real problem for
Churchill was the fact that his proposals, like all the core strategic proposals
set before the War Cabinet at this time, targeted vulnerable neutrals and not
Germany. This brought with it a variety of intractable political, diplomatic,
ethical, and military problems that will be explored in more detail when the
plans themselves are addressed in a subsequent chapter.

For all Churchill's frustration at process, the MCC's foray into strategy
was comparatively brief. The consolidation of the Finnish option occurred
primarily at the War Cabinet level. The MCC became absorbed again in
more discussion of supply matters under Churchill's relentless inquisition
of the army and air force. From mid-February until early March the MCC
met rarely. Its rejuvenation coincided with the failure of the Finnish option
and the ascendancy of Churchill and his pet offensive schemes: the Narvik
plan and Royal Marine. By this time these were the only offensive options
available to the Allies to salve the humiliation of Finland's capitulation.

A Question of Executive Authority

With the rebirth of the Narvik scheme and War Cabinet support for Royal
Marine in early March 1940, Churchill's influence grew within the War
Cabinet and the MCC. From March onward he also became a regular presence at SWC meetings. Given his significant new role in the development
of strategy, there was even less need for a minister for the coordination of
defense. At the end of March 1940 Chatfield again offered Chamberlain his
resignation, and this time it was accepted. This change coincided with others
in the War Cabinet, including the demise of Kingsley Wood as secretary of
state for air. Churchill remained first lord and was elevated to the chairmanship of the MCC.[56] In a note to Chamberlain he thanked the prime minister
for the confidence being shown in him and indicated he would "try his best
to deserve it."[57]

At its most cynical, Churchill's promotion to chairman of the MCC has
been characterized as a political move by Chamberlain intended to ensure that
should the Norway strategy or Royal Marine come unstuck, Churchill would
be held responsible.[58] This is a bleak perspective and fails to acknowledge

the circumstances of the time. It made eminent sense to give Churchill a supervisory role over the two impending Allied initiatives, which, although they had been adopted by the War Cabinet quite independently of his agitation, were Churchill's conceptions. Given the other, albeit minor, ministerial changes, the promotion also provided an element of continuity. However, it is also probable that in offering him the chairmanship, Chamberlain was seeking to link Churchill more directly to the recommendations and decisions that emanated from the MCC.[59] Chamberlain was not banking on the prospect of failure or the hope that Churchill might be shown up for the policies he had promoted; rather he was hoping his new role would promote more caution and less excess. Churchill's new position might have proved a boon for him had it not been that under his chairmanship the MCC was required to undertake the most challenging element of its brief: the guidance of military operations during the Norwegian campaign, which began on 9 April. In the absence of executive authority, his chairmanship proved a considerable challenge for him.

With few exceptions, the historical assessment of Churchill's performance as chairman of the MCC is negative, and he is blamed for much of the folly of the battle for Norway. Churchill gave his own assessment of his role as chairman in *The Gathering Storm*, in which he wrote that he had "an exceptional measure of responsibility, but no power of effective direction" and that matters were complicated by the fact that "many important and able men had a right and duty to express their views on the swiftly-changing phases of the battle."[60] Although a somewhat self-serving assessment of the MCC's limitations, these observations nevertheless accurately reflect the problems inherent in its structure, all of which were seriously exacerbated the moment Britain began fighting a "hot" land war. While the recommendations emanating from the MCC were generally accepted without demur by the War Cabinet early in the campaign, this situation changed within days when Chamberlain and Halifax, much as they had done over the Narvik plan months before, added an ultimately decisive political dimension to the discussion of strategy. The pressure brought to bear on Churchill to shift the focus of Allied action from Narvik to Trondheim placed him in a situation in which he would more likely be supervising failure in Norway than success, and his reputation has suffered ever since. However, although Churchill was justified in identifying in *The Gathering Storm* the serious flaws inherent in the MCC, he is much less persuasive in inviting us to extrapolate that had more executive control been vested in him, all would have been better for it. It is likely nothing could have saved the Allies in Norway, and Churchill played his own part in extinguishing what little hope there was.

Nevertheless, Churchill's failure as chairman has been much overstated and unfairly related. The way he conducted business as the new chairman is the explanation most often given for this crisis. However, while there is some truth to the criticism, this explanation does not satisfactorily acknowledge the enormous pressures placed on him by the inadequate decision-making structure, conflicting views of strategy within the War Cabinet, and the rapidly changing course of events.

Churchill's efforts to accommodate the political dimensions of the campaign led to the key crises of its early weeks: the decision to take Trondheim and then the decision to abandon it. In late April Churchill attributed this debacle to his lack of authority, and he wished not to return to the chairmanship of the MCC unless this matter was addressed.[61] Chamberlain viewed the issue of Trondheim quite differently. In a letter to his sister, Hilda, he noted that Churchill had changed his mind four times over Trondheim but had, in the end, conceded that it was best they had not persisted with the attempt to take it. Chamberlain was concerned that Churchill's ambiguous role within the MCC allowed the first lord to disassociate himself from recommendations emanating from it as and when it suited. Of Churchill's indecisiveness over Trondheim, Chamberlain wrote that he did not "blame W.C. for these natural alternations"; rather he was frustrated that this episode did not "square with the picture the gutter press and W.C.'s friends try to paint of the supreme War Lord."[62]

If Churchill's views on Trondheim were self-serving, so too were those of Chamberlain. It was he, Halifax, and the Foreign Office that had been most insistent on the switch from Narvik to Trondheim. Nevertheless, there was truth in his comments on Churchill's selective recollection of events. Churchill had agreed to, or had been influential in, all the changes in strategy, and he subsequently wished he had not. The Trondheim affair, therefore, produced a situation in which Churchill wanted more authority and Chamberlain was keen to give it, but the motivation of each was very different. Churchill was no longer willing to accept responsibility for decisions that he believed were not his. Chamberlain was, just as at the beginning of April, continuing to seek a solution that would tie Churchill more closely to MCC recommendations and compel him to accept his share of responsibility for them. This would make Churchill a more effective contributor to the war effort and make him less likely to press unwise or foolish proposals. Chamberlain's personal challenge was to find a way to give Churchill more authority without making this absolute. He accepted Churchill's central role in the formulation of strategy and the conduct of operations, but he "could not accept a proposal which would make him [Churchill] sole director of military policy without safeguards which would ensure the Cabinet getting the independent advice of the Chiefs of Staff before taking decisions."[63] If Chamberlain had a mind-set at the end of April 1940, it was that he was very keen to find a war leader who could take the burden of fighting the war from him. This might have been Churchill. In denying him this role, Chamberlain was being driven not by personal animus but by a concern that Churchill was not quite up to the job. This had as much or more to do with Churchill's lapses in judgment than Chamberlain's purported prejudices.

At the end of April, Churchill was made "responsible on behalf of the Committee for giving guidance and directions to the Chiefs of Staff Committee" and could summon that committee or members of it at any time he considered necessary.[64] Thus was executive control of sorts given him. He recognized the limitations of the proposal but was personally confident the system could work. The period between Churchill's promotion within the MCC and his becoming prime minister was so brief it is not possible to assess the merit of the new system or to deduce how well Churchill might have exercised his increased influence.

As the new British leader, and strongly supported by the people who brought him to the position, Churchill revamped the decision-making process, and the MCC disappeared. He made himself minister for defense and operated in direct consultation and discussion with the COS, although he still took all, or at least most, proposals to the wider War Cabinet for confirmation. This new structure was in a state of flux for the first week or so of his administration, and several important decisions were tediously slow. Over time, however, Churchill's centrality in the decision-making process was almost certainly advantageous. John Colville, now as Churchill's secretary, was inspired by his "ceaseless energy" and the fact that he was always full of fight and "thrive[d] on crises and adversity." These characteristics were undoubtedly very important for the times ahead. Tellingly, however, Colville also commented on Churchill's newly found caution. In response to one questionable proposal, he recorded, "Winston answered that our hands were too full elsewhere to enable us to embark on adventures; such is the change high office can work in a man's inherent love of rash and spectacular action."[65]

While Churchill's administrative changes worked well in the circumstances that were presented to him after 10 May 1940, it is far from certain that had such a change occurred any earlier, the British war effort would have been better for it. Churchill was a benefactor of circumstances that made his role as war leader much less complicated than that of his predecessor. As cataclysmic as the invasion of France and the Low Countries was, it simplified matters strategically. Britain was now fighting the principal enemy on the principal front; neither he nor his government were required to devise and prosecute dubious plans to fight Germany through vulnerable neutrals, a problem that had been at the heart of Phoney War politics and strategy. Moreover, it is difficult to contend that Churchill ought to have acquired more influence earlier and that this would have been to the Allies' advantage. Churchill was a more responsible leader than he had been a follower, and once invested with the power he had long sought, he displayed an unexpected wisdom in its application. The problem for both Churchill and Chamberlain during the Phoney War was that it was always far from apparent that Churchill was capable of exercising such authority successfully. It is interesting to record how relieved, and not a little surprised, Chamberlain was to discover Churchill was more responsible as prime minister than he ever thought he would be or could be: "I must say that Winston has shown up well so far. . . . He does take the opinions of the staff and doesn't attempt to force different views upon them or to shoulder off his colleagues."[66]

Conclusions

This study of Churchill as War Cabinet minister and, in particular, his contribution to the LFC and the MCC identified his big picture view of the war and his determination to adopt a broad oversight of Britain's war effort.

He sought to maximize the potential of all three services while avoiding absolute priority to any, a legacy of his experiences of World War I. His focus was, nevertheless, first and foremost on the rapid growth of the army, for here was the greatest deficiency and need. He believed Britain must do its bit in France lest French morale or French forces collapse before Germany's propaganda and armies. He argued that a fifty-five-division army was the minimum at which Britain should aim and believed it was within Britain's capacity to fulfill this. As important, he believed that many more divisions could be put in the field within the first year of war. The requirements of the other services did not need to encroach on this expectation. As far as the navy was concerned, its requirements would not be as great as they were during World War I; in terms of capital ships, and much to the chagrin of his sea lords, he contended that Britain already had forces in excess of likely needs. When it appeared Britain might fail to meet his nominated benchmarks, Churchill's agitation transmuted into a relentless determination to prove more could be done.

To this end, with the assistance of Lindemann, he challenged every time frame, every need, any perceived indulgence or excess, and any failure of his sister services. Additionally, he challenged the principles and practices that were the foundations of the RAF and War Office war effort: the levels of mechanization and motorization of the army and the training and reserve practices of the air force in particular. Even the financial calculations of the Exchequer were open to criticism and comment to ensure more forces were put on the front line more quickly. No area of policy was immune from Churchill's inquisition, and this was a heady burden of self-imposed responsibility.

While Churchill's purpose might have been sound, his manner and method were not. The positive consequences of these inquiries were negligible.[67] This is not to suggest that the war economy was working to capacity or that things could not improve or be better done. Rather, it is to contend that Churchill's and Lindemann's criticisms often missed their mark. Given the limited resources available to Lindemann's committee and the short time frames often imposed on its investigations, this was not surprising. What was surprising was Churchill's willingness to place great store in the conclusions drawn and recommendations made by Lindemann when he must have recognized the limitations of his assessments at this time in the war. With only the imprimatur of the first lord to support him, Lindemann likely could not secure access to the departmental resources needed to give his appreciations the depth and accuracy needed.[68]

Churchill's strong personal views and preconceptions combined with Lindemann's sometimes dubious appreciations to produce a mixture of under- and overestimation on many subjects. Typically, his attitude was about hurrying things on, doing more with less, and doing so in shorter time. Lindemann's assessments almost invariably reinforced these views.[69] Given Britain's challenging strategic situation and evidence that things could be done better, Churchill's desire to hurry the war was to be expected; he erred on the side of "hurry" as much as others erred on the side of complacency, but on occasion Churchill was also guilty of this latter sin. His conviction that the merchant marine, supported by the Royal Navy, had British trade sufficiently under control to justify a relaxation of certain elements of government import and export policy, including rationing, proved unsound.

Although Churchill was undoubtedly genuine in seeking and maintaining economy, he proved incapable of imposing and maintaining this at the Admiralty. This had much to do with an excessively optimistic outlook regarding the growth of the navy, his all too hopeful views on the anti-U-boat war, and his failure to satisfactorily anticipate expenditure blowouts caused by enemy action (such as the impact and consequences of the temporary abandonment of Scapa Flow). Less forgivable was the waste in time, money, and effort in meeting several of his personal ventures and schemes and in accommodating his wider strategic vision. Too often in these instances the due diligence expected of others was absent.

Churchill's frustration with the structure and nature of the decision-making process was justified. As an instrument intended to formulate and guide the War Cabinet in matters of strategy, the MCC was flawed. It was born of a hodgepodge of ideas and aspirations, and certain apprehension regarding Churchill, and then transformed into something it was not meant to be. Its deliberations rarely saved time and instead contributed to delay and duplication, and through this produced frustration from all quarters. The MCC was an even less successful body when its members attempted to address the fast-flowing demands of the Norwegian campaign. Nevertheless,

Churchill contributed significantly to the MCC failure to fulfill what little potential it had. This was not least because he filled many of its hours with the minutiae of supply issues and because he was so reluctant to take no for an answer on any issue that conflicted with his own view of the war or failed to meet with his strategic aspirations.

At the heart of many of these problems of process was the absence of a consistent executive influence in the formulation of strategy; this might have prevented much of the duplication and time wasting that frustrated Churchill. Chamberlain can be held responsible for not filling this void; it is much less clear that he can be blamed for not allowing Churchill to do so. The absence of executive authority within the MCC had more desperate consequence during the Norwegian campaign. That it was most efficient when Chamberlain chaired its meetings owed much less to Chamberlain the man than to the executive authority he held as prime minister. It was an injustice to Churchill to blame him for the failure of this body during the Norwegian campaign when it so clearly had a great deal to do with the instrument itself. Nevertheless, Churchill's own performance limited the influence he was able to wield and the confidence he was able to instill. This was a problem for Churchill and for Chamberlain; the latter was looking for a warrior in whom he could place complete trust, but Churchill had too often demonstrated he was not quite the man for the job.

FIVE

"DON'T HURT THEM, DEAR!"
Air Policy, the French, and Royal Marine

There were four avenues through which Churchill could encourage Britain to take the war to Germany: land, sea, amphibious operations, and air via the new and, according to some, potentially decisive strategic bomber. Action on land was constrained by French determination to assume the defensive in the West, and Britain had long accepted that the western front was a French domain. Land operations in southern Europe were compromised by a variety of political issues and, more particularly, the Italian threat in the air and at sea. The war at sea began almost immediately and was prosecuted with vigor. Churchill's efforts to hurt Germany with superior sea power in amphibious operations (Catherine) were constrained by a great number of political and operational difficulties. Three other important initiatives—the War Cabinet's Finnish option, Churchill's Narvik scheme, and Operation Royal Marine—were compromised by other factors. The Finnish option and Narvik plan are the subjects of the next chapter. Royal Marine, Churchill's scheme to mine the Rhine River—and its intimate links to matters of Allied air policy and fears over German retaliation—is discussed here.

The fourth avenue of attack—the strategic use of British airpower—faced its own obstacles. The first of these was British (and Allied) bombing policy, the essence of which was to avoid harming civilians, or rather to avoid being the first to do so. A powerful influence working against the escalation of air warfare was President Roosevelt's call at the start of the war for the belligerents to avoid civilian casualties. The second obstacle, intimately linked to the first, was the enemy's much larger air force, which invited fears of retaliation and escalation. Moreover, every day without unrestricted aerial warfare permitted Britain's own powers of retaliation to grow stronger. A third factor was that the Germans declined at the start of the war to conduct unrestricted air war against Britain and France, and neither country was disposed to disturb this situation while they were rearming. A fourth factor was interallied disagreement over the circumstances that would justify bombing Germany.[1] Because of these issues, and despite bombs being dropped on Polish, Norwegian, and Danish territory, not a single Allied bomb was dropped in anger on mainland Germany for the entire period of the Phoney War. Chamberlain's wartime critics and some postwar historians denounced this policy for its pusillanimity.[2]

This chapter will explore the issues and policies surrounding the use of the air weapon and assess Churchill's attitude toward the restrictions these imposed on the aggressive prosecution of the war. This analysis will question the view that Churchill was a uniquely determined warrior during this time. It will be shown that despite occasional frustration he was a strong supporter of Britain's conservative air policy. He supported this policy as part of the long war grand strategy: that Britain be left alone to build its war effort while constricting Germany's own via blockade. An important influence on Churchill was his concern that should Britain be first to "take the gloves off" in the air war, it would have a negative impact on American public opinion. He feared this would make America even more reluctant to aid the Allies in their war with Germany.

Any assessment of Churchill's attitude toward the air war must recognize his thinking involved two elements—not always consistently defined or separated. The first was his view of how Britain should respond to the pinprick German aggression that characterized most of the Phoney War. This was German action that could not be considered decisive or potentially decisive under War Cabinet guidelines and that would not justify taking the gloves off. War Cabinet policy (heavily influenced by the COS and the air force, the latter of which would necessarily be responsible for retaliatory measures) was to respond not to all provocation—even on a like-for-like basis—but only in circumstances that would be demonstrably to Britain's advantage and would justify the attrition of British air resources. Further, the cabinet intended not to precede Germany in any aggression; Britain might react but would not initiate, even if some limited advantage was to be gained. Although in general agreement with these principles, Churchill became increasingly uncomfortable with the restrictions imposed, not least because he believed the actions he proposed were reasonable and would not precipitate escalation.

The second element was Churchill's views on enemy action that should be deemed decisive and that, therefore, should justify bombing military and industrial targets and possibly causing civilian casualties. On this issue Churchill proved remarkably conservative. He was content, along with most civilian members of the War Cabinet, to set aside the evidence of the Polish campaign, which appeared to present ample justification for a more aggressive air policy. As to the specifics of British policy, he accepted that a large-scale land or air attack on Britain or France causing large numbers of civilian casualties (it was often—but not always—accepted that the former would lead to the latter) or a large-scale air attack on Britain's maritime trade (which Churchill himself had described as "potentially mortal") would justify escalating the air war. However, he was inconsistent and indecisive when Britain and France clashed over the question of how Britain should react in the air to a German invasion of Belgium or Holland and whether this should also be deemed decisive.

From the earliest days of the war, the COS argued that an attack on the Low Countries must be viewed as decisive and be followed by the bombing of the Ruhr—the heart of German industry—by Britain's main striking force of heavy bombers. By mid-October the War Cabinet agreed with this principle, although the issue of timing remained. The French, however, proved extremely reluctant to view an invasion of the Low Countries as decisive and were ardently opposed to Britain's intended response for fear it would lead directly to the bombing of France. For the entire period of the Phoney War, these issues were a major point of contention between the Allies, yet the dynamics and consequences of this disagreement remain misunderstood. Churchill shared his prime minister's anxieties, and those of the French, over the escalation of the air war, and in the first days following the German invasion of the West in May 1940, he hesitated to accept an attack on the Low Countries was cause enough to take the gloves off.

One other extraordinary element to this study of Allied policy must be considered. In some respects it is the most important. This is the extent to which Allied disagreement over air policy contributed to the disastrous military strategy adopted by the French during the Battle of France. There is an inadequately explored and inadequately understood link between British air policy and the adoption of the tragically flawed Dyle plan and the

Map 5.1. Northwestern Europe and the North Sea

subsequent Breda variant. This plan required Allied forces entering Belgium to take up lines along the River Dyle. The Breda variant was the movement of substantial mobile French forces to take up positions in Holland at the far left of the Allied line. This strategy proved a disaster for the Allies because it helped deny the French the necessary reserves to interdict the Germans' masterful sickle-cut strategy via the Ardennes.

In his postwar writing Churchill was critical of the Dyle plan and contended that the Chamberlain administration ought to have explored the plan more searchingly. This criticism ignored the extent to which British agitation—and in particular British air policy—influenced western front strategy. Churchill's criticism also concealed his personal contribution to this misfortune.

Air Bombing Policy: The Early Months

The essentials of Allied war strategy and air bombing policy were established well before the invasion of Poland and before Churchill joined the War Cabinet.[3] When he acquainted himself with these matters, he did not dissent. Allied strategy was to be defensive at the outset, while executing the greatest measure of economic pressure against Germany and building military strength sufficient to permit a turn to the offensive. A conservative air policy suited this approach because it limited the likelihood of escalation and the harm that would be done to Britain's rearming efforts, including of Bomber Command, which was well short of desired strength. As for Poland, once the invasion had begun, it was accepted that nothing in the air could be done to save it; the salvation of Poland was to be achieved through the ultimate victory of the Allies.[4]

Britain's heavy bomber force, or Main Striking Force (MSF), numbering approximately three hundred first-line aircraft, was for many the jewel in the crown of the RAF. It was generally acknowledged that this weapon, once unleashed, could have a decisive impact on the war. Until decisive events presented, or until the War Cabinet, in consultation with the French, altered policy, the activities of the heavy bombers would be confined to the bombing of the fleet at Wilhelmshaven and German ships at sea and the dropping of propaganda leaflets. The MSF was not intended to be frittered away on incidental action or employed tactically. Support for this policy was pervasive within the War Cabinet and was strongly advocated by the COS, but also by the RAF, the Royal Navy (which did not wish to invite an escalation of air attack against shipping), and Churchill himself.

It was, of course, always the British government's intention to support the French, and subsequently BEF, forces tactically in France in the event of any kind of land offensive.[5] This support would be provided, not by the heavy bombers, but by squadrons of light and medium bombers allocated for operations on the western front.[6] Fighters too were allocated, although the numbers provided were a matter of some concern to the French.

Just how, when, and where Britain's bombers—heavy, medium, and light—would be used depended, for the most part, on the Germans, for it was not expected the French would launch a major offensive of their own in the early stages of the war. However, this reactive policy looked set to end as early as the first hours of the conflict when the War Cabinet mistakenly apprehended that the French might bomb targets in Germany as soon as hostilities were declared.[7] As will become clear as this chapter progresses, there was never the slightest possibility this would occur; nevertheless, the War Cabinet sought reassurances the French were not planning air action that would result in civilian casualties.[8] Confusion continued into 4 September. Poland was under attack, and nothing was being done to help. Churchill proposed action to relieve pressure on the Poles, and he suggested air operations against the Siegfried line, which was then thinly held by the enemy. The War Cabinet generally accepted the suggestion. Its members thought that a combined plan to relieve pressure on Poland was necessary, and they instructed the COS to contact General Maurice Gamelin. This contact would also allow the government to "discover the French Army Plan and the best means by which our Air Striking Force could collaborate."[9] It was apparent, nevertheless, that the War Cabinet intended only to use the air weapon as part of a serious combined operation with the French.

By 5 September the War Cabinet was more fully apprised of French intentions. Gamelin planned a slow and methodical movement of French forces up to the Maginot line and then a reconnaissance in force to test the strength of the Siegfried line. Thereafter, the French army would begin "leaning against the Siegfried Line." The French move was to be supported, much as Churchill had wished, by ten squadrons of the Advanced Striking Force (ASF). As for the MSF, the policy remained not to "fritter [the heavy bombers] away on unremunerative tasks" or to undertake operations that risked civilian casualties. The meeting of British and French staff also concluded there should be no attack on German oil supplies for the present to avoid possible retaliation to Britain's own stocks, especially those stored along the Thames. The chief of the air staff (CAS), Cyril Newall, emphasized his policy was not merely to hold back the air force for retaliatory measures but to wait for a project that offered potentially decisive results. These included the oil plan, the Ruhr plan, and the aircraft industry plan.[10]

Discussion indicated that fear of retaliation and concern for civilian casualties were governing influences on decisions. Some War Cabinet members, Churchill and Chatfield among them, thought Germany had already indicated intention to ignore the rules of war through such action as the sinking of *Athenia*, and they believed Britain should act accordingly.[11] Even Chamberlain wondered if, rather than doing nothing, the RAF could act in a way that would invite retaliation and therefore permit the air force to take action against its nominated targets. Ironside put an end to all such speculation by bringing discussion back to Gamelin's plan, which, he thought, would be interrupted by an escalation in the air war. If Gamelin was not permitted to carry out his plan, it would, Ironside argued with considerable overstatement, "mean to all intents and purposes, the end of the Western Front as a theatre of War." The meeting concluded that the air force should take no action and instead preserve its forces to assist the French on or after X day, the undisclosed day upon which Gamelin would move into the Saar.[12] Ironsides' recommendations assumed a serious land operation from Gamelin, but this did not develop. By early October French forces had withdrawn to their own lines.

Britain's conservative bombing policy was challenged a second time on 9 September. Evidence from Poland suggested the Germans had begun unrestricted bombing, and this had led to heavy civilian casualties. In response to this news, and without having first discussed the matter with the rest of the COS, CAS Newall suggested to the War Cabinet that Britain now had sufficient justification to undertake similar large-scale attacks against Germany. He believed such an attack could "render the most valuable contribution to the final conclusion of this war."[13] The JPS was set to reviewing air policy in light of Newall's suggestions, and on 11 September the COS and War Cabinet reaffirmed the existing principles of air policy and the decision to prepare to support Gamelin's offensive.[14] No strategic air action would take place in support of Poland.[15]

In all the above, there was little or no dissent from Churchill. Indeed, he had given his views on air policy to Chamberlain in a wide-ranging letter on 10 September. He had expressed admiration for Newall's "spirited mood," which, he thought, "may play its part very shortly," but he was "in full accord" with Chamberlain's view, which, he gathered, "was for waiting." Churchill believed the Allies should not take the initiative in the bombing war "except in the immediate zone in which the French armies are operating, where of course we must help."[16] He thought that it was in Britain's interest the war should "be conducted in accordance with the more humane conceptions and that we should follow and not precede the Germans in the process." Further, he believed Britain needed time to prepare air defense and it was not in British interests to provoke the interruption of munitions production. He was also reluctant to upset neutral opinion, and he had in mind Roosevelt's plea of 1 September to limit the air war.[17] Finally, he considered it "idle" to believe that anything that could be done in the air could save Poland.

Despite these views Churchill showed concern over the self-imposed idleness of Britain's bomber force. At the 14 September War Cabinet meeting, he asked if it would be possible, "without going beyond our current policy," to find strategic military objectives that were away from civilian populations and attack these even if it invited retaliation. The SSW counseled against this. Churchill believed targets should be worth attacking and must not be too expensive to attack; it was important to keep "our small and inferior air force 'in being' against a time when it would be vital."[18]

No member of the Cabinet, Churchill included, saw virtue in frittering away Britain's bomber forces on indecisive bombing operations, and few wished to risk retaliatory measures. It was certain the War Cabinet placed too much store in keeping Britain's heavy bomber force for the decisive moment in the belief it could make a decisive difference at any point in the near future, but it was a compelling justification for doing little at the time. It was also impossible to ignore the threat the Luftwaffe posed to France in the event of aggressive air activity; this had to be factored into British air policy. Churchill took the issue no further.

The collapse of Poland and the French withdrawal from the Saar removed any immediate motivation to act aggressively against Germany in the air. Contrary to expectation, no significant German air threat developed, and the War Cabinet and the COS decided that full advantage should be taken of this hiatus. Churchill remained conservative in his approach to bombing and, except regarding the use of naval power, supported the wider policy of sitting tight and rearming. In late September he wrote his appreciation of the strategic situation in the shadow of the German and Soviet occupation of Poland. He believed Hitler should "stew in his own juices during the winter" while Britain developed its armaments and built its alliances.[19] Thereafter, his views changed little. In a speech in November, he declared, "I do not doubt myself that time is on our side," and in another in January he declared, "I am quite clear that our policy has been right."[20] He added to this latter declaration his conviction that if the Germans did not escalate their war effort on the land or in the air, the Allies would have won the first campaign of the war.[21] Also in January, in a personal reply to Lord Trenchard, Britain's most ardent advocate of strategic bombing—who had written to Churchill selling the virtue of an air offensive—Churchill wrote, "The time has not yet come when it is in our interest to initiate general and unlimited air war."[22]

Despite his endorsement of air policy and the broader policy of sit tight and rearm, Churchill occasionally chaffed at the constraints these policies imposed on reasonable defensive measures or retaliatory action for German deeds already done. Two episodes stand out. Each pertained to the War Cabinet's responses to the German magnetic mining threat that emerged in November. Churchill wanted to attack the island air bases used by aircraft responsible for some of the mining. This fell outside bombing guidelines, and the air force could offer only more regular patrols near the bases.

The second measure he proposed was Operation Royal Marine, a plan to mine enemy waterways with fluvial mines. Although this plan was initially rejected by the government's legal experts and was also criticized by the RAF, it fairly quickly received the endorsement of the War Cabinet. However, French military and political opinion proved an insurmountable obstacle. Churchill became deeply resentful of the French attitude, and he wrote as much, pointedly and unjustly, after the war. He was unwilling to acknowledge that the French rejected Royal Marine for the same reasons he and the British War Cabinet, over many months, declined to bomb Germany: a fear of retaliation and escalation in the air war.

Royal Marine

The Admiralty began investigating the idea of laying mines in Germany's waterways in the first weeks of the war.[23] At some point in November—perhaps earlier—naval staff put to Churchill the idea of using floating mines in Germany's inland waterways as a proportionate retaliation for the German magnetic mining program. Churchill had discussions with Pound and Phillips and authorized further development. He also instructed his staff to explore the juridical justification for the scheme, his own suggestion being the losses that had occurred in the Thames through magnetic mines.[24] As soon as the appliances were ready in large numbers, a continuous discharge into the Rhine would take place, and Churchill set naval staff to devising the appropriate weapon. He also ensured that General Gamelin was acquainted with the plan, and the latter expressed considerable interest.[25]

Churchill intended to introduce Royal Marine to the War Cabinet when he proposed another retaliatory measure for the magnetic mining program: the stopping of German export trade proceeding in neutral shipping. However, he discovered the air force, via the work of Major Millis Jefferis, was working on a similar scheme with mines to be delivered by aircraft.[26] Thereafter, Churchill thought in terms of an expanded plan that would involve simultaneously mining from land and air into rivers, estuaries, and canals. On 24 November he gave his delayed presentation to the War Cabinet. He explained that ten thousand mines could be ready to place in the Rhine by the end of January as a "retaliatory measure." He sought and received approval for the project on the understanding that the final decision would be made once the mines were ready.[27] Thereafter, Churchill conveyed this information to Gamelin and General Alphonse Georges, and they again endorsed the concept. However, his plan would soon run into trouble.

The first obstacle to Royal Marine developed in early December when the RAF produced two negative papers against the mining plan and Churchill's proposal to bomb the seaplane bases on the island of Sylt.[28] The deputy director of plans, Air Commodore Alfred Conrad Collier, was concerned that action would invite a much larger German attack against naval and air bases, shipping, and possibly shipbuilding yards and aircraft factories. In short his paper repeated the accepted thesis that Britain had more to lose than to gain in an escalated air war.

Collier's paper was accompanied by an appreciation by the Foreign Office's legal expert, Sir William Malkin, on the legal aspect of Royal Marine. Malkin had concluded "the mining of inland waterways in Germany other than the Kiel Canal is illegal and cannot be undertaken at the present time as retaliation." Churchill exploded with indignation when he read Malkin's paper. He crossed out the paper's title and wrote instead: "Some funkstick in the Air Ministry running for shelter under Malkin's petticoats."[29] He wrote to the secretary of state for air, Kingsley Wood, in the hope that this did not reflect his views on the matter.[30]

As it turned out, Wood was more receptive to the mining proposal than Churchill had anticipated. During the War Cabinet of 10 December, it was agreed that given Germany's disregard for international law, retaliation should be based on the expediency of options open to Britain rather than strictly legal matters.[31] While this did little to alter Britain's policy toward bombing German island bases, it left the door open to Royal Marine, and in due course the War Cabinet endorsed the Royal Marine proposal.[32]

Blocked over Sylt but encouraged by the War Cabinet's response to Royal Marine, Churchill immediately wrote a persuasive justification for the operation. Mindful of Collier's criticism of palliative measures, Malkin's various legal strictures, and the pervasive anxiety over risks to civilians, he argued that while Royal Marine would inflict "damage on the enemy . . . which will . . . be substantial," it would be achieved with "the minimum effusion of blood."[33] It was, therefore, neither a mere "palliative" measure so disliked by the air force nor an unlawful or provocative response to German aggression, as feared more generally by the War Cabinet. Over the following months Churchill repeated these principles in his communications with the French. With great vigor and commitment, the first lord, in unison with the air force, pressed forward with preparations for Royal Marine. On 6 March he received a green light from the War Cabinet. This decision coincided with the imminent collapse of the War Cabinet's Finnish option and a growing need for some kind of relatively benign military action to offset the consequences of this. Whether this strong support for Royal Marine would have been forthcoming except for the failure of the Finnish option is moot; nevertheless, permission was given to implement the plan after consultation with the French. This represented another significant step away from the War Cabinet passivity of early months.

Churchill now had to bring the French on board. He seemed hopeful in this regard; after all Gamelin had several times expressed support for the mining plan. Churchill was to be profoundly disappointed with what he would subsequently characterize as the "don't hurt them, dear!" attitude of the French. Immediately after the 6 March War Cabinet meeting, he sent his emissary, Rear Admiral John Fitzgerald, to France with a letter to inform Gamelin that the operation awaited his signal.[34] Gamelin responded that while he agreed in principle with the project, "he was doubtful whether the French were prepared for possible reprisals and wondered if it should not be delayed until it could be combined with some unspecified other operation."[35]

For Churchill this was frustrating news, but there had long been signs the French would hesitate at implementing the project according to a British timetable. Churchill had envisaged a constant and ongoing campaign of mining, begun at a moment most propitious for the Allies, that would produce long-term disruption to German inland trade and industry. For him Royal Marine represented an appropriate retaliation for the German misdeeds. The delay in its implementation had been primarily a matter of preparation. Quite early, however, Gamelin had indicated that he did not think of Royal Marine as an independent operation but one that would coincide with major land operations in the West.[36] Unless or until the Germans attacked in the West, it was evident Gamelin did not intend for Royal Marine to take place.

On 16 March Churchill attempted to persuade Gamelin to support Royal Marine with a sophisticated line of argument that contended France had little to fear from the plan. He wrote that the British government "did not consider that the fluvial mines . . . would logically entail reprisals against the French Air factories." The operation had been conceived as an "exact measure of retaliation for the illegal and inhumane methods of warfare directed against the coasts and harbours, [and] shipping of this island." He thought that while the Germans might naturally reply with attacks on French and British inland waterways, they would need some time to prepare this response, which in any event would not be as advantageous to them as would be the attack on the Rhine for the Allies. If the Germans attacked French or British air factories, they would invite attacks on targets that had long been studied. Churchill also repeated the argument offered to Kingsley Wood several months before: the Germans would not need a pretext to escalate the war; they would do so when it suited. Therefore, it made no sense to hold back for fear of retaliation on an aggressive action that could do the Germans considerable harm.[37]

These arguments failed to appreciate how vulnerable the French felt to air attack and tended to overlook how recently Britain had been converted to a more aggressive stance. Moreover, Churchill's argument regarding pretext was problematic. Hitler might not be constrained by law, but he was just the kind of man to be provoked by action, lawful or otherwise; it was this awareness that animated the French. They were not open to risk, and as will be considered later in this chapter, there had been abundant evidence to demonstrate this to Churchill in their prolonged disagreement over the application of Britain's heavy bomber force should the Germans invade Belgium or Holland. Inevitably, France's proximity to Germany, its limited strength in the air, and Britain's reluctance to commit substantial fighter forces to the Continent ensured that the French view of the right time to risk escalating the air war was markedly different from their ally's.

Air Policy and the Western Front: Britain and France in Conflict

As the events outlined demonstrate, the British War Cabinet had a disturbingly limited understanding of how the French proposed to fight the war in the West. The obverse was almost as true as far as air policy was concerned, and there was a pressing need for both sides to establish common ground. Although Churchill did not expect a German attack in the West following the defeat of Poland and was content to let the Germans stew over winter, the French soon acquired intelligence a decision would be sought during October and November, and this gave rise to discussion of several issues, including additional British fighter support in France. By degree this latter issue evolved into a wider discussion of Allied air policy and, in turn, exposed a disturbing difference between the Allies regarding the importance of Belgium and Holland in western front strategy. The process by which this difference was discovered, and its implications for the Allies, can be summarized as follows:

In the opening weeks of the war, British plans—particularly air policy—were built around the expectation that little could be done (partly because little had been planned) to prevent the Germans' occupying Belgium and Holland or some portion of each. This assessment applied much more to

Holland than to Belgium (because it was more distant from France). This potential loss of the Low Countries exposed Britain (as it did France) to a heightened German air threat; there was a particular concern that German light and medium bombers could thereafter be escorted by fighters over southern England.

Also, at this time there was considerable doubt over what Allied forces would or could do if Germany attacked Belgium (and this was the main reason why the British anticipated losing the Low Countries). The French had long expressed their intention to enter Belgium if invited and take up one of several lines of defense. The depth of the advance would be influenced by several factors but principally the timeliness of the invitation and the success of Belgian resistance. At all costs an encounter battle was to be avoided, and this was always an important consideration for Gamelin and for the British. In the early weeks of the war, the uncertainty surrounding these matters left the British General Staff reluctant to have the BEF leave prepared lines along the Franco-Belgian border; its first priority was to get to its lines and consolidate its positions. The French too wondered at their prospects for an advance into Belgium any deeper than the Scheldt. In the best of circumstances, therefore, it was highly probable the Germans would occupy a considerable portion of the Low Countries following an invasion.

When, therefore, Gamelin asked for additional Hurricane fighter squadrons to be based in France (there were then four Hurricane squadrons based there), the British declined. If the Germans secured most of Belgium and Holland, they might thereafter concentrate on a great air attack against Britain. If that occurred, all available squadrons would be needed in England. The British argued that additional fighter squadrons requested by Gamelin could operate—perhaps with even greater efficiency—from airfields in Britain; nevertheless, they proposed to make all the preparations necessary should it be decided to send more squadrons. Rather than more British fighters in France, the British offered another solution they thought would meet the needs of both countries. If the Germans attacked, Britain's heavy bombers would launch an attack on the Ruhr. The Germans would be compelled to redirect elements of their bomber forces to attack Britain in retaliation and would be met—to advantage—by British fighters. The French offered no response to this suggestion at this juncture, but the Ruhr bombing plan quickly became central to Anglo-French discussions—and disputation.

During October the British attitude to a deep advance into Belgium gradually changed. The early resistance to a move into Belgium, as per French plans, had little or nothing to do with the proposition itself, but with its timing. The BEF needed to get to France and establish itself in prepared lines before it contemplated moves that might expose it to encounter battles with the German armies. Once the BEF was established on its lines, other influences came into play that gave the British government reason to support some kind of advance, always assuming that an encounter battle could be avoided. The British had readily accepted the advantages offered by a movement into Belgium. It would shorten the Allied lines, permit the Allied armies to support and secure the assistance of eighteen to twenty Belgian divisions, and keep the German air threat at a suitable distance from Britain's shores. At first glance, therefore, there was little to separate the British and French attitude to the Low Countries. Each country considered it important to secure a position in Belgium. Assistance to Holland was always recognized as more problematic.

With Poland defeated by the end of September, the British War Cabinet began in earnest to discuss the ramifications of German control over the Low Countries. The issue of the Low Countries had typically been addressed in the context of land warfare, but much of this renewed discussion took place with air policy in mind. On 13 October the service ministers, Churchill among them, and the COS convened to decide if a German invasion of the Low Countries should be added to the short list of events considered decisive enough to justify unleashing Britain's heavy bombers against Germany. The meeting concluded that existing policy be amended to read that Britain should begin bombing prescribed targets in Germany's industrial heartland, the Ruhr, "if the Germans launched an attack on France or ourselves which looked like being decisive and had involved either appreciable casualties to civilians outside the military zone [i.e., anywhere in England or the back areas of France] *or a violation of Belgian neutrality*" (italics added). This amendment was put to the War Cabinet the following day but met resistance. No issue was taken with the wisdom of defining an attack on Belgium or on Belgium and Holland (it was assumed at this time that both countries would likely be invaded simultaneously) as a decisive event, but Chamberlain, Halifax, and Hoare did not think that a German violation of Belgium neutrality should automatically precipitate the bombing of the Ruhr.[38] Halifax worried the Allies would be accused of being the first to take the gloves off unless it could be established that the Germans had first caused large numbers of civilian casualties during the invasion. Chatfield argued that a German attack would cause "tremendous suffering" to the Belgian civilian population and that this would amply justify such action. Churchill too saw no problems with the proposal and thought the idea of incidentally causing German civilian casualties by bombing targets in the Ruhr "less shocking" than the Belgian casualties that would occur as German forces moved through Belgium. Nevertheless, the more cautious view prevailed, and the policy proposal was adjusted to read that an invasion of Belgium that "caused significant numbers of civilian casualties" would precipitate the bombing of the Ruhr.[39] This amendment, however, proved much too much for the French.

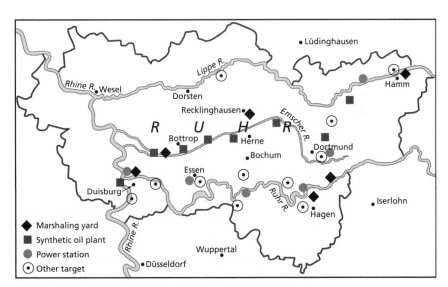

Map 5.2. The Ruhr: Germany's Industrial Heartland. From the start of the war, the RAF had extensive plans ready for bombing Germany and, in particular, the Ruhr area. Neither side, however, was inclined to be the first to "take the gloves off" in the air war and the region was not bombed until 15 May 1940.

French Resistance

Although the War Cabinet had balked at an immediate escalation in the air war in response to an invasion of the Low Countries, its members recognized the need to respond forcefully to this threat. There were a variety of influences at work. First, strategic bombing could do material harm to Germany's war effort. Second, attacking targets in the Ruhr could materially delay a German offensive. Third, German control of the Low Countries would provide depth to their defenses and make any subsequent attacks on Germany much more costly. Fourth, the air force believed that the Ruhr offensive would be best timed to coincide with German aggression in the West. Finally, public opinion would demand that German aggression against Belgium or Holland or both be responded to with full force. With such influences driving British policy, the War Cabinet was taken aback by the strong French reaction to its new policy proposal when this was conveyed to them in mid-October.

In a letter of reply Gamelin argued that all bombing efforts should be concentrated on German columns, railway lines, and airfields; an attack on the Ruhr would not slow a German advance. Not even a successful German occupation of the Low Countries would justify taking the gloves off in the air war unless the Germans first did so against Britain and France. Gamelin acknowledged that a German occupation of the Low Countries presented a serious threat because the enemy would secure air bases closer to Britain and France, but neither he nor the French high command wished to see Germany bombed until, at the very earliest, spring 1940. Even if Belgium were invaded "totally or partially," Gamelin believed Britain and France would be advised to "play for time."[40] Perhaps most telling in his communication was his sanguine observation that Belgium would, after all, offer "a battleground upon which we will be able to use, with every chance of success, the powerful air and military weapons which will then be at our disposal."[41]

As far as the British were concerned, these sentiments were at odds with the attention the French had hitherto given to the Low Countries.[42] The British had never intended to neglect the tactical support of the armies in France, but this support would be given by light and medium bombers and this was known to the French. The heavy bombers were not suited to the tactical role outlined by Gamelin, and if not used to attack the Ruhr, they would not be used at all. Moreover, attacking strategic targets would, it was believed, have an important if not an immediate impact on a German invasion.

Rather than sharing the British War Cabinet's conviction that an invasion of the Low Countries was a decisive event, the French, it appeared, did not consider Belgium or Holland of crucial strategic value. British anxieties went one step further. Suspicion arose that the French might be willing to see Belgium and Holland overrun by the Germans with hardly a fight if France were left alone during the oncoming winter. Gamelin's letter added new import to the observations CAS Newall had made at the War Cabinet on 7 October, when he noted the French general's comment that the Germans might attack and occupy the Low Countries in the autumn and not attack France.[43]

It is possible Gamelin's apparent ambivalence to the Low Countries' importance was being misunderstood and misinterpreted. However, the possibility that before the onset of winter the Germans might attack Belgium and Holland or perhaps Holland alone, and not France, was being canvassed during this time as a real prospect. Moreover, whenever Gamelin discussed plans to enter Belgium, he had always appended the caveat that an invitation had to be offered and offered in a timely manner for Allied forces to advance. Although a reasonable condition to set, this undoubtedly added to British uncertainty over just how much of the Low Countries—if any—would be denied the Germans. If the French were desperately keen to be left alone for as long as possible—even at the expense of German control of one or both of the Low Countries—a British air attack on the Ruhr would be unwelcomed by them. Yet Britain now believed this attack was very much in its own best interest.

General Ismay, then secretary to the COS, was aware of the implications of Gamelin's October correspondence, and at the beginning of November, he proposed the COS review their recent air policy memorandum in light of it.[44] Ismay thought the COS had to determine the importance to be placed on a German invasion of Belgium and also the action to be taken if this occurred in the near future. Perhaps more important, he believed the COS had to decide how to interpret Gamelin's reference to "playing for time." Air staff, he noted, interpreted this as meaning the French did not consider a German invasion of Belgium as decisive. During the next two weeks these investigations, combined with further developments in British air policy, became intimately entwined with Allied liaison over an imminent German invasion of Holland to produce a significant and fate-filled development in western front strategy: the Dyle/Breda plan.

The Coalescence of Land and Air Policy

While at Ismay's request the COS reconsidered their attitude to the strategic importance of Belgium and the recommendation that Britain meet a German invasion with everything available, including an attack on the Ruhr, the JPS completed an assessment of a German invasion of Holland during which Belgium did not remain neutral and invited in the Allies.[45] The committee concluded nothing could be done by Britain and France on land to assist or save Holland and efforts in the air could only be minor and ineffective and would invite retaliation from the Germans. The appreciation also provided a disturbing list of consequences of German control of Holland: an increased air threat to Britain; enhanced opportunities to harass east coast trade; the exposure of Belgium to a future attack from the north and east; and German control of the Scheldt, which would afford them complete control of navigation of the estuary and the approaches to Antwerp. In response to the report, the disconcerted COS briefly explored the possibility of a military advance through Belgium to Holland, but CIGS Ironside explained he had discussed this with Gamelin already and had concluded that without Belgian support, an advance to the Scheldt was probably the best to be hoped for.

The COS presented this report to the 6 November War Cabinet, and cabinet members were greatly concerned about the consequences of German control of Holland and dismayed so little could be done to prevent it. Kingsley Wood believed German control of Holland ought to be resisted at some level. Churchill worried German control of Holland could be mortal to Britain, and he proposed that if the Germans made even a limited attack on Holland, Britain should be prepared "to retaliate immediately by attacking the Ruhr."[46]

At this juncture neither the JPS nor the COS had considered the desirability of the Ruhr plan as a response to an invasion of Holland, but this was in the JPS pipeline. Nevertheless, the War Cabinet proposed the French be informed of this new report and also the tenor of the War Cabinet discussion, which presumably included sentiments expressed in regard to the Ruhr plan. Thus, by the end of 6 November, the French were aware the War Cabinet wished to implement the Ruhr plan in response not only to an invasion of Belgium but also to an invasion of Holland in which Belgium was not attacked but invited in the Allies. Of course, British air policy regarding a German invasion of Belgium was, as per Ismay's instruction, still under review; this policy could change, but War Cabinet sentiment about Holland suggested it would not.

The new JPS appreciation of the Belgium issue was considered at the COS meeting the following morning, during which perceptions of French ambivalence toward Belgium were noted: "Originally the French had been in agreement with ourselves in thinking that a German invasion of Belgium would be a decisive event, and that all possible measures should be taken against it. Latterly, it appeared that the French had modified their view, and were disposed to deprecate any whole-hearted action against Germany until the Spring."

The new JPS appreciation concluded that whatever the outcome of the defense of Belgium, every effort must be made to slow a German attack and permit an Allied advance into Belgium. Although Gamelin was apparently content with a modest movement to the Scheldt in the best-case scenario, the JPS considered it extremely desirable to save as much of Belgium as possible. Even if gains were small, it would be a "grave error" not to inflict heavy casualties on German forces as they advanced toward the Franco-Belgian border. This would require a maximal effort in the air, including the implementation of the Ruhr plan.

During these discussions Ironside remarked he had just heard the French had offered to send troops to Walcheren, an island in the Scheldt estuary, and also to Dutch territory south of this. This was a significant and unexpected enlargement of the commitment—or potential commitment—the French had hitherto made regarding the Low Countries. The novelty of this plan and its timing are best explained—especially with Gamelin's October correspondence in mind—by the French receipt of the latest COS paper on the German threat to Holland and the accompanying evidence that the War Cabinet was determined to respond with the bombing of the Ruhr. Arguably, in offering these significant extensions to likely French action, Gamelin was not primarily concerned with protecting British interests but with deflecting Britain from prosecuting the Ruhr plan.

On the morning of 9 November, Newall and Ironside met with Gamelin and Georges to discuss these latest developments in land and air policy in light of an imminent threat to Holland. The details of the meeting were conveyed to the War Cabinet later in the day.[47] This was the War Cabinet's first serious discussion of the French reaction to British plans to bomb the Ruhr, although it took place in the absence of Chamberlain, who was unwell. Ironside explained that assuming a Belgium invitation, the French intended the Allied armies to first move to the line of the Scheldt. If time permitted, an advance would be made to the line Givet–Namur–Wavre–River Dyle: the Dyle line. This more or less conformed to the existing British preference—which was to defend as much of the Low Countries as possible while avoiding an encounter battle. Primarily because of the collective desire to avoid such a battle, the British did not object at this juncture to the precondition of Belgian cooperation, although it would subsequently become a major issue.

Ironside went on to mention Gamelin raising "a new feature of his [military] plan," intimations of which he had heard two days before. If Allied forces moved into Belgium in support of Belgium and Holland, two French motorized divisions would advance on the far left of the Allied lines to secure two key islands in the Scheldt.[48] This apparently would take place whether or not the Allies were subsequently able to advance to the Dyle, but an advance to the Scheldt was assumed. This was not a hypothetical move. Gamelin was preparing it in response to an imminent invasion of Holland and had already given instructions to the French 16 Corp to move to a position in France that would allow it to achieve this objective.

These discussions no doubt went some way to assuaging British concerns the French did not consider an invasion of Belgium a decisive event, and this in all probability was Gamelin's intention. If the French could provide a successful military response to an invasion of Belgium and Holland that secured important parts of both countries, the British would have less cause to implement the Ruhr plan. The problem with these efforts to deflect the British from this plan was that their strategy remained contingent on being invited into Belgium in a timely manner. This precondition—and the uncertainty it engendered—was destined to play havoc with French efforts to meet British needs and to secure their own; so long as there remained a prospect Belgium and Holland would be lost to the Germans, neither party could feel confident about the path that would be taken by the other.

If, as is contended here, Gamelin's Walcheren plan was conceived to deflect the British from the Ruhr plan, it was an abject failure. The Walcheren plan was not seen as especially practical, and the COS was not sure why it had been put forward. A subsequent JPS assessment of the proposal argued the occupation of this territory would not make Britain more secure and would redirect British air support—which the French hoped to get for the operation—from more pressing needs.[49]

When the War Cabinet turned to the French attitude to the Ruhr plan—a discussion that had followed the revelation of the Walcheren plan earlier that day—it took a direction that would have caused Gamelin much anxiety. Ironside explained the French remained "uncompromisingly opposed" to the implementation of the Ruhr plan in response to an invasion of Belgium, Holland, or both. They argued it would not stop the Germans from over-running the Low Countries and would invite attacks on British and French factories.[50] All bombing should be concentrated on the movement of enemy troops, their communications, and their transport.

This attitude toward the Ruhr plan continued to make no sense to the British. By this time there was no doubt the French understood the strategic bomber force would not be used in, and was unsuited for, the tactical operations they proposed. It appeared, therefore, they were refusing to permit an operation that would slow a German advance and increase the chances of the Allied armies reaching their preferred objectives: islands of the Scheldt and the River Dyle. Thus, despite Gamelin's efforts over Walcheren, fears remained that the French cared little for the Low Countries—especially Holland—and that they were not taking British needs seriously.

The sentiment of the War Cabinet was decidedly against the French obstruction. In what became a permanent change of heart, Samuel Hoare argued the Ruhr must be attacked as soon as an invasion began lest a fleeting opportunity to hurt the Germans be lost. Pound reiterated the COS conclusion that the French did not consider Holland a "vital matter." He and Newall believed Britain's medium bombers should be used to slow the German advance while the heavy bombers, which were unsuited for such an operation, should attack the Ruhr.[51] Wood, Newall, and Pound all argued that Britain already had sufficient justification to bomb the Ruhr and should dispense with the existing preconditions (evidence of civilian casualties) and do so as soon as Holland was attacked.

Churchill supported these strong views but also accepted that if the French refused to budge on the Ruhr issue, the government must defer. Thereafter, however, his position regarding the defense of Holland and an escalation in the air war became rather obscure and confused. Later in the discussion, perhaps as a way of resolving the impasse with the French, Kingsley Wood returned to the air force's traditional fallback position regarding Holland: rather than bombing the Ruhr, the British could encourage the Germans to bomb Britain (would this not require bombing Germany first?) and wear down the enemy's bomber force while the Allies conserved their own. However, a policy that would permit the bombing of Britain without a serious retaliation against Germany was surely impossible, and the idea did not gain traction. Churchill was among those who demurred in support of the accepted orthodoxy. Whether or not the bombing of the Ruhr followed automatically or awaited evidence of civilian casualties, he thought an attack on the Low Countries must be resisted because it would expose Britain's "great centres of industry" and would increase the depth of German defenses between Britain and the Ruhr. The problem with Churchill's position was the consensus view that the strongest resistance to a German invasion required an attack on the Ruhr (by heavy bombers that would not otherwise be used), and Churchill had already conceded this could not take place if the French objected. It took Churchill five months to reconcile this inconsistency, and he ultimately did not suggest greater aggression but rather pulled away from bombing Germany and encouraged a closer accommodation with the French.

At the 9 November War Cabinet meeting, cabinet members resolved to tell Chamberlain that they were strongly in favor of "an immediate and heavy air attack on military objectives in the Ruhr" if Belgium and Holland or Holland alone (if Belgium did not remain neutral) were invaded and that the French should be told this as soon as possible.[52] Despite strong support for a similar policy regarding an attack on Holland alone, with Belgium remaining neutral, this issue was left in abeyance until it was studied by the JPS.

In preparation for the discussion with Chamberlain, on 11 November the COS prepared another appreciation of air policy with Gamelin's comments in mind. The service chiefs explored the French view that all air support should be concentrated on advancing columns, railway lines, and airfields and also their view, expressed in October, that the Ruhr should not be bombed "even if Belgium were invaded 'totally or partially.'" They also addressed the disconnection between French determination to advance as far into Belgium as possible and their unwillingness to employ all the airpower available to achieve this. After weighing the advantages offered to British and French strategy by an attack on the Ruhr, the COS concluded this attack must take place. Further, the paper recommended the air staff be permitted to initiate the bombing of the Ruhr without reference to the War Cabinet as soon as an invasion began.[53]

Meanwhile, the COS considered the just completed JPS assessment of air policy in the event of Holland being invaded and Belgium remaining neutral. Against all expectation the JPS had come out against the position the COS had assumed, that the circumstance be treated as would an invasion of Belgium. The JPS maintained that taking the gloves off in the air war must coincide with major movements on land and that this would not occur if Holland were invaded and the Belgians did nothing. The COS demurred and instead proposed to emphasize to the War Cabinet the shocking political impact of an invasion of Holland in which the Allies failed to offer "effective resistance." However, apart from a single paragraph in their report, there is little evidence the issue was pressed.[54]

On 14 November, and following an MCC review the night before, the new COS air policy was put before the War Cabinet for a final time, this time with Chamberlain in attendance. The cabinet members agreed that the Ruhr plan should be implemented in response to an invasion of Belgium and Holland or an invasion of Holland alone in which Belgium invited in the Allies. However, determined not to be accused of being the first to take the gloves off, Chamberlain again demurred at the proposal that an invasion of the Low Countries automatically precipitate the bombing of the Ruhr. Instead, he proposed a novel proposition that did not bear on evidence of civilian casualties and, instead, seemed to be a concession to the French. Rather than bomb immediately, he thought a decision to proceed should await evidence an invasion of Belgium and Holland was developing "decisively."

Ironside argued strongly that the bombing of the Ruhr would have a material impact on the German campaign, would serve to slow their advance, and would help Allied forces secure their preferred positions in Belgium and Holland. It was to the Allies' advantage not to delay. Despite these views as offered by his chief of staff (who was possibly representing the combined views of the COS rather than the view of the army), Secretary of State for War Hore-Belisha expressed sympathy for Chamberlain's position, which he thought was also the position of the French. This was a surprising position for Hore-Belisha to take. The COS reckoned that any delay to await evidence of the invasion developing decisively would make it more likely an invasion would develop precisely in this manner.[55] Hore-Belisha, like Chamberlain, was sufficiently concerned by French anxieties over the German air threat to risk delaying the Ruhr plan. Churchill's main contribution was to assert that arguments for and against the Ruhr plan were finally balanced but that he thought the Ruhr operation should go ahead.

Given the equivocation that had taken place, it is unsurprising the decision was postponed. With fears of an invasion abating—and winter ahead—the matter could be readily held in abeyance. Nevertheless, although an air attack on the Ruhr would now likely await evidence of a German invasion developing decisively, the War Cabinet had reaffirmed the right to take the gloves off in the air war in defense of Belgium. It now required that this again be made clear to the French.

A different conclusion had been reached regarding an invasion of Holland. The JPS had come out against an attack on the Ruhr in defense of Holland, unless the attack was accompanied by a movement of troops or a great battle. Without Belgian cooperation, there would be neither. Of all the parts of the air policy puzzle—and its consequences for Allied land policy and Anglo-French relations—it was the prospect of doing almost nothing in response to a German invasion of Holland alone that most bothered the COS. The service chiefs feared this would have serious diplomatic repercussions. More than this, once Holland was occupied, it meant in all likelihood there would never be an advance into Belgium. Surrendering Holland, therefore, meant surrendering Belgium. As to Churchill's attitude to this hole in British air policy and Allied land policy, there is no evidence he took exception to it. The uncertainty surrounding Holland ensured that when spring approached, these issues would be revisited in a way that would see British air policy dominating Allied strategy. Indeed, British air policy had already had a decisive and fate-filled impact on western front strategy.

The Dyle Plan and the Breda Variant: A French Plan or British?

When on 10 November the JPS submitted to the COS its assessment deprecating Gamelin's Walcheren plan, it put forward two alternative plans, both of which were deemed preferable to the French plan.[56] One of these plans, the preferred option—if circumstances would permit—was what is now almost universally accepted as Maurice Gamelin's own initiative: the Breda variant of the Dyle plan. The second, less aggressive option proposed the Seventh Army advance to a position in the rear of Antwerp. Although preferring the Breda option, the JPS considered it unlikely the French forces could arrive in time to anticipate the Germans. During discussions on 12 November, the British liaisons explained British concerns to the French and put forward the Breda option, although they did so without the reservations outlined in the JPS assessment. They subsequently explained its advantage as providing depth to Allied defense. The French staff was unreceptive and instead argued the virtues of its own plan but promised to put the British alternatives to Gamelin. During the meeting General Pierre Lelong noted that the Breda plan "was stretching the line excessively and he would be surprised if General Gamelin agreed to this proposal."[57] On 15 November the French confirmed their determination to occupy the islands of the Scheldt, believing this was essential to secure the left flank of Allied forces whether on the Dyle or on the Scheldt.[58] It was this plan that was confirmed at the SWC on 17 November. Nevertheless, Gamelin had taken on board the British Breda alternative, having remarked that a single French division might be sufficient to secure the Scheldt islands and that, therefore, another could advance to Breda. Over the next several months, his interest in and commitment to the Breda variant would continue with ever more forces being committed to it.

The facts outlined turn the historiography of the origins of the Breda variant on its head. The most high-risk element of the French strategic plan—the

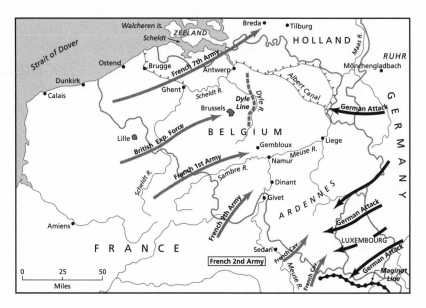

Map 5.3. Germany invades the West, 10 May 1940. Immediately following the German invasion of France, Belgium, and Holland, the Allies initiated the Dyle/Breda plan. This joint Anglo-French strategy required a deep advance into Belgium and southwest Holland. It placed the Allied forces precisely where the Germans wished them to be.

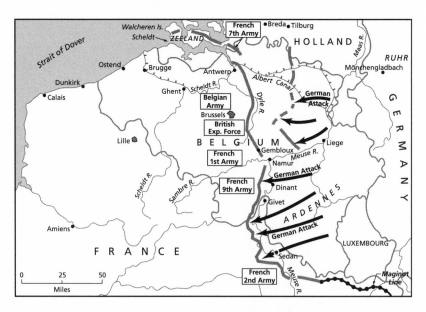

Map 5.4. Crisis at Sedan. By 13 May, it was becoming clear to the Allied forces that the main weight of the German armored attack was not in the north but through the Ardennes.

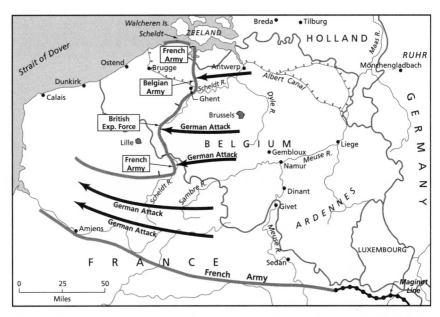

Map 5.5. The Sickle's Cut. By 20 May, the German envelopment of British, French, Belgian, and Dutch forces to the north was far advanced. Within ten days, British and French forces were evacuating in large numbers from the beaches of Dunkirk in a desperate effort to save themselves.

extension of the Allied line into Holland—was not a French conception but an English one. Although the relentless northward movement of Allied forces had begun because of French anxieties over the Ruhr plan, it had developed because the British saw merit in a military link with Holland. Gamelin was happy to oblige. The new plans had little or nothing to do with the fate of the Belgian and Dutch people, and everything to do with British and French determination to limit the German air threat to their respective countries.[59]

At the SWC on 17 November, Chamberlain strongly put the British air policy to the French, but unsurprisingly given the equivocation of the War Cabinet, he wilted before Premier Édouard Daladier's resistance. The precise timing of the Ruhr plan—and the circumstances under which it would be implemented—was placed on hold. Chamberlain made at least one thing clear (although the French no doubt already understood this): the British would suspend a decision on an automatic Ruhr offensive if the French attempted to occupy as much of the Low Countries as possible and a battle did not develop decisively. Daladier declared that if the plan succeeded, "German aviation would not have gained an appreciable advantage and the general strategic situation of Britain and France would not have been substantially changed."[60] In other words there would be no need to take the gloves off in the air war.

Whatever his personal view of the merit of entering Belgium, Gamelin was now locked into a deep incursion to avoid that which the French feared most: unrestricted aerial warfare. Further, it could not have escaped him that at some point he could face a decision to enter Belgium uninvited or be forced to accept the Ruhr plan in defense of Holland. What he certainly would not have foreseen was what eventually transpired: that the British would press him to enter Belgium to create the circumstances under which they could justify the implementation of the Ruhr plan—the precipitation of a decisive land battle—Gamelin did not welcome any of these decisions because he believed success against the Germans, a successful advance to preferred lines, and the avoidance of an encounter battle depended on cooperation that might not be forthcoming if the Allies forced their way through Belgium.

The British War Cabinet decision to hold off on bombing the Ruhr until there was evidence of an invasion developing decisively was weak, but given French intransigence, it was probably inevitable. It was a decision in which Churchill played an important part. He had accepted that arguments for the immediate prosecution of the Ruhr plan were "finely balanced"; he had accepted that should the French object, their views must be respected; and finally, he accepted that there would be time enough to establish the decisive moment in a land battle in which to initiate the Ruhr bombing. Among the ministers, only the much-maligned Hoare was ardently opposed to the SWC resolution.[61]

The COS did not revisit the issue of bombing policy again until late March, a mere six weeks before the invasion of France and the Low Countries, and bombing policy was not a serious topic of MCC, War Cabinet, or SWC discussion until April, when Churchill proposed important amendments to existing policy. During these new discussions Churchill's views had more in common with Chamberlain's and the French leaders' perspectives than they had with the aggressive policies of the COS and RAF. In the days immediately preceding the German assault in the West, Churchill was among the most hesitant toward taking the gloves off, and he was so for the first days of his premiership. As prime minister, Churchill would adopt precisely the position taken by Chamberlain in November; he would wait and see if the battle for France and the Low Countries developed decisively. Before exploring the period of late March to early May 1940, it is appropriate to consider briefly the discussion of air policy and plans for action in Scandinavia—and Churchill's contribution to them—and to assess how these compared with policy decisions made for the western front.

Air Policy and Scandinavia

The military plans pertaining to Finland and, subsequently, Norway are considered in detail in the next chapters. It suffices here to record that the COS and the War Cabinet recognized, from at least the end of January, that a probable precondition for Scandinavian (Swedish and Norwegian) cooperation with Allied strategy would be a commitment to treat an air attack on Scandinavian territory as though it were an attack on Britain or France.[62] Chamberlain raised this issue at the SWC on 5 February, but Daladier failed to address it in his general discourse.[63] The issue was broached again by the COS on 2 March and discussed in the War Cabinet on 4 March as part of desperate last-minute attempts to secure Scandinavian support for the Finnish option.[64] During the War Cabinet meeting, CAS Newall referred to the 28 January report that he was concerned might have led the government to believe the COS thought an attack on Scandinavian cities should be treated precisely as if it were an attack on London. He explained that the report ought to have been interpreted as posing a question rather than making a recommendation. After all, he declared, "we could hardly be expected to consider air attack on Trondhjem, for example, as the equivalent of air attack on London. If we did, it would mean we should have to start bombing Berlin, and this would almost certainly lead to retaliation against London itself."[65]

Newall thought such an assurance should not be offered unless the Scandinavians demanded it. Here was cold, calculating pragmatism at work. Although present, Churchill did not disavow these sentiments, and there is little doubt he was in sympathy with them. With Swedish support then so unlikely in any circumstances, Chamberlain decided to defer the question until the situation arose, and there the matter rested until the German invasion of Norway.

Air Policy Revisited: March, April, and May 1940

The issue of air policy reemerged in late March. Over the next six weeks, Britain and France revisited at length many of the arguments of September–November 1939, and the gaps in policy filled. Britain also sought and secured a French commitment to enter Belgium as soon as Belgium or Holland was invaded and whether or not the Allies were invited. The War Cabinet finally decided to take the gloves off in the air war and finally secured French agreement to this. However, having achieved these significant amendments to air policy, the War Cabinet hesitated. Following Germany's invasion of the West on 10 May, the enemy was left largely untouched by Britain's heavy bombers for five days. Churchill played a central role in this delay.

The catalyst for the renewed interest in air policy in late March was another perceived threat to Holland. This threat began to stir all the old British anxieties and encouraged efforts to address what the COS believed was unfinished business. Intelligence was suggesting Germany would attack Holland and then conduct an air assault on Britain. The British and French staffs were as one in wanting the Belgians to assist the Netherlands in the fight, but they worried the Belgians would not do so if they thought the Germans would respect their neutrality. The British considered the Belgians even less likely to act if, rather than invading the Netherlands, the Germans merely pressured the Dutch into ceding bases for their use. Either scenario was problematic for the Allies' preferred strategy and especially for British self-interest. If the Allies were invited in by the Belgians in time, Gamelin would advance Allied forces as deeply as possible into Belgium, and this would have limited the air threat to Britain. However, time was critical to all these plans. If the Belgians were hesitant or uncooperative, the French would not advance beyond the line of the Scheldt, and even this move was not certain. The British also remained apprehensive that rather than accept the risks of a move forward, the French might use Belgian obstruction to stay put. If the Germans did not initially threaten the Belgians, they would not immediately threaten the French.

Acting Unilaterally: Britain Pressures the Belgians

All these concerns and anxieties began to reemerge when on 18 March, amid ongoing efforts to engage with the Belgians, Churchill argued before the

War Cabinet that the Belgians would be encouraged to invite the Allies in if they were told the Allies would come in whether invited or not. Churchill's suggestion was duly adopted, and this message was given to Belgium and Holland on 20 March, along with a request that each begin serious discussions with the other and the Allies. The War Cabinet's warning to the Belgians was conveyed to the French and appeared to have the sympathy of France's new prime minister, Paul Reynaud, but Gamelin subsequently expressed his strong opposition to entering Belgium unless the Allies were invited to do so. What is of interest here is that around this time Gamelin gave his final endorsement to the Breda variant of the Dyle plan. Whatever his reluctance regarding Holland, he was continuing to prepare for the possibility of a deep advance into Belgium and Holland.

In a memo in late March, Ironside conceded Gamelin's view that without Belgian cooperation, military support for Holland would be extremely dangerous and should not be promised, but there ended British sympathy for Gamelin's views. It was evident that the French general's entire western front policy and his extensive planning continued to be contingent on the degree and timeliness of Belgian cooperation; at a pre-SWC meeting on 28 March, Gamelin informed the COS that he had authorization to advance into Belgium only after an invitation had been offered. This position was no longer acceptable to the British. They expected the French to commit to a move into Belgium if the Netherlands were invaded. This was important for several reasons, some of which were intimately linked to British air policy: it would force the Belgians into the war because it would compel a German attack on Belgium; it would precipitate the great movement of armies deemed the necessary precursor to take the gloves off; and if the Allied armies did not advance into Belgium in response to German invasion of Holland, they would not be able to do so later for fear of being outflanked. Perhaps most important of all, if the French refused to advance, the Allies would respond to an invasion of Holland with nothing more than inconsequential air attacks from medium bombers flying from England or flying around Belgium from bases in France. For Chamberlain and his government in late March 1940, this would have been political suicide.

It was, therefore, essential the precise nature of French intentions toward Belgium and Holland be established, and this was put on the agenda of the

SWC meeting of 28 March. Unfortunately, conclusions fell short of clarity, and these issues were subject to further discussion throughout April. At the SWC Chamberlain tackled Reynaud by presenting a variety of scenarios. In the only significant advance, he secured agreement that the moment the Germans invaded Belgium (or Belgium and Holland), the Allies would enter Belgium, with or without invitation. This, at least, eased concerns the French would permit the Germans to establish themselves in Belgium without a fight. On the question of an invasion of Holland alone, the French were calculatedly vague. Despite Gamelin's extensive planning to address this threat, when asked what would happen if Holland were invaded and the Belgian army went to its aid, Reynaud offered nothing more than "the Allies should come to the assistance of the Low Countries." As to the questions of what would be done if Holland were invaded and Belgium remained aloof or if the Germans merely occupied certain Dutch island bases—the most recent British concern—Reynaud merely suggested the Allies "should retain the freedom to decide what action to take at the time."[66]

As frustrating as Reynaud's answers were, his evasion had its foundations in practical matters. The truculent attitude of the Belgians, who had repeatedly refused to engage in discussion on military cooperation, was compelling the French to weigh their actions in the context of varying degrees of resistance. Belgian noncooperation was considered more likely in any situation in which Holland was attacked and Belgium left alone. Chamberlain understood this and acknowledged it. However, the British continued to be anxious over a threat that manifested against Holland alone. They worried the French might yet balk at action on land and in the air that would bring the war to France any earlier than absolutely necessary. That this remained a driving force in French thinking—especially among its politicians—became apparent in the subsequent weeks.

Churchill, Royal Marine, the Ruhr, and French Anxiety

While these issues were developing during the first days of April, Churchill was personally exposed to the degree to which French anxiety over the German air threat remained a powerful influence on French military policy. During the 28 March SWC, Chamberlain had secured a reluctant commitment from Reynaud to begin the Royal Marine operation at the earliest opportunity. Several days later this decision was vetoed by Daladier for fear the plan would invite retaliation against French aircraft factories. A deeply frustrated Churchill set off to Paris to persuade the French to reconsider. Churchill failed in his mission and instead immediately set about a reassessment of Britain's air bombing policy to more satisfactorily meet the needs of the French. It is probable Churchill took this path because he recognized the French reaction to Royal Marine—which was to hesitate and delay—would be duplicated in their reaction to any proposal to escalate the air war if Belgium or Holland were invaded.[67] Rather than have Britain's strategic bomber force sit idly awaiting French concurrence in the bombing of strategic targets in the Ruhr, he sought to have it involved more intimately in the great land battle, and he proposed a number of possible objectives with this in mind.[68]

Although he suggested attacks on German oil resources—a suggestion from which he eventually withdrew—Churchill eschewed other objectives in the Ruhr and instead proposed nodal points on German roads and railways and bottlenecks in German communications, such as Aix-la-Chapelle and München-Gladbach. He also sought to involve the French more intimately in the selection of targets for the heavy bomber force.

These proposals were discussed by the MCC over two days in early April. Unsurprisingly, the air staff was resistant to the proposed changes. In contrast, the secretary of state for war and CIGS, the latter of whom had long accepted the air force's reluctance to use heavy bombers in tactical operations, were encouraged by Churchill's line of argument and supported his ideas. Newall put the air force case strongly, but in the end the air staff capitulated, albeit temporarily. The targets for the heavy bombers—or a small percentage of them—were, per Churchill's suggestion, expanded to include tactical objectives, such as rail communications (in particular marshaling yards) focal points within Germany or on the Belgian-German border, bridges and defiles, and fleeting targets. Oil refineries remained on the list of targets—perhaps a reason why the air force had surrendered to the MCC's recommendations—but it was not at all clear why this was so. The French were certain to view attacks on oil installations as an invitation to unrestricted air warfare and, therefore, certain to resist them. Wider operations against the Ruhr, most particularly east of the Rhine, were otherwise put on hold. They might take place under certain circumstances, but they would not be part of a first response; any decision to take the gloves off would require further consultation with the War Cabinet, which, at this stage, might still have felt compelled to consult the French.

Churchill undoubtedly believed his intervention had achieved changes in air policy that met French needs while also meeting British. It would involve the heavy bombers more closely in the land battle. However, all his efforts were quickly undone by the JPS, which had been busy reviewing Allied action that should be taken in response to an invasion of Holland alone, one of the unresolved elements of the recent SWC discussion.

The Search for Common Ground

On 7 April the COS began considering a JPS appreciation of action to be taken if the Germans invaded Holland. In combination with the COS's thoughts on air policy, JPS's conclusion offered the War Cabinet an answer to the difficult question of Holland, which had defied resolution; unfortunately, the recommendations manifestly increased French anxiety over being drawn into a major land and air battle they did not deem necessary. The most significant element of the JPS appreciation was its conclusion that potential Belgian resistance did not preclude an advance into Belgium or even an advance to preferred lines of defense on the Dyle. The committee anticipated Allied mobile units advancing rapidly to the Dyle defensive line while other units advanced to the line of the Scheldt. If the Belgians resisted but did not cause excessive delay, these latter units would also move on to the Dyle line. This would take place with due regard for the safety of the forces. In an instant the single impediment to an Allied advance into Belgium in support of Holland had been removed. As for air policy the COS simultaneously recommended that an invasion of Holland be treated as decisive and be responded to with the bombing of the Ruhr. The existing policy—which in November had been influenced by the JPS's conviction the Ruhr plan must be accompanied by a "great movement of armies"—was then confined to "some half-hearted attacks on the German columns advancing into Holland."[69] However, if, as was now proposed, the Allied armies entered Belgium as soon as Holland was invaded, the air force would have the great movement of armies necessary to implement the Ruhr plan, or a version of it. Gamelin, when presented with the latest British thinking, was about to find himself in an extraordinary position. Months earlier he had been able to stall the Ruhr plan with his Dyle/Breda variant, which offered the prospect of securing large areas of Belgium and Holland. Now he was being pressed to advance into Belgium to provide the military preconditions for what he feared would be a major escalation in the air war.

These developments were interrupted two days later with the German invasion of Norway. This brought the Allies to another SWC meeting on the afternoon of 9 April. Most of the discussion surrounded Norway, but Holland and Belgium were also discussed. Reynaud briefly outlined the advantages of the Allied armies taking up advanced lines in Belgium: it would shorten the front, it would help protect industry in northern France, and it would give France the support of the Belgian army. This was all standard stuff from the French. However, thereafter, in what was a significant retreat from his statement at the 28 March SWC, he indicated the Allies would enter Belgium "provided the co-operation of the Belgian army could be secured." He gave no guidance on what this cooperation would entail or how far in advance of need this cooperation would be required. Another important issue germane to French western front policy and the use of air power was raised when Chamberlain revisited the question he had put before Daladier in February over Norway: How would the French react to a Norwegian request to bomb Germany in support of their fight for survival? Reynaud said the answer to "full-scale air warfare was to be sought in the present state of their [Allied] air forces."[70]

The contrast between these views and the direction taken in the JPS/COS discussions two days earlier is extraordinarily marked. Whatever the British determination to defend Holland—and perhaps even Belgium—by attacking with the full force of British airpower against Germany, it was not shared by the French. The modest advances in Allied cooperation and understanding of western front policy established in late March were evidently not what they had appeared.

The JPS/COS proposals were put before the MCC and endorsed at a meeting of 10 April. Two days later they were put to the War Cabinet.[71] If Holland were invaded and Belgium left alone, the COS believed it essential to immediately advance into Belgium regardless of the Belgian attitude. If the Allied armies did not do so, a German advance would quickly outflank the Belgian lines. Allied forces should advance, with caution, at least to the Scheldt. If cooperation was forthcoming, the Allied armies would advance to the Namur-Antwerp line.

As far as air policy was concerned, the secretary of state for air informed the War Cabinet that if Germany invaded Holland and Allied armies entered Belgium, "he had no hesitation in recommending that air action against the objectives proposed [those recently amended as a result of agitation from Churchill] should be initiated without a moment's delay." He thought the great air battle should coincide with the great land battle, and he expressed concern the French might refuse to enter Belgium and leave action to the air force if Holland alone were invaded. Unless a strong Allied response was immediate "the effect on world opinion might be disastrous."[72]

Just as he had five months before, Churchill concurred but repeated it "would be necessary for the French to agree." However, he was also convinced that a "successful German advance into Holland would constitute such a dangerous threat to Belgian defenses that it would be necessary at all costs for Allied Armies to advance to the Antwerp-Namur lines."[73] As far as he was concerned, there could be no compromise on the Dyle plan, and he no doubt accepted that an air attack on the targets proposed would help facilitate this deep advance.

These views were immediately conveyed to the French and met with the usual reservation: an advance should be conducted with the cooperation of the Belgians.[74] As for air policy the French Committee of War was opposed to Churchill's new air bombing regime and emphasized it "is not in the French interests to initiate any action against factories and other objectives which would affect the civilian population."[75]

Allied western front policy—on land and in the air—was in crisis and regarding not only Holland but Belgium as well. Over the next several days, further discussion followed and was summarized in a COS memorandum of 19 April that cited the conclusion of British Air Liaison Officer Arthur Barrett: Even in response to an attack on Belgium, Gamelin's strictures would prevent "our initial attacks being against anything other than German columns or roads."[76] They would also prevent attacks against defiles in Germany west of the Rhine. The French were rejecting even those targets that Churchill had pressed the air force to adopt in lieu of industrial targets farther east and that he had considered more relevant to the battle at hand. The COS was concerned Gamelin's policy would materially affect efforts to arrest the advance of German forces and compromise the Allies' capacity to advance to their preferred lines. The COS believed the French would resist air action even more stubbornly in any situation in which an attack on France itself might be avoided. This raised the old specter that in the event of a German invasion of Holland, if the Belgians hesitated to assist the Dutch or were not immediately invaded themselves, the French might not advance, and the entire Low Countries would be lost to the Germans without a fight.

French Capitulation, British Hesitation

Apart from the concerns surrounding the Norwegian campaign, the resolution of these issues became the centerpiece of Anglo-French discussion at the SWC of 22 and 23 April. On 21 April the War Cabinet convened a special meeting to consider the Holland and Belgium dilemma and to establish a line of argument. The COS believed there was no point in discussing matters further with the French and proposed the French be informed that the British would not hesitate to use their heavy bomber force against military objectives, both west and east of the Rhine, if Holland or Belgium were attacked. If the French would not concur, Britain should "reserve the right to independent action." Although present at the meeting, Churchill played no role in this discussion, but Chamberlain agreed with these sentiments and "hoped that the War Cabinet would leave it to him and his colleagues" to convert the French. He was as good as his word.[77]

Chamberlain was now determined to gain French support for the Ruhr policy but also to gain a guarantee from the French to advance into Belgium to support Holland and to do so as aggressively and as quickly as possible. Reynaud resisted, and during this discussion he exposed his country's desperate hopes for the Norwegian campaign to extricate France from the dilemmas of western front policy. He suggested the Allies should concentrate on Scandinavia and resist all distractions, even perhaps "the temptation to intervene in Belgium, a course which, he admitted, had certain advantages, but which also presented dangers arising from Allied inferiority in arms and aviation." As for plans to bomb German territory and, in particular, targets east of the Rhine, he sought to have these put before the French government before a decision was made; pressed by Chamberlain, he finally conceded that no further reference would be required in response to an invasion of Belgium and Holland.[78]

The French, at last, had given ground to meet Britain's own needs for self-preservation.[79] Among the concessions made was to invest the British War Cabinet with full responsibility for the decision to begin bombing the Ruhr, east and west of the Rhine. This did not mean, however, that the RAF was now at liberty to act as it saw fit, for having secured the right to do so, the British War Cabinet immediately began to reconsider the circumstances under which it would unleash Britain's heavy bombers against the German military machine. Although the War Cabinet rejected the more absurd limitations on air action requested by the French, Churchill and Chamberlain soon resurrected the two old bogies that had plagued air policy discussion in the earlier months of the war: Should a German invasion automatically initiate elements of the bombing regime considered most likely to lead to escalation, or should this await evidence of substantial civilian casualties? Also, should a less bold move await evidence that a German attack was developing in a decisive manner? Churchill's scruples were based on two concerns: fear of British action in the air that was not fully justifiable in the eyes of the world and fear of prematurely inviting escalation and retaliation in the air war. If, despite the vast movement of armies, a great land battle did not develop, it would be difficult to justify bombing the Ruhr and risking civilian deaths. If an invasion was successfully arrested or the advance of armies did not result in them joining in decisive battle, it would be unwise to prematurely precipitate unrestricted air warfare by bombing east of the Ruhr (that is, in areas not immediately linked to the battles at hand). This attitude, in most respects, mirrored the French perspective the War Cabinet had just spent considerable energy overcoming. Newall despaired. Having secured French acquiescence, he had thought British air policy was decided; now all again was under review.

At the beginning of May, a mere ten days before the Germans launched their campaign in the West, the War Cabinet still feared the Germans would give their attention first to Holland and then escalate the air war against Britain. The latest intelligence suggested an occupation of the Netherland islands, with the most likely target being Texel. The War Cabinet sought to know if such a limited attack—which might preclude the clash of armies—would be sufficient justification to bomb the Ruhr. At the 1 May War Cabinet meeting, nearly all members accepted it would. Churchill shared this view and declared the most effective response would be to attack the Ruhr. Even Halifax did not demur. Chamberlain also agreed, although he thought it desirable that the COS produce a review. Thereafter, this apparently united support for the Ruhr plan began to disintegrate, and Churchill was a major—and perhaps even the main—contributor to this disintegration.

Unsurprisingly, the COS review repeated the long-held conviction that an attack on Holland would be preliminary to a major escalation in the air war against Britain and should, therefore, be met with full force. Churchill hesitated, and on 2 May he asked if the bombing of the Ruhr should be automatic or subject to final approval from the War Cabinet. The secretary of state for air reminded the War Cabinet that the existing guidelines already permitted immediate attacks on a catalogue of targets in German territory, including troop concentrations, marshaling yards, lines of communications, and oil refineries, but considering the possible German reaction to these operations, he would try his best to consult the War Cabinet before taking action.

There matters stood for the next five days when, on 7 May, the War Cabinet again asked if the bombing of the Ruhr would be automatic or referred to the War Cabinet. Chamberlain apprehended the invasion of Texel—the latest threat—might not be followed immediately by a German invasion of Holland. Would such a limited offensive provide sufficient justification for bombing the Ruhr? Further, the French, despite their current commitment, might hesitate to enter Belgium in response to such a limited German assault. The concern was that either circumstance would deny the Allies the great land battle considered a prerequisite for escalating the air war; a mere movement of enemy troops into Holland appeared not enough. Chamberlain wanted assurance, in any scenario, that marshaling yards would not be automatically attacked unless they were occupied by German troops.

The COS then threw in a new complication that began the collapse of a policy eight months in the making. The most controversial target for the heavy bombers then agreed to was the oil refineries in the Ruhr. It had somehow been accepted an attack on these would not necessarily invite an escalation in the air war, possibly because these objectives were not close to civilian populations. The COS now pointed out these targets would be difficult to detect except in moonlight. If they were not attacked for want of the necessary visibility, Bomber Command would be back to square one: the vast majority of heavy bombers would not be used strategically; only a small number would attack marshaling yards and other such targets. If action were required during limited or no moonlight, it would be preferable that heavy bombers attack self-illuminating targets, such as coking ovens and power plants; but these were not currently on the list of acceptable targets. If coking ovens and power plants were attacked as substitutes for oil refineries, it would even more likely precipitate unrestricted aerial warfare.

If these concerns were insufficient to turn the minds of doubters, the secretary of state for air worried whether the existing heavy bomber force was sufficiently large to do the job it was hoped it would do. He concluded, nevertheless, that circumstances would demand an immediate attack on the Ruhr. Chamberlain, however, was unnerved and asked if, after all, it would not be wiser to concentrate on marshaling yards alone because this would be less likely to bring on retaliation against industry in Britain. This gave the army the opportunity to turn the entire focus of the heavy bomber force to the main battle. In the absence of Ironside, the recently appointed assistant chief of the Imperial General Staff (ACIGS), John Dill, suggested the full attention of the heavy bombers be applied to marshaling yards. Newall was unimpressed. He pointed out that an attack on marshaling yards would bring on unrestricted bombing just as certainly as an attack on other targets. He evidently still believed the heavy bombers' strategic role more important than any tactical assistance they could offer.

It was now Churchill's turn to get cold feet over the Ruhr. This manifested with respect to not only the air force's strategic plans but the tactical elements he had been instrumental in developing as targets for Britain's heavy bombers. He considered it "very dangerous and undesirable" to take the initiative in opening unrestricted aerial warfare.[80] He pointed out that Britain had only a quarter of the striking force, and he worried, if the British took the first steps, they would not thereafter be able to appeal to the United States for assistance.

The CAS and secretary of state for air pushed their case. Hoare pointed out that 80 percent of German industry was in the Ruhr and that, as a target, it had "no counterpart" in the UK. Churchill had said as much in the past,

Winston S. Churchill served as First Lord of the Admiralty in Neville Chamberlain's wartime government. This photograph was taken after he became Prime Minister and Minister of Defence. *Naval History and Heritage Command*

The Chamberlain War Cabinet, September 1939. *Front, left to right:* Lord Halifax, John Simon, Neville Chamberlain, Sam Hoare, Lord Chatfield. *Back:* Kingsley Wood, Winston Churchill, Leslie Hore-Belisha, Maurice Hankey. As discontent with the direction of the war grew, Chamberlain received considerable criticism for the perceived shortcomings of this body. His most severe critics sought the adoption of a smaller Lloyd George–style War Cabinet of World War, the removal of the "old appeasers," Hoare and Simon, and a greater role for Churchill. Chamberlain resisted the first two demands but afforded Churchill two promotions before resigning on 10 May 1940. It was not enough to save him. *Fremantle/Alamy Stock Photo*

The Prime Minister and his First Lord of the Admiralty: Chamberlain and Churchill in conversation. The relationship between these two men has been much analyzed, with the consensus being that they shared little regard for each other. But their relationship was stronger, and the differences between them fewer, than is claimed. During the Phoney War each man required the support of the other and each gave it. *The Print Collector/Alamy Stock Photo*

The Board of the Admiralty in session, 6 December 1939. Around the table, *left to right*: Geoffrey Shakespeare (Parliamentary and Financial Secretary); Rear Admiral H. M. Burough (Assistant Chief of the Naval Staff); Vice Admiral Sir Alexander R. Ramsey (Fifth Sea Lord); Rear Admiral T. S. V. Phillips (Deputy Chief of Naval Staff); Admiral of the Fleet Sir Dudley Pound (First Sea Lord); Sir J. Sidney Barnes (Deputy Secretary); Sir Winston Churchill (First Lord of the Admiralty); Sir Archibald Carter (Secretary); Admiral Sir Charles Little (Second Sea Lord); Rear Admiral Bruce Fraser (Third Sea Lord); Rear Admiral G. S. Arbuthnot (Fourth Sea Lord); and Captain A. U. M. Hudson (Civil Lord). *Heritage Partnership Ltd./Alamy Stock Photo*

General (later Field Marshal) Lord Edmund Ironside was the Chief of the Imperial General Staff during the Phoney War period. His views on Churchill were mixed. Ironside was an ardent advocate of the Finnish option. He was also a strong supporter of Operation Hammer, the proposed amphibious assault on Trondheim during the Norwegian campaign, although he shared Churchill's initial apprehensions. He was not, as is often contended, cajoled by Churchill to support Hammer. *Official Government Photograph/Creative Commons. This scan is taken from* The Ironside Diaries, 1937-1940; *Constable, 1962 /The War Office*

Admiral Sir Dudley Pound was First Sea Lord to Churchill during the Phoney War and one of three members of the Chiefs of Staff Committee. Pound has been criticized for not standing up to Churchill on important issues. Although he rarely tackled Churchill head on, Pound always stood his ground on matters he considered important. When concession was made, it was often because he shared Churchill's views, or did not consider the matter worth disputing. *World History Archive/Alamy Stock Photo*

Three U-boats of the Type VII class that became the German workhorse during World War II. The larger size of this U-boat and the German emphasis on its production signaled the intention to operate well beyond Britain's waters in this new war. The Germans began with fifty-six U-boats, of which only thirteen were combat-ready Type VIIs. Construction of new boats barely kept pace with losses during the Phoney War period. U-36 was lost with all hands, December 1939; U-28 survived fifteen months of war before becoming a training boat; U-26 was sunk in July 1940. *Naval History and Heritage Command*

As First Lord, Churchill resisted the Admiralty's construction of new battleships beyond the completion of the *King George V* class. He believed new (*Lion*-class) battleships would not be constructed in time to participate in "this war." He preferred to modernize several *Royal Sovereign*–class battleships. HMS *Vanguard* (above) was his compromise with the Admiralty. Using spare 15-inch guns, it was hoped this ship could be constructed within three years. *Vanguard* was completed too late to participate in World War II and was the last battleship constructed in Britain and the last battleship ever launched. *Naval History and Heritage Command*

British Wellington Bombers, 1939. The Wellingtons, along with Whitleys and Hampdens, constituted the British strategic (heavy) bomber force in which great hopes were placed. Early in the war, these aircraft all proved extremely vulnerable to German fighters, forcing them to subsequently operate only at night. This manifestly increased the challenges of finding and accurately bombing German military and industrial targets once permission was given to do so on 15 May 1940. *Sueddeutsche Zeitung Photo/Alamy Stock Photo*

Kingsley Wood, Churchill, and Anthony Eden, 10 May 1940. Wood was the Secretary of State for Air before switching places with Sir Samuel Hoare to become Lord Privy Seal at the beginning of April 1940. Eden was Secretary of State for Dominion Affairs but not formally part of Chamberlain's War Cabinet. Wood and Eden were both supporters of Churchill's premiership and both acted as confidants in the days immediately prior to Chamberlain's resignation. When Churchill assumed office, Wood became Chancellor of the Exchequer and Eden Secretary of State for War, until he replaced Lord Halifax as Foreign Secretary. *Fremantle/Alamy Stock Photo*

Winston Churchill sitting alongside other members of his War Cabinet. *Back row, left to right*: Mr. Arthur Greenwood, Deputy Leader of the Labour Party; Mr. Ernest Bevin, Minister of Labour; Max Aitken, 1st Baron Beaverbrook, Minister of Aircraft Production; Sir Kingsley Wood, Chancellor of the Exchequer. *Front row, left to right*: John Anderson, 1st Viscount Waverley, Lord President of the Council; Sir Winston Churchill, Prime Minister of the United Kingdom; Clement Attlee, Lord Privy Seal; Antony Eden. After taking office in May 1940, Churchill governed with a comparatively small War Cabinet. This conformed to the expectations of those who helped bring him to power although, unlike Chamberlain's critics, Churchill preferred its members have working portfolios. *World History Archive/Alamy Stock Photo*

but now he argued the best "counter was the land battle." Dill pointed out that the Germans might invade Holland but only invade Belgium up to the Albert Canal. If, as planned, the Allied armies advanced only to Dyle, no great battle would ensue; by implication the heavy bomber force might sit idly while an invasion of the Low Countries took place.

The meeting concluded with Chamberlain instructing the COS to consider prospective targets for the heavy bombers if Holland or Holland and Belgium were attacked. On 8 May air policy was discussed a final time before the German invasion of the Low Countries. This discussion was primarily centered on a limited German attack on the Netherland islands, but the conclusions reached extended to a more general attack on Holland or Belgium. Chamberlain began by making a clear distinction between attacks on marshaling yards and oil targets. If marshaling yards were in use, they were clearly a military target; oil targets were deemed to be much less so, although he conceded the issue was a matter of degree. He also conceded that attacks on marshaling yards were just as likely to result in civilian casualties and, therefore, would invite retaliation.

Churchill took Chamberlain's hesitation even further. He was consumed by the need to secure the necessary justification for escalating the air war and proposed that neither marshaling yards nor oil targets be attacked until the great battle began. He feared France might not yet move into Belgium if Holland were attacked, and even though they might know German troops were on the move, their bombing actions "would be very much criticized." Once the great battle had begun, "the thunder of battle would cover the attacks on the German marshalling yards, even those resulting in heavy casualties to civilians."[81] These were extraordinarily conservative recommendations for Churchill—the British Bulldog—to make, and they were not accepted by his colleagues. Nevertheless, new restrictions were proposed. Attacks on marshaling yards could proceed without reference to the War Cabinet if German troops were moving through them toward the front. This concession did not apply if the Germans launched an attack on the Netherland islands alone. All other targets of a more strategic nature were to be subject to further approval and evidence that a great land battle had begun.

Not all the 8 May discussion was policy; it stood as recommendation only. The COS was instructed to consider these recommendations when reassessing objectives for the heavy bombers. Thus, two days before the German invasion of the West, the War Cabinet, with Churchill's considerable support, was on the cusp of denying the air force nearly all initiative in the use of the heavy bombers. Despite the COS repeated calls to the contrary, the greater part of this force was to await the course of events; except for limited areas, German territory would not be bombed unless or until there was clear evidence of a decisive battle having begun. An invasion of the Low Countries was not enough.

"Don't Hurt Them, Dear!"

On 10 May, the day of the German invasion and the last day of Chamberlain's premiership, there were three War Cabinet meetings. At the 8 a.m. meeting Newall put the case for an attack on the Ruhr, but the War Cabinet demurred. Heavy bombers could attack targets west of the Rhine, but they must otherwise await further information on German activities and civilian casualties. At the 11:30 meeting it was noted that the French were "putting it about that the GAF [German air force] had confined attacks to aerodromes and other strictly military objectives" and that this appeared more or less correct. Chamberlain believed it was important "not to do anything which could render us liable to be accused of having initiated unrestricted air bombing."[82]

A decision was deferred until 4:30 p.m.—Chamberlain's last War Cabinet as prime minister—when Newall announced, with obvious frustration, that there were still no definite indications the Germans were bombing other than military objectives. Between the meetings Churchill had shown some initiative on this issue and had sent a message to Gamelin explaining the British were now "inclined to attack targets in the Ruhr including marshalling yards and oil refineries"; he wished to know if Gamelin supported this. Gamelin was probably surprised to be asked because, following the SWC decision of late April, Britain was free to do as it wished, and Gamelin replied as much.[83] At the 4:30 meeting Newall again put the case it was time to attack the Ruhr, but Ironside resisted the proposal and argued they ought to wait and see how the battle developed. Deceived by the disposition and nature of German attacks, he was doubtful whether an invasion of Belgium in strength was taking place. Churchill, who was in the thrall of the "decisive battle" conception, proposed a postponement of twenty-four hours before attacking the Ruhr. He did so despite acknowledging full justification existed for attacking refineries and other such targets.[84]

The confusion surrounding Chamberlain's resignation and the establishment of Churchill's new War Cabinet meant this delay would be forty-eight hours and not twenty-four. A considerably truncated War Cabinet (Churchill, Halifax, Chamberlain, and the three chiefs of staff) met twice on 11 May but did not discuss air policy. The next War Cabinet did not take place until 10:30 p.m., 12 May (now with Eden, Albert V. Alexander, and Archibald Sinclair present). Newall explained the COS had met, as per the instructions of several days earlier, and had determined that on military grounds it was vital the Ruhr be attacked as soon as possible. He reminded those gathered that issues of moonlight made it necessary that attacks on oil refineries take place soon. In what was likely viewed as vindication for air force policy, Newall also referred to reports of heavy losses that had occurred among the tactical bomber force. With some pointedness he then reintroduced an old theme to justify the prosecution of the Ruhr plan. Rather than prolong further bomber losses in the area of the advances, the Ruhr might be bombed to draw off German bombers to attack Britain. In a reversal of his earlier position, Ironside accepted Newall's contention the heavy bombers ought not be risked tactically and endorsed the CAS's proposal. However, Ironside worried, if Britain were heavily attacked, there might be a greater reluctance to send fighters to France in support of the BEF. Pound also supported Newall, but Churchill maintained his equivocal approach. He conceded Britain was no longer bound by scruples, and he believed the United States would no longer be averse to a change in bombing policy. Nevertheless, before committing the government to bombing the Ruhr, he wanted to consult the two new War Cabinet members, Clement Attlee and Arthur Greenwood, who had yet to attend the Cabinet.[85]

A decision was thus postponed until 6:30 p.m., 13 May. During this meeting Churchill laboriously set out the pros and cons of the Ruhr case. Views were split along the usual lines, with Newall and Hoare strongly in favor of an immediate attack on German industry and Dill, again in the absence of Ironside, arguing that the heavy bombers give their full attention to marshaling yards "on to which we could not direct too great a scale of attack." New members Eden, Attlee, and Alexander weighed in on the side of hesitation, whereas Greenwood supported immediate action. Eden and Chamberlain repeated Ironside's concerns that a German riposte to an attack on the Ruhr might make it impossible to send more fighters to France for the great battle. Of course, there was never a possibility the Germans would have their attention deflected from the main prize.

Churchill, as Chamberlain before him, used the lack of consensus to hesitate further. He was not convinced his great battle was "developing. . . . No great mass of troops had yet come forward." He proposed the decision be put off for another three or four days "to make sure if the great battle had started or not," although the situation would be reviewed daily.[86] Churchill was confused by the deep armored incursions and assumed that without support of infantry, these would be defeated or forced to retreat. His decision to delay was made despite the CAS warning that the nighttime Ruhr operations must take advantage of the waxing moonlight or be seriously disadvantaged.

It was not until 15 May that Churchill agreed to the Ruhr plan. By this time the decision was not tied to a desire to strike a heavy blow against the Germans but to a desire to limit further harm to Britain's tactical bomber forces and to the War Cabinet's growing reluctance to send more fighters to France. This decision to attack the Ruhr represented an extraordinary backflip in the rationale for bombing the Ruhr and was at odds with the guiding principles behind the conservative bombing policy Britain had maintained since the beginning of war. More significant, this flip in rationale contradicted an air policy that had materially influenced the disastrous military dispositions adopted in response to the German invasion of France. Over the previous nine months the War Cabinet had helped build a western front strategy around a determination not to expose Britain to an air threat via a German lodgment in the Low Countries. Having suffered substantial and deleterious air losses in defense of France and the Low Countries, the War Cabinet was now accepting enthusiastically Hoare's suggestion that the best way to aid the French would be to draw a German bombing attack to Britain; the best way to do this was to implement the full Ruhr plan. At last Churchill was amenable to risking an escalation in the air war. He, like all members of the War Cabinet, could see it would fulfill multiple needs.

It would (it was claimed) attract German bombers to Britain and relieve pressure on France; it would, as many times argued by Newall, inflict material harm on the Germans; and perhaps most important, and as clinically declared by Pound, it would provide "a conclusive reason for refusing the request of the French" for more fighters. Nevertheless, Churchill asked one more time if the United States would accept it as a "reasonable and justifiable retaliation." Remarkably, Halifax put Churchill's mind at rest on this point when he declared that the operations were "fully justifiable" provided they were directed at military objectives. Chamberlain too argued that it would "be wrong to stay our hands any longer." The die was cast, but Churchill had hesitated until the end.

Conclusions

For the entire period of the Phoney War, Churchill's view of the air threat and the limitations this threat should place on Britain's use of its own air weapon differed little from those of many of his colleagues and his prime minister. Churchill's determination to take the war to the enemy did not extend to the war in the air. His views differed from those of other members of the War Cabinet only to the extent that his were less "hawkish" than some. Moreover, in most respects Churchill's view of the air threat differed little from the argument the French used to delay Royal Marine, an argument Churchill much reviled.

All these matters were well hidden in Churchill's own writing on World War II. The air policy debate around Belgium and Holland and the use of Britain's heavy bomber force is largely ignored in *The Gathering Storm* and *Their Finest Hour*, the two volumes that address the Phoney War and the first few days of Germany's invasion of the Low Countries. In reference to Royal Marine, Churchill argued that Daladier contrived a "special" excuse to avoid its implementation. Of the entire Royal Marine episode, Churchill wrote the following in *The Gathering Storm*: "On the one side endless discussions about trivial points, no decisions taken, or if taken rescinded, and the rule 'Don't be unkind to the enemy, you will only make him angry.' On the other, doom preparing—a vast machine grinding forward ready to break us."[87] Churchill's assessment could describe, with equal aptness, prolonged discussion over bombing policy and Churchill's contribution to it.

By omitting a discussion of air policy, Churchill did much to obscure the limitations of his own offensive spirit. As far as the Allies' sit-tight-and-rearm policy was concerned, he was much more in tune with War Cabinet air bombing policy than is generally supposed. He certainly chaffed at the restrictions air policy imposed on aggressive action in minor instances, like Royal Marine. It was the French, not the British, who obstructed Royal Marine, and the French objected to the operation for the reasons Churchill hesitated to take the gloves off in the wider air war: the threat of retaliation and national self-interest. Churchill's motivations were also tinged by anxiety over the reaction of the United States to greater aggression in the air; nevertheless, his criticism of the French, although in many respects justifiable, was hypocritical. At the very least, it failed to acknowledge that France had more cause to be anxious about the air threat than Britain had.

This chapter also explored the close link between British air policy and French land policy. It has been suggested elsewhere that the French Dyle plan was an unselfish action to accommodate British concerns that a German occupation of Belgium would increase the air threat to Britain.[88] The evidence adduced here suggests this plan was symptomatic of a great divide. The fate-filled Dyle plan and the Breda variant were influenced much less by a desire to protect Britain from the German air threat than by a French desire to protect itself from the same threat. The French knew—for Chamberlain had made it plain—that the more of Belgium and Holland saved from the enemy the less cause Britain would have to bomb the Ruhr and invite the unrestricted aerial warfare that Gamelin, Daladier, and Reynaud feared.

As one of three service ministers, Churchill played his part early in the war in pressing the aggressive Ruhr policy on the French in support of the strong views of the COS. However, he shared many of Chamberlain's doubts this was the correct path to follow. Nevertheless, under constant pressure from the COS and air staff and supported by the secretaries of state and Churchill as first lord, Chamberlain eventually secured permission from the French to act unilaterally against the Ruhr. Denied still was permission for the RAF to take the gloves off without further reference to the War Cabinet. Churchill and Chamberlain each demanded the unequivocal evidence that German action in the West was likely to be decisive and that it fully justified a decisive change in air policy; an unprovoked assault on the Low Countries, let alone Germany's brutal air action in Poland, apparently remained insufficient justification for action against Germany's large industrial targets and even tactical targets vital to successful military operations. This hesitation to attack strategic targets likely had no significant impact on the Battle of France or the effectiveness of the subsequent Ruhr operations, the value of which was much overrated at the time (so too were the abilities of the heavy bombers involved in the Ruhr plan). However, Churchill did not know how ineffectual these operations would be. Rather he, like everyone else, expected these operations, once begun, to have a considerable impact. Yet before unleashing this weapon, Churchill reset conditions the COS had spent months contesting, even though he knew the delay would undermine the bombers' effectiveness.

Churchill's determination to have the heavy bombers adopt a tactical role in the early battle, although having some merit, reaped few rewards. Unable to attack strategic targets in the Ruhr, the greater part of Britain's heavy bomber force sat idly for the first five days following the German invasion. If Chamberlain's reluctance to escalate the air war against Germany is to be judged a weakness, it was a weakness shared in full measure by Churchill. If the French had adopted a "Don't be unkind to the enemy, you will only make him angry" approach to Royal Marine and their air policy, this attitude was largely replicated by Churchill in his support for Britain's own air policy.

Churchill's last-minute hesitation to take the gloves off—and his last-minute willingness to see German airpower redirected to Britain—effectively undid nine months of British agitation to ensure Allied forces advanced as deeply into Belgium as quickly as possible after a German attack. To secure Britain from the German air threat, the French were increasingly squeezed into a position in which the Allied armies had to advance into Belgium in any and all circumstances. Gamelin developed a plan to make this move as viable as possible and to meet British needs, but the original Breda variant was a British initiative, and not Gamelin's.

It is possible the French would have made the decision to advance deeply into Belgium independently of British pressure; they had long been aware such a move had certain advantages. However, British pressure was almost certainly influential in discouraging the French from exploring more closely the risks involved in this maneuver; it also no doubt encouraged the precipitate and aggressive way Allied forces eventually undertook it. The Dyle/Breda plan, commonly recognized as a French disaster, should more reasonably and more accurately be considered an Allied folly, and possibly even a British folly. Churchill, as one of the first and most famous chroniclers of this great conflict, ought to have done more to acknowledge this.

The common thread in this study of airpower and Royal Marine is the determination displayed by the British and French to fight the war with as little harm as possible to their respective countries. This, after all, was the essence of the sitting-tight-and-rearming long war view with which Churchill agreed. This approach to the war also manifested itself in two other important strategic initiatives during the Phoney War: Churchill's Narvik scheme and the War Cabinet's own Finnish option. Churchill subsequently lamented the passing over of the Narvik plan for the Finnish option as a consequence of the War Cabinet always taking "the line of least resistance." It will be argued the difference between this attitude and Churchill's own willingness to fight the war via three friendly neutrals is only a matter of degree.

SIX

LINES OF LEAST RESISTANCE
Narvik and the Finnish Option

For much of the Phoney War period, two offensive plans were at the center of War Cabinet discussions: Churchill's Narvik operation and the Finnish option, the War Cabinet's convoluted plan to secure Swedish ore by helping Sweden and Finland fight the Soviet Union.[1] The Narvik operation did not take place until April 1940, much too late to do the Germans harm. The Finnish option collapsed in early March. In January 1940 a frustrated Churchill attributed the failure to implement the Narvik scheme to the "immense walls of prevention" put in place by a government that had made it impossible to "gain the initiative."[2] In March he was still blaming a government that had "never done anything but follow the line of least resistance."[3]

Lord Halifax, Churchill's primary interlocutor in these communications, took another view. He expressed dismay at taking a "different line" over the Narvik operation but believed "one can but do one's best to form a judgment, and reach a decision, to the best of one's capacity as the problem presents itself."[4] In his March reply Halifax declined to accept Churchill's apportionment of blame for the inertia of the period and asserted, "The events have followed naturally and inevitably from circumstances that no Government resolution or energy could have surmounted."[5]

The aim of this chapter is to determine the extent to which Churchill's criticism was deserved.[6] Was he justified in blaming failure and inertia on a pusillanimous government determined to take a line of least resistance, or were these shortcomings and disappointments a product of other factors, including practical difficulties inherent in the proposals under consideration, the influence of Britain's French ally, and Churchill himself? Also assessed is the merit of Churchill's entire Scandinavian mind-set. It was one thing to have a strategic "vision"; it was quite another for it to be viable and likely to be achieved.

Map 6.1. Scandinavia

Narvik and Swedish Ore

At the beginning of World War II, most of Germany's ore supply was drawn from Sweden. During the ice-free months in the Baltic—approximately May through December—most ore to Germany was shipped through the port of Lulea, deep in the Gulf of Bothnia. For the rest of the year, when the Baltic was frozen, the ore moved through the Norwegian port of Narvik and down the Norwegian Leads. Except for British scruples toward entering Norwegian territorial waters, this left the ore eminently exposed to interception. Churchill drew the War Cabinet's attention to the issue of Narvik ore in September, but it was not until April 1940 that the Royal Navy acted against the Narvik trade by laying a minefield.

The delay in the prosecution of this operation is commonly attributed to unnecessary obstacles put before it by a prime minister unreasonably set on avoiding conflict at all cost. Halifax is often mentioned as a contributor to this behavior.[7] While these assertions hold some truth, they are open to amendment. Although Chamberlain and the War Cabinet avoided action that might escalate the war prematurely and undermine Britain's own war effort, they did not exclude action to compromise Germany's capacity to wage war and, thereby, improve chances for a successful compromise peace initiative.[8] Thus, in December, when circumstances allowed for an indirect approach to hurt the German war effort and, therefore, created the opportunity for action less likely to unite the German people, the Narvik operation was received with interest by Chamberlain and by members of the British and the French governments.

The problem with the indirect approach represented by both the Narvik operation and the Finnish option was that it became little more than an attempt to fight the war by proxy via Norway, Sweden, and Finland, and this was inherently fraught. Try as they might, the Allies were able to neither cajole nor compel these countries to accommodate their strategic needs. It is here, rather than in the deliberate obstruction by Chamberlain and Halifax, that one will find the best explanation for the failure of these plans.

As for all plans for action, Churchill's Narvik scheme had to pass the "palliative" test; that is, it must have a real possibility of hurting the enemy while offering few risks, or at least limited consequences, for the Allies. These strictures were persistent guiding principles of COS deliberations throughout the Phoney War. When put to the test, Churchill's Narvik operation did not quite stack up. The folly was that the Finnish option somehow did, despite fairly obvious reasons why it was never likely to succeed and was very high risk.

The general resistance to palliative action, rather than any deep-seated anxiety over the escalation of the war from Chamberlain or Halifax, helps explain why the Narvik ore issue, first mentioned by Churchill in September, was not acted on until December. To this can be added Churchill's own reservations and also matters of common sense: there were few ore ships leaving Narvik in the fall; Britain was negotiating access to Norway's tanker fleet, and neither Churchill nor the government wished to put these negotiations at risk; action against the ore trade would risk Britain's own supply of ore and other metals that traveled through Narvik; and the Admiralty was uncertain over the value of the scheme. The naval staff was initially not convinced it was worth stopping this source of ore to Germany. Once Lulea reopened, the trade would be resumed, and the Germans would presumably do everything possible to make up any shortfall in their supply. Finally, the War Cabinet was justifiably cautious about acting against a friendly neutral. The potential political ramifications of such an action were a considerable preoccupation.

The catalyst for Churchill resuming his interest in the Narvik operation was intelligence acquired in mid-November that the Narvik ore trade had resumed. Nevertheless, he remained cautious about any precipitate action and viewed the Norwegian charter agreement as a priority.[9] It was only at the end of November, after the Ministry for Economic Warfare (MEW) had provided him with an explosive appreciation of the ore situation, that Churchill began pressing in earnest for action against Narvik. The MEW report asserted, "A complete stoppage of Swedish exports of iron ore to Germany now would, barring unpredictable developments, end the war in a few months." The memo concluded with similar force: "The future course of the war might well be deeply affected by the defeat of supply of Swedish ore between now and next May."[10]

The MEW report was an extraordinary document and, because of its grandiose claims, also extraordinarily irresponsible. Its import was that Germany's economy—and its capacity to wage war—could be seriously compromised by nothing more than denying the country a single winter's supply of ore via the southern Swedish port of Oxelosund and the Norwegian port of Narvik. Although stopping the supply via Oxelosund was more problematic, the Royal Navy had the capacity to sever the supply via Narvik. The report, however, was a grossly exaggerated assessment of the likely harm that cutting off an ore supply would do to the German economy. The Germans were never desperately short of ore and had taken steps to minimize risks by importing more ore in the prewar period.[11] Additionally, they were mining and using their own low-grade sources; this was undoubtedly an expensive and inefficient process, but it helped meet their immediate needs.[12] They had sufficient ore to wait out the winter and begin importing ore via Lulea in mid-spring.

Unsurprisingly, the memorandum captured Churchill's attention, and this was very probably what was intended.[13] Churchill wrote to Pound insisting that the Admiralty must "arrive at a clear policy" on Swedish ore. He noted the naval staff had cast doubt on the value of stopping the ore trade, but the MEW had informed him "nothing could be more deadly to the German war-making capacity . . . than to stop for three or even six months this import." Churchill immediately began exploring ways in which the navy could stop the flow of ore via Narvik and prevent the other German efforts to mitigate the early freeze in the Baltic. The most important of these was his proposal to mine the Norwegian waters at critical points to force the trade into open waters and facilitate its interception.[14]

Churchill was now willing to put into second place the significant obstacles to action at Narvik. The tanker agreement with Norway had yet to be sealed, but he wrote, "It may not . . . be possible to wait." Given the importance of Norwegian ships to Britain's survival and the navy's responsibility for maritime trade, this was a remarkable choice of priority for a first lord. It was also an important indication of the degree to which, in naval matters, Churchill was prepared to put offensive action ahead of actions designed, first and foremost, to secure Britain's own capacity to wage war. Others were more cautious. Churchill put his mind to the issue of a satisfactory casus belli for action in Norwegian waters, a vital issue if the War Cabinet was to agree to the proposal, and he saw promise in the Germans' recent action to challenge Sweden's territorial limits.[15]

Churchill brought up the issue of the Norwegian ore trade to the War Cabinet of 28 November, but there is no evidence he drew attention to the MEW report in his possession. His Narvik proposal was met with reservations. Halifax considered it important that the government investigate the economic ramifications of the proposal for Germany and for Britain. The possibility and consequences of German retaliation also had to be considered.[16]

Nevertheless, the War Cabinet requested a detailed assessment of the proposal from the MEW and the COS. Thus, in early December the Narvik operation hung in the balance.

The Finnish Option

On 30 November the Soviet Union invaded Finland. This would soon have a significant impact on War Cabinet policy and bear heavily on Churchill's Narvik aspirations, although he initially saw it as a positive for his various offensive plans. He thought the Soviet threat might solve the most intractable problem facing any operation in Scandinavia, including Catherine: Swedish cooperation. Fear of the Soviet Union might cause the Swedes to seek Allied protection, allowing the Allies to gain a foothold in Scandinavia without necessarily going to war with Russia. This "would open up prospects in the Naval war which might be most fruitful."[17] However, rather than facilitating the Narvik operation as he hoped, the Soviet threat quickly became one of two insurmountable obstacles for Churchill's proposal.

Things began to unravel for the Narvik operation with the new MEW report, a draft of which was ready by 12 December. This report backed away from the grander consequences of denying Germany ore via Narvik. The MEW now contended that while stopping this trade would cause the Germans "acute industrial embarrassment," a "decisive advantage" could be achieved only if it were followed by the stoppage of ore via Lulea.[18] If, therefore, no way could be found to stop this latter trade, the War Cabinet would likely conclude that taking action against Narvik would not be worth the potential consequences.[19] Churchill recognized this problem immediately and argued in a 16 December memorandum that the Narvik operation would be only a first step to stopping all ore to Germany. However, he offered no direction as to the "next step"—the stopping of ore via Lulea—beyond declaring that after the Narvik operation, "the prevention of the reopening of Lulea may become a principle Naval objective."[20] Such vague propositions did little to advance the Narvik operation, and on 20 December Halifax got to the nub of Churchill's problem when he noted the MEW equivocation over the value of Narvik alone. It was evident the future of the plan hinged on finding a way to stop the flow from Lulea in the summer.[21] The COS also argued that a decision on the Narvik operation should be based on the precise effect on

Germany of this project against the value of stopping all ore.[22] If a way could be found to follow the Narvik action with successful operations against the Gallivare ore fields and Lulea, then Narvik might yet proceed. If it could not, the Narvik operation was likely to be deemed of doubtful efficacy. If a solution to the entire ore problem could be found, and if this solution would be compromised by the prosecution of the Narvik plan, it was equally likely the latter would be sacrificed to the former.

Halifax thought the only way to stop all ore to Germany would be to "involve Sweden in war, either against Germany, or against Russia over Finland."[23] One solution to this problem immediately presented itself. This was the French, British Foreign Office, and COS initiative already under consideration to offer Sweden assistance should it be threatened by the Soviet Union for the help it was giving Finland: the Finnish option. If an offer of assistance were accepted, it would draw the Swedes to the Allied side, possibly result in a request for military assistance, and thereafter facilitate the control of the Swedish ore fields by British or Allied forces. The proposal was premised on the belief that the Swedes and Norwegians feared the Soviet Union more than they did Germany. However, the plan was also driven by several other, extraneous strategic and political influences: assistance to Finland and Sweden would help the Allies keep the Soviet Union embroiled in its war with Finland, and this would limit the economic support the Allies assumed the Soviet Union was giving Germany. The Finnish option would restrict the ability of either country to wage war in the Balkans, where the British War Cabinet, if not the French, believed the Allies were more exposed and less capable of taking action.[24]

Given the Foreign Office's hopefulness surrounding Swedish fear of the Soviet Union as a catalyst for action in Scandinavia, COS support for this idea, and the other perceived advantages of the Finnish option, there was really no contest between it and Churchill's Narvik plan. When these proposals were discussed at the 20 December MCC meeting and the War Cabinet meeting of 22 December, Churchill supported the proposal to offer assistance to Sweden. None of the possible disadvantages, he believed, would outweigh the value of stopping the supply of ore to Germany. This included the possibility of war with the Soviet Union, which "was a risk we should have to run."[25] However, Churchill argued this initiative be accompanied with action against the flow of ore via Narvik and Oxelosund, and he made light of the uncertainty that would follow: the government should "advance with our eyes fully open to the fact that we could not possibly precisely know what would be the next step we should have to take." Unfortunately for Churchill, the consequences of the Narvik operation—that is, the alienation of Norway and Sweden—were eminently foreseeable and would make stopping the ore trade via Lulea impossible.

At the end of December it appeared inevitable that Churchill's Narvik plan would be subsumed by the Finnish option. Remarkably, and in contrast to the accepted view of his resistance to action, Chamberlain several times breathed life into Churchill's plan.[26] The prime minister was interested in the idea of separating Germany from its supply of ore, and despite his anxieties over palliative measures, he was receptive to the view expressed by several members of the War Cabinet on 26 December that it was better to do something now to hurt Germany than to wait and possibly lose the opportunity.[27] Thus Chamberlain sought to test the proposition that the Narvik operation and the Finnish option were incompatible. He suggested that the Swedish fear of the Soviet Union was so great that it would override the negative impact of the Narvik operation if this accompanied the Allied offer of assistance. Fear of the Soviet Union would also stop Norway and Sweden from temporizing.

This appreciation was not supported by the COS, which by late December was concerned that Finnish resistance had been so successful that Norway and Sweden were now less fearful of the Soviet Union and would be less inclined to accept any threat of action against Narvik accompanying the démarche of assistance.[28] At the 27 December War Cabinet, Churchill and Chamberlain attempted to get around this obstacle by arguing that the Finns' success would be temporary and that the Soviet threat would return in the spring and so, thereafter, would Swedish anxiety. They believed the Swedes would "protest" about the Narvik operation but not be permanently alienated. This was a particularly dangerous line of argument for Churchill to adopt because, in making this case, he was endorsing the two great threats to the Narvik operation: the Finnish option and the Soviet threat scenario. His endorsement would prove just enough to encourage the War Cabinet to persist with the Finnish option and not enough to persuade it to go ahead with the Narvik operation.

During these last days of December and into January, Churchill adopted two other lines of argument in his efforts to activate his preferred scheme. He contended that far from compromising the Finnish option, the Narvik operation would be the essential catalyst. The moment Britain acted against the Narvik ore, Germany would act in southern Sweden, and this would force Norway and Sweden into the war.[29] It was most unwise to argue the Narvik operation would precipitate a violent German response against Sweden and Norway while the War Cabinet was building a strategy based on Scandinavian cooperation. Churchill must have been conscious of the risks involved in pressing this line, but he seemed not to care. Over the following weeks, he would, as and when it suited, brazenly interchange between two mutually exclusive arguments in support of the Narvik operation. When the situation warranted, he would push the Narvik plan as the "essential catalyst" to Lulea because it would prompt German aggression and force Scandinavian cooperation. When it appeared that the Narvik operation might yet proceed, despite concerns over its impact on the Finnish option, he would argue Norway and Sweden had nothing to worry about because it was not in the Germans' best interest to act against them. Such flexible, but inconsistent, lines of reasoning did little for his credibility as a strategist.

Another more aggressive line of argument that Churchill used repeatedly was forceful action against Norway and Sweden to secure the Gallivare ore fields. He believed, and argued, the Allies could develop sufficient force to occupy the ore fields in the face of Norwegian and Swedish resistance. This was an assertion entirely without foundation and would, again, have done little to demonstrate Churchill's credentials as strategist. As Ironside and the COS explained several times, control of Narvik was not the ticket to the Gallivare ore fields, but Swedish cooperation was.[30]

The COS came out against the combined démarche and the Narvik scheme in two important papers on 31 December.[31] Each put the emphasis on Swedish cooperation and concluded that the Finnish option was the best way forward; the Narvik operation would compromise this larger scheme. At a practical level the COS was concerned that the army needed time to prepare forces for operations in Scandinavia, whether to resist the Soviets or the Germans. As Churchill had unwisely but correctly pointed out, an immediate naval operation against the Narvik trade risked precipitating a German response in Scandinavia, and for this the Allies were ill prepared.

Churchill despaired when he read the papers condemning the Narvik operation, and he wrote a compelling memorandum in response. While he agreed with elements of the COS reports, he concluded that their effects

> will lead to a purely negative conclusion.... The self-contained project of stopping the ore from Narvik and Oxelosund must not be tried because it would jeopardise the larger program. The larger program must not be attempted unless Sweden and Norway co-operate.... But is there any prospect of Sweden and Norway actively co-operating of their own free will to bring about a series of operations which ... will:
> a. Ruin the trade of their ironfield and the shipping which carries it.
> b. Involve them in war with Germany.
> c. Expose the whole southern part of both countries to German invasion and occupation.[32]

Nothing written by Churchill during this time more clearly represents his frustration than this note. However, his comments, while accurate in many ways, did not quite represent the tenor of War Cabinet discussions or his own views. No one expected the Swedes or Norwegians to cooperate of "their own free will." They would need to be coerced to take the risks Churchill had outlined, and this coercion was expected to be generated by the Soviet threat. Chamberlain, Halifax, and most particularly, the Northern Department of the Foreign Office held this view, but Churchill also endorsed it as a path to success and, thus, had contributed to the impasse.

In early January it was not Churchill but Chamberlain—and to a lesser extent, Halifax—who resurrected the Narvik scheme after the COS reports. Intelligence showed that while the Narvik operation would upset the Norwegians, it would not offend the Swedes. This intelligence suggested the Swedes expected, even hoped, the Allies would take action against the Narvik ore trade because this action would help them justify rationing the Germans during the summer. Additionally, another COS investigation had concluded that if the Germans took aggressive action in southern Norway in response to the Narvik operation, it would be satisfactorily contained and would not harm the Finnish option. Although he still sought reassurance that the Narvik operation would not compromise the larger plan, Halifax was receptive to the COS conclusions at the War Cabinet of 3 January. Churchill seized on

Halifax's softening attitude and attempted to ameliorate anxieties further with his first guile-filled volte-face regarding the likely German response.[33] Germany would not, after all, attack Norway or Sweden because this would be against its best interests. Even if Germany did act, its action would be contained to southern Norway, and the Norwegians would join the Allied side; none of this would compromise the critical relationship with Sweden and the vital Finnish option. With this anxiety removed, the War Cabinet concluded that the government could send a formal warning of the intention to block the Narvik ore trade, although the action itself would await the Scandinavian response.

It is important to emphasize the Narvik operation remained a possibility during the first week of January not because Churchill claimed it would only do good but because Chamberlain, Halifax, and the COS had accepted it would do no serious political or military harm. Despite Churchill's efforts to make action against Narvik ore the essential catalyst in a successful Scandinavia strategy, the thinking of the War Cabinet remained that this strategy hinged on the Soviet threat and the Scandinavian reaction to it. So long as the Narvik operation could go ahead and not affect this plan, it made sense to begin compromising the German ore supply at the earliest opportunity, even if, as Chamberlain concluded on 3 January, it was not possible to make any decision about Oxelosund. This situation is inconsistent with the view of an evasive and war-shy Chamberlain blocking Churchill's offensive initiatives at every turn. Through Chamberlain's intervention, the Narvik operation had been drawn back from the brink several times. Churchill's efforts to do as much had done the opposite.

The War Cabinet's delusion that Sweden would be indifferent to any plan that might bring the war to Scandinavia was quickly shattered. The Norwegians objected strenuously—which was unsurprising—but, more important, so did the Swedes. Remarkably, this was not the end of the Narvik operation. Chamberlain and Halifax were sufficiently influenced by comments made by the Swedish minister in London, Bjorn Prytz, to believe that the official Swedish response might be mere bluster and bluff. Over the next several days, several alternative solutions were discussed, but the Narvik plan remained a possibility, albeit remote. It was thought that, instead of aggressive action by the Allies to deal with Germany's ore supply, the mere threat of this operation might be enough for the Norwegians and Swedes themselves to act to curtail this trade.

Halifax reviewed the Narvik problem at the Foreign Office on 9 January, but unsurprisingly, this meeting reaffirmed the Foreign Office conviction the Soviet threat would ultimately determine Norwegian and Swedish action.[34] By 11 January the decision on the Narvik operation had again been reduced to Sweden's likely response to it. A final decision awaited Halifax's discussion with Markus Wallenberg, a Swedish banker and representative of the Swedish Trade Commission who was due in London. The discussions of this meeting, along with opinions offered by Dominion representatives and Ironside's reaffirmation of the Finnish option, proved decisive to burying the Narvik plan. Halifax concluded it was not possible to retain the goodwill of the Swedes if the Narvik operation went ahead, and without this support it was impossible to stop all ore.[35]

During these decisive few days, Churchill's primary contribution was to argue vociferously that it was only by force or threats that the Allies could hope to move the Norwegians and Swedes: "We should have to make them more frightened of us than they were of Germany."[36] Here, perhaps, was the key to the entire problem. It had been the German threat to Sweden that had compromised all discussions from the beginning. The tragedy of the discussions within the War Cabinet and the folly of Churchill's relentless pursuit of the Swedish ore problem were that this objective was beyond fulfillment short of invading Sweden, which was not possible, or getting the Germans to do so. But the Germans did not want to invade Sweden, and the Swedes were determined to give them no incentive to decide otherwise. No contrivance of the British War Cabinet or Churchill's own plans had ever been likely to change this. Churchill, of course, long argued the Narvik operation would be the catalyst for German action against Scandinavia, and this would provide the necessary foot in the door. However, this strategy would work only if the Germans attacked Sweden. Instead, they successfully attacked and occupied Norway—always a more likely option—and thereby destroyed the foundations of Churchill's own solution to the Scandinavian problem.

Despite Churchill's occasional efforts to initiate the Narvik operation during February and March, the War Cabinet, through the Foreign Office, remained stubbornly supportive of the Finnish option.[37] However, in early

February it belatedly recognized that something more than fear of the Soviet Union was needed to animate Sweden. Maintaining its almost unbroken record for foolish ideas, the War Cabinet adopted the idea put forward by the lord privy seal that the Allies should offer direct military assistance to Finland itself.[38] The Finns would be asked to make a formal request for military aid, to which the Allies would respond. Lest they earn the acrimony of world opinion, the Swedes were expected to permit the passage of these Allied armies through their territory. The War Cabinet recognized, at least, that the Swedes would do this only if the Allies could protect them from a German invasion. Thus did the Finnish option evolve, inexorably, into a substantial military operation. Forces were needed to occupy at least three Norwegian ports, to support the Swedes in southern Sweden, to occupy the Gallivare ore fields, and to help fight the Soviets in Finland. However, only a small portion of the forces available would be destined for Finland itself, an important factor in Finland's decision not to accommodate this dubious Allied strategy.

Churchill was most often on the fringe of these decisions, always preferring his Narvik solution. Nevertheless, it is impossible to separate him from the plan. While he doubted it would succeed, he had not eschewed the essential principles on which the Finnish option was based, including the conviction that war in Scandinavia would be good for the Allied cause and that the opportunities to secure Swedish ore would be worth the risk of war with the Soviet Union. He showed no greater capacity than other members of the War Cabinet to recognize the inevitable fruitlessness of the entire northern strategy. It is disturbing to read the War Cabinet minutes of this time and discover how often the fairly obvious and essentially insurmountable obstacles to a successful northern strategy were canvassed and, as often, how these concerns were overlooked, discarded, or forgotten in the policy finally reached. There had, for example, always been much to suggest that the Soviets were not colluding with the Germans but acting entirely in self-interest in its action in Finland, much as were the Allies in conceiving a strategy that would place the war in the very middle of Scandinavia, embroil three neutrals, and keep the fighting some distance from the French frontier. That the Soviet Union was not in any real sense an ally of Germany was cause enough not to add this country to a list of enemies.

The Finnish option also hinged on the Foreign Office's conviction that after Finland the Soviets would move into Sweden or at least that the Swedes believed they would. That this was considered possible despite the German need to protect its supply of ore, or that in the circumstances it was ever thought the Soviets would consider such a move, is difficult to understand; this perspective is even more difficult to understand when the existing conviction was that the Soviet Union was militarily weak. It made no sense to imagine that the Soviet Union would risk war with Germany to acquire Swedish ore, nor did it make sense to believe the two countries had an agreement that would place Swedish ore in the Soviet orbit.

Churchill had oftentimes displayed a certain perspicuity toward Russia's motives and actions, but this insight was ultimately sacrificed to his hopes regarding Swedish ore. Certainly, he had always believed that war with the Soviet Union could be avoided under the Finnish option strategy, but this risk had grown exponentially with the plan to send Allied forces to Finland.

It was fortunate for the Allies that the Finnish appeal for aid never came; that Churchill and the War Cabinet ever thought it would is the extraordinary element of this period. The Finns grasped early the realities of their predicament and the weakness of the Allies. The Allies could not possibly offer enough support, and in sufficient time, to make a difference. Further, the Finns did not see how this help could be rendered without Swedish cooperation, and they knew this would not be forthcoming. The Finns also saw no virtue in encouraging the Germans into Scandinavia. This would not help them in their war against the Soviets, and any threat from Germany would ensure assistance from Sweden would be reduced to a trickle. As for the Swedes themselves, they were more animated by the German warning that should Allied soldiers set foot in Sweden, the Germans would retaliate. Allied policy continued to be guided by the naive belief that the Allies could compete with this. Always more likely than a successful Finnish venture was what actually came to pass. The Finns wisely used the threat of Allied intervention in Scandinavia to their advantage. The Soviets did not want conflict with the Allies and were prompted to negotiate with the Finns. The Finns were required to make serious concessions, but the result was always better for them and for the Swedes, who encouraged them to make peace, than it would have been had Allied assistance been sought.

In the final rundown of the Finnish option in early March, Churchill balked at failure and sought to bully Britain's way into Sweden.[39] Against type Chamberlain endorsed the idea, arguing that it would be "fatal to abandon the expedition altogether merely because we had received a diplomatic refusal from the Scandinavians to our demand for passage."[40] Action would show the sincerity of Allied efforts; its failure could then be laid at the feet of the Norwegians and Swedes. The Finnish capitulation arrived just in time to avoid this folly. Churchill tried a last time to force a landing in Norway and take advantage of the forces accumulated for this purpose.[41] However, without the cover of assistance to Finland, this was a step too far for the War Cabinet. Moreover, such action would not do what Churchill claimed; it would not give the Allies access to Gallivare.[42] These early days of March were the low point for British strategy and Churchill's own strategic aspirations, and this low point prompted Churchill's letter to Halifax that began this chapter. Churchill had suffered a second and almost simultaneous blow. Several days earlier the French had vetoed Operation Royal Marine. These moments, however, were a turning point.

Churchill Ascendant: The Resurrection of the Narvik Plan and Royal Marine

The collapse of the Finnish option left the British and French governments in fear of a strong political backlash at home and abroad. Almost immediately they set about finding a replacement for the plan. The only two viable proposals available were the Narvik scheme and Royal Marine, and Churchill suddenly found his strategies at the center of Allied strategic planning. The difficulty was that the British wanted Royal Marine and doubted the efficacy of the Narvik operation, while the French had the opposite view. The French priority remained for action in Scandinavia, to keep the war as far away from France as possible. Daladier, desperate to retain his leadership after the collapse of the Finnish option, pressed for an operation against the Narvik ore trade and a forceful occupation of key ports in Norway. Additionally, the French returned to their old proposals for action in southern Europe, including against the Russians. As for Royal Marine, the French had already sought a two-month delay.

The British War Cabinet was now shy of action that might incite the Russians and more interested in establishing a trade relationship with them.

The War Cabinet had moved beyond the Narvik operation, believing that a future initiative must save face and assuage neutral anxieties and public opinion, and this could not be achieved at the expense of a neutral. The great hopes for stopping Swedish ore and seriously hurting the German war effort had been surrendered. There was no way of getting to Gallivare, and the Baltic would soon be free of ice. The Narvik operation was now even less worthwhile than it had ever been. Much more attractive to the War Cabinet was Royal Marine, which struck directly at the enemy and would therefore impress the neutrals but would not unduly escalate the war or lead to violent retaliation. Palliatives were now the order of the day.

On 19 March the War Cabinet decided to confront Daladier over Royal Marine, but before it did, Daladier was replaced by Reynaud. On 26 March, and following receipt of Reynaud's analysis of the strategic situation, the War Cabinet conceived a quid pro quo proposal to address the ongoing disagreement in the British and French strategic views: the British government would undertake the Narvik operation, minus the forced landings recommended by the French, if the French would do Royal Marine.[43] The War Cabinet believed action against Norway must be offset by direct action against Germany via this latter operation.[44] The proposal was agreed to by Reynaud at the SWC meeting of 27 March, but several days later, under pressure from Daladier, the French reneged.[45] On 1 April Chamberlain, with Churchill's support, decided to call the French bluff: "No Royal Marine, no Narvik."[46] Churchill was soon set off to France to persuade the French to undertake Royal Marine, but instead he recommended Royal Marine be postponed and the Narvik operation proceed on its own. Lest nothing at all occur as a result of French stubbornness, Chamberlain and the War Cabinet decided to proceed with the mining operation against Narvik.

Such were the extraordinary political dimensions behind the final resurrection of Churchill's Narvik operation. It was no longer his plan but that of the French and a reluctant War Cabinet. It took place not because it would cause major harm to the Germans but because a show of force was needed and this would help the government out of a fix with the French, who wanted much more drastic measures and continued to entertain potential conflict with the Soviet Union. The operation could not be justified by the possibility that the Germans would react violently and take action in Scandinavia, although this remained a possibility. Churchill now doubted the Germans would respond forcefully. Since the surrender of Finland, it had been generally and dangerously assumed that the Germans no longer had cause to be anxious over their supply of Swedish ore; instead, it was expected Germany and the Soviet Union would redirect their aggression elsewhere. It was hoped that the Narvik operation would at least draw German attention back to Scandinavia. Neither the Narvik operation nor Royal Marine signified the War Cabinet's determination to escalate the war. It certainly did not represent the British War Cabinet's surrender of its long war strategy. Three memorandums—one by Hankey, another by the COS, and a third by Halifax—were written at this time, and all recommended Britain return to its pre–Finnish option posture: time was still on the Allies' side, direct confrontation with Germany was to be avoided as much as possible, action in southern Europe—a proposal of the French—was also to be avoided, and economic measure increased.[47] In early April the green light was also given to Oxelosund on the understanding that sabotage could not be traced to the Allies. There would be no more proactivity beyond these measures. The focus was now on the spring campaigning season and a possible assault in the West. The best-case scenario was that the Narvik operation and Royal Marine might distract the Germans from this action. If the Germans launched a major attack in Scandinavia, it would delay action in the West or reduce the strength of the German blow.

Churchill and the War Cabinet were completely misreading German intentions, and Soviet. The Soviets were keen on rapprochement, while Hitler's attitude to action in Scandinavia was hardening, not softening. The activities of the Allies over the preceding three months had convinced him and his advisers that Allied respect for Scandinavian neutrality could not be guaranteed, and in the circumstances, Norway should be occupied. The arrival of spring and the freeing from ice of the entrance to the Baltic would make a decisive German operation possible. Moreover, the Germans had hit on that which was never satisfactorily grasped by Churchill, the COS, or the British War Cabinet: successful action against Norway would remove the need for a much larger campaign against Sweden. Unfortunately, and despite months of focus on Scandinavia, when the Germans set in motion their plan for the invasion of Norway in the early days of April, Churchill and the War Cabinet were ill prepared for its clinical, meticulous, and brilliant execution.

Conclusions

Despite Churchill developing an interest in Narvik very early in the war, it would take until April 1940 for this comparatively minor operation to be implemented. The primary reason for this delay was that the War Cabinet was not persuaded the Narvik operation was worth doing alone. This perspective reflected the basic foundations of War Cabinet strategy during this time: operations must be worth doing and must be certain to do more harm to the enemy than to the Allies themselves. In the context of the Narvik plan, economic and political issues discounted it as a stand-alone operation. During December the War Cabinet conceived the Finnish option, which offered the prospect of stopping all ore. This need not, in the first instance, have compromised the Narvik operation; combining the two operations would have compounded the harm done to the Germans and achieved this harm more quickly. Unfortunately for Churchill, the Finnish option required the cooperation and friendship of Sweden and Norway, and both could only be undermined by the Narvik plan.

Churchill was unsuccessful in his efforts to sell the Narvik operation as an essential catalyst to successful action in Scandinavia. His arguments were not persuasive, and he could not break through the consensus view that the Finnish option was the best strategy to pursue. Particularly unsatisfactory and unconvincing from the point of view of the War Cabinet and COS was Churchill's repeatedly expressed determination to use force against Norway and Sweden if all else failed.

Rather than accepting these explanations for the delay of the Narvik plan, Churchill contended it was a lack of will within the War Cabinet and a determination to "take the line of least resistance." However, Halifax was justified in arguing that many of the problems experienced were inherent in the situation the War Cabinet faced and the strategies themselves. With few exceptions the historical view has been that Chamberlain and Halifax were deliberately and calculatedly obstructionist, but this has been challenged here. Each—although Chamberlain more than Halifax—made real attempts to advance the Narvik operation, but they ultimately spoke out against the operation's prospects and reward. Moreover, these two men were not alone in their criticism of the Narvik operation; this is often ignored. The MEW, the COS, and in particular, Ironside and the Northern Department of the Foreign Office were all influential in establishing the priority given the Finnish option. Churchill made his own contribution to this by endorsing the Soviet threat scenario.

The Finnish option was, from beginning to end, complete folly. Its viability hinged on assumptions that were never likely to be fulfilled, yet there always appeared a genuine conviction within the War Cabinet, and especially the Foreign Office Northern Department, that they might be. The German threat was decisive throughout, and there was never a serious possibility that the Swedes would accommodate Allied aspirations, especially when the Allies were offering so little. The only slim hope for the scheme was further Soviet aggression, but there were many reasons why this prospect was remote. The collapse of the strategy was as timely as it was predictable, and undoubtedly saved the Allies from a much greater disaster than that which subsequently befell them in Norway.

The reemergence of the Narvik scheme in the aftermath of the Finnish option failure had little to do with Churchill. After four months of advocacy by Churchill, the Narvik operation finally met the needs of War Cabinet policy, but not in the manner the first lord had conceived. Britain was in desperate need of a comparatively benign palliative operation that would help the British secure their preferred option, Royal Marine. Together, the development of these plans made March a seminal month for Churchill and placed him at the center of Allied strategy; it did not, however, prove a period of vindication. Churchill's opportunity to bask in the light of success was cut short by French intransigence over Royal Marine and then by the German invasion of Norway on 9 April. This would be the greatest disaster of the Phoney War and one to which Churchill would make his own unfortunate contribution. Moreover, his long-held conviction that war in Scandinavia would be to the advantage of the Allies proved without foundation.

SEVEN

NORWAY, PART 1
A Failure of Preemption

In the early hours of 9 April 1940, the Germans invaded Norway. Churchill had long believed such an invasion would be a great advantage because the Allies' subsequent support of Norway would provide a gateway to the Gallivare ore fields and give Britain naval bases along the Norwegian coastline. Instead, the invasion proved a disaster for Britain, France, and Norway and shattered many of Churchill's cherished and long-held assumptions.

Although the British government had made preparations, albeit perfunctory and limited, to deal with a German response to Wilfred, the operation involving the mining of the Norwegian Leads, and had warnings of imminent German action, the Royal Navy failed to prevent the Germans' occupying all the important west coast ports of Norway as far north as Narvik. This chapter will assess Churchill's contribution to this failure with a focus on the 7–8 April period of missed opportunity, during which Churchill and the Royal Navy had within their reach a decisive victory against the German forces then in transit.

Churchill's assumptions regarding German aggression against Norway were reflected in his limited preparations for a campaign in Norway and in his response to the intelligence of imminent German action during 7–8 April 1940. These assumptions will be explored, and the impact on Churchill's actions—or inaction—assessed. Also considered will be others' contributions to the decisions that caused the failure, with particular attention given to First Sea Lord Sir Dudley Pound. Churchill and Pound made serious errors of judgment, but these occurred in circumstances very different from those described in the existing historical record. Several controversial issues will be reexamined, including the misunderstanding surrounding a breakout of Germany's capital ships and the decision to disembark the landing forces for Operation R4, the British plan to occupy Stavanger, Bergen, Trondheim, and Narvik should the Germans react to Wilfred. This latter episode was not the decisive error it is generally painted.

Although this investigation will establish responsibility and apportion blame, it will concede that responsibility could never be absolute. The vagaries of war, good luck and bad, the unforeseen and unpredictable elements that form part of any battle or campaign, all played their part. Nevertheless, a primary conclusion will be that Churchill must bear a heavy burden of responsibility for lost opportunities of those vital two days.

Flawed Assumptions and Poor Preparation

The preparation for the Narvik operation, which began in the last days of March 1940, coincided with ever more frequent intelligence suggesting imminent German action in Scandinavia. Despite this intelligence Churchill and the War Cabinet doubted the Germans would react to the mine-laying operation, and they gave little thought to the Germans' taking action independently of it.

As an earlier chapter has shown, the Allies believed German attention was focused on Holland at this time. Nevertheless, intelligence continued to hint at action somewhere in Scandinavia—and most likely against Norway—and there was reason to take this seriously. The warmer months would not only open the Gulf of Bothnia and provide Germany access to Lulea, they would, several weeks before this, free the Great Belt from ice and expose Norway to a German invasion through the Skagerrak and Kattegat.

On 26 March information came in via the British minister in Stockholm regarding impending German moves. Swedish intelligence believed the Germans were concentrating aircraft and shipping for operations against Norwegian airfields and ports, "pretext being disclosure of allied plans of occupation of Norwegian territory." Admiral Phillips took seriously this and other intelligence and wrote to Churchill on 28 March that it appeared the Germans were preparing for action against southern Scandinavia. He recommended that whether or not German action was taken independently, or as a result of Britain's action against Norway, this would offer a "last opportunity to try to get to the Swedish ore fields via Narvik before the ice breaks up."[1]

As a result of this communication, Churchill raised the matter of troops for Norway at the War Cabinet of 29 March. He drew attention to the possibility the Germans might take forcible action in Norway and suggested "we should continue in a state of readiness to despatch a light force to Narvik, and possibly also the force that had been planned for Stavanger."[2] Churchill's recommendations bore the hallmarks of afterthought and a general lack of conviction that the German threat would arise; also complacency was evident as to just how serious this threat might be. Furthermore, the recommendations showed a complete lack of interest in the integrity of Norway itself. There was no thought here of the possibility Allied troops might be required to offer large-scale support to the Norwegians for the defense of their country. Further still from Churchill's mind was any thought of the potential political ramifications if the Allies did not send substantial assistance when called for. Churchill made no mention of the importance of Bergen or Trondheim, despite these ports routinely being nominated as objectives of considerable strategic importance.

Churchill was not alone in his complacency; it was pervasive and extended to his War Cabinet colleagues, the JPS, and the COS, and this must temper any criticism of him on this point. On 31 March the COS circulated a report that outlined the likely German response to Wilfred.[3] The prospect of a full-scale German invasion to secure all of Norway was not among the possibilities canvassed, despite the ongoing intelligence of impending action in Scandinavia. Thus, even though the COS took the issue of invasion more seriously than Churchill did, plans to combat this threat were only marginally more thoughtful. The service chiefs accepted nothing could be done at Oslo but proposed two battalions be readied to occupy Bergen and two battalions prepared for Stavanger. A single battalion would be sent to Trondheim as a second echelon. Like Churchill, the COS gave priority to Narvik despite no one seriously believing this port was under threat from the Germans. Three British battalions were to be sent there, plus a French contingent, the purpose of which would be to move into Sweden should the opportunity arise.

Although these limited dispositions assumed assistance from the Norwegians, they suggested several other assumptions were at work: First, that a German reaction was unlikely. Second, that a German reaction would most likely be limited to southern Norway. Third, if the German reaction escalated, the Royal Navy would facilitate an adequate movement of troops as and when required. Certainly, the COS counseled against preparations for major operations in Norway and Sweden to combat a German invasion;

it preferred instead to be ready for operations in the West. There was perhaps a fourth assumption at work in the COS recommendations: that whatever the Germans might do, Norway would be defended only in so much as it helped secure Narvik.

Of enormous importance to planning for a German response to Wilfred was clear and accurate intelligence followed by a timely and appropriate reaction. As a result of Phillips' agitation, the COS made special arrangements to acquire "the earliest possible authentic information of a German move against Norway or Sweden." To help estimate the value of information, it was decided the reliability of the source of information would be indicated in these reports.[4] Unfortunately, no guidance was offered as to how to react to intelligence deemed less than absolutely reliable. Were responses to be guided by the risks of inaction toward a particular piece of intelligence or entirely by doubts over the reliability of the source?

The COS warned of the need for celerity in the dispatch of the expeditionary forces and portentously observed, "The first news received of a German move against Scandinavia will very possibly be vague and unconfirmed, and many hours may elapse before full confirmation can be obtained." Again, no guidance was given as to how to reconcile the precondition of celerity with "vague and unconfirmed" intelligence.[5] Timing was everything, especially if the Germans were to be preempted in southern and central Norway, where the Germans might quickly dominate the air.

Preemption

The Admiralty response to the available intelligence was a woeful, sustained bungling, save for some judicious decisions by Admiral Forbes. The Germans preempted the Allies at all key ports at the start of the Norwegian campaign. The path to failure began with matters of intelligence. There was ample and remarkably accurate intelligence available, but it was ignored not so much for its source but because it did not conform to existing expectations, Churchill's among them. At the War Cabinet meeting of 3 April, Oliver Stanley explained he had been given a somewhat garbled account the Germans were collecting "a strong force of troops" at the Baltic port of Rostock with the avowed intention of taking Scandinavia. Halifax noted the most recent telegrams from Stockholm tended to confirm this, and that substantial numbers of Germans were "aboard ship in Stettin and Swindemunde harbours." Churchill "doubted the Germans would land a force in Scandinavia" but noted all necessary preparation had been made for the landings "should they prove necessary."[6] At the COS meeting the following day, Ironside said the Germans were focused on Western Europe and "any diversion to Scandinavia would be to their serious disadvantage and was therefore in his opinion unlikely."[7] He demurred from any premature withdrawal of regular forces from France to address this threat and recommended only preparations for small reinforcements when needed.

At the Admiralty news of German activities against Norway or Sweden also continued to meet a wall of doubt. On 4 April news was received the Germans were targeting Narvik with a landing on 8 April. The deputy director of the Operations Division (Home), Captain Ralph Edwards, wished to take precautions against this possibility but noted in his diary, "In the opinion of the Intelligence and the High Command, the German High Command would never allow such a 'mad expedition to sail.'"[8] His concerns received no more interest two days later, when he recorded, "Some indications of a German move in the not too distant future against Norway. My own personal point of view is that it is only a matter of hours . . . but I am in the minority."[9]

With the exception of Edwards, the doubt surrounding German action was universal. Churchill, Ironside, military intelligence, the Foreign Office, and the higher echelons of the naval staff, including naval intelligence, all failed to place adequate store in intelligence of impending German action in Norway. Churchill, more than some, could be forgiven for his ongoing blindness to events. Invariably overlooked in studies of this time is that from the morning of 4 April until the evening of 6 April, he was in France trying to persuade the French to adopt Royal Marine. It is not clear how up-to-date he was kept on intelligence reports, but it is probable his absence from the Admiralty denied him the awareness required to adopt a more cautious attitude to Norway. Pound was away from the Admiralty on a fishing trip during 7 April and did not return until around 8 p.m. It is therefore probable Churchill and Pound did not discuss developments regarding Scandinavia for the three days leading up to the invasion of Norway. This ought to be kept in mind when considering Churchill's subsequent failures. Nevertheless, it is difficult to understand why Churchill failed to show greater caution to the important intelligence received earlier on the day of his return (6 April), especially given its corroboration of other information. Evidence suggests it might have been inaction against his better judgement.

Intelligence via the U.S. ambassador in Denmark indicated Hitler had given "definite orders to send one division in ten ships to land at Narvik on 8 April, occupying Jutland on the same day but leaving Sweden." A subsequent telegram stated these troops had been embarked on 4 April.[10] By the time the Admiralty circulated this information to, among others, Admiral Forbes, who received the warning only in the afternoon of 7 April, it had added to it, "All these reports are of doubtful value and may well be only a further move in the war of nerves."[11] These final comments represented the intelligence system at work. DCNS Phillips saw the telegram and signed off on it. This was surprising given Phillips' role in preparing the military and naval response to German action. A decision to circulate this message with the qualification raises questions as to what intelligence would have been deemed "of value" and caused the Admiralty to be more proactive. Certainly, the telegram was not designed to engender a heightened alertness in the commander in chief. Fortunately, despite this extra brick in the wall of doubt, Forbes would take more judicious action in response to the German threat than is commonly assumed.

When it came, the German invasion was a shocking turn of events that shattered Churchill's long-held illusions about the Narvik scheme. He had maintained Britain's overwhelming naval power would allow it to fight a war in Scandinavia to advantage. He further believed that should the Germans invade, only southern Norway would fall, and this would make little difference to Allied plans. Churchill's tune quickly changed in the aftermath of the successful German occupation. He stood in Parliament and lashed out at the Norwegians with a desperate apologia for Allied incompetence. Of the information of German preparations known to the Allies, he declared: "No one could tell when they would be used or against what peaceful country they would be used."[12] At the War Cabinet meeting midday on 9 April, he told his colleagues, "We could not have prevented these landings without maintaining large patrols continuously off the Norwegian coast, which would have been wasteful of our naval strength."[13] These statements mocked the preemptive plans of Operation R4.

For all the foregoing criticism of Churchill and the Admiralty and the wall of doubt leading up to the German invasion, Churchill's Operation Wilfred and R4 plan had serendipitously placed the Royal Navy in a better position than it might have been otherwise to respond to the German invasion. The German timetable had been decided quite independently of the Narvik mining plan, yet by coincidence major British naval vessels were simultaneously in the vicinity of Germany's northernmost objective, Narvik, and other, much more substantial forces were readied to respond to a German reaction. Thus, despite the extraordinary complacency of Churchill and the Admiralty up to 7 April, all in Norway was by no means lost; the main German forces had yet to move and would be highly exposed when they did. The preparation for, and the prosecution of, Wilfred and the subsequent landings (Operation R4) ought to have been enough to destroy the German invasion effort at Bergen, Trondheim, and Narvik. Yet these opportunities were lost. Churchill must bear much, but not all, responsibility for this.

Flawed Decisions and Faulty Dispositions

The activities that occurred in the Admiralty War Room during 7–8 April are important to an accurate assessment of Churchill's contribution to the failure to preempt the Germans in central and northern Norway. One of the most important (and influential) sources available to the historian is Captain Edwards' diary and his subsequent elaborations on it. Edwards saw firsthand and was sometimes directly involved in the decision-making process.[14] This source has not been used with adequate caution—in part because historians have been unaware of its various versions—and this has led to error in the historical record and to an unnecessarily jaundiced assessment of Churchill's role at important junctures. There are at least three versions of the elements of Edwards' diary that pertain to this campaign: the original and two other expanded versions; additionally, there is a fourth version of several pages in Stephen Roskill's handwriting.[15] The versions are sometimes in conflict. Careful reading of all is required to draw clear and accurate conclusions.

The historical consensus—heavily influenced by Roskill's official history, *The War at Sea*, and his subsequent volume, *Churchill and the Admirals*—is that the Navy misread the invasion of Norway in the critical days of 7 and 8 April as an attempted breakout to the Atlantic by Germany's heavy ships.

The blame for this is usually directed at Churchill.[16] Because of this misapprehension, all naval dispositions had as their primary focus the prevention of the breakout and, subsequently, the interception of any ships that might seek to return to Germany. It is accepted that an early consequence of this misjudgment was the disembarkation, or abandonment, of all the military forces destined for Stavanger, Bergen, Trondheim, and Narvik under Operation R4 in the evening of 7 April. This is considered a pivotal moment in the early days of the campaign, and Churchill is, again, often blamed. However, the episode was by no means pivotal, did not occur in the evening of 7 April, and was an error made by Pound, not Churchill.

Edwards' diaries reveal that Pound returned to the Admiralty from a fishing trip around 8 p.m., and he, not Churchill, was the key decision maker that evening and the following day. Churchill certainly offered opinions, but where these conflicted with those of his staff, he deferred. The diaries also suggest that Pound (and less consistently, Phillips), rather than Churchill or Forbes, was preoccupied with the battle cruiser breakout and made the controversial decision to disembark the R4 landing forces.

In the elaborations of his diary—although not in his original diary, where fewer judgments were made—Edwards consistently maintains that Pound's actions on the evening of 7 April contributed most to the missed opportunities that followed. In contrast, Edwards shows Churchill as receptive to the possibility that the battle cruiser threat was a mask for an operation against Norway rather than the other way around. The diary also suggests Churchill was receptive to the possibility a breakout was occurring in conjunction with an invasion. That Churchill was willing to contemplate these possibilities, despite the doubt he had entertained, was not surprising. Given his personal investment in Norway and Narvik, it is difficult to imagine him redirecting all his attention to the prospects of a decisive naval battle, as has been argued in a variety of sources.[17]

In contrast, Pound was predisposed to assume that German activity in the North Sea represented a breakout and that the Norway intelligence had been a ruse to conceal this. Undoubtedly influential in shaping Pound's assumptions was the navy's view, as enunciated by Vice Admiral Thomas (Hugh) Binney in October 1939, that "the main aim of C.in C. Home Fleet is to prevent ships escaping into the Atlantic." Moreover, Binney had warned:

"Any action by the German forces in the South Part of the North Ocean is likely to have for its object a diversion during which other forces may endeavour to escape."[18] Pound had already responded with considerable anxiety to this particular threat in the first week of the war. He wrote to Forbes after the event: "I must say I was obsessed by the idea that, if the Germans wished to make the heaviest attack on our trade, they must send out practically every available ship instead of keeping them or some of them in the North Sea."[19] The parallels between this evidence and the events of 7–8 April are manifest. When Pound returned on 7 April and learned that Edwards had been proposing that an invasion of Norway was imminent, he "went for [Edwards] like a pick-pocket for—as he put it—trying to lead the Naval staff away from the main objective which was the defense of the Atlantic trade routes."[20]

Rather than being entirely preoccupied with a breakout, Churchill is several times recorded as being receptive to the possibility there was more afoot: "In the early part of the evening [of 7 April] D.C.N.S. and the 1st Lord agree with me that this might well be part of the heralded attack on Norway, but when the Commander-in-Chief finally went to sea, 1st Sea Lord and D.C.N.S. strongly advised against ordering the Commander-in-Chief into the middle of the North Sea, which would have been the correct strategic position if our first care was Norway."[21] Another entry from the evening of 7 April (but probably written before Pound's return) has Churchill supporting Edwards' warnings about Norway with the declaration, "I believe the boy is right." Edwards wrote, "For a short while plans for dispositions to meet the possible Norwegian attack were in process of preparation."[22] This is supported by another, apparently overlooked, source. Roskill's handwritten "Transcript of RAB Edwards' Contemporary Notes on Norway" records the following about Churchill's reaction to Edwards' concerns over the movements of the Home Fleet during the evening of the seventh and morning of the eighth. It is apparent that this is another version of the events mentioned previously with the key difference being that at some point, probably after Pound's return, Phillips had a change of heart about the battle cruiser threat:

> WSC [Churchill] while still worried about Wilfred agreed (?) both CNS
> & DCNS were obsessed by the BC [battle cruiser] menace . . .

Then meetings and discussions went on all night. WSC disagreeing with C in Cs movements (to the North) & I confess I agree with WSC. C in C has gone off with (his fleet?) up North leaving the Norwegian menace uncovered. However they decide to leave the C in C to act as he thinks fit. Why we always interfere when we shouldn't and leave C in C alone when we ought to guide. They were all worn out.[23]

From the evidence of Edwards' diary, one must conclude Pound was the key decision maker and Churchill, apparently against his better judgment, deferred to the first sea lord on the vital issue of the battle cruiser breakout versus an invasion of Norway. This is not a picture of Churchill dominating proceedings but of Churchill wanting to undertake precautionary measures with the Home Fleet in defense of Norway and not being able to secure the support of his staff.

The timing of the order for disembarkation of the R4 forces has also been wrongly related. The misapprehension over this has helped sustain the historical view that Churchill and Pound made a premature and precipitate decision to discard Operation R4 for the bigger prize of the German battle cruisers.[24] As inaccurately, Churchill has been criticized for making this decision without consulting the MCC or the War Cabinet in a further demonstration of high-handedness.[25] Given the import of this criticism of Churchill, it is appropriate to consider the decisions that compromised the landing operations in some detail.

The first point to make is that two significant orders were given in relation to R4 forces, but only one involved disembarkation of troops.[26] The first was to meet the needs of the 2nd Cruiser squadron on evening of 7 April. Earlier that day, following a warning of a German battle-cruiser force heading north (Admiralty telegram [AT] 0808/7),[27] Commander of the Second Cruiser Squadron (CS2) Rear Admiral Frederick Edward-Collins raised steam in his force of three Polish destroyers and the light cruisers *Galatea* and *Arethusa* and informed Forbes he would be ready by midday if needed. Forbes had decided that there would be no movement in response to the enemy sightings until he had received reports of a bombing attack on the German force. Whatever the results of this attack, Forbes did not intend to use CS2 to pursue the enemy because at 11:59 a.m. he tasked Edward-Collins to act as "force R" as per the guidelines of Plan R4 and to deal with any seaborne expedition the Germans may send against Norway. He further instructed Edward-Collins' force be ready at two hours' notice from 4 a.m., 8 April.[28] These instructions soon changed when, at 2:20 p.m., 7 April, Forbes belatedly received the infamous AT 1259/7, which warned of an attack on Narvik and Jutland but was amended to suggest the intelligence was of doubtful value.

It has been generally assumed that Forbes accepted the qualification in this telegram and did not act in response to it. This assumption has helped skew the story of 7 April—including Churchill's involvement—toward the misunderstanding that all were focused on the battle-cruiser threat alone. In fact, Forbes acted wisely and decisively to the possibility the intelligence regarding Narvik might herald a wider threat to Norway. His first move was to reinforce substantially Edward-Collins' CS2 strike force R. His second was to bring forward the time of its departure. At 4:07 p.m. on 7 April, Forbes instructed Edward-Collins to leave port immediately. The four destroyers of D6, then supporting a convoy, were ready to join him and to sail to N 58°30', E 3°30'; they would arrive there at 7 a.m. on 8 April. This disposition would place Edward-Collins' force about sixty miles from Stavanger on the southwestern tip of Norway.[29] Forbes added to the CS2 force another light cruiser, HMS *Sheffield*, and four large Tribal-class destroyers.[30] This gave Edward-Collins a strike force against a threat to Norway totaling three light cruisers and eleven destroyers.

Within an hour and a half Forbes was compelled to make some difficult decisions that forced amendment to these plans. At 5:35 p.m. he received AT 1720/7, which belatedly updated news on the German battle-cruiser force heading north.[31] The force was now reported as two cruisers, one *Scharnhorst* class (battle cruiser), and ten destroyers. This was a much larger force than originally reported, and Forbes likely thought it would require a larger response from the Home Fleet.[32] He immediately ordered that available destroyers be ready to depart and gave numerous instructions for other preparations. At this point the Admiralty, specifically Phillips, sent Forbes AT 1808 (received by Forbes at 6:20 p.m.), which read, "Forces detailed for Plan R4 may be used as convenient to bring enemy surface forces to action."[33]

Over the next hour Forbes made several new dispositions. He rescinded his orders regarding *Sheffield* and the Tribals; these ships would no longer join Edward-Collins off Norway but would join Forbes in the pursuit of the German battle-cruiser force.[34] This left Edward-Collins short of the substantial force Forbes had intended to give him to deal with a possible threat against Norway. At this point CS2 was reduced to two light cruisers, three lesser Polish destroyers, and the four destroyers of D6, which, having arrived at Rosyth, required several hours to refuel. Moreover, there was now no possibility CS2 could be at the nominated position by 7:00 the next morning.

However, presumably as a substitute for *Sheffield* and the four Tribals, Forbes gave instructions at 7:15 p.m. for the eight destroyers of D4, which were in Rosyth in support of the First Cruiser Squadron (CS1) and their embarked *Rupert* forces, to raise steam to depart with CS2. Captain Edwards referred to these decisions and dispositions in his original diary entry of 7 April when he wrote, "Plan R4 to go 'by the board' in many cases in order to supply enough destroyers to meet other requirements."[35] This entry, coupled with several serious inconsistencies and contradictions in Edwards' postwar elaborations, has led historians, beginning with Roskill, to conclude the disembarkation of R4 forces occurred in the evening of 7 April as a result of Churchill and Pound's narrow-minded focus on the battle-cruiser problem. This interpretation is incorrect. Rather, it is apparent that one of the consequences of Phillips' AT 1808/7 was to facilitate the reinforcement of CS2, destined for the southern tip of Norway as a strike force in response to AT 1259/7, regarding the possible threat to this country. That Forbes and the Admiralty maintained the strike force component of R but forsook the landing component is best explained by concerns over Germany's large ships and the threat they offered to any vessel carrying soldiers. As for Pound, it is probable he had yet to return from his fishing trip and had no role in these decisions.

Where then did Churchill fit into these decisions? As noted, Edwards claimed he had been making some progress with Churchill and Phillips regarding Norway. The disposition of CS2 and its reinforcement is probably further evidence of this. It seems that Churchill, possibly Phillips, and certainly Forbes were taking precautionary action against a threat to Norway. It is difficult to assess the consequences of the decision to deny the landing forces embarked on the cruisers of CS1 their destroyer escort on the subsequent prosecution of the R4 plan. Had these subsequently crossed to

Norway—perhaps to Stavanger and Bergen—they would have been more exposed to enemy forces. However, given that CS2 was already in the region to act in support, the Admiralty decision to proceed with the R4 plan would not seem to have represented an undue risk. The decisions of the evening of 7 April were not terminal to R4; they did, however, suggest that the Admiralty might balk at sending amphibious forces to sea while Germany's big ships were about; indeed, this is precisely what happened.

When Admiral Forbes set off with the Home Fleet to intercept the German battle cruisers along their last known bearing, he had—with the support, or at least the acquiescence, of Churchill and Phillips—ensured that a powerful strike force had been disposed against possible action in Norway. It is important to note that Forbes had left alone the four large cruisers, their embarked forces, and the other R4 forces then in the Clyde, including the destroyer escorts. Had he been entirely preoccupied with the battle-cruiser threat, as was supposed by Captain Edwards, it is unlikely he would have done so. A similar observation can be made regarding Churchill and Phillips.

As earlier discussion pointed out, this acknowledgment of the Norwegian threat stalled with the arrival of Pound around 8 p.m. in the evening. Thereafter, as Edwards' diary tells us, Churchill continued to express anxiety over the northerly movement of Forbes' fleet, but Pound was unwilling to direct him otherwise; his focus remained firmly on the possibility of a breakout. Nevertheless, Pound did nothing at this point to alter Forbes' instructions to CS2, which was still destined for southern Norway. Presumably, he too deemed it an appropriate precautionary measure, although he might also have viewed CS2 disposition as a potential blocking force against the German forces already at sea should they attempt to return home.

This explanation of events shares little in common with current assessments. The evidence suggests that during the afternoon and into the evening of 7 April, Churchill became increasingly alert to the possibility of a threat to Norway and acquiesced in several dispositions that reflected this—most notably, Forbes' decision to direct a strong force of cruisers and destroyers to the southern tip of Norway to act in the capacity of a strike force. Churchill's anxiety continued into the evening, when Forbes set off to the northward, but against his better judgment, the first lord deferred to his first sea lord's supervision of operational matters. Nowhere to be found in this picture is the big gun and battleship man dominating discussion and transfixed by the prospect of a second Jutland.

The second decision regarding the R4 force—the disembarkation orders for Rosyth and the Clyde—was more significant. The CS1 war diary records that the orders for the Rosyth force were made verbally by the commander in chief, Rosyth, to Commander of CS1 Vice Admiral John Cunningham at approximately 11:30 a.m. on 8 April and that this was confirmed later in AT 1216/8.[36] At around this time, instructions were given to the cruisers and destroyers then in the Clyde and destined for Trondheim to abandon their transports and head to Scapa Flow.[37] Despite Roskill's assertions to the contrary, it is certain Edwards made the call to commander in chief, Rosyth, and was instructed to do so by Pound. Edwards recorded in his diary, "We needs go and remove all the soldiers from the R.4 plan ships, or rather I was told to call up Rosyth and tell them to instruct C.S.I. to do so in the morning." Edwards spoke out against the decision, but for a second time in as many days, he was reprimanded by Pound: "I protested but received a curt answer from the 1st Sea Lord and also a 'bottle' for trying to suborn the staff away from their proper objective—the Battlecruiser."[38] Churchill's involvement in the decision is unclear, but it is likely he was aware of it and agreed to it.

The view that the decision was made while Churchill was in denial about a German threat to Norway is incorrect. The decision to disembark the R4 forces and to abandon the Clyde transports coincided almost precisely with an Admiralty telegram to Forbes and others that warned the German threat to Narvik noted in AT 1259/7 might be true. This coincidence presents a new and critically important historical question. What possessed Churchill to acquiesce in a decision that neutralized the landing forces of R4 at the time he was presented with the conditions and circumstances for which R4 had been conceived?

There were four influences at work. The first is the German battle-cruiser force itself. Churchill would not have wanted soldiers and transports on the high seas while this was about. Second, the cruisers at Rosyth no longer had a destroyer force in support, and this might have caused extra anxiety. Third, as was evident in his action to this point, Churchill was being cautious in challenging the recommendations of his sea lords. Fourth, and most important, Churchill had concluded that by the late morning of 8 April, he had been presented with a scenario that did not require the R4 forces and was potentially better than that for which he had planned. This was because he had unwisely convinced himself that the sole target of German aggression along Norway's western coastline was Narvik.[39] The intelligence conveyed to the Admiralty on 6 April and repeated to the commander in chief, Home Fleet, on 7 April stated the Germans intended to occupy Narvik and Jutland. No other objectives were mentioned. Churchill was taking this at face value. At the War Cabinet of 11:30 a.m., 8 April, during which Churchill related the latest naval dispositions, including the decision to disembark the R4 forces, there was no mention of a possible threat to southern or central Norway. During discussion of the German objective, the only suggestions recorded were that the German Narvik assault might presage their occupation of Lulea once the ice melted, and *Gneisenau* might head for the trade routes after the forces had been landed. The disembarkation order for the R4 forces came at a time when the Admiralty mistakenly believed it was dealing with these prospects alone. This is the best explanation for the fact that despite knowledge of the threat to Narvik, the disembarkation continued uninterruptedly. When Churchill spoke at the War Cabinet, the disembarkation order was eminently reversible had any member of the cabinet questioned the Admiralty's assumptions, but none did. The disembarkation order was made at a time when Churchill believed British forces were already well placed for several great successes. Of Churchill's demeanor at this time, Ironside recorded, "He was like a boy this morning describing what he had done to meet the Germans."[40]

Churchill's assessment of the situation was not unreasonable given his understanding of the existing naval dispositions. At midday on 8 April he believed the Royal Navy had substantial forces, including a battle cruiser, between Narvik and the German forces converging upon it; courtesy of Forbes' forward thinking, the Navy soon had CS2 and fifteen destroyers operating as a strike force at the southern tip of Norway against any further threats from the south and as a bar to a retreat of the German forces from the north. Farther south were British submarines, recently reinforced as a precautionary measure. Additionally, there were the substantial forces of the Home Fleet. The freeing of the CS1 heavy cruisers was intended to ensure the location and destruction of as much as possible of the German force at sea.[41] However, circumstances were not as they seemed, and Churchill was destined not to meet the Germans as he expected. The catalyst for failure was not the disembarkation of the R4 forces, but the persistence of Churchill's belief the only threat to Norway was at Narvik. This misreading of events, combined with and influenced by a series of operational misjudgments—some forgivable, others less so—ensured that Trondheim, Bergen, and Narvik, one after the other, were opened to the enemy and produced the disaster of the Norwegian campaign.

The Vagaries of War
Narvik

One of the first misfortunes to begin unraveling Churchill's optimistic appraisal of events was a product of poor communications, and there would be more to follow. Barely one half hour before the Admiralty warned the fleet that Narvik was a possible target for the German forces, it instructed the mine-laying force in the Vestfjord (D20) and the destroyer force patrolling the field (D2) to join the battle cruiser HMS *Renown*, which had been acting in support.[42] This instruction has baffled historians because *Renown* was, by this time, some distance from Vestfjord proceeding to the support of the destroyer, *Glowworm*, which was to be sunk by the German heavy cruiser, *Hipper*.[43] In joining the *Renown*, therefore, the mining forces would leave Narvik open to the Germans.[44]

The instruction has been viewed as utterly foolish, and Churchill and Pound have received much criticism for it.[45] The criticism is undeserved because neither Churchill nor anyone at the Admiralty, nor even Forbes with the High Fleet, was aware that *Renown* was no longer standing by at Vestfjord.[46] This was because either Vice Admiral William (Jock) Whitworth had not sent a communication regarding his intentions to go to the assistance of the *Glowworm* or it had not been received.[47]

The most likely reason for the Admiralty directive was to concentrate all available forces against the threat from the south. Although *Renown* was always intended to remain in close proximity to the D2 destroyers after the mines had been laid, the D20 minelayers were to withdraw and, at the time of the Admiralty telegram, were already on their way out of the Vestfjord to rendezvous with another force much farther to the southwest.[48] Evidently, the Admiralty now wished this force to remain to help protect the fjord.

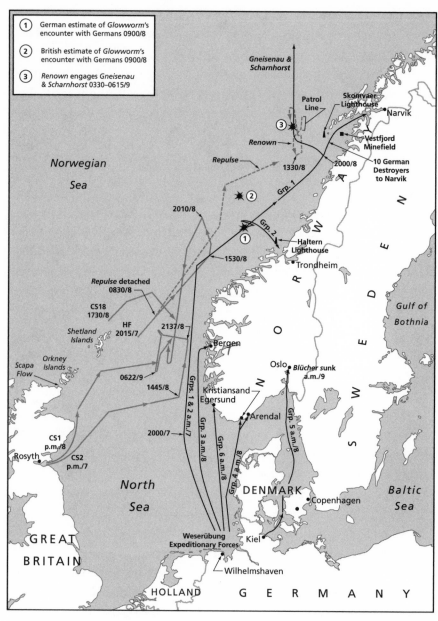

Map 7.1. The German Invasion of Norway. Naval movements, 7–9 April. Flawed assumptions, poor decision making, faulty naval dispositions, and the interminable fog of war ensured that, despite Britain's belief that it controlled the seas, the Germans secured all their major objectives in the early hours of 9 April 1940.

These circumstances also explain why the Admiralty instructed the destroyers to move *Renown* rather than the other way around; this instruction has been a source of more criticism. In any event it made much sense for the many to converge on the one. Although it is always assumed to be the case, it is not clear if D2 immediately left the Vestfjord to find *Renown* as instructed. If it did, it would likely have moved to *Renown*'s midmorning patrol lines before its journey south to *Glowworm*. This move would not have left D2 far distant from Vestfjord. To this extent the withdrawal of the destroyers from Vestfjord at this juncture was far from critical; the misfortune was that they were subsequently not directed to return until too late.

Ignorant of all this drama and confusion, Churchill was more than hopeful the German forces heading north would be intercepted in or near the Vestfjord. At the late morning War Cabinet meeting of 8 April, he declared of the German forces heading to Narvik: "It was calculated that if they were unopposed, they would reach there about 10 p.m.; but they would no doubt be engaged by His Majesty's ships *Renown* and *Birmingham*, and the Destroyers which had been laying the minefield, and an action might take place very shortly."[49] Churchill added, cautiously, that this "should not be on terms unfavourable to us." He had no idea that *Renown* did not know where *Birmingham* was, that neither ship was in the most likely path of German forces heading to Narvik, and that soon neither would be with the mine-laying force.

There was, of course, still much time to save the situation and mask Vestfjord with a substantial force against the enemy. But Whitworth's muddled thinking and unwelcomed bad weather, rather than the Admiralty or Churchill, stopped this happening. When at 11:14 a.m. Whitworth received the Admiralty warning that the German threat to Narvik was possibly true, he might have wondered why, only a little earlier, the Admiralty had given instructions that left the Vestfjord open to this threat. He might not have understood that neither the Admiralty nor Forbes knew where he was. Forbes only learned Whitworth's approximate position at 12:34 p.m., when he received a message sent by Whitworth at 11:06 a.m. giving his position at 10:30 a.m.

If Whitworth's rush to the south to support *Glowworm* had made the convergence of the mining forces on *Renown* difficult, his response to the warning regarding Narvik now made this much more so. Rather than turn north and regroup with the destroyer force, Whitworth changed his course to the southwest, where he anticipated he would be in position to intercept this new threat to Narvik at 1:30 p.m. At 12:46 p.m. Whitworth gave D2 his anticipated location at 1:30 p.m. and instructed these forces to spread themselves to receive either *Renown* or the enemy. It is difficult to determine precisely where D2 would have been spreading its forces because details of D2 movements at this time have not been found by this writer. This force might have remained in Vestfjord or returned to *Renown*'s patrol lines of earlier that day; it was indeed at the latter point that *Renown* and the destroyers met later in the day.

Whitworth now had a change of heart. Having reached his desired interception position at 1:30 p.m., he belatedly concluded that in declining visibility and with only one destroyer in support, he had little or no chance of finding the enemy. Instead, he turned to the northeast to rendezvous with his mine-laying force off Skoemvaar Lights (west of Vestfjord), where he had begun his southward journey five hours earlier. Despite the warning about Narvik, the most likely route to Vestfjord remained open to the Germans.

Despite all the confusion Whitworth's search to the southeast had presented a real opportunity to locate the German force heading to Narvik. It would certainly have neutralized the unfortunate consequences of the Admiralty's decision to direct the destroyers to *Renown* while the latter was off in search of *Glowworm*. Had Whitworth informed his destroyers to sweep toward his proposed point of interception, it would have manifestly increased the prospect of Whitworth achieving his objective. This would not necessarily have been to the advantage of his ship or his destroyers. He would have been converging on a stronger force, and unlike in the circumstances of the following morning, when *Renown* clashed with an evasive *Scharnhorst* and *Gneisenau*, Commander Günther Lütjens would have been compelled to fight to protect his destroyers and their embarked military force.

The reasons Whitworth offered for surrendering his search for the Narvik force are not readily reconciled with the availability of his own destroyer force. It is possible that wisdom got the better part of valor, or he lacked conviction that any force had Narvik as an objective. Certainly, there appears to be a stubborn reluctance to take the Narvik threat seriously. There is no evidence to suggest that as Whitworth turned northward, he had this threat in mind. He was close to, but certainly not in the likely path of, a force heading to Narvik, nor as much as we can estimate, were his destroyers. This would not be the end of his carelessness.

At 3:15 p.m. Whitworth received information that a German force had been discovered moving west off Trondheim. The force was wrongly identified as a battle cruiser, two cruisers, and two destroyers; it was in fact Group 2, the breakaway force, including *Hipper* and four destroyers that were marking time before entering the Trondheim fjord the following morning. Whitworth set about assessing this new intelligence. He believed this force was likely that which had attacked *Glowworm* (and was correct) and might have one of four possible objectives: (1) it might return to Germany because *Glowworm* had discovered the force moving in the southward direction just before it fell silent; (2) it might be headed to Iceland, with a breakout to the Atlantic thereafter, because it currently appeared to be bearing westward; (3) it might be moving to Murmansk, where Whitworth thought there might be a German tanker available to refuel the smaller vessels in the force; or (4) it might be headed, as part of a larger force, to Narvik. Left unclear was approximately where Whitworth imagined the rest of the force: north or south of this force off Trondheim. Just like Forbes (who will be discussed later), Whitworth gave not a moment's thought to the possibility this was a breakaway destined for Trondheim.

Whitworth concluded that with the Home Fleet to the south, he did not have to worry about this possibility. Neither did he pursue the Iceland alternative; this might have been because the Home Fleet and *Repulse* squadron changed bearing to address this threat. Instead, he decided to defend against a northward move, although not, in the first instance, the threat to Narvik that concerned at least some elements in the Admiralty. Rather than address, once and for all, the open door to the Vestfjord, he proposed his destroyers adopt a patrol to the west of the Lofoten Islands (and Vestfjord) with *Renown* fifty miles farther north.

These dispositions disconcerted the Admiralty, which at 5:22 p.m. sent a telegram warning Whitworth that the force discovered off Trondheim was only part of the force sighted the evening before and that, therefore, the other part might still be destined for Narvik. Only a few minutes before Whitworth had finally rejoined his destroyers twenty miles southwest of Skomvaer Lights and was proceeding to farther north and west of this position, away from the Vestfjord.

Two hours later an exasperated Admiralty explicitly instructed that Whitworth's task was to concentrate his forces to intercept any German force proceeding to Narvik. Time was certainly running out to address this threat. Tragically, weather conditions had now reach gale force, and Whitworth decided to remain west of the Lofotens until the bad weather abated. He thereby surrendered his last hope of intercepting the Narvik destroyers and, instead, found himself confronting *Scharnhorst* and *Gneisenau* early in the morning of the ninth, after they had peeled off from the destroyers. Whitworth's own destroyers were strewn about well to the west of Vestfjord and were ill prepared to rectify the situation. Thus were the circumstances that gave Narvik to the enemy.

Trondheim

In many respects the episodes surrounding Trondheim were the most unfortunate, not least because subsequent Allied control of Trondheim would have offered some prospect of building a satisfactory military response to the German invasion. Forbes had two opportunities to act against Group 2 before it occupied Trondheim. The *Glowworm* incident again played an important and inadvertent role in the first of these.

When Forbes had learned of the threat to *Glowworm* earlier in the morning, his force was some three hundred miles south of the location provided by the ship. He directed the battle cruiser *Repulse*, along with the cruiser *Penelope* and four destroyers, to proceed at high speed to provide support. This move offered the possibility that *Repulse* would have discovered *Hipper* and the rest of Group 2 at some point in the afternoon. After the sinking of *Glowworm*, not only did *Hipper* spend almost an hour in efforts to rescue the British ship's crew but the Weserubung plan required that Group 2 remain in the vicinity for many more hours before entering the Trondheim fjord in the early morning of the ninth. Unfortunately, *Repulse* was advancing on a position at least sixty miles farther north of the position where *Glowworm* and *Hipper* had made contact, and this was likely sufficient for the two forces to miss each other. In his most recent book Geirr Haarr has argued that during its contact with the German forces, *Glowworm* provided the wrong latitude, or at least the information given was incorrectly decoded. There are strong reasons to believe Haarr is correct. The Germans record the *Glowworm-Hipper* contact at a similar longitude but farther south. The Home Fleet war diaries also hint at an error.[50] Had *Glowworm*'s correct coordinates been known and had Forbes not directed the *Repulse* force to head west when Group 2 was subsequently discovered bearing west, a clash between the *Repulse* force and *Hipper* would have been probable and the story of the Norwegian campaign very different.

The second opportunity for success against Group 2 was offered at 2 p.m. on the eighth, when an aircraft discovered this force but wrongly identified its composition. Given Group 2's proximity to Trondheim and the threat to Narvik that was by then animating the Admiralty, the Allies might readily have concluded this was an invasion force destined for Trondheim with a breakaway group advancing on Narvik. As we have seen, the Admiralty subsequently grasped the latter but failed, along with everyone else, to deduce its true objective. Forbes, however, concluded it was another force altogether—perhaps because of its erroneous composition—and that its objective was a breakout to the Atlantic.[51] He adjusted his progress to the north and then northwest for interception. Even more unfortunately, he instructed *Repulse*, *Penelope*, and their destroyer support to do the same, although this force was subsequently redirected to the support of *Renown* off Narvik. Along with *Repulse* and *Penelope* went the best existing prospect for the interception and destruction of *Hipper*.

Forbes has rightly been much criticized for this unfortunate error in judgment, but there were circumstances in mitigation. First was the mistaken identification of a battle cruiser off Trondheim (rather than *Hipper*, a heavy cruiser), a prime candidate for a breakout. Second, when discovered, this force was moving westward. Third, despite the warning about Narvik, the prevailing assumption was that Narvik alone was at risk in the north. Thus, rather than imagine that Narvik and Trondheim were at risk, Forbes concluded that Narvik was at risk in combination with a breakout of one or two battle cruisers in the north. A fourth factor in the mitigation of Forbes' reasoning, including his assumption that the Trondheim force was an entirely new force, was *Glowworm*'s incident and the erroneous coordinates.

It was always reasonable to assume that *Glowworm* had clashed with elements of the large German forces (Group 1 and 2 in company, or recently separated) that had set Forbes off to the north the previous evening and that, by the late morning of the eighth, were considered a serious threat to Narvik and the Atlantic. Forbes, however, was unable to reconcile the previous evening's coordinates for the large force advancing north with those of the force that attacked *Glowworm* in the midmorning of the eighth. Nor could he reconcile this with the force newly discovered off Trondheim. By his reckoning the large force sighted the night before could not have advanced that far north to attack *Glowworm* at that latitude.[52] His conclusion was that this must be a second force. We now know that his deduction about the northward movement of Lutjen's force was sound. It was probably too much to ask that rather than conjuring a second force, he conclude *Glowworm* was actually attacked farther south. Also, given the presence of a battle cruiser and the westward movement of this force, it is not unreasonable that he drew the conclusion he did.

Censuring Forbes, along with Pound and Churchill, on the issue of a breakout—largely incorrectly in the case of the first lord—has perhaps failed to adequately acknowledge the dilemma with which all were faced. At no time during 7–8 April were circumstances such that effort could be concentrated on an invasion over a breakout. The advantages to be gained by the destruction of the German naval forces were considerable and could not be ignored. Further, a successful breakout would have been an enormous drain on British resources and would certainly have made the subsequent conduct of the Norwegian campaign much more difficult.

Despite all these concessions offered in support of Forbes' assessment of events, he surely should have sent a naval force to Trondheim to investigate more closely and should have masked Trondheim against further possibilities. Forbes ought to have appreciated—just as Churchill ought to have—that the occupation of Narvik by the Germans made little sense without control of Trondheim and perhaps the whole of Norway. Forbes ignored any potential threat to Trondheim, but neither Churchill nor the Admiralty gave him cause to do otherwise.

This was not the end of the comedy of errors, or the end of the consequences of misreading events off Trondheim. At 8 p.m. on 8 April, Forbes gave up the pursuit of the force he imagined was breaking out to the west and turned due south in response to Admiralty instructions (AT 1842, received by Forbes at 8:10 p.m.) that his objective was now to prevent forces in the north returning and to intercept other forces moving northward off southern Norway. He was so willing to undertake this dramatic turnabout, and indeed had already begun to do so, because he believed the breakout force had likely eluded him by movements to his south and east and was now racing for home closer to the Norwegian coast. Indeed, it was probably Forbes' own deductions that prompted the Admiralty to direct him to prevent northern forces returning. Of course, no such movements were in train. Group 2 was still biding its time off Trondheim and with not a single British vessel to be found.

Forbes' belief that the force discovered off Trondheim was now heading for home set in motion decisions and dispositions that undid all the good he had done with his placement of CS2 as a strike force between Stavanger and Bergen. The result was the completion of the German trifecta along the coast of Norway: a free passage to Bergen for Group 3. These events as they unfolded in afternoon and evening of 8 April (as with most events of that day) had nothing to do with ignorance of the German threat to Norway; this had been understood since the late morning, although for much of that afternoon understood primarily in the context of a threat to Narvik. Nor were they a product of a preoccupation with a breakout; this anxiety bore only slightly, if at all, on the decision and dispositions made. Rather, it was the deep, dark fog of war at work.

Bergen

The decisive influence on events in the evening of 8 April were the phantom forces imagined by Forbes and the Admiralty and addressed in the AT 1842: Forbes' breakout force was now breaking for home, and others were moving northward from the Great Belt. Still ignorant of Group 3, the Admiralty believed the southern forces, or elements of them, might have Bergen and Stavanger as their objectives. The worry existed that the two might rendezvous as early as 5 a.m. on 9 April about 60° north (AT 2102/8), although to what end was anyone's guess. To these threats Forbes directed his attention. As for the threat to Narvik in the north, this continued to cause much concern but appeared adequately covered by Whitworth's force, with *Repulse* on its way to help. A threat to Trondheim, if it had ever figured in his mind, was forgotten.

The challenges facing Forbes were considerable. He was only guessing at the whereabouts of the breakout force, and the Admiralty's assessment of movements off southern Norway was just as speculative. Fortunately, CS2, still south of Bergen and the closest force to the Norwegian coast, was well placed to intercept either threat, should it develop. CS1 was also about, as was a French squadron. As it turned out, CS2 was also well placed to intercept Group 3, which, unknown to anyone, was still silently moving northward to Bergen. Unfortunately, although CS2, the other cruisers, and their destroyer escorts were a great boon, they were also an anxiety until Forbes arrived in support against the two phantoms believed to be bearing on them. This fear ultimately determined the redisposition of CS2 in the late evening of the eighth, which gave the only German force in the area—Group 3—a clear run at Bergen.

In the first instance the Admiralty's focus was on the northern phantom force. Included in AT 1842 was a recommendation that CS1 conduct a northward sweep from its position west of CS2 while the latter acted as a strike force between E 1°50' and E 2°35' at its existing latitude. As part of this screen, the Admiralty proposed that Admiral Geoffrey Layton, CS18, also at sea, patrol identical lines of longitude farther north. CS2's disposition, still to the south of Bergen, suggested the Admiralty was also concerned about protecting Bergen, but the squadron was too far to the west to intercept enemy forces destined for this port.

It was Forbes' prerogative to amend the Admiralty's dispositions, and he did so almost immediately. He instructed CS2, CS1, and French cruiser *Emile Bertin* to form an east-west patrol line by 5 a.m., 9 April. The cruisers were to operate in pairs, twenty miles apart, and at 5 a.m. were to advance NNW until they joined his fleet. CS2's *Galatea* and *Arethusa* were the farthest east of these pairs and would now be even closer to the Norwegian coast and Bergen. This new disposition placed Group 3 in considerable peril. At some point in the morning, *Arethusa* might have been within twenty miles of the Bergen force. Even had Group 3 passed safely by, CS2 would still have been in close proximity at the nominated time for Group 3's landing at Bergen, and this might have made an important difference to events there.

Although Forbes' patrol line manifestly increased the threat to Group 3, this was not its primary purpose; it was only an unintended consequence. After all, Group 3 was unknown to him. The patrol line's primary purpose was to maximize the chances of locating the northern phantom force while gradually concentrating the Allied cruisers for their protection and, presumably, in preparation for major operations should the northern and southern forces unite.

Forbes' plan was insufficiently cautious for the Admiralty. Despite AT 1862 having advised something similar, the Admiralty now feared Forbes' weak and dispersed cruiser patrol line would "be caught between two enemy forces with our battle fleet 135 miles away" (AT 2252/8). The cruisers were instructed to converge and then move immediately to the Home Fleet. Thus, at the last moment, was the way opened for Group 3. The Admiralty instructions were as inexplicable as they were extraordinary. Had the northern force existed and had it been moving south as was thought possible, it would have been given an easy passage south.

During the early morning of 9 April, the cruiser squadrons slowly joined Forbes as he continued south. Admiral Layton's CS18 was the first to find him, and CS1, CS2, and *Emile Bertin* joined him about 9:30 a.m. By the time this enormous force was united farther to the south and west than CS2 had been the night before, the Germans had been in Bergen for many hours. When Forbes and the Admiralty belatedly sent a cruiser and destroyer force to attack the Germans at Bergen (a subject for the next chapter), the force faced a northeastern movement into heavy seas before the excursion was canceled and substituted with an aerial assault. As for Trondheim, nothing could be done. The last hope was Narvik, but this had already been lost; the Allies just did not know it yet.

Thus were the circumstances that, one after the other, opened Trondheim, Narvik, and Bergen to the Germans. There was no German force escaping south, nor one attempting a breakout to the northwest, nor a substantial force moving north; the forces sighted in the bight all had much more southerly objectives: Egersund, Kristiansand, and Oslo.

Such were the vagaries of war, on which success and failure were finely balanced and which defied the apportionment of blame and responsibility. These events had their foundations in two errors of judgment: Churchill's assumption that Narvik alone was threatened by German forces and assumptions surrounding a German breakout to the Atlantic. Perhaps more accurately, it was the belief these events were occurring in combination that was important. But it is not to these errors of judgment that one can directly and absolutely attribute the subsequent failures at Narvik, Trondheim, and Bergen. Circumstances off Norway only became irredeemable well after it was apparent that Norway was under threat and well after concerns about a breakout had ceased to guide decision making. Trondheim and Bergen were redeemable for a long time after the threat to Narvik was understood. Bergen was redeemable long after it was evident all of Norway was threatened. The cause of failure at Trondheim and Bergen was not that the navy was too late but that circumstances developed in a way that encouraged Forbes and Pound, like Churchill, to believe they had these objectives well covered. In addressing the threats as they arose, they imagined they were always protecting the vital points along Norway's west coast. In truth, and in every respect, they repeatedly exposed them to the German onslaught.

What, if anything, could have altered this disastrous chain of events? One is ineluctably drawn to the conclusion that had Churchill recognized earlier that, whatever the early intelligence suggested, it was unlikely Narvik alone was under threat, the results at Trondheim and Bergen would have been very different. A less laser-like focus on Narvik would have encouraged a different perspective toward the German forces discovered off Trondheim. Although Forbes might still have rushed off to the north-northwest, an effort might have been made to mask Trondheim, and this would have discovered Group 2. Had this occurred, Bergen would also have been saved, and perhaps Stavanger too. The specter of the southward movement of the Trondheim phantom, which so influenced the dispositions off Bergen and, by degrees, opened this port to Group 3, would never have developed.

We might return for a moment to the question of the premature disembarkation of the R4 forces and ask at which point, if any, these military forces might have made a difference in a way that the naval forces freed of them did not. This is a step into counterfactual history and is fraught, but some reasonable claims might be made. Likely no difference would have been achieved at Narvik. The forces destined for Trondheim were never intended to move until two days after the first British landings, so these do not have a place in this consideration of the might-have-beens. As for Bergen, there was time enough to land a force there, but CS2 would have done all that was necessary for success against Group 3 without the R4 forces. Had the R4 forces been available in the afternoon or evening of 8 April, they might have been landed, but would this have occurred in the circumstances that developed and subsequently caused the Admiralty to withdraw all the cruiser forces from the area? Had the R4 forces been landed and Group 3 subsequently destroyed, or turned about, would this have made a significant difference to the campaign? It is surely doubtful the occupation of Bergen would have proved of great advantage to the Allies. Given the dominance of German airpower that far south, it was never likely these landings were sustainable; reinforcement would have been difficult and so, too, an eventual evacuation.[53]

Possibly the wisest and most propitious amendment to the action taken by the Admiralty on the evening of the eighth would have been to direct the CS2 force into Bergen fjords rather than to the Home Fleet. This would have successfully masked Bergen from Group 3 and protected CS2 from the two phantoms until Forbes' arrival. In this scenario the R4 forces would not have been needed, although any subsequent landings of military forces would have been highly problematic.

There is one final element to the disaster of 7–8 April that must be addressed in any assessment of culpability and responsibility of these vital two days. This is the appallingly inept handling of the crisis by the Norwegians themselves. Haarr records that soon after the 11:30 a.m. 8 April War Cabinet meeting, the Admiralty requested a meeting with a Norwegian envoy "regarding a matter of utmost importance." The Norwegian vice consul was subsequently informed that German operations against Narvik were suspected and that their forces could arrive before midnight on 8 April. This information was conveyed to Foreign Minister Halvdan Koht by phone from London at 3 p.m., but he did not act on it because he believed "the British Navy would take care of it" and, in any event, there were Norwegian naval forces and army units at Narvik that could deal with the threat.[54] A subsequent Admiralty telegram arrived at the Norwegian Foreign Office at 6 p.m. and was copied to Norwegian naval staff, where it arrived at 7:05 p.m. Despite these communications the Norwegians did little. They showed a similar indifference to warnings in the midafternoon of the eighth, when Bergen was also under threat. Still, the British government and, more particularly, the Foreign Office and Admiralty—the latter even through Churchill himself—ought to have done more to rouse the Norwegians. No doubt this process would have been complicated by the British mine-laying operation that had taken place in the early morning of the eighth, but a more vigorous attempt should have been made. That stronger warnings were not given is perhaps best explained by Churchill's conviction the Royal Navy would intercept the German forces and had matters in hand.

Conclusions

Churchill's performance as first lord in the days preceding the German landings in Norway leaves much to be desired. However, his shortcomings were not a product of bombast, bullying, and the domination of events—all of which are central to the existing assessments—but of a failure of imagination, poor deduction and analysis, and for a time, a seriously misplaced single-mindedness. His shortcomings were, in stark contrast to existing assumptions, also a result of a willingness to defer to—rather than to interfere in—the recommendations and advice of Pound and his naval staff on critical operational matters. On occasion a more assertive Churchill would have made a significant difference.

This chapter has challenged and, hopefully, dismissed the accepted emphasis of most historical analysis in explaining these themes: the centrality of a preoccupation with a breakout to the Atlantic, ignorance of a threat to Norway, and the disembarkation of the R4 forces. It has been contended that failure in Norway can never be satisfactorily or adequately explained through the personal failings of Churchill, Pound, or Forbes. Misfortune and misadventure, not readily accounted in terms of blame and responsibility, played their critical parts. If one is to search for Churchill's unique culpability and the element of his reasoning that exposes him to greatest criticism, it is his assumption, for much of 8 April, that Narvik alone was exposed to the German threat. This appears to have made a decisive difference.

EIGHT

NORWAY, PART 2

Fighting the Campaign

ollowing the failure to prevent the German occupation of all the key points along the Norwegian coast, the Allies opened the second chapter of the Norwegian campaign with the effort to retake them. This involved naval action at Narvik and Bergen and, subsequently, landings at various points along the coast to facilitate the capture of Narvik in the north and the city port of Trondheim in central Norway. Within three weeks Allied forces had abandoned central Norway, but they finally captured Narvik in early June and promptly evacuated the town as the fighting in France reached its climax.

Churchill is accused of imposing his strategic vision and generally making an unfortunate contribution to this indecisive, opportunistic, and chaotic campaign. Inept personal intervention in naval operations and indecision over the order in which the ports were to be retaken are focal points of criticism of his role. Narvik was initially given priority, but within several days focus was redirected to Trondheim. It is generally contended that the initial attention on Narvik was a result of Churchill's preoccupation with Swedish ore and that he entirely ignored the wider strategic requirements of a campaign to save Norway.[1] When focus was redirected to Trondheim, a switch for which Churchill is often held responsible, this served only to divide Allied resources and make impossible the achievement of either objective.

This chapter will consider the merit of these criticisms and assess Churchill's contribution to the misfortunes and failures of the Norwegian campaign. His role will be considered alongside those of other key players in the context of a challenging and rapidly changing strategic, political, and operational environment. This context is essential for an accurate and fair assessment of Churchill's performance, and it will be analyzed here through the six phases of the campaign.

Playing Catch-Up: Naval Operations in Bergen and Narvik

With the greater part of the British fleet at sea, efforts were begun to redeem the situation along the Norwegian coast. All plans for preemptive landings were in disarray; inevitably naval action or air operations—from distant Britain or from HMS *Furious*—were the only offensive options possible. Initially, instructions were issued to prevent consolidation at Narvik, Trondheim, and Bergen, but this would disperse forces and expose them piecemeal to the large German ships, the whereabouts of which were unknown. New orders were given to concentrate on Bergen and Narvik.

In the influential work of Roskill and Barnett, the subsequent naval operation against Bergen has been characterized as a missed opportunity and that against Narvik as a tragic error of judgment. Each unfortunate episode is attributed to the unwelcomed interference of Churchill and Pound, who as usual are viewed as making decisions in unison.[2] However, as in much analysis of this time, the culpability of each is likely overstated; their decisions were not unreasonable in the circumstances, and the negative consequence of their input is not as clear as claimed.

Like Churchill and Pound at the Admiralty, Admiral Forbes understood the urgent need to act at Bergen and Trondheim (Narvik had adequate forces nearby), and at 6:20 a.m. on 9 April, he indicated his intention to send two cruisers and six destroyers to attack the enemy off Bergen (the first of the cruiser squadrons had just joined him). Forty-five minutes later he added he could send aircraft from carrier *Furious* sometime on the tenth. Coincidentally, in a telegram marked 8:20 a.m. (and received at 8:45), the Admiralty requested Forbes prepare a plan to attack Bergen, assuming defenses were still in the hands of the Norwegians. Forbes' original proposal was approved at 10:25, and several minutes later he was informed that reconnaissance confirmed at least one Koln-class cruiser present. Forty minutes later, with the arrival of the other cruiser squadrons (CS1 and CS2), Forbes added two more cruisers and one more destroyer to his Bergen force; the cruisers would block the two exits to the fjord while the seven destroyers advanced on Bergen from different entrances. These ships departed at 11:25 a.m. Forbes informed the Admiralty of their departure, although not the reinforcement, and at 12:30 he received a prompt warning in reply that it could no longer be assumed Bergen defenses were still under Norwegian control. In a telegram marked 1:57 p.m. (and received at 2:38), the Admiralty canceled the attack. Another telegram subsequently explained this decision had been based on Forbes' earlier reference to using aircraft from *Furious* the following day. The Admiralty recommended this plan proceed, with *Warspite* in support. Evidently, the Admiralty had concluded the risks of advancing the attack with surface craft outweighed the risks of delay. To prevent the enemy's escape from Bergen, the Admiralty instructed Forbes to ensure that cruiser forces patrol both entrances; with the enemy so contained, the surface operations no longer appeared critical.[3] In addition to the proposed attack with *Furious* aircraft—fully endorsed at this time by Forbes—there was to be an attack by Bomber Command aircraft that afternoon and by skua aircraft early the following morning.[4]

Shortly after the cancellation of the surface attack, news came from reconnaissance aircraft that there were two cruisers at Bergen. Also present was the artillery ship *Bremse*. When the British attacked from the air the following day, they found only the damaged cruiser *Königsberg* and duly sunk it. Postwar analysis—including confirmation that Bergen defenses were not yet in German hands—has helped characterize the "missed opportunity" of Bergen and invited censure of Churchill and Pound, but the notion of a missed opportunity is dubious at best. A positive outcome of a clash between seven British destroyers and two German cruisers with *Bremse* in support was possible but by no means likely. Had the naval attack proceeded, the British cruisers were not to enter the fjord but merely stand guard; thus, had all the German craft been discovered on the ninth, there would have been seven destroyers fighting two cruisers, one of which was seriously damaged (although ready for battle). When Layton learned of a second German cruiser, he wrote, "the prospects of a successful attack now appeared distinctly less."[5] As for the operation itself, the squadron would not have arrived until dark and had to consider not only the enemy ships but also U-boats and mines. There was, too, the air threat during the remaining daylight hours. Indeed, along with the rest of Forbes' force, Layton's force was attacked by German aircraft on the afternoon of the ninth and lost the destroyer *Gurkha*.

After the German air attacks, Forbes proposed that the southern reaches of Norway be left to British submarines and aircraft. Given this recommendation it is probable that had the Admiralty not canceled Layton's attack, Forbes would have done so. Notably, Forbes also reneged on his decision to use *Furious* and her aircraft against the enemy forces at Bergen, contending the risks were too great. One can speculate if the risk would have been taken had *Furious* had its fighters on board. One can speculate too about the potential success at Bergen had *Furious* joined the fleet earlier; *Furious'* late arrival, as we know, was an error of judgment jointly shared by Churchill and Forbes, who were not inclined to give the carriers their due.

Overall, it is difficult to accept that the decision to cancel the Bergen operation deserves a place on the list of Admiralty failings induced by Churchill and Pound. Important evidence suggests the decision was prompted by the Admiralty's mistaken belief that Forbes had sent only the two cruisers and six destroyers he originally proposed to the fight; it was not aware of his reinforcement.[6] If this was the case, the Admiralty was surely acting wisely, even if its wisdom was based on a faulty reckoning of events. This episode highlights the hazards of Admiralty interference and the largely unexplored issue of radio communication problems. Several messages were sent and not received, and this created challenges for all concerned. There was also an apparent absence of communications at vital junctures.

As for Churchill's personal involvement and the degree to which he has been held culpable for this episode, it is likely he was not aware of the decision to rescind the Bergen operation until after the event. In a postwar defense, his principal private secretary, Eric Seal, claimed he recalled Churchill learning of the cancellation via Pound upon returning from a War Cabinet meeting.[7] Seal thought Pound himself had been pressured to agree to the cancellation by other staff. The timing of the telegram canceling the attack—1:57 p.m.— makes this recollection plausible. Immediately before the telegram was sent, Churchill was in a War Council meeting. As to the extensive discussion in the Admiralty about the Bergen attack, we have the evidence of Edwards' diary, which Roskill himself used.

Similar confusion, delay, and much criticized Admiralty input occurred during operations at Narvik. For much of 9 April, hope existed that the Germans had not occupied Narvik. Instructions were sent to prevent the Germans' reaching the port, but for the reasons outlined in the previous chapter, the available forces failed to do so. Efforts by Whitworth to redeem the situation were complicated by his clash with *Scharnhorst* and *Gneisenau* (the latter of which was assumed to be *Hipper*), which drew him even farther from the Vestfjord. During the chase his destroyers became detached, and he instructed them to return and guard the fjord. Further intelligence indicated a small German force had landed at Narvik. With *Renown* now somewhat distant, it fell to this destroyer force to advance on Narvik. The captain of D2, Bernard Warbuton-Lee, stopped at the pilot station on his way. He learned that six large destroyers and a submarine had passed during the night; there were, in fact, ten large enemy destroyers spread about the fjord. Warbuton-Lee forwarded this intelligence to Forbes, Whitworth, and the Admiralty and expressed his intention to attack at dawn. The Admiralty—almost certainly on this occasion Churchill and Pound together—replied that in the circumstances, only the captain could decide to attack. Warbuton-Lee set off early the following morning with four destroyers in support and surprised several German vessels in the process of refueling. Two were sunk, and three more were subsequently damaged. Unfortunately, the British force soon found itself under attack from other German destroyers emerging from the arms of the fjord. Warbuton-Lee's vessel was sunk as was another. Warbuton-Lee lost his life.

Postwar criticism points to the risks involved in Warbuton-Lee's force advancing against a larger enemy force while reinforcements (among them *Repulse* and the cruiser *Penelope*) were not far distant. Whitworth contemplated proposing that Warbuton-Lee await these ships but felt constrained by the Admiralty intercession, which had bypassed the chain of command. The might-have-been had reinforcement occurred has been built on the resounding success of the force that entered the fjord several days later with *Warspite* in support; the remaining German destroyers were all sunk without loss. Again, the criticisms of Churchill and Pound have lacked balance. There were always more than naval matters at stake in an early attack at Narvik and a more immediate need for action. The COS had already met and concluded that Narvik had to be captured as quickly as possible because the port was needed as a base for all other operations. Indeed, extensive naval preparations had been undertaken to put this port to full use. It was evidently desirable to attack the German forces before they completed the disembarkation of their matériel. As it was, Warbuton-Lee's easy early successes occurred because several destroyers were refueling. The earlier the fuel tanker present was sunk the better. Much time and opportunity had already been lost by the forces disposed at Narvik, and there is little doubt that the Admiralty's frustration over this had encouraged the direct communication with Warbuton-Lee; nevertheless, the decision to attack was left to him. Moreover, despite the direct intervention of the Admiralty, further suggestions from Forbes or Whitworth proposing the reinforcement of Warburton-Lee were surely not precluded, but none was forthcoming.

In assessing Churchill and Pound's culpability, it is important to recognize that neither was being as calculatedly reckless as has been suggested. Churchill (and presumably the Admiralty more generally) believed Warbuton-Lee was advancing with nine destroyers and not five. Warbuton-Lee elected to leave behind the minelayers, which had neither guns nor torpedoes aft. It is moot if knowledge of Warbuton-Lee's decision would have prompted the Admiralty to postpone the attack, but it is certain that Churchill at least believed the D2 captain was entering the fjord with superior numbers. No one knew of the ten destroyers, although all ought to have been aware that several German destroyers were unaccounted for and might have found their way to Narvik. To this extent, the responsibility for what subsequently took place should be more broadly spread than Churchill and Pound.

Regarding actions at Bergen, Churchill and Pound are criticized for not taking risks against a potentially superior force, and regarding actions at Narvik, they are criticized for doing the opposite. The criticism is always more than censure of the interference itself and involves judgment about the consequences of the interference. Yet the action taken in each circumstance appears eminently reasonable, even if the consequences were unfortunate. There was less cause to act immediately at Bergen, and there were considerable risks in doing so. At the Admiralty's behest plans (however unsuccessful) were put in place to prevent the enemy's escape and permit air attacks on the morrow. There was a pressing need to act at Narvik, and it seemed the forces available were as strong as or even superior to the enemy.

The censure of Churchill and Pound—particularly by Roskill and Barnett—is buttressed by somewhat too generous speculation as to the probable consequences had they not interfered, but rather than achieving greater success, immediate action at Bergen and delay at Narvik might have produced results that were no better and possibly much worse. Instead of focusing on the personal failings of Churchill and Pound and the perceived consequences of Admiralty interference, these events are, again, more appropriately assessed in the context of the vagaries and misfortunes of war.

Which Port First?

The first decision facing the Allies on 9 April was which port to retake first? There is no doubt that Churchill's primary interest in Norway was the capture of Narvik, but he shared this interest with most members of the War Cabinet, all of whom recognized the port's importance in the ore trade and its value as a possible route to the Gallivare ore fields. Nevertheless, it is not clear this was the determining influence in the War Cabinet's decision to make Narvik its first strategic objective. Although the War Cabinet had hitherto shown little interest in the people of Norway, once the extent of the German operations was understood, the British government's intentions were to regain as much of Norway as possible; moreover, there was never any doubt that a southern objective was highly desirable if this were to be achieved.[8] Whether this objective should be Bergen or Trondheim (or perhaps, initially, even Stavanger) was of some dispute. In making a judgment on this matter, the views of the French had also to be considered. They believed Narvik should receive priority initially but eventually redirected their attention to Trondheim in unison with the British government, although for slightly different reasons. Ultimately, in these very early days of the campaign, the decision to focus on Narvik was determined not by what was best for Norway or for Allied ore policies but by what was considered possible with the resources available.

At the War Cabinet meeting of 10 April, Chamberlain explained that Narvik would receive priority because no other objective seemed immediately viable.[9] Several factors had led to this conclusion. First, the Allies had only light and limited forces near to hand. Second, it was difficult to know the size of the German forces in each port; assumptions about numbers led to the conviction that only one port could be immediately retaken. Third, and most important at this time, it was difficult to establish the level of resistance the Norwegians would mount against the Germans, and it had to be assumed that the enemy forces in Bergen and Trondheim would be reinforced from farther south before successful Allied action could occur. A fourth influence was concern that the Norwegians might choose capitulation over resistance;

in this case, it was probable that no attempt would be made to retake any of southern or central Norway and that all effort would be concentrated on Narvik. A final factor was that Narvik was less exposed to German airpower.

Nevertheless, despite these eminently sound reasons for concentrating on Narvik and, of course, its value regarding Swedish ore, Trondheim and Bergen were not ignored in these initial deliberations. Plans were prepared to secure lodgments farther south with a second echelon of troops, but there was no intention to use these in major operations against Trondheim or Bergen until Narvik had been retaken.[10]

Churchill offered another reason why Narvik should be retaken first, and he was supported in this by Pound. He believed it was critical for Britain to secure a naval base in Norway to match the advantages gained by the Germans farther south. Churchill's public statements regarding success in Norway were sometimes extremely optimistic and suggested an unrealistic appreciation of the military realities facing him. However, his private communication to Pound displayed an awareness of the challenges ahead and a certain perspicacity that only in the north could the Germans be fought to advantage: "It is immediately necessary to obtain one or two fuelling bases on the Norwegian coast. . . . Now that the enemy have bases we cannot carry on without them. . . . Unless we have this quite soon we cannot compete with the Germans in their new position. . . . Narvik must be fought for. Although we have been completely outwitted, there is no reason to suppose that prolonged and serious fighting in this area will not impose a greater drain on the enemy than on ourselves."[11]

Thus, for Churchill, Narvik was more than a route to Gallivare, and in arguing its priority and advantage, his voice was only one among many. The War Cabinet gave Narvik priority for rational and what were perceived as sound operational reasons. Nevertheless, the tension in the "Narvik first" rationale was inescapable, ate away at its viability, and made it increasingly indefensible. Whatever the advantages of a base and whatever the immediate challenges were to action farther south, the longer southern and central Norway were left alone, the greater the effort that would be needed to dislodge the German forces there. Furthermore, the "Narvik first" approach would mean that should they resist, the Norwegians would bear the full burden of battle farther south without Allied assistance. As soon as it became obvious the

Norwegians would fight, the Narvik strategy became an untenable political and moral proposition, to say nothing of the questionable military wisdom of allowing the Norwegian forces to face the Germans alone.

Churchill, the MCC, and the War Cabinet deliberated these dilemmas over the next several days. It was far from clear if the immediate recapture of Trondheim was militarily viable, but the British War Cabinet and the MCC were increasingly compelled to consider the needs of the Norwegian people in their wider strategic objectives; this was something that had never figured in discussions of a northern strategy. German preemption had forced a choice between Narvik and Norway.

Trondheim

On 14 April, four days after the War Cabinet had given priority to Narvik, their focus shifted to Trondheim. The sudden change and its consequences have been attributed to a considerable degree to Churchill's indecisive leadership and bullying nature.[12] However, the dominant players in this change of strategy were Chamberlain and Halifax.[13] Churchill's role was that of facilitator, albeit a not entirely effective one. It was an unenviable role in which successful outcomes were much less likely than failure. Although there is no doubt Churchill ought to have acted more cautiously in supporting the switch and less precipitately in proposing a plan to retake Trondheim, it is doubtful if the need to recapture this port could have been resisted. Moreover, it was not Churchill alone who supported the change in strategy. The move from Narvik to Trondheim had the support of Phillips and Ironside.

The first tentative step away from Narvik to Trondheim was made by Admiral Phillips at an Admiralty staff meeting on the evening of 11 April. He questioned the wisdom of the War Cabinet's decision to send all available troops to Narvik and noted that this decision had been made when it was thought the Norwegians might come to terms with the Germans.[14] Now that this concern no longer existed, he considered it essential to get a footing in Namsos in preparation for action against Trondheim. This was an eminently sensible idea if one wished to avoid an opposed landing in the future, and it had first been considered by the COS on 10 April. The proposal resulted in a meeting later that evening between Churchill, naval and air staff, and Ironside.[15] Churchill suggested the diversion of part of the force destined for

Narvik, but Ironside feared this would herald a division of effort between two objectives and deny success at either, and so nothing came of it.[16]

However, whether or not Churchill or Ironside liked it, the days of the "Narvik first" strategy were numbered. Over the next several days the decision was taken from their hands by the growing political, moral, and military need to help the Norwegians via Trondheim. These inexorable forces were bolstered by the War Cabinet's hope that control of Trondheim would give the Swedes the confidence to join the Allies or, at the very least, would prevent Sweden surrendering to German demands. The champions of these views were Chamberlain, Halifax, and Alexander Cadogan, and they dominated the decision-making process. Churchill was less than enamored with these efforts to secure Swedish support. He knew Trondheim was important if the Allies intended to help the Swedes; this had been part of the Finnish option. But now that it was possible the Allies might gain access to Gallivare via Narvik, he viewed large-scale assistance to Sweden via Trondheim as a price too high to pay for the control of Swedish ore. If assistance was to be offered to Sweden, it should be via Narvik. He was prepared to sacrifice much of Sweden to the Germans so long as the Allies controlled Gallivare, and he did not want a situation to develop in which the Allies would have to sustain the Swedes "as long as the war lasts."[17]

On 12 April Churchill informed the War Cabinet of his discussion with Ironside the previous evening and expressed their collective view that nothing be done to interfere with Narvik. Chamberlain explained that he had also given thought to a landing at Namsos and noted that the Swedes had been emphasizing the importance of the port of Trondheim.[18] Churchill explained that retaking Trondheim would be a substantial undertaking since it would "no doubt" be reinforced by the Germans from Oslo, a point of view that Chamberlain had held a mere two days earlier and that had helped determine the "Narvik first" policy. However, Churchill was not blind to the pressing need to succor the Norwegians and Swedes, and he made an important concession, which would soon have significant ramifications: it might, he suggested, be possible to use the Chasseurs Alpins at Trondheim if Narvik was captured quickly. These French alpine troops had been destined for the Swedish border after the occupation of Narvik in the hope they might eventually occupy Gallivare, but as Churchill now acknowledged, if Sweden were hostile, they could not be used, and if Sweden were friendly, they need not be used.[19] It was probable, therefore, that the Chasseurs would be surplus to need at Narvik, or would quickly become so.

The pressure for Churchill to redirect his energies to Trondheim continued at a second War Cabinet meeting later in the day when Halifax argued that while Narvik was of military importance, its capture would have less political effect than action farther south. Halifax warned that "the enemy was thrusting to the southward from Trondheim and northward from Oslo," and if the forces joined, they would control all of southern Norway.[20] Here was the dilemma of the "Narvik first" strategy, but Churchill was shy of the only action by which Trondheim could be recaptured before it was relieved from Oslo: a rapid, direct, and dangerous amphibious assault. Churchill warned of a "bloody repulse" at Trondheim and noted that a British landing at Narvik might occur in a matter of days, presumably hoping, therefore, to defer a decision on Trondheim. In a further effort to deflect Chamberlain and Halifax, he reminded the War Cabinet that plans for Trondheim continued to be studied, as did plans for small landings at Molde and Namsos.

Churchill's mention of a series of small landings set in motion a new chain of events. The COS and JPS plans for these landings were to have been implemented as forces not needed at Narvik became available. However, Churchill's reference to the landings resulted in them being brought forward to help salve War Cabinet anxieties over Norwegian and Swedish morale. They would soon become the platform for larger and more immediate operations in central Norway.

Later in the afternoon of 12 April, Churchill took his limited landings proposal to the MCC meeting. There it was agreed that plans should be drawn up under the code name Maurice. As agreed at the meeting, Churchill wrote a rationale for Maurice for discussion with the secretary of state for war, Ironside, and subsequently, the War Cabinet. The landings would encourage the Norwegians in their defense and provide "evidences of the Allied intention to throw substantial forces into Norway," and this, Churchill hoped, might also influence the Swedes.[21] The landings would also prepare jumping-off points for future operations against Trondheim; some landings could be withdrawn as necessary after the enemy had been drawn to them. In the meantime they would confuse the Germans.[22] In the immediate term this

action to the south would be a demonstration, a diversion, a bluff—preparation for significant future action rather than significant action itself.[23]

The rationale bore the hallmarks of Churchill's faith in the flexibility of sea
power, but unless the landings served a distinct tactical purpose—either to
provide direct help to the Norwegians or to directly threaten the Germans—
they were likely to cause less anxiety and fewer problems to the enemy than
they would cause the Allies in their execution. This was particularly so when
the main enemy response would probably come from German airpower,
which had a mobility and economy of effort against which the navy could
never hope to compete. Despite the hopefulness of his proposal, Churchill
was aware of its ramifications and later wrote, "We are irresistibly drawn into
all kinds of improvised operations with raw, half-trained troops."[24] However,
at this stage he could see no other way to sustain the Norwegian war effort
while avoiding a deleterious overcommitment in the south, which neither
he nor Ironside wanted until after Narvik had been secured.[25] Moreover,
there is no evidence that the idea of these landings was challenged by naval
or military staff. Unfortunately for Churchill, his proposal not only failed
to deflect the War Cabinet from a southern front but contributed to the very
problem he had hoped to avoid.

Churchill put his diversionary stopgap measures to the War Cabinet the
following morning (13 April), but Chamberlain and Halifax continued to
maintain that Trondheim should be attacked as soon as possible and hoped
the French Chasseurs Alpins would be used there. Churchill and Ironside
again demurred; Narvik was imminent while Trondheim would necessarily
be a "more speculative affair."[26] Neither man wished to seek the diversion
of the Chasseurs Alpins until the Allies were established at Narvik, lest this
French force "be committed to a number of ineffectual operations along
the coast." Nevertheless, Churchill's resistance to Chamberlain and Halifax
continued to erode, and he somewhat offhandedly suggested that the German
forces at Narvik might be invested so that more immediate action could take
place at Trondheim.[27] After much debate Churchill and Ironside secured a
delay in the decision over Trondheim that was conditional on explaining
to the Swedes, "While the importance of Trondheim as a focal centre was
recognised, it was considered Narvik was vital as a naval base" and must,
therefore, take priority.[28]

However, the political and military pressure for immediate large-scale action in central and southern Norway was unrelenting. During 13 April a telegram from Otto Ruge, the commander in chief, Norwegian forces, warned that if he did not receive "'assistance at once, ie. today or tomorrow' the war would be ended in a few days."[29] While Ironside appeared inclined to view such communications as exaggerating the Norwegian need, they could not be ignored.[30] Unless the British War Cabinet was prepared to surrender Norway and its hopes for Sweden, a change of policy toward Trondheim was irresistible. To this point, Churchill had identified two circumstances in which action against Trondheim might be brought forward. The first was a successful coup de main against Narvik, which would free a substantial force immediately. The second was that if the capture of Narvik were long delayed, it might be decided to invest Narvik and concentrate on Trondheim. In the meantime Churchill and the COS would proceed with plans to land some four thousand infantry of the second echelon of forces "at suitable points on the coast to secure a lodgment from which large forces would be directed against Trondheim" at a later date.[31] Churchill was required to make one more concession to the War Cabinet on 13 April; he agreed to ask the French to allow the use of the Chasseurs Alpins other than at Narvik.

The intensity of political pressure being brought to bear on Churchill and Ironside for a change in strategy against their better judgment is evident in Cadogan's diary: "P.M., J.S., Sam H and H[alifax] impressed by message showing that Narvik alone is no good and we *must* attack Trondhjem (easier to do now than in a few days when it will be reinforced). Winston against. . . . But we got something out of him. . . . Reluctantly sent telegram to Paris asking . . . to divert *Chasseurs Alpins* from Narvik to elsewhere."[32] The challenges these circumstances presented for Churchill were considerable. Politics and diplomacy were now dominating strategy in a manner that had not been anticipated. In the criticism of the decisions Churchill subsequently made, this is often overlooked.

Pace, Audacity, Speed: Operation Hammer

The dilemma that dominated all considerations for operations in central Norway was how to recapture Trondheim with the forces available before it was reinforced by the Germans. There appeared to be no answer to this problem, save for the two propositions Churchill had put forward regarding Narvik. In the evening of 13 April, it appeared that the first of these might be possible. The Admiralty received news of a resounding naval success at Narvik. News also came forward from Vice Admiral Whitworth claiming the Germans at Narvik were thoroughly frightened and a landing should be made as soon as possible. Churchill, and most likely Phillips, believed they now saw a way to deal with the question of Trondheim. Narvik might, after all, be taken by a coup de main with a relatively small force, and therefore, resources could be more rapidly switched to central Norway.[33] More than this, Churchill's staff suggested to the first lord that naval action at Trondheim might also provide the conditions for a coup de main there. Soon, this proposal for an amphibious assault was given the code name Hammer. These matters were discussed at a specially convened MCC meeting at 10:30 p.m., whereupon it was agreed that if, in Churchill's opinion, information suggested Narvik could be taken quickly, the "W.O. and Admiralty in consultation, should without further reference to Committee, make arrangements for diverting the 2nd Brigade of Narvik forces to Namsos."[34] The COS was to consider a plan for a direct assault on Trondheim, "bearing in mind the need to effect a landing at Trondheim as soon as possible."[35]

Most historical analysis contends that later in the evening of 13 April or early the following morning, Churchill, in his capacity as MCC chairman, unilaterally demanded the diversion of the 146 Brigade to Namsos against Ironside's vehement objections.[36] This version of events is based on Ironside's postwar recollections in *The Ironside Diaries* and is an important pillar of the view that Churchill exercised an unconscionable and aggressive influence on strategy during the campaign. There is, however, no evidence beyond Ironside's recollections to suggest this meeting took place. Rather, there is evidence that Ironside confused and conflated the events of the evening of 13 April with the late night / early morning meeting of 11–12 April (discussed earlier).[37] This error has been compounded by the editors of Ironside's diaries (and perhaps by Ironside himself), who erroneously record the following as an entry for 1 a.m., 13 April, when it was in fact an entry for 1 a.m., 14 April:

> The Navy have had a very fine effort in Narvik, redeeming completely their mistake. . . . The enemy appears to have evacuated the town. . . . There should not be so much difficulty in mopping up the remains of

the force. . . . The Navy now wish to repeat the process at Trondheim. They have put up a completely new plan—which has the disadvantage of taking some time to execute. I said we must go on with our Namsos landing which can now be increased by one of the brigades.[38]

This entry is largely consistent with the tone of the decisions made at the 10:30 p.m. MCC meeting. Moreover, the decision to divert the 146 Brigade was not made unilaterally by Churchill in the late night of 13–14 April as claimed in *The Ironside Diaries* but through consensus during the afternoon of 14 April and only after two COS meetings, a War Cabinet meeting, and a meeting of the MCC. At this last meeting, it was recorded, "The Chiefs of Staff expressed the view that owing to the necessity of getting to the Trondhjem area as soon as possible, it was better to divert one of the Narvik brigades there immediately."[39]

There is no doubt that by the evening of 13 April, Ironside was as aware as Churchill that preparation for action at Trondheim must begin in earnest. Furthermore, not only did he cooperate with the diversion, he was willing to take a gamble on Hammer as well. The main reason Ironside was willing to accept the move away from Narvik and to accept the change in Maurice from a series of minor operations to something much more substantial was because these changes included the prospect of a direct and rapid assault on Trondheim. In a continuation of the 14 April entry, Ironside wrote, in what can only have been a reference to the future Hammer operation: "Anyway, the thing is pace, audacity, and speed. We must take a chance. Any scheme which means delay must be rejected."[40]

Throughout this time the pressure being brought to bear on Churchill continued unabated. Cadogan again recorded the significant influence that he and Halifax were having on strategy and policy: "I hope we have liquidated N[arvik] and—still more—purged Winston of the Narvik obsession. Let's now leave that alone, and get on with Trondheim, which is the only thing that matters in the Scandinavian eyes."[41] Cadogan's diary entry demonstrates the extent to which Churchill was being led by events rather than leading them. It was his staff, rather than he, that conceived the assault on Trondheim. Ironside's support for the plan, although perhaps given reluctantly, was not forced by Churchill. Together, they had accepted that a military effort in central Norway was essential, and both accepted that the best, if not the only, way to deal with the problem was a direct thrust at Trondheim via Hammer. Four episodes over the next three days, 15–17 April, provide further evidence that Churchill was by no means alone in pushing Hammer or the wider strategic agenda. Ironside made a substantial contribution to this new strategic direction, but the most significant force in its advancement was Chamberlain.[42] These episodes have typically been used to illustrate that Churchill was at the center of all major decisions. This was much less the case than has been assumed.

The first episode pertains to the pressure Churchill purportedly brought to bear on the COS to ensure Hammer took place. The evidence points not to Churchill but to Ironside, who dominated COS discussions on the subject and marginalized the JPS report that counseled against a direct assault at Trondheim. The JPS believed this action too risky and recommended, instead, the development of the Maurice landings north and south of Trondheim. Despite JPS's recommendation, when the COS considered the report in the afternoon of 15 April, it requested that plans be made for a direct attack on Trondheim, either in conjunction with or independently of forces operating from Namsos and Andalsnes.[43] Ironside's diary shows that it was he who was most insistent that Hammer take place and that he believed the operation could be successful despite German airpower. His diary recorded criticism of JPS member John Slessor, who had "produced a theory that if we took the place [Trondheim] it would be no good to us because we couldn't use it . . . owing to the air." Ironside pointedly noted that after these comments had been made, a report came in about the destroyer *Somali*, which had been attacked off Namsos by the Luftwaffe. The Germans had "dropped eighty-eight bombs in two hours and had never had a bomb within two hundred yards. . . . We then went on to make a plan. . . . I was pretty forceful in what I said and I forced the Committee to continue planning. We are now at a critical moment of the war from a moral point of view and we must expect to suffer casualties."[44]

Churchill's support for Hammer was also influenced by the limited success German aircraft were experiencing against Allied forces at this time. On 17 April, when Churchill wrote to Forbes to encourage him to undertake Hammer, he declared: "All that has happened makes me sure that Hitler has made a grave strategic blunder in giving us the right, as we have always had the power, to take what we like on the Norwegian coast. . . . All yesterday, the 16th, he was bombing our transports and our landed men at Lillesjonas and Haugesand and off Namsos, yet so far as I know not one man has been killed or one ship struck."[45] On 15 April Churchill had been much more cautious at the War Cabinet: "The First Lord impressed upon the War Cabinet the very hazardous nature of this Operation, not only on account of the terrain and of the exposure of the landing forces to air attack, but also owing to the fact that the majority of the troops to be employed were not highly trained."[46] Unfortunately, the good fortune the Allies had hitherto experienced at the hands of the Luftwaffe was not to last, and efforts to support operations on land became highly problematic owing to the relentless and increasingly effective German air presence.

Despite the foregoing evidence of Ironside's strong support for Hammer, the view developed among some members of the War Cabinet that Churchill was manipulating COS support for the operation. This brings us to the second episode used to demonstrate Churchill's disastrous domination of events. In the evening of 15 April or the morning of 16 April, Churchill informed the secretary to the MCC, General Ismay, that he strongly disagreed with the COS's views regarding the attack on Trondheim.[47] Ismay was worried that a "first-class row" would break out if Churchill chaired the meeting at which the plan for Hammer was to be discussed. He consulted Chamberlain's secretary, Sir Horace Wilson, who consulted Chamberlain, and they decided the prime minister would take the chair. However, it transpired that Ismay's anxiety was largely unjustified, that Churchill was in general agreement with the Hammer plan conceived by the COS, and that the crisis did not really exist.[48] The single point of dispute between Churchill and the COS was the former's concern that neither the number nor quality of the forces available was adequate for the central thrust of Hammer, and on this point Churchill was likely correct. He was particularly concerned that Ironside did not intend to employ the Chasseurs Alpins, the force diverted from the Narvik operation at the request of Chamberlain and Halifax. Ironside had decided to use them as part of the northern pincer via Namsos, in part because the French had requested the Chasseurs not be used in an opposed landing.

Churchill's anxieties were compounded by another issue, this time much more of his own making. In conceiving his proposal for a move from Narvik to Hammer on 14 April, he had hoped for a seamless transition that would allow him to transfer the regular 24th Guards Brigade from Narvik for the assault at Trondheim. However, by the next day he was forced to acknowledge that "Narvik would have to be fought for" and that the guards would probably not be available.[49] Moreover, by 16 April Major General P. J. Mackesy was making clear that nothing could be expected at Narvik without reinforcements, but his only source of reinforcement was the Chasseurs Alpins, now destined for Namsos. Thus, rather than rapid success at Narvik followed by more rapid success at Trondheim, Churchill feared both operations would be stalled for want of adequate forces at either place; the guards brigade would languish at Narvik while Hammer would be denied the Chasseurs Alpins. All the foregoing makes clear that Churchill did not try to force Hammer on the COS; what he attempted to do was ensure that sufficient experienced soldiers were committed to the decisive thrust.[50] It must be recognized, however, that the problems Churchill now faced were partly of his own making.[51]

The dispute over forces for the direct assault led to an intervention for which Churchill has been roundly condemned, and this leads to our third episode.[52] Churchill proposed to Chamberlain that Mackesy should be pressed to make a direct assault at Narvik at the earliest opportunity so that the guards brigade might yet be used in Hammer.[53] The pressure brought against Mackesy was certainly unpleasant and has reflected poorly on Churchill. However, the first lord alone was not responsible.[54] The telegram Churchill sent to Mackesy and Cork decrying the "damaging dead lock and the neutralisation of one of our best brigades" was drafted by the first lord but was discussed by the COS and the MCC and, after a minor amendment, endorsed by everyone, including Chamberlain.[55] Moreover, an equally objectionable joint Admiralty/War Office telegram of 18 April, which informed Mackesy that his actions, still expected to be aggressive and immediate, should be based on "having no more troops than you have at present," was sent at the suggestion of Ironside, not Churchill.[56] Even Churchill's subsequent belligerent attitude to Mackesy was paralleled in every way by Ironside. Further, while Churchill was instrumental in having Mackesy subordinated to Cork in an effort to ensure more aggressive action at Narvik, Ironside had contemplated replacing him altogether as early as 18 April.[57] Churchill's and Ironside's behavior toward Mackesy was unfair; they had halved his force and denied him any hope of reinforcements. Now Churchill required him to perform miracles at Narvik to ensure success at Trondheim with Hammer. However, it is also important to appreciate that Chamberlain and Halifax were placing enormous pressure on military strategy and that Chamberlain fully supported Churchill's actions. Chamberlain and Halifax were also responding to political imperatives that could not be addressed other than by the aggressive methods proposed. Such were the pressures and improvised nature of the Norwegian campaign.

One can now turn to the fourth episode that took place between 15 and 17 April. This anecdote further undermines the argument that Churchill bullied the COS to support Hammer and reinforces the central role of Chamberlain in the development of the operation. After the brief War Cabinet meeting of 16 April, several members of the cabinet expressed concerns that they were being asked to endorse policy, most particularly, Hammer, without being apprised of the views of the JPS and COS. Among the most animated of these men was Hankey, who saw parallels to the process that led to the abortive Dardanelles campaign of 1915.[58] Chamberlain had chaired the MCC meeting regarding this plan the day before and must have been aware that, if the COS was responding unwisely to pressure, it was the political pressure he and Halifax were applying. Nevertheless, the prime minister organized a private meeting with the chairman of the COS, Sir Cyril Newall, and asked if the COS had been providing its honest and open views. Newall confirmed the committee had. At the next day's War Cabinet meeting, Hankey made a point of asking Newall if the COS agreed with the MCC's Hammer plan. Newall said it did, noting: "The operation was of course attended by considerable risks; but the risks were not out of proportion to the value of success if achieved. The Military value of success should not be rated too highly, but it was clear that the political and moral advantages that would result from the capture of Trondheim, would be very great."[59]

This was not a strong endorsement of Hammer, and it reinforces the fact that the COS was making a judgment based on the political and moral imperatives emphasized by Chamberlain in previous days. The pressure Churchill had brought to bear had been primarily to ensure that if it were to be done, it be done properly, and there was much to be said for this as a wise course of action.

Shifting Breeze of Opportunity or Relentless March of Events?

In the afternoon of 19 April, British strategy underwent another transformation. Hammer was canceled and replaced by Operation Maurice and Operation Sickle, a plan to capture Trondheim in a pincer movement. The change occurred with extraordinary rapidity. Operation Hammer was affirmed at an MCC meeting chaired by Chamberlain at 10 a.m. on 19 April and was rubber-stamped by the War Cabinet at 11:30. At 1 p.m. a note was circulated by Pound requesting a meeting of the COS at 2 p.m. to discuss his proposal to replace Hammer for an envelopment strategy.[60] The COS met and was unanimous in its support. The records show that Churchill was present at the COS meeting for some of the time, although there is no record of his contribution to it.[61] After the meeting he immediately consulted Chamberlain about the change of plan and the latter agreed to it. The new strategy was then set before a late evening MCC meeting chaired by Chamberlain, during which it was also endorsed unanimously. The following day the plan was accepted by the War Cabinet.

Pound's reasoning for a switch to an envelopment strategy was the success of the landings at Namsos and Molde, north and south of Trondheim, although this was probably a foil for his ongoing concerns over the risks the operation presented for the navy. Pound believed it made sense to exploit these landings rather than continue with the direct assault, which had always been recognized as extremely hazardous. He expressed grave reservations over the risk to his ships during the long approach to Trondheim, especially given German superiority in the air. Subsequent discussion identified several advantages of the new plan: it would avoid the direct bombardment of Trondheim and the certainty of Norwegian deaths, and it would avoid the embarrassment of a failure of the direct attack. Perhaps more important, although it would delay the capture of Trondheim, it would bring forward direct contact with Norwegian forces in the south.[62] Finally, the cancellation of Hammer freed naval and military forces, which "seemed to open the possibility of earlier and more direct operations for the capture of Narvik itself."[63]

In *The Gathering Storm*, Churchill claimed he disapproved of the COS's sudden change in strategy, but there is no contemporary evidence to show this.[64] The notes he composed for discussion at the late evening MCC meeting indicated no particular objection to the proposal and even said, "We move from a more hazardous to a less hazardous operation."[65] Churchill too was concerned by the possible consequences delaying the implementation of Hammer would have on the Norwegians, and he continued to have reservations regarding the limited forces committed to the operation. However, that his response was so muted after he had been such a determined advocate of Hammer is best explained by the fact that the change offered a solution to the deadlock he and Ironside had created at Narvik. As a result of the pressure brought to bear on Cork and Mackesy, there was now a possibility of action there. A difficulty was that Cork wanted HMS *Warspite* for bombardment, but this ship had been withdrawn for use at Trondheim in the direct assault.[66] Immediately Hammer was dropped, and before the MCC on the evening of 19 April, Churchill sent a telegram to Cork explaining, "We have altered the emphasis of operations against Trondheim in such a way as to place *Warspite* and her escorting destroyers at your disposal."[67] Churchill also suggested that the Canadian forces earmarked for Trondheim be redirected to Narvik, where they might "enable the Commander to undertake the necessary offensive steps."[68] Churchill had not yet given up on central Norway, although he was now emphasizing the challenges of remaining there. On 20 April he wrote a note intended to draw the War Cabinet's attention to Narvik.[69] He spoke out even more strongly in the War Cabinet itself, contending, "It was of the utmost importance not to have our attention diverted by operations elsewhere from our principal objective, which had always from the very start been the control of the Gallivare ore fields."[70]

Whatever Churchill's true motivation in accepting the end of Hammer, it was always a decision beyond his power to resist, and it is difficult to hold him responsible for the farce that followed. Almost as soon as the decision was made, grave doubts about the efficacy of the new strategy began to emerge from the people who had endorsed it. The argument developed that success in central Norway would depend not so much on the ability to land troops, but the capacity of the ports to sustain and supply them thereafter.[71] The concept of a pincer movement was also challenged. The secretary of state for war explained to the War Cabinet on 20 April that the new plan could not really be considered a pincer movement because, until the threat farther south was dealt with, it could be a month or more before the southern forces could begin their northward drive toward Trondheim.

The northern pincer movement was also declared highly problematic. Major General Adrian Carton de Wiart, tasked with moving on Trondheim via Namsos, telegraphed that "further disembarkation of men and *materiel* at Namsos is impossible unless enemy air activity is restricted."[72] This was a problem that Ironside had discounted only two days earlier when he stated to the MCC meeting, "There was no need to feel undue anxiety in regarding the position of the troops both in the course of disembarkation and subsequent land operations."[73] On 21 April Ismay noted considerable difficulties with facilities for unloading military stores and poor communications with the interior which "even if we were not hampered in other ways [such as air attack] would present considerable difficulty."[74] The difference between these views expressed on 20 and 21 April and those presented by Pound on 19 April and endorsed by the COS, Churchill, and Chamberlain on the same day are extraordinarily marked and best explained by German air success. That a decision made one day could become almost redundant the next reinforces the forlorn nature of the campaign and illustrates the challenges faced by the decision makers. The devastating effect of German air attack in central Norway was eminently foreseeable; it is unlikely, however, that this would have caused the Allies not to have taken action there. For all the criticism of Churchill and the ad hoc nature of the Norwegian campaign, it must be borne in mind that Britain and France were locked into the enterprise whether they wished it or not. From the beginning, improvisation was always the order of the day.

In a further illustration of the challenge Churchill faced in striking the ideal strategic and operational line during this time, Pound's efforts to protect the fleet with a movement away from Hammer on 19 April were followed several days later by Phillips' proposal, also with the fleet in mind, to return to it. Phillips, like most members of the War Cabinet, had grave concerns about Italian activity at this time and believed that a prolonged campaign in central Norway was incompatible with meeting the threat in the Mediterranean. He preferred instead to return the focus to Narvik. At the COS meeting of 23 April, he flagged the possibility of a return to Hammer, or a modified version of it, as the only way to deal quickly with the problems in central and southern Norway.[75] He expanded on these views in a lengthy memorandum on the matter two days later, the sentiments of which were essentially a more emphatic version of the War Office paper of 21 April quoted previously.[76] Phillips' memo was a significant value judgment. Narvik was important; the rest of Norway was not, or at least not as important as the Mediterranean; and the navy could not do both. Instead of a return to Hammer, a decision was made to abandon central Norway altogether.

The Surrender of Central Norway

By the fourth week of April there was a growing consensus that fighting in central Norway was probably unsustainable, that preparations should be made for evacuation, and that Allied energy should be returned to Narvik. Churchill's mind had already moved in that direction. However, a decision on these issues was neither his nor even the British government's alone to make. Despite the priority the French had originally given to Narvik, they were now convinced that Trondheim was the key to everything, including to Swedish ore and Swedish cooperation in the war. Intelligence was leading the French to believe that Sweden might soon be invaded by the Germans. It was their firm conviction that Norway was just the Germans' first step to this. Much as Chamberlain and Halifax had argued a week before, the French believed Allied control of Trondheim would somehow influence the Swedes or, just as desirably, encourage the Germans to take action against Sweden. The capture of Trondheim, therefore, represented the best way to get to Gallivare. However, the minutes of the SWC meeting of 22 April indicate that Churchill, Chamberlain, and Ironside were already less than keen to continue the effort in central Norway and that they worked hard to downplay the prospects for success. Instead, they promoted a renewed focus on Narvik.[77] The French, supported by the British Foreign Office, carried the day, and despite British misgivings and warnings, the meeting accepted that Trondheim and Narvik remained joint priorities.

However, it was one thing to desire Trondheim; it was another to capture it. Inevitably, it fell to Churchill to help find a way to make capturing Trondheim a success. It was becoming abundantly clear the Allies would not secure Trondheim before it was reinforced from the south by the Germans; Trondheim was already being reinforced daily via air transports. The only solution open to the Allies was to revisit Hammer or a version of it, just as Phillips had said.[78] In what is considered yet another example of Churchill's whimsy, he broached the issue with Pound on the 24 April, arguing, "Without Trondheim it is difficult to believe the Norwegian Southern Front can be held."[79] On 25 April Pound took the matter to the COS, where it was concluded that a modified Hammer was not worth the risk because it would demand more of the Allies than of the enemy.[80] At the War Cabinet the following day, it was mentioned that the naval effort required to sustain the fight in central Norway would prevent Britain taking the requisite action should the Italian threat develop.

There is no evidence that Churchill "quite improperly" applied pressure to the COS to attempt another Hammer; moreover, the proposal is generally inconsistent with his attitude to the fighting in central Norway.[81] From the beginning Churchill had been shy of a situation in which the Allies might be caught up aiding Sweden via Trondheim.[82] He had always thought the best route to Gallivare and the Swedish ore—the route that would limit Allied obligations to Sweden—was via Narvik. He had only succumbed to an operation at Trondheim when it had been politically impossible to do otherwise and had promoted Hammer as the best military solution. Now, neither Churchill nor Chamberlain demurred from the COS recommendations at the 24 April MCC meeting that central Norway be evacuated. Rather, Churchill argued that nothing had really been lost by Allied efforts in central Norway and that the important thing was to secure Narvik as a base for land or air operations against Lulea.[83] Later in the morning, the War Cabinet decided, with virtual unanimity and much relief, to get out of central Norway.

Thus, in a space of some ten days, Allied strategy had moved from Narvik to Trondheim via Hammer, to Trondheim via Maurice and Sickle, then back to a modified Hammer and Narvik, and finally to evacuation in central Norway and a concentration on Narvik alone. The characterization of Churchill's mind being "puffed this way and that by the shifting breeze of opportunity" does not do justice to the problems faced, nor does it accurately reflect who was making the decisions.[84] Throughout Churchill was being led by events and influenced by advisers who were also struggling to hold a consistent line. There is no evidence that Churchill was dominating discussion or commanding strategy or that it was this that fueled the disaster the Allied forces were facing. The first lord was being repeatedly defeated by the pace of German movements, their superior position, and in particular, their command of the air. In the circumstances, the challenges for Churchill were considerable.

It is symptomatic of the dilemma Churchill faced in fighting the Norwegian campaign that he has been criticized for not attempting to capture Trondheim and then criticized for promoting the one plan that might have made this possible, Hammer.[85] In this campaign there were no easy options. As to the matter of Churchill's whimsy, he was, despite his assertion that the new envelopment plan was less hazardous, very much aware of the challenges the strategy imposed. At the War Cabinet of 20 April he, along with the secretary of state for war, warned of the threat of air attack and the need for an adequate base and secure lines of communication if operations in the south were to be successful. In the event these requirements were unattainable and the air threat too great.

Although the British War Cabinet was now convinced evacuation of central Norway was essential, the French instinct was to stay. At the SWC of 27 April, French ambassador Charles Corbin warned that they would lose altogether the influence they had over Sweden and also the best chance they had to solve the ore problem.[86] So entrenched were the French hopes for economic warfare to provide them with salvation from another conflagration on the western front that surrendering the idea of capturing Trondheim, as remote and as valueless as this was likely to be, was a deeply disturbing prospect. The decision to evacuate went ahead. In nearly all the discussion with the French, the dominant player was not Churchill but Chamberlain. Chamberlain's sense of obligation to the Norwegians by this time had largely dissipated. The Allies had done what they could, and two days later he declared that he "had little sympathy for the Norwegians," noting rather cruelly and inaccurately that they had put up little resistance.[87] Although Churchill showed a little more compunction by suggesting that some of the Allied forces be dispersed into the wilds of Norway to fight on, he was largely a like-minded and earnest deputy when it came to withdrawal. This was entirely unsurprising given his earlier opposition to the central Norwegian strategy.

To Stay or Not to Stay? Exiting Norway

More militarily questionable than the decision to evacuate central Norway was the decision to continue the battle for Narvik. With the Germans in control of central and southern Norway, it was surely only a matter of time before Narvik would be lost to the Germans.[88] Churchill was certain the Allies should remain in Norway, and there was little or no dissent on the matter. The limited discussion that took place on the subject tended to assume, for several important political reasons, that Britain must stay. All the War Cabinet participants understood there would be a political price to pay, both at home and abroad, for surrendering central Norway, although they never fully appreciated how severe this would be. On 27 April, following the line of argument Churchill had adopted at the MCC on 24 April, Chamberlain suggested they justify the withdrawal to the nation by arguing the fighting in central Norway had been only a temporary diversion to help secure Narvik.[89] There could, therefore, be no thought given to stopping their efforts to take this town, at least in the immediate term. Another reason for persisting in northern Norway was the hope it would be secured as the seat of power for the Norwegian government.[90] This semblance of concern for the Norwegians was linked to fear over the consequences of withdrawal; after all, an objective of this last incarnation of Narvik had been to impress on neutrals and warn potential belligerents that the Allies were capable of taking effective action against Germany. An evacuation would hardly meet this objective. Additionally, there were concerns over the potential consequences for Allied efforts to secure Norwegian tankers if they abandoned the fight in Norway. That the Norwegians would deny Britain this resource was unlikely, but it did cause anxiety for a time.[91]

Narvik was also sustained by continued hopes regarding Sweden and Swedish ore. It was Churchill who most commonly propagated these hopes, but they were not his alone.[92] He believed the Germans would not be content to accept the surrender of its Narvik contingent and would insist on sending forces via Sweden to help them. This, he expected, would open opportunities to deal with Gallivare and Lulea.[93] If Germany left Sweden alone, Churchill intended to secure an ongoing supply of ore for Britain. As late as 31 May, Hugh Dalton of the MEW was arguing that so long as Narvik was open, the Germans would be faced with a dilemma: either "allow us to draw supplies . . . or carry out their threats and invade Sweden," a win-win situation for Britain.[94] Dalton gave no thought to the improbability of trade via Narvik with the Germans in command of the rest of Norway.[95] If Britain could not secure its own ore supply, then Narvik would be used as a base from which to launch land and air attacks against Gallivare and Lulea to compromise the ore trade with Germany. In the death throes of the Norwegian campaign, the land attacks were again recognized as nonsense, but Churchill placed the air operations among his highest priorities, and this required an air base at Narvik.[96] It was, however, foolish to imagine that an airstrip could be built to accommodate enough bombers to satisfactorily achieve Allied objectives, while also being home to the desperately needed fighter force required to protect Narvik and the airstrip itself against the German air forces farther south. The action would also lead to serious conflict with Sweden.

It was folly for Churchill and others to have thought it possible to retain Narvik as a useful operational port or air facility or to consider the advantages to be gained thereby would make worthwhile the effort required. Narvik would have been subjected to constant attack from the German air forces and constant siege from German forces moving northward; lines of supply and communications would have been exposed to aircraft, U-boats, and surface craft working from Trondheim. Estimates of the resources required to keep Narvik were substantial. Churchill projected a force of some 35,000 troops, and the requirements for antiaircraft guns would have cut deeply into the needs of ADGB. Nevertheless, it is remarkable that until mid-May hardly a voice was raised to question the effort required to retain Narvik and northern Norway.[97] The COS and the JPS were not asked to give their opinions, nor were they offered, but papers written warned of the considerable matériel drain that would result from persistence in northern Norway. Only around 20 May, after a second JPS report argued, "The security of France and the United Kingdom is essential, the retention of northern Norway is not," were plans for evacuation authorized. Even then, a final decision was postponed.[98] If not for the enormous demands of the war in France, Churchill could likely have continued the effort in northern Norway, despite the overwhelming German forces in the south, the certainty of defeat, and dubious merit of staying.[99] However, he was only one among many who were reluctant to surrender the hopes regarding Swedish ore. The collapse of France provided Germany with access to French iron ore, and only then did the last hopes for a short war via the cessation of Swedish ore supplies finally die.

Conclusions and a Question of Sea Power

Churchill, as first lord and a member of the MCC, was always an important participant in the decision-making process during the Norwegian campaign, but he was less influential in determining the direction of Allied strategy than is generally supposed. He was most often only one among many in the strategic decision-making process and often not the most important. His interference in operational matters, particularly at Narvik via Cork, was undoubtedly wrong, but the facts were that the most significant of these interventions received the full endorsement of the prime minister, the secretary of state for war, and the CIGS. Furthermore, criticism of his interference in naval matters fails to address the fact that Churchill's role as first lord and chairman of the MCC produced a unique dynamic in the operational decision-making process that blurred the lines of responsibility. Chamberlain was aware of several of the more egregious examples of Churchill's interference, but he did nothing to stop them; on several occasions he gave Churchill his full support.

Any assessment of Churchill's performance in the Norwegian campaign must recognize that Chamberlain and Halifax's insistence on operations in central Norway produced a strategic situation in which the likelihood of success was remote and attended by great risk. This placed Churchill, as chairman of the MCC, in a profoundly difficult situation. At the heart of Churchill's problems was that from the early hours of 9 April, German success had irretrievably altered the risk-reward scenario of the entire northern strategy in a way that made the campaign of doubtful efficacy. From the beginning, operations in Norway, and possibly Sweden, had been based on the dubious assumption that fighting in this theater would impose a greater burden on the Germans than on the Allies while also offering the prospect of denying Germany access to Swedish ore. Churchill championed the view, also accepted by the COS, that sea power would allow the Allies to match or exceed the effort needed by the Germans to capture and control Norway via the long and limited lines of land communications. However, all this presupposed Allied control of Bergen, Trondheim, Narvik, and possibly Stavanger as well. Churchill had never expected that these objectives would have to be fought for from a position of significant disadvantage. Despite Churchill's initial and more public optimism, 9 April gave the advantage to the Germans and presented the Allies with a conflict they were not likely to win, except at considerable cost, but had to fight. The anxieties exhibited by Forbes, then Pound, Phillips, and finally Churchill, from mid-April reflected their separate appreciation that the risks were not justified by the potential rewards. In due course a similar and belated conclusion was drawn over Narvik.

Churchill's conception for Norway must be judged not only by the campaign that was fought but by the campaign he had expected to fight. Had the Allies secured Bergen and Trondheim, as they might have done but for the confusion of 7–8 April, could they have fought to advantage the Germans in Norway? Had the Norwegians not been taken so completely by surprise, could they not have made a prolonged fight of it? It seems likely that Allied control of the limited internal lines of communication to Trondheim, combined with an air presence there, would have ensured the Germans paid a much higher price for success, and this might have been enough to change the dynamics of the operations in Hitler's eyes. However, had Hitler persisted in Norway, it seems equally likely that in time the Germans would prevail. Although one must consider the advantages that would have been offered to the Allies by control of a major port, it is doubtful they could have matched the German buildup via southern Norway, especially given Germany's rather bloodless coup in Denmark and the advantages this offered for its lines of communication. Britain's much longer lines of supply and communication were subject to interdiction in a way that the German lines were not. British submarines suffered grievously in the Skagerrak, and the longer days of summer would make operations there almost impossible. The Allies were, therefore, not able to interrupt German communications to the extent it was hoped. British aircraft could do even less, and it was a burden the air force was reluctant to fulfill. The Royal Navy would have been exposed to U-boats and a constant attrition from German aircraft, as would all the men and matériel landed. In time the risk to the navy had to tally significantly in any decision to persist in Norway, and Trondheim or not, this would have told on any decision to stay in Norway.

In their attempts to ameliorate the defeat in Norway, Churchill and Chamberlain referred to the substantial naval losses incurred by the Germans. It was, however, only the problems the Germans faced with their magnetic torpedo mechanism during the early days of the campaign that saved British naval forces from similarly shocking losses. One might speculate on the impact these losses would have had on Churchill's career had they occurred. Fate would ordain that he would not be held culpable for Norway; this failure, and a great deal more, would be placed at the feet of Chamberlain. Such good fortune might well have deserted Churchill had German torpedoes worked as expected.

For Churchill, Norway was always about using sea power to wrest the initiative from Germany; if Germany responded to the Allied threat to its ore supply, it would draw German forces away from France and deny them a decision there. However, the diversion of effort did not prevent Germany from attacking in the West. Rather than deflecting Germany from a decision in France, the already overburdened Royal Navy was faced with an even greater responsibility: the supply and perhaps rescue of the BEF, a situation that at any time might have been, and eventually was, compounded by Italian action in the Mediterranean. The Norwegian scheme had, as expected, drawn a much larger German force to Norway than was sent by the Allies. The misjudgment made by Churchill and others was that the Germans could not afford to send this force. Moreover, the logistical effort needed to sustain the fighting in Norway was much less for the Germans than that demanded of the Allies and the Royal Navy. In the circumstances, Churchill and the members of the British War Cabinet, not Hitler, were called on to make stark choices in Norway. It had taken the prospect of defeat in France before Churchill finally grasped that the Royal Navy did not have resources enough at this time for extraneous ventures.

NINE

FIRST LORD TO PRIME MINISTER

At the end of April 1940, Churchill and Chamberlain understood a political price would be paid for the withdrawal from central Norway. Neither had any idea just how high this price would be, nor did they know that Chamberlain alone would be required to pay it. Within ten days of Chamberlain's informing the Commons of the abandonment of the efforts to capture Trondheim, Churchill was prime minister and had begun to form a new government. The catalyst for this monumental change was a two-day debate on 7 and 8 May—now referred to as the Norway debate—that was followed by a division in the House of Commons that effectively became a de facto confidence motion. The government won the motion by a significant, but nevertheless substantially reduced, margin over previous divisions, and two days later Chamberlain offered his resignation.

Inevitably the juxtaposition of failure in central Norway, the Norway debate, and Chamberlain's resignation has created inextricable links between these events. Cause and consequence appear fairly clear, but this neat assessment has always been problematic. The problem arises not for the fact of Chamberlain's resignation but because he was replaced by Churchill, who was viewed by many as a major contributor to failure in Norway.

This chapter has two primary aims. The first is to explore the link between the Norwegian campaign and Chamberlain's resignation and to offer an alternative assessment. It is argued that Norway was not the primary cause of Chamberlain's eclipse. The misfortune surrounding this campaign and the reaction to it were important catalysts, but influences that long preceded Norway caused these events and reactions to precipitate such extraordinary change. To a considerable extent, these influences made Chamberlain's fall unsurprising, if not inevitable. That Norway was not central to Chamberlain's fall also explains Churchill's rise.

The second aim is to consider the Churchill-Chamberlain relationship in the weeks leading to Chamberlain's resignation. The focus here is their respective view of events and the contribution of each to the process that led to Churchill becoming prime minister in the early evening of 10 May. The evidence adduced shows Churchill was much less ambitious—and much less aware of his own destiny—than he and some historians would have us believe. It also shows that Chamberlain was much less limpet-like in his determination to retain power than is often contended.[1] This investigation advances a major theme of this study: that even at this most tense of times, Churchill's relationship with Chamberlain proceeded on a basis of coopera-tion rather than competition. Until almost the moment he became prime minister, Churchill was very much aware his own best interests were closely linked to Chamberlain's continuation as prime minister. Chamberlain was no less aware of Churchill's importance to his government.

These issues are developed in several parts. The first outlines the broader challenges facing Chamberlain and his government during the latter stages of the Phoney War and the extent to which they ensured failure in Norway would be a catalyst for significant change. An important objective is to explain why Churchill oftentimes found himself cocooned from criticism despite being a member of a much reviled War Cabinet. This analysis sets the parameters for a consideration of the political and military events as they unfolded—primarily within the House of Commons—from March through May 1940. This begins with the reactions to, and consequence of, the failure of the Finnish option and ends with the failure in Norway.

The considerations of events within the House are complemented by an exploration of antigovernment activities and anti-Chamberlain opposition that developed outside the House during April and May. Considered also will be the actions, attitudes, and expectations of Churchill and Chamberlain as the failure in Norway developed and the opposition to Chamberlain and his government grew as a consequence. The conventional perception of these times is of a Churchill-Chamberlain relationship primarily characterized by mutual suspicion; any hint of cooperation or goodwill was merely cal-culated and superficial.[2] This view has been encouraged by the assumption that Churchill was deeply discontented with the government in the dying days of the Phoney War and that he was in sympathy with the agenda of Chamberlain's critics. It also assumes that Churchill believed he would be better off without Chamberlain than with him and that he might even be able to assume the leadership. These perspectives are not strongly supported by the evidence. It is likely that almost until the day he became prime minister, Churchill gave little thought to the premiership because he believed his lack of support within the Conservative Party put this beyond him. All his actions and attitudes were, therefore, guided, not by premiership aspirations, but by the expectation he would—post-Norway debate—in any likely scenario continue as Chamberlain's warlord within a revitalized War Cabinet.

Rather than being hostile toward Chamberlain and the direction of the government, Churchill was, by May 1940, generally supportive—sometimes strongly so—of government policy. Perhaps more important, he was at odds with several of the changes sought by the most vociferous of Chamberlain's critics, and this is an important point of analysis. As for Chamberlain, there is little doubt he anticipated Churchill having a major role within his government, whatever the outcome of the Norway debate. The notion of a scheming, calculating Chamberlain contemplating Churchill's demise in order to save himself is difficult to reconcile with firsthand evidence and requires reassessment.

The Seeds of Chamberlain's Demise

An important influence in Chamberlain's fall was his prewar critics' unrelenting determination to view his wartime "sit tight and rearm" policy as merely an extension of prewar appeasement rather than in any way as a wise, or judicious, or necessary path to take. An important influence in Churchill's rise was that these same critics believed he shared their anxiety and frustration over this policy and that a different war—a better war—would be, and would have been, fought under him as prime minister or minister for defense. At the very least, the war fought under him would have been more aggressive and more successful and preparations more earnest.

In drawing these distinctions between the policies Churchill might have adopted and those of Chamberlain's government, the latter's critics were not interested in, or even aware of, the challenge of being suitably proactive during the Phoney War. They offered few, if any, concessions for the inertia of Britain's French ally or the limited and problematic opportunities for proactivity. In contrast, concessions were given Churchill. His silence on policy—or his occasional effusive acknowledgment of the advantages of being left alone (for example, his occasional comments on the advantages of air policy)—was viewed as a virtuous loyalty to the prime minister and to cabinet solidarity rather than as genuine support for policies the critics considered fundamentally flawed. Despite tacitly, and oftentimes explicitly, acknowledging the merit of the "sit tight and rearm" approach, Churchill was forever identified with the more aggressive and proactive approach some members of the House clearly desired. He needed do nothing and gain advantage from impatience and frustration. An added bonus for Churchill was the kudos he secured from the achievements of Britain's most active service, the Royal Navy. The sinking of *Graf Spee* and the capture of *Altmark* did much to link him to successful aggression.

In early May Chamberlain reflected on the dilemma he had faced as prime minister. Critics always asked, "Why are we always too late? Why do we let Hitler take the initiative? Why can't we have some plan which would take him by surprise. The answer . . . is simple enough. . . . Because we are not yet strong enough."[3] Chamberlain's "sit tight and rearm" policy had always been a response to this problem, but whatever its military virtue, it was politically fraught. In a personal and political sense his great mistake was not the policy but that he imagined his parliamentary critics—including those within his party—would be as willing as he to accept the policy's merit and to show patience in regard to it. He was naive to believe they would forget he was a primary reason why Britain was not yet strong enough to do other than sit tight.

The Critics and Their Demands

It was always those least able to forgive Chamberlain's prewar appeasement policies who were his most ardent critics once the war began. This opposition coalesced for a time around a variety of figures, including Anthony Eden (the "Glamour Boys"); Leo Amery, whose own group absorbed many of Eden's supporters once the latter entered the government; and Member of Parliament (MP) Clement Davies, who was chair of the All Parties Action Group. Churchill also had a retinue of loyal and determined supporters whose aspirations were decidedly anti-Chamberlain, but there is little evidence that Churchill either encouraged them or cooperated with their activities once he returned to government. A similar observation can be made of Eden.

From late February 1940, a new grouping developed around Lord Salisbury and included elements of all these groups. This group evolved into the Watching Committee, which had its first formal meeting in early April. The Watching Committee's primary objective was not removing Chamberlain (although some of its members hoped for this) but rather guiding him toward a more effective prosecution of the war. Chamberlain's resistance to their counsel, and the course of subsequent events, especially in Norway, hardened some members to the belief that his premiership must be terminated.[4] Others, of course, had long held this view.

In addition to this internecine collection of critics, there were the opposition parties. The most important of these was the Labour Party under Clement Attlee and the Liberal Party under Sir Archibald Sinclair. These parties had only a fraction of Conservative representation in the House, but they became increasingly important for their refusal to contemplate participation in a national wartime government with Chamberlain as its leader. Labour's cooperation in government was particularly important because of its close links to British trade unions and labor. Each party had been invited to be part of the government at the start of the war but had declined. The refusal to participate in government became important when members of the Conservative Party and, ultimately, Chamberlain himself determined a truly national government was necessary to fight the war; it is, therefore, the opposition to Chamberlain from within his own party that primarily concerns us here. Chamberlain had always been able to rely on the vast majority of Conservative members who were personally loyal to him. However, in the aftermath of Norway, and urged on by senior members of their own party, a considerable number abstained in the censure vote, and this made a decisive difference. Few, however, imagined the consequences.

That Norway had the impact it did—especially in the matter of abstentions—had less to do with the failures of the campaign than with Chamberlain's failure to listen and attend to the concerns of party members over a period of several months. One of the requests most commonly made of Chamberlain was to make changes to his War Cabinet to admit more talent and to secure greater efficiency. For some, the removal of those most tainted with the brush of appeasement—Hoare and Simon—would have been sufficient. Others, among them Amery and, subsequently, Salisbury, wanted the War Cabinet restructured to mirror that of David Lloyd George in World War I or, at least, to mirror their perception of this structure. In time they added to their demands the establishment of a genuinely national government and, ultimately, the potential replacement of Chamberlain as prime minister. Chamberlain had contemplated and then rejected his own version of a small War Cabinet at the start of the war. Churchill had not been keen on the idea, preferring, instead, the hands-on role of first lord. No doubt the role of minister for defense was not in the offing in September 1939.

Despite this pressure Chamberlain resisted change. He was not persuaded the existing structure was flawed or was in any way failing to meet the needs of the British war effort. His resistance to the small War Cabinet concept might also have been because, within such a structure, Churchill would have most likely overseen the armed forces. Yet in April and early May, this was the direction of things anyway, and he no doubt had concluded that a small War Cabinet that included himself and Halifax would have been more than adequate to contain Churchill's excesses. Chamberlain's resistance might, therefore, have been little more than a stubborn and misguided determination not to be pushed.

If his critics considered Chamberlain's reluctance to listen mere hubris, it was, to some degree, a matter of the kettle calling the pot black. Many were driven by a similar high-mindedness and an equally deep-seated conviction they were right. They accepted without question that action somewhere would certainly be to the Allies' advantage, and they believed inaction, especially in the air, was neither wise nor moral once Hitler had demonstrated his willingness to do as he wished in Poland and, subsequently, Norway. Rarely did they offer cogent alternatives or potential answers to the intractable problems that beset proactivity. Their opposition was magnified by their views—often mistaken—that efforts to become strong enough were insufficiently earnest and by their anxiety the enemy was arming much more aggressively than Britain was—when, in most respects, it was not.[5]

Chamberlain's refusal to make adequate concessions ensured his critics attributed any and all shortcomings to his failure to make the changes pressed on him. They were never of a mind to concede that for a time at least, Britain, tied as it was to an even more hesitant ally, was destined to react rather than initiate and to suffer trial and tribulation before the might of German forces. Norway was, therefore, a prophecy fulfilled; here was an unnecessary disaster, the root cause of which could only be Chamberlain's leadership and administration. The solution was a new cabinet, possibly a new leader, and certainly new policies.

Circumstances ensured Norway was an extraordinarily potent catalyst for change. Apart from being at the end of a long line of perceived failures, it appeared, initially, to be a battle that could be won. Unlike Poland or Finland, Norway offered a comparatively level battlefield: German military might versus Britain's dominance at sea. Yet even here the Chamberlain government failed. It was not only the failure itself but the nature of its unfolding that brought Chamberlain down. At its start both Churchill and Chamberlain had provided much hope for a different result, and the Commons carried these hopes with it for three weeks before having them seriously undermined on 2 May, when the withdrawal of forces south of Trondheim was announced. Two days later, hopes were shattered altogether by news of the abandonment of central Norway. All this took place within days of the long-scheduled 7 and 8 May debate, ensuring wounds would still be red and raw.

The Norway debate was of unparalleled passion and put on trial not only Norway but Chamberlain's entire past performance. In the final analysis it mattered not that attribution of past disappointments or a satisfactory understanding of cause and effect were adequately determined or that perception as much as reality was guiding events. Change was nigh, as one MP remarked: "The lesson we have learned from the Debate is that if you sit on the safety valve of a boiler the boiler will, in the end, blow up. And that is what happened in the Debate. Regrettable though it was I think it was absolutely inevitable."[6]

Growing Discontent inside the House: Finland

Opportunities in the House of Commons to discuss and criticize the general conduct of the war were few. Unsurprisingly, these arose primarily at moments of crisis or soon thereafter. The two months preceding the 7 and 8 May debates were unique in offering several opportunities for such discourse. These were important occasions for members to vent their frustrations, but it did little to diminish them. As one disappointment followed another, and there was little evidence forthcoming that guidance was being heeded, this frustration increased manifold. It was a downward spiral that relentlessly eroded the faith of many of Chamberlain's strongest supporters.

The first period of significant debate on the course of the war in 1940 occurred after the surrender of Finland and the failure of the Finnish option in early March. The second, although circumscribed, occurred in the days immediately following the German invasion of Norway. The final period was during the first eight days of May but, more particularly, the 7 and 8 May debates. Many of the key players in the May debates are found at work in mid-March in the debate over Finland, and here, also, are to be found their core grievances.

Despite disappointment over Allied failure to help the Finns, this episode was not seen by Chamberlain's most severe critics as a decisive opportunity to force major change within his government. It was, nevertheless, an important part of a process that would bring it down. Debate in the House generally acknowledged that efforts to aid Finland had been problematic because this assistance had potentially involved an abrogation of, or infringement on, the neutrality of Norway and Sweden, and this did not sit well with many members. Some critics were loathe to condemn the failure of plans to help Finland because they considered the enterprise had been unwise, even foolish, and were relieved it had not come to pass. Instead, the plan was criticized as a dubious conception indecisively prosecuted. Some were more strident. Labour MP Colonel Josiah Wedgwood declared: "I cannot believe any Staff College man in this country can have supported this expedition to Finland as a deliberate and well-conceived military adventure."[7] These sentiments reflect the conclusions of this study regarding the efficacy of the plan. The point here, of course, is that such criticism, directed primarily at the personality of Chamberlain, was more appropriately directed at the entire administration, including the COS and Churchill.

Despite the tempered nature of the censure, critics used the failure of the Finnish option to chastise Chamberlain's government for a general lack of initiative; most critics assumed the government ought to have done better. Attlee took the opportunity to declare "initiative must not be left for Herr Hitler. You cannot have a policy of wait and see." Sinclair had a bit each way, simultaneously demanding initiative and caution: "Flashy adventures . . . will spell defeat, and playing for safety will certainly ensure defeat. We must seize the initiative and hold it both militarily and politically."[8]

As was their custom, neither man offered suggestions as to how initiative might be seized, and on this point, it is instructive to consider an example of the challenge already faced by Chamberlain in achieving a proactivity suitable to the Labour opposition. During February Churchill had used the *Altmark* episode to resurrect his Narvik plan. Chamberlain finally came down against this for several reasons, many of which have been discussed. One factor that counted against Narvik was Attlee's reluctance to accept the *Altmark* incident as sufficient cause to infringe Norwegian rights. (Sinclair, however, endorsed the idea.) Thus, it was probable that had Chamberlain accepted *Altmark* as cause enough for Narvik, and had he done so in the name of proactivity, he would have been strongly criticized by the Labour Party for doing so.

Other elements of the Finnish debate indicated the extent to which Chamberlain had already created circumstances from which he could not extricate himself. One of his most vociferous Conservative critics, Richard Law, observed how often Chamberlain and other members of his government had over the years spoken in "the midst of some wreckage of policy. . . . Each time it happens, it makes the next time easier and the next time more likely." Finland's surrender—explained by some as a result of Allied parsimony, hesitation, and indifference—was merely another example of this process. It was readily accepted that more dynamism would have made a difference when it almost certainly would not.[9]

Law's criticism was also of a strain commonly heard but not easily combated; it reflected a heartfelt concern for the weak and vulnerable countries that continued to be threatened by the dictators. There was a desperate desire to arrest the dictators' assault on the small countries of Europe. This sentiment was no less strong within the government, but whatever the public display, the War Cabinet's decisions were coolly and clinically calculating in their assessment of British self-interest. Churchill was among the most cautious in offering matériel support unless he was persuaded such assistance would bear directly on the ultimate defeat of Germany. In condemning the Chamberlain government for its coldhearted parsimony critics were also condemning Churchill, but it was not clear this was ever understood.

Although considerable frustration manifested from the failure to help Finland, not all was directed at Chamberlain personally; much was directed at the structure of the War Cabinet. Even Law avoided specific reference to the prime minister in his criticism; instead, he was one of those seeking to restructure the War Cabinet: "This is a matter, not of personalities, but of organization."[10] National Labour MP Commander William King-Hall saw things differently and emphasized the personalities that made up the government, although he too avoided criticism of Chamberlain. In an entertaining moment he likened Chamberlain to a battleship, alongside whom sat "a battlecruiser [Churchill], not exactly a streamlined vessel but a formidable ship which delivers powerful broadsides against the Nazis." As for the rest he thought them not quite so impressive: "drifters, trawlers, dredges and other auxiliary vessels all having their useful functions to perform but not designed by God or Man to be in the line of battle." Later, he declared more succinctly that "the present War Cabinet has not got the drive and decision which I think it should have if we are going to get out of this war in the way which everybody believes and hopes and wills, that we shall."[11] In due course this call for a change in personalities, most notably Hoare and Simon, coalesced with the small cabinet mantra. There is some irony to be found in the ongoing vilification of Hoare. As has been seen he was one of the most persistently determined advocates of an aggressive air policy, first as lord privy seal and then as secretary of state for air. He was often more so than Churchill, the recognized firebrand within the cabinet.

At the end of the Finland debates Chamberlain's concessions were minor and reluctantly given. He acknowledged things could be better done and claimed he had "no rigid mind upon matters of administration and the machinery of government," but he believed there was a "right time and wrong time for everything."[12] He argued the Finnish problem had little to do with the machinery of government and everything to do with obstructionist Norway and Sweden. He was not persuaded his ministers were doing anything other than a good job. He did not intend to discard Simon or Hoare, and their prewar history apart, there was little genuine reason for doing so.

Nevertheless, at the end of March several significant initiatives were in the War Cabinet pipeline, although it is difficult to determine the extent to which these were prompted by the pressures of domestic politics or the post-Finland international political situation. The discussion within the War Cabinet, and the papers written by its members at this time, suggested that little or no store was being placed in the views of government critics and instead that initiatives were being taken in response to the wider strategic and political situation. Indeed, several cabinet members counseled against being pressured into adventures. The War Cabinet shared the Commons' view that neutrals' confidence must be restored and this required action, but it viewed the solution quite differently. Beyond the short-term plans for Norway and Royal Marine, the government had no intention to ramp up aggression and pursue the initiative as some within the House would have wished but instead intended to return to its "sit tight and rearm" posture and prepare for the imminent prospect of a German offensive in late spring. There was much wisdom in doing so.

At the beginning of April, Chamberlain made his modest changes within the War Cabinet, and this included strengthening Churchill's role in the MCC. It is, again, difficult to assess the extent to which this promotion was designed to assuage government critics or merely reflected the practical reality of Churchill's two pet projects being at the forefront of British policy. If this were a measure intended to mollify critics, it was not a success.[13] Churchill's new role was not well understood (nor was the actual functioning of the MCC at any time), and when his promotion was subsequently explained, it was criticized for imposing an excessive burden on him.

Unfortunately for Chamberlain, the Narvik initiative and Royal Marine were unknown—as was French resistance to the latter—before the German invasion of Norway, the next and final crisis of his government. Thus, as this new and most dramatic of threats developed, there was little to suggest Chamberlain had been listening; despite these initiatives, he remained exposed to the "do nothing" tag.

Inside the House of Commons: Norway

The new crisis for Chamberlain began in the early hours of 9 April with the German landings in Norway. As momentous and shocking as this event was and despite the admonishments delivered during the previous month, it was not an immediate disaster for him. After all, no one yet knew if in subsequent days and weeks they would be celebrating victory or mourning defeat. Nevertheless, comments from within and without the House underscored the extent to which failure in this new challenge threatened Chamberlain's government and his leadership.

Unfortunately for Chamberlain, buoyed by the optimism Churchill had displayed at the late morning War Cabinet meeting of 9 April, the prime minister began this new campaign by immediately committing a cardinal sin: he was unwisely upbeat in his speech to the House that afternoon. After providing general, but necessarily uncertain, details of German movements, he declared: "I have no doubt that this further rash and cruel act of aggression will redound to Germany's disadvantage, and contribute to her ultimate defeat." In response Attlee said little beyond offering support for the Danes and Norwegians and expressing his hope "that aid will be given in full, and that it will be speedy, and that it will be effective." Sinclair also hoped British action would be "prompt, swift and effective."[14]

Some MPs were more anxious. They were already alert to the extraordinary nature of German success and their questions anticipated the difficulties both Chamberlain and Churchill would face when this was more fully understood. Liberal MP Geoffrey Mander wanted to know if it were true that the Germans had occupied Narvik and Bergen, a fact he considered "remarkable . . . a very astonishing and startling thing," while the "British Fleet held the seas." Chamberlain confirmed reports the Germans had landed at Bergen but expressed his doubt regarding Narvik. He could offer no more information but promised Churchill would update events in due course. Overall, the response of the House was muted.

Churchill gave his much-awaited overview of events in Norway to the House on 11 April. Two aspects of the speech had a particular bearing on the debates of 7 and 8 May. First, was the extent to which it ignored or concealed the unfortunate events of 7 and 8 April (considered in chapter 7). In the decisions of these two days Churchill's greatest failures were to be found; it was unsurprising, therefore, that these days received scant attention in his speech and were scrupulously avoided thereafter. Thus was he protected from the most damning criticism he could have faced over Norway. The extent to which this silence represented a wider War Cabinet conspiracy of silence that helped him retain sufficient credibility to be considered an alternative prime minister is considered later in this chapter.

Churchill's speech was also important because it gave even more cause for optimism over the outcome of the campaign than had Chamberlain's. This was despite recent news that the Germans had also occupied Narvik.

This hopeful message was followed by almost three weeks of silence, broken occasionally by further indiscrete and inaccurate news of success in Norway; thus, when news of defeat spread at the beginning of May, the disappointment was palpable and prolonged. This would redound much more on Chamberlain than on Churchill.

Churchill began his 11 April speech with details of the British mining operation that had coincided with the German action. As to the circumstances that permitted the Germans to secure the major ports along the west coast—the issues to which he was personally most vulnerable and exposed—he was vague and evasive. German success was a result of the nature of war at sea, the profound difficulty in discovering German naval movements, and the shortcomings of the Norwegians themselves.

Although many were impressed by the vigor of Churchill's speech—and some commended him for it—not all were satisfied by the reasons he gave for German success. Harold Nicolson was an unsatisfied observer and noted that Churchill did not explain how it was the Germans had gotten past the Royal Navy. It was Churchill's good fortune that Nicolson and others took this question no further, for it protected him from a potentially career-ending censure.

If obfuscation on this issue was of immense importance to Churchill's reputation, it was also highly problematic for Chamberlain. Inevitably, when the House became aware of the considerable intelligence surrounding a possible German invasion of Norway, the issue of how the Germans managed to get by the Royal Navy became even more incomprehensible. Why had the government been so unprepared? The obvious riposte would have been to explain the extensive preparations of ships and men under Operation R4, but the House would then have demanded to understand why, despite these preparations, the Germans had succeeded. On subsequent occasions there were searching questions on this issue—and several vague answers given—but none within the House was ever permitted to grasp how closely run were the events of these two days, nor the extent to which Churchill and the Admiralty were responsible for the Navy's failure to seize the opportunities offered.

It is difficult to determine how calculatedly complicit the War Cabinet was in limiting exploration into this critical period, but evidence suggests its members were cognizant that the less said the better. In early May, while drafting his speech to the House of Lords for the Norway debates, Halifax told a confidant that nothing negative could be said in regard to Churchill, and he made reference to the latter's order to disembark the R4 forces.[15] It is apparent Halifax and probably others viewed this as a significant event, although this study has argued that it was not. Nevertheless, the extent to which this detail alone, had it been known to the House, might have seriously compromised Churchill can be estimated by Sinclair's observation during his speech on 7 May: "If the expeditionary force had been available a day or two earlier, it could have struck with naval support before the German air force had settled in the Norwegian aerodromes and brought in supplies."[16] As for Churchill's other errors of judgment, including his conviction Narvik alone was the target of German aggression, it is probable that no one who attended the War Cabinet, other than Churchill and Pound, fully understood their consequences.

Whatever the extent of the War Cabinet's awareness of the Admiralty's shortcomings, Chamberlain would have appreciated that the more these vital two days were shrouded in mystery the more his critics would be permitted to draw their own conclusion. In these circumstances it would not be Churchill or the Admiralty bearing responsibility for this folly, but Chamberlain.

No doubt Churchill was aware of the can of worms that would be opened if scrutiny of 7 and 8 April occurred. This can be glimpsed in his explanation on 11 April as to why the mining forces, working in Norwegian waters and supported by HMS *Renown*, had failed to discover the German forces before they arrived at Narvik. These forces, he said, had been immediately withdrawn from the Norwegian coastline to avoid a confrontation with the Norwegians. We know, of course, the mining forces had been instructed to fall back on *Renown*, not only to permit concentration but to intercept and engage the enemy heading for Narvik. Instead, incomplete knowledge of *Renown*'s whereabouts effectively opened the door to Narvik. No such explanation was ever offered to the House.

In the immediate term Churchill's 11 April assertion that the Germans had made a grave strategic error in Norway and that the Royal Navy would take a heavy toll on them instilled enormous confidence. It helped boost his stocks and stay further censure of Chamberlain, but it was evident a crisis would ensue if results failed to meet the expectations he had fostered. Albert Alexander, who was Churchill's most astute (but nevertheless unsuccessful) inquisitor during the May debate, was generous in his praise of Churchill's positive message. He thought that if the government applied the note of determination conveyed in Churchill's speech to the battle for Norway, it could "look to support for that type of action and vigor in prosecuting the War from all members of the House." Sinclair adopted a similar tone when he suggested success in Norway would be an opportunity to efface past examples of vacillation and ineffectiveness.[17] Norway, therefore, was an opportunity for redemption or a likely spur for significant change. On 11 April both Churchill and Chamberlain remained optimistic. Their optimism would not last, nor would the hopes of the House.

Despite the reserved nature of the criticism and an endorsement of Churchill's fighting speech, Chamberlain's critics did not miss the opportunity to take a further swipe at the prime minister; many resented the emotional roller coaster to which they had been subjected over the previous two days. Following Chamberlain's optimistic comments on 9 April, news had come in confirming the capture of all the major west coast ports, including Narvik; this was followed by inaccurate news—subsequently corrected—of resounding Allied success with the recapture of Narvik and Trondheim and then news of naval losses at Narvik. This variously fueled anxiety, hope, disappointment, and then anger, a stress-filled experience that was not forgotten in the May debates. Sinclair returned to a now well-worn theme when he declared that there was "no service" in minimizing Germany's latest success and that it was not desirable to "prophesy smooth things to the people. Keep a firm grip on reality. . . . When I hear responsible ministers and public servants saying that Hitler has 'missed the bus' and that we have turned the corner, I am not impressed."[18]

This reference was, of course, a response to Chamberlain's faux pas of early April, but it was also criticism of his 9 April optimism, which was quickly followed by the conflicting and deflating news via the BBC and newspapers. The criticism also reflected a longer-term frustration with Chamberlain's perceived inclination to minimize the consequences of failure.[19] Still, many critics remained uninclined to attack Chamberlain even as they were prepared to attack his government. One implored him to get rid of his "duds"; another accused him of being too influenced by "personal likes and dislikes" and of rejecting obvious talent (with the exceptions of Churchill and Eden).[20] This criticism would not go away.

Overall, the debate pointed to a willingness—at least among Conservatives—to chastise Chamberlain for his optimistic statements while accepting Churchill's at face value. Much of this criticism was of a carping quality, but there was sufficient amount of it to suggest that the lack of accurate information, rendered openly, honestly, and accurately, was a genuine concern. It was not, however, an issue that could be immediately or easily remedied and was certainly not something for which Chamberlain personally could be justifiably held to account.

For entirely practical reasons of security, the discussions of 11 April were the last on Norway in the House until 2 May. The silence would weigh heavily against the government because the next detailed news provided by the government was of failure and withdrawal. In the interim, members gleaned knowledge of events in Norway from the radio and British newspapers— sometimes fed by inaccurate reports from Sweden and elsewhere—and also from gossip and rumor, including that from returning servicemen. Some members—among them those least disposed to Chamberlain—acquired intelligence from deep within the Admiralty via Commander Robert Bower, who was more than willing to report the worst of news and often did so inaccurately. The frustration that developed over too little information, and too much misinformation, was also manifest on 7 and 8 May.

Beyond the House: Salisbury and His Committee

Despite matters in the Commons being in abeyance as success or failure was played out in Norway, the key government critics escalated their change agenda during April. Lord Salisbury's Watching Committee had its first formal meeting on 4 April. Three days later Chamberlain received clear evidence his recent War Cabinet initiatives had done nothing to assuage his critics when Salisbury visited him and declared his committee's unanimous conviction that a small executive-style War Cabinet was necessary. This reflected the committee's concern that the existing government was ineffective and inefficient, a belief most surely reinforced by Germany's successful occupation of Norway. Chamberlain was unimpressed and expressed his doubt the public would wish to see the service ministers divested of their positions in the War Cabinet.

Salisbury also expressed concern about Churchill's new role as chairman of the MCC while he retained his position as first lord. Salisbury's view was that these roles were incompatible and demanded too much of Churchill. Chamberlain demurred and noted Churchill had "not asked in any way to be relieved" of this double responsibility.[21] Salisbury then raised the question of adding new blood to the cabinet. In a reply that was certain to upset his critics, some of whom considered themselves suitable replacements for existing ministers, Chamberlain spoke of a dearth of talent, a circumstance he attributed to the great losses of World War I.[22] Inevitably, the discussion moved to Norway, and Salisbury warned that "unless we were successful . . . the results would be serious." It is likely that Chamberlain had some awareness of this, but at this juncture he thought all would be well. Thus, his response to the warning was little more than to take umbrage and declare that the neutrals were largely at fault for their existing dilemma. It is certain Salisbury drew nothing positive from his interview. As for Chamberlain, he evidently felt sufficiently confident at this time to ignore his fellow party men and carry on as he was. In any event there would have been no opportunity to make the changes suggested in the midst of the existing crisis.

By mid-April concerns over the War Cabinet structure began to coalesce with anxiety over—or a new strategy toward—Churchill. He had looked very tired during his 11 April speech, and when rumor spread in mid-April that he had sought the support of Chamberlain to chair the MCC meetings, an explanation for this was fatigue brought on by his dual role as MCC chairman and first lord. Thus, although Churchill's greater role within the War Cabinet was welcomed by Salisbury and his supporters, these men became increasingly convinced this reform was, at once, too much and not enough.

Having achieved little or nothing with Chamberlain, Salisbury sought a meeting with Churchill on 19 April and covered similar territory with him. Salisbury explained the Watching Committee's preference for a small War Cabinet, which, among other things, would see its members divested of portfolio responsibilities, including the three service ministers. Much to Salisbury's frustration, Churchill was "resolutely opposed to any change which would deprive him of this great position of authority and usefulness [the Admiralty] in order to be a mere chairman without power." As the conversation progressed, Salisbury grasped Churchill's existing role as chairman did not confer the authority he and others had believed, and this might largely explain why Churchill was so unreceptive to the idea of losing the Admiralty. Salisbury explained he did not "contemplate any diminution of Churchill's authority," but apparently Churchill feared otherwise.[23]

On 24 April Salisbury wrote to Churchill of the most recent Watching Committee meeting and clarified that its members did not wish to deny him the Admiralty except to place him in "a still better position to control under the Cabinet the operations of the War." He expressed the committee's concerns over his dual role and mentioned also their anxiety, based on Churchill's own comments, that the government currently had "no Minister of Defense at all."[24] Salisbury concluded that "so long as the success of the Norwegian campaign continues, criticism in this head will die down." This comment is important for two reasons. First, it reflected the extent to which Norway was being viewed as a decisive event in Chamberlain's government and potentially in the work of the committee itself; that is, success in Norway would reinforce Chamberlain's leadership, and failure would seriously undermine it. Second, the comment showed a surprising confidence in the progress of the Norwegian campaign as late as 24 April. This was an indication of how little people outside the War Cabinet understood what was taking place.[25] By this time the War Cabinet was fully aware of the parlous state of operations in central Norway and was well on the way to its decision to withdraw. The extent of the shock, therefore, to which the Houses of Parliament were soon to be exposed is to be understood.

Churchill's response to Salisbury's inquiries opens some important questions regarding his relationship with these party activists, his pursuit of the premiership, and also the strength of his relationship with Chamberlain fewer than three weeks before he became prime minister. It also offers another perspective on the anti-Chamberlain movement and Churchill's part in it. By 24 April Churchill was fully aware he had strong support in the Watching Committee and among other government critics. He must also have been aware this support would shelter him from much of the fallout should the Allies fail in Norway. Additionally, he could not have failed to appreciate that despite his own reservations about the committee's small cabinet plans, including the potential loss of the Admiralty, he would be empowered under the committee's agenda. With these assumptions in mind, Churchill's actions at this time are not readily explicated.

The day he received Salisbury's letter expressing the Watching Committee's preference for a small cabinet, with him playing a dominant role within it, Churchill drafted his letter to Chamberlain that began: "Being anxious to sustain you to the best of my ability, I must warn you that you are approaching a head-on smash in Norway." In this letter Churchill declined to resume the chairmanship of the MCC unless he was given more power. Given the coincidence of this correspondence with his communication from Salisbury, it is difficult to imagine other than the former was influenced by the latter.

Churchill's letter, we know, was not sent, for by coincidence Chamberlain invited him to a meeting that evening during which the issue of the MCC and his role in it were thrashed out. In a subsequent letter to his sister, Chamberlain explained the meeting had been prompted by news Churchill had been "complaining bitterly of being 'thwarted' and not having sufficient powers."[26] This most likely pertained to the issue of Trondheim and the indecision that had surrounded it. Be this as it may, it was, according to Chamberlain, a positive discussion during which Churchill professed his loyalty but also expressed his concerns over the functioning of the MCC.[27]

Others, such as Colville, were much more critical of Churchill's actions and motivation at this time, and these assessments have dominated analyses and reinforced the perception of division between the two. However, it is far from clear this existed at a personal level, and it is desirable to consider other reasons why Churchill chose this juncture to warn Chamberlain of the "head-on smash" he was facing over failure in Norway. We have, of course, the analysis of this letter and his discussion with Chamberlain offered earlier in this work; Churchill was reluctant to continue accepting responsibility for decisions he believed were not his own and for which, if they led to failure, he might be called to account. This explanation was offered in the context of the practical challenges of the Norwegian campaign. It is also possible that in his discussions with Chamberlain, Churchill used the knowledge of Salisbury's support to get what he wanted from a perceived position of strength. However, it is even more reasonable to imagine that despite Salisbury's efforts to allay his fears, Churchill worried he might be less influential under any changes being pressed by the Watching Committee than he would be under Chamberlain if the latter acquiesced in his further empowerment. Furthermore, Churchill would have understood that in pushing for, and then accepting with considerable enthusiasm, a greater role in the War Cabinet under Chamberlain, he was defusing a major source of criticism directed at Chamberlain's government. Salisbury had noted the call for change would lose its force if things went well in Norway; Churchill already knew that things were destined to get worse. A man more attuned to his destiny, or with one eye determinedly on the premiership, would surely have acted otherwise.

There was, perhaps, another factor providing direction to Churchill's actions. Although his discussions with Salisbury indicated the Watching Committee's willingness to have him play a major role in military matters, there is no evidence either Salisbury or his committee saw Churchill as a potential alternative prime minister. Given these circumstances, it is unsurprising that Churchill would have been keen to see Chamberlain remain in power rather than be replaced by some uncertain other; this might have been Halifax, who Churchill likely considered less amenable to his ideas than Chamberlain was, or any of a number of Chamberlain critics.

If Churchill's vision for the future was Chamberlain as prime minister and he as a putative minister for defense, a precedent could be found in World War I, when a plot was launched to place Lloyd George in control of a small War Cabinet while H. H. Asquith was retained as prime minister to run the nonmilitary side of the war. The parallels are compelling. In late April 1940 Churchill's purpose would have been to achieve this objective while avoiding the acrimony that accompanied Lloyd George's actions.

For all the assumptions, both contemporary and historical, that Churchill was at serious odds with the direction of the government at this juncture and that he was pushing a personal leadership agenda, there is a strong case to be made for the view that Churchill considered Chamberlain integral to his own future. The extent to which Churchill was less than enamored with the interference of the Watching Committee and not in sympathy with government critics can be illustrated further by a consideration of the committee's growing determination to implement a more aggressive air policy. This was an agenda very much at odds with Churchill's own convictions. By late April it was increasingly evident that Chamberlain's critics believed the best—perhaps the only—way to seize the initiative in the war and to secure support from wavering neutrals was to begin bombing Germany. They were being influenced by the ongoing agitation of Lord Trenchard and also their own discontent with the government's hypocrisy in permitting Norway to be bombed while maintaining a veto against the bombing of Germany.[28] For many, among them Amery and Salisbury, it seemed that the War Cabinet was content to see Norwegians bombed but not Germans, and indeed it was. The difficulty for the Watching Committee and its effort to secure Churchill's support for a more aggressive air policy in response to events in Norway was that Churchill was not in sympathy.[29]

In late April, alongside Chamberlain and Halifax, Churchill was the most conservative member in the War Cabinet regarding any premature escalation in the air war. Thus, at the end of April he was at odds with two core initiatives of the Conservative critics. He was not enamored of the Watching Committee's small War Cabinet—especially now he had secured even more authority in the MCC—and he was strongly opposed to a more aggressive air policy. He was fully aware of the practical implications of such a change and the serious obstacles before it. He was also more aware than Chamberlain's critics of the extent to which Chamberlain, in recent weeks, had sought to drive a more proactive and aggressive agenda.

Having received only modest interest in their causes from Chamberlain and Churchill, a deputation of senior members of the Watching Committee, among them Amery and Trenchard, visited the third of the big three, Halifax, on 29 April.[30] A new topic for discussion—also of most recent debate within the House—was concern over supply and the insufficient voting of funds in the budget, but beyond this the agenda was fairly predictable: the government's ongoing failure to secure the initiative and concerns over the intelligence failure that had, apparently, helped the Germans to secure Norway. The principal topic, however, was the committee's determination that air attacks on German objectives should begin. In his responses Halifax offered little more than had Chamberlain and Churchill. He believed that as far as supply was concerned, "everything required to be done would be done." As to seizing the initiative, he argued that democracies were always at a disadvantage against countries like Germany. Considerable time was required to marshal forces, and meanwhile Germany could act at any time along interior lines in any direction. This in essence was Chamberlain's thesis—that Britain should be aggressive when it was capable of being so and that in the interim it could expect to be on the defensive. As for the intelligence failure of Narvik, Halifax explained away this much as others had: the government had known of the assembly of forces in the Baltic but had not known where they would be used. Little more was said on this issue, ensuring that the failures of 7 and 8 April remained a mystery. In response to the committee's determination to escalate the air war, Halifax cautioned those present against pressing a strategy "to which our experts advise is for the best in winning the War merely because it was showy (or some word to that effect) . . . as things now stand our experts [the COS] would still be against an air attack on Germany."[31] This was an important observation. It accurately identified the extent to which the War Cabinet was being guided by professional advice in its policies; the growing consensus among critics was that it was doing quite the opposite and that this idleness was down to Chamberlain. The critics' position was much as it had been when they chastised the political decisions surrounding the Finnish option. Had those challenging Halifax on air policy been exposed to the unanimous views of the COS—as had the War Cabinet—it is difficult to imagine any would have continued to press Trenchard's views, regardless of how uncomfortable they felt with existing policy.

At the end of April there was little common ground between the three key members of the War Cabinet—Chamberlain, Churchill, and Halifax—and the core Conservative critics. Chamberlain had been courteous but dismissive, Churchill had been interested but hesitant on the issue of a small cabinet (and had, presumably, informed them of his own reluctance to escalate the air war), and Halifax had been pragmatic in response to the agenda being offered. In assessing the merit of the Watching Committee's criticism of policy, it is far from clear its proposals were superior. Churchill, Chamberlain, and Halifax were dealing with the practical challenges of fighting the war alongside a cautious ally. The Watching Committee's anxieties were justified on many issues: the Germans were always one step ahead of the Allies, the Allied air policy was lacking integrity, and it was certainly desirable to find the ways and means to take the initiative. However, the committee's solutions were not necessarily practicable or immediately desirable. Moreover, the government's essentially defensive posture was a matter of not only French intransigence but the COS conviction this was the best way forward, especially given the imminence of the campaigning season.

Again, the dilemma for Chamberlain was that whatever the merit of his approach—a "sit tight and rearm" policy—it was the least persuasive response to accusations of "doing nothing." Chamberlain was as aware as anyone of the need to give the perception of strength in the absence of strength, but there was little or no common ground with his critics as to how this ought to be done. This applied, in most respects, to his critics' potential champion, Churchill.

Overall, it is not at all clear that the policy changes being proposed would have led to a more successful prosecution of the war. It is possible that matters might have been decidedly worse, and this evidently was the concern of the COS. As to what Churchill's contribution might have been had he been given more power at this or an earlier juncture, much evidence has been presented to suggest that had he gotten his way entirely, things might have been much worse. However, as to the matter of an escalation in the air war, it is probable there would have been little or no change.

Rather than champing at the bit for change, at the beginning of May 1940, Churchill was more amenable to Chamberlain, to the government, and to his role in it than he had been at any time in the war. There is much else that incidentally points to Churchill's contentment with the direction of things, albeit at a time of considerable anxiety over Norway. Several other episodes provide evidence of his loyalty to Chamberlain and also hint at remarkably limited aspirations right up to 9 May. On 1 May Churchill had one of his periodic talks with W. P. Crozier, during which he spoke of his recent promotion in the MCC. Few outside the War Cabinet officially knew of this; Chamberlain made it widely known only during the debate on 7 May.[32] Churchill's promotion proved another failed opportunity by Chamberlain—if he viewed it as such—to neutralize criticism of his government by giving Churchill more power. The promotion was too little too late, and it failed to meet the small cabinet demands of the critics or to assuage ongoing concerns over Churchill's dual role. Furthermore, when revealed, it tended to absolve Churchill of responsibility for much of the Norwegian debacle; it made little sense for Chamberlain to have given more authority to Churchill if he had been a major contributor to failure in Norway.[33]

Crozier began his discussion with Churchill with reference to what had evidently become a topical issue: his chairmanship of the MCC in combination with his role as first lord and the burden this placed on him. Churchill responded enthusiastically, "But now I have more powers—I've got more powers! (He seemed very pleased about this)." He dismissed the issue of stress: "I don't feel the strain. I can do it."[34]

Three days later Churchill met Lord Camrose, publisher and editor in chief of the *Daily Telegraph* who, as always, kept a meticulous record of the discussion. Camrose recorded, "He (C) was on excellent terms with the PM, better than ever before. He had told the latter that he did not want to continue as Chairman of the Ministers' Committee and carry the responsibility without any power. The latter had acquiesced, and as from 1 May he would have the right to attend and take the Chair at the meetings of the joint staffs." That Churchill was excited about his new role was reinforced by his declaration that he had shown the document to Lloyd George, who had said to him that "it was exactly the same authority he (Ll G) had failed to secure from Asquith" during World War I. These comments from Churchill also indicate the extent to which his horizons, even at this late juncture, did not extend beyond a position akin to a minister for defense. Whether or not Churchill had in mind the fate that subsequently befell Asquith (he was succeeded by Lloyd George) when he drew these parallels is moot. Churchill informed Camrose of his meeting with Lord Salisbury, who had told Churchill he had been having meetings with some fifty people who all believed Churchill "should be given the powers and facilities which were now his."[35]

Churchill's contentment with his new circumstance four days before the Norway debate seems clear. The record of his conversation with Camrose indicates he anticipated continuing his work with Chamberlain, a man whom he had long forgiven for his past failings: "He [Churchill] thought they would get through the debate all right, but a number of people were out for the PM's blood—people who have never forgiven him for Munich."[36]

Lord Camrose also recorded several more general observations from Churchill about the lack of wisdom Chamberlain had shown in selecting his cabinet and the men he might have included in the government. These included Sinclair, who Churchill claimed he could have brought in to Chamberlain's government. Sinclair, he said, "would have represented a million

Liberals . . . who would now have been supporting the Government instead of running them down." Churchill would also have had Duff Cooper, Amery, and "others in too—not left them to become the fierce critics and rallying points for opposition. Sinclair was one of his oldest friends and he regretted very much that they should have been in opposition to each other." Camrose concluded: "I could not help feeling that he was not quite happy with the present make-up of the Government, that he was a little afraid of criticism from the Liberal and Conservative side, and that he was not quite the master of himself or cool politician that the PM is."[37]

Nothing in these records suggests that Churchill imagined he might be in line for the premiership or that in the turmoil of the time, he was taking measures to make this possible. If anything, apart from his concerns about the makeup of the War Cabinet, Churchill's focus was entirely on shoring up the government's position, rather than on taking advantage of any potential collapse.

In the days leading to the Norway debate, Churchill appreciated that the best way to limit the harm done by the withdrawal from central Norway was to capture Narvik. The day after his discussion with Camrose, he telegraphed Lord Cork approving Cork's intentions to be more aggressive at Narvik: "Urgency of Narvik," Churchill wrote, "is extreme."[38] Again, a more calculating Churchill would have been aware that success at Narvik would have done much to extricate Chamberlain from the serious political predicament he was in.

Just as there is little evidence that Churchill was working toward the premiership or was seriously at odds with the government, there is little persuasive evidence Chamberlain was playing any kind of deep game in his relationship with Churchill. There is little doubt, as recorded by Minister for Information Sir John Reith, that Chamberlain was frustrated by "Churchill's reputation so inflated and based on broadcasts" and that he was anxious about rumors Churchill "was being tempted to lead a revolt against the P.M.," as recorded by Henry Channon. However, these were essentially unsurprising responses to concerns, as recorded by John Colville, that Churchill's "satellites (e.g. Duff Cooper, Amery, etc) were doing all in their power to create mischief and ill-feeling."[39] These men were certainly doing this, but it is difficult to describe Amery, for example, as in any strong sense a satellite of Churchill.

There is, therefore, a certain irony in Harold Nicolson's records from several days earlier, which said, "The Tapers and Tadpoles are putting it around that the whole Norwegian episode is due to Winston."[40] Nicolson would have written this with disapproval, and historians have frequently referred to this diary entry to indicate the improper behavior of the Chamberlain camp toward Churchill. However, if this were the tenor of whip activity, it might just as readily be seen as a necessary response to the misinformation being spread about by hyperactive Chamberlain critics who were determined to place responsibility for failure in Norway and elsewhere entirely at the prime minister's feet.

That Chamberlain might have been willing to see the activities of Amery and others countered with some debunking by his own supporters is surely unsurprising, but this does not imply personal animus toward Churchill so much as self-preservation.[41] As much as the records of Reith and Channon build a picture of dislike, they are at their least persuasive when purporting to know Chamberlain's inner thoughts; they are no more persuasive than the commentaries of Churchill's supporters that imply they knew his. Of Chamberlain, Reith concluded, "There is no doubt how he feels about Churchill," while Channon expressed the view that Chamberlain was playing a "deep game" and had given Churchill "more rope" by making him "what amounts to the Director of Operations."[42] To further illustrate the dubious accuracy of Channon's appreciations, one can cite his diary entry of 25 April. He recorded a conversation with Alex Dunglass, Chamberlain's parliamentary private secretary: "Dunglass pumped me; did I think that Winston, the man who has never been right, should be deflated, was the moment ripe to begin to sell him? Ought he to leave the Admiralty? Evidently these thoughts are in Neville's head."[43]

What was in Chamberlain's head that day was not the deflation of Churchill but a draft outline of the new powers to be given to him within the MCC, an outline he subsequently set before his advisers for critical comment. Unlike some of his arch-supporters, Chamberlain accepted that any mischievousness was being done by Churchill's supporters and not Churchill himself.[44] His comments to his sister of 4 May indicate an attitude toward Churchill that he had held for some time: he believed that Churchill wished to work with him and that he was valuable to his government and the Allied cause, although he believed him not quite the warlord and salvation the public imagined. "I am extremely anxious not to have any breach with him for that would be disastrous for the Allied cause and I am sure he does not want one. . . . How thankful I must be that the good British public does not know the truth & persists in ideas which recall the Kitchener legend. Winston changed his mind *four times* over Trondheim."[45]

Despite Channon's speculation, and an equally bleak perspective from Churchill's own supporters that he was being set up for failure, it is nonsense to imagine Chamberlain would have given Churchill his new MCC role if he did not recognize that despite his occasional waywardness—including his supposed shortcomings over Trondheim—he knew more of war than anyone else in the cabinet. A war was being fought, after all, and political history tends to forget this. Although there is certainly an element of churlishness in Chamberlain's letter, there is little doubt that Chamberlain accepted Churchill was important to Britain's war effort and to any Conservative government, whether or not he, Chamberlain, was at its head. However, the prime minister also believed that Churchill needed supervision by more cautious and steadier minds, and this would be provided by him and by Halifax.[46]

If, as the rumor mill suggested, Chamberlain was either colluding in or turning a blind eye to the machinations of the party whips in May or earlier to undo Churchill, it would have been extraordinarily unwise political behavior—so unwise as to make it implausible. Chamberlain had promoted Churchill at the beginning of April and again at the end. Although the latter promotion was officially known only to War Cabinet members, courtesy of Brendan Bracken it quickly became an open secret. It is impossible to imagine that Chamberlain would have simultaneously conspired to blame failure in Norway on Churchill's incompetence. Such, however, are the circumstances supporters of this conspiratorial view would require us to accept. A no more certain path to shattered credibility for Chamberlain could be imagined.

The Withdrawal from Central Norway and Its Consequences for Chamberlain

On 2 May Chamberlain announced to the House the withdrawal of forces south of Trondheim. That the government intended to withdraw from central Norway—a process already begun—was not immediately told, although to some it was already known. The impression given was that troops being withdrawn from Åndalsnes were to be used farther north and that Trondheim remained a prospective target. This impression was intended to deceive the Germans, but while many now understood the full extent of withdrawal plans, the news probably deceived a great many within Parliament and caused them to cling to hopes soon shattered. The ruse may have been a necessary military deception, but it was also a political disaster. Five days before the Norwegian debate, members were again to be misled and let down.

Even at this late juncture Chamberlain was largely ignorant of the hornet's nest being stirred by this repeated disappointment. He, like all members of the War Cabinet, underestimated the resentment developing over Norway. On 30 April he informed Attlee and Sinclair of the withdrawal from Åndalsnes and the plans for the withdrawal from central Norway. He thought they had taken the news well, and he told the War Cabinet, "No difficulty need be anticipated in the House of Commons."[47] However, he immediately noted that both men had wished to know why Churchill's promise to cut German supply lines to Norway had not been fulfilled—surely a sign of challenging questions ahead.

Chamberlain's political radar failed him as badly regarding his own party. The War Cabinet or the Admiralty had been leaking like a sieve, and the news of the withdrawal had quickly reached Leo Amery by the ever-mischievous Commander Bower soon after Amery's meeting with Halifax on the twenty-ninth. Amery's diary conveys a sense of cataclysm in response to the withdrawal that would have shocked Chamberlain. Amery's writing made clear the government could not expect the soft landing that it was hoping for and that Chamberlain expected. Critics were not about to accept Norway as anything other than unmitigated defeat, yet the government's strategy was to argue otherwise. Amery rushed about gathering as much information as he could and finally found Samuel Hoare, to whom he declared the withdrawal "meant the end of HMG [her majesty's government]." Hoare replied only that "they had to do what they thought right."[48] For a time Amery contemplated action to reverse the withdrawal decision and was willing to support Sir Roger Keyes' ongoing efforts to lead a naval attack on Trondheim. Amery's diary records a variety of largely inaccurate reasons why the attempt to take Trondheim had been abandoned, among them that Churchill had declined because "he is so obsessed now with the fear of Italy that he won't risk a single old ship."[49] It was not Churchill who was preoccupied with the Italian threat but senior naval staff, principally Phillips, and there was much cause to be anxious.

By the following day Amery was recording, even more inaccurately, that the "decision to scuttle" was down to the French, who, "of course, care less about Norway and do not realise its bearing on the sea issue and want their hands free to deal with Italy." Nothing could have been further from the truth. Amery consulted Attlee about the capture of Trondheim, but Attlee accepted the false assumptions about the French and concluded the decision to withdraw was "irrevocable and [he] saw no use in an emergency secret session or in asking Neville to give last minute considerations to Keyes' plan."[50]

Chamberlain's 2 May announcement to the House met another comparatively subdued response, but it had little to do with the temper of its members. As always they felt constrained by the military circumstances of the time; those more fully informed would have known the evacuation from Namsos was in train. Amery noted in his diary, "No debate, everyone wisely preferring to leave things till next week, but the House greatly worried."[51] Nevertheless, the rumor mill was running at full tilt and was feeding a determination to see the failure in central Norway produce definitive political change. Amery continued to receive intelligence, frequently inaccurate, but always provocative, from a variety of sources. On 2 May he again met Bower, who told him "definitely that the Staff plan for Trondheim was both 'Hammer' and 'Pincer' and that the hammer part was over-ruled by the Cabinet. Winston apparently acquiescing (another story I was told was that it was settled between Neville and Winston, the latter never very keen on Trondheim and frightened of naval losses!)."[52] As for a store of evidence against British air policy, Amery recorded Bower's claim that the War Cabinet agreed after only two days to bomb Stavanger airfield "on the condition that only six bombers" were used.[53] Later in the day Amery attended an "emergency conclave . . . to discuss line for next week's debate." At this stage he intended only to push for "national government and War Cabinet," but the Labour Party ensured this meant the end of Chamberlain, if not the rise of Churchill.[54]

Two days later, and a mere three days before the debate, Harold Nicolson was still recording the fallout from Chamberlain's 2 May speech: "I find there is a grave suspicion of the Prime Minister. His speech . . . has created disquiet. The P.M. said that 'the balance of advantage rested with us' and that 'Germany has not attained her objective.' They know this is simply not true. If Chamberlain believed it himself, then he was stupid. If he did not believe it, then he was trying to deceive. In either case he loses confidence." Nicolson's distress was compounded by the uncomfortable question of who could replace Chamberlain: "We always say that our advantage over the German leadership principle is that we can always find another leader. Now we cannot." He wrote, "Eden is out. Churchill is undermined by the Conservative caucus. Halifax is believed (and with justice) to be a tired man."[55]

Inside the House: The Progress of the War Debate, 7 and 8 May

The debate of 7 and 8 May has been considered in detail by historians. The focus is invariably on the major—some say decisive—speeches of Keyes, Amery, Lloyd George, and a few others. The extent to which the rhetoric of these speakers contributed to Chamberlain's downfall is difficult to assess; it is likely, though, that the temper of the first day speeches encouraged the Labour Party to reverse its decision against a division and also contributed to the results.[56] Similarly, the strength of feeling within the House encouraged the high abstention rate that was at least as important in Chamberlain's decision to resign as the no votes of his party critics. However, rather than discuss the impact of the speeches, the purpose here is to explore briefly the substance of the criticism and the government's defense and to understand why Churchill walked away comparatively unscathed. The object also is to consider the attitude of Churchill and Chamberlain to the circumstances that began to emerge around the leadership.

The debate was never meant to be about Norway but the progress of the war; unsurprisingly, Norway became central to it.[57] Both opposition and government forces prepared their cases with care. Chamberlain's opening speech received extensive input from his private secretaries and War Cabinet secretaries, Arthur Rucker, Wilson, and Bridges, and it was viewed by the three service ministers and also Halifax and Hankey. The extent to which the Conservative critics cooperated in their preparations is less clear, but Amery's reference to an "emergency conclave" suggests there was some level of coordination. As for the government, Churchill was aware of what

Chamberlain intended to say and of his positions on core issues; it is unclear if Chamberlain or anyone else reviewed Churchill's speech, although his War Cabinet colleagues must surely have had some idea as to the direction he would take. As last speaker Churchill would have been expected to rebut his critics, yet he did little of this. His introductory remarks made clear he had a prepared path and he intended to follow it. This mortified his interlocutors, who sought answers to a great many questions but received little satisfaction.

The decision to have Chamberlain begin the debate and Churchill to finish was an article of faith between the two men. Chamberlain had much more to lose than Churchill in the circumstances, but there was never any doubt, despite speculation, that Churchill would defend the government. Even at this late juncture, he saw his future with Chamberlain, not without him. Of course, it has to be acknowledged that Churchill would alienate many more than he would win over by criticizing Chamberlain, but he was not of a mind to anyway. In the circumstances a strong defense of the government was inevitable. Churchill's own best future lay with Chamberlain, and this was despite knowing his speech would be followed by a division. The development of Chamberlain's speech indicates he and his secretaries, Rucker and Wilson, who drafted an early version, always had more than Norway in mind when defending the government. In draft and final form, the speech was essentially a response to, or a rebuttal of, the already well-known criticisms of the government's running of the Norwegian campaign and other criticism, now familiar to the reader, that had been plaguing the government over the preceding months.

Chamberlain dealt first with the concerns of the Norwegian campaign: the frustration surrounding rumor and misinformation that built and then dashed hopes. He then challenged the contention Norway had been a disaster. It was not, he declared in response to a newspaper article of several days earlier, comparable to Gallipoli, and he spoke against premature judgment and made mention of the serious toll taken on the Germans. His speech also addressed the reasons the forces gathered for the Finnish option were disbanded, and he challenged the assumption this was a cause of failure.[58] He explained why most, but not all, the soldiers gathered for Finland had departed for other roles. Some, he pointed out, were sent to France, where they were no less readily available for action in Norway than they might have been in Britain. As for shipping, it was desperately needed elsewhere and could not be held ready for the mere prospect of action in Norway. Nevertheless Chamberlain emphasized that forces were kept ready to "occupy certain Norwegian ports if the country's neutrality had been previously violated."[59] This was as close as he permitted the House to come to an understanding of R4 preparations or the events of 7 and 8 April.

The government's explanation of German success was as it had been in early April: the German attack had nothing to do with the mining operation and had begun before the mines were laid; the Norwegians contributed significantly to the overwhelming German success; there were also the inherent challenges of finding the enemy forces at sea. The issues of Trondheim, the decision not to move forward with the naval assault, and the subsequent decision to withdraw from central Norway were also addressed. The critics were not inclined to accept the explanations at face value; none seemed persuasive. The issue of Trondheim was a difficult one for the government and Chamberlain, and Churchill knew it. A more successful rebuttal of the mischievousness that had already been achieved by Keyes before the debate was constrained by a need to conceal certain issues from the enemy. It was not, for example, desirable to dwell too long on the air threat to Allied warships as a primary reason for withdrawal from central Norway. Churchill was subsequently greatly bothered by his inability to challenge the criticism over Trondheim more directly; he might have been relieved the intense focus on Trondheim served as a distraction from the first two days of the campaign.

Digressing occasionally, and sometimes unwisely, to address heckling, Chamberlain's discourse moved from Norway to more general matters. These included the repeated accusations of complacency. A minister, he declared, "who shows confidence is complacent. If he fails to do so, he is defeatist." He took exception to criticism of his declaration that "Hitler had missed the bus"; in this case he thought his words had been twisted "out of their meaning."[60] He also tackled those whom he believed had been attempting to divide his War Cabinet: "Attempts have been made to separate them from one another, to suggest that this Minister or that Minister is more responsible than his colleagues for this or that action. Such suggestions are as unworthy as they are unfounded. There is no division among us. None of us has attempted to intrigue against any other. All of us have but one thought and that is how we may each of us make our best contribution to winning of the war."[61] These latter claims would have invited ridicule then, as they would undoubtedly do now from some historians. This chapter suggests that there was more truth here than has been supposed, at least as far as Chamberlain and Churchill were concerned.

Chamberlain followed these comments with a consideration of the much-vaunted small War Cabinet. He explained that he remained unconvinced of its efficacy. This did not mean he was unreceptive to change, and he referred to his recent promotion of Churchill within the MCC as an example of this. He concluded by imploring the Labour opposition to lend its support to a national government. This received in reply an emphatic no, an indication that Labour remained implacably opposed to joining the government while Chamberlain was PM.

Although Chamberlain's speech had anticipated much of the criticism that followed, the critics developed their own prepared lines of argument while ignoring, dismissing, or belittling Chamberlain's case. Unsurprisingly, given the evasion the government applied to the subject, members sought an explanation for the inexplicable success the Germans had in securing all the major ports of Norway despite intelligence of a significant German buildup in the Baltic. The second significant issue, again despite Chamberlain's explanation, was Trondheim. The focus of questions was the War Cabinet's initial preference for Narvik over Trondheim and thereafter the balking at landing at Trondheim itself. The latter criticism was built around the bombast of Sir Roger Keyes and his belief this operation ought to have taken place. Whether or not his rendition of events was accepted by most members of the House, it furnished critics with ample grounds to accuse the government of further ineptitude, complacency, and weakness.

In seeking to understand the completeness of German success, the critics targeted several aspects of the government case. The War Cabinet had admitted its awareness of German activity in the Baltic during March and acknowledged there had been moves afoot for action somewhere in the region. They, therefore, continued to challenge the decision to disband the military forces and the shipping held in support of the Finnish option, especially given that, almost immediately thereafter, the War Cabinet reenergized the Narvik mining plan, an operation the government must have anticipated would invite an aggressive German response. The questioners displayed little understanding of the chronology of these events, and constrained by a need to conceal certain issues from the enemy, including matters surrounding Royal Marine, the government did little to correct them.

Oliver Stanley came closest to a coherent, if incomplete, answer to why the Germans had been so successful in securing Norway's west coast. He explained the government had not ignored the prospect of a German response but had not imagined this would ever extend to the ports of Bergen, Trondheim, and Narvik. It is possible the War Cabinet thought it better to concede this point than to explain how opportunity was first given and then lost.

The penultimate speaker on the final day of debate, A. V. Alexander, soon to be Churchill's replacement as first lord, pressed the government most on these early days. Churchill as last speaker would not be drawn, and instead he made light of Alexander's extensive catalogue of questions. He argued that to address these one by one would not meet the needs or expectations of the House, and instead he proposed to "answer the principal questions in a general account."[62] In short, he stuck to script, said exactly what he wished to say, and then left the stage as the last to speak. At one point, earlier in the debate, he famously declared he took full responsibility for the actions of the Admiralty and his share of the burden. In fact, Churchill did not and was never required to. His failure and the failures of the Admiralty in the decisive moments of the Norwegian campaign remained unexposed.

The relevance of these issues to the Churchill-Chamberlain relationship is considerable. Rather than Churchill carrying the burden of Chamberlain's failings, which is the generally accepted assessment of the events of 7 and 8 May and certainly the perception of critics within the Commons, it was very much the other way around. Again, it is desirable to explore Chamberlain's motivation. This issue is clouded by the fact that while a full disclosure of the events of 7 and 8 April would have been better for Chamberlain relative to Churchill, it would have been very much worse for Chamberlain's government. A charitable, but nevertheless reasonable, conclusion is that more than his own demise, Chamberlain feared the complete collapse of the Conservative government and the potentially devastating loss of public trust in their great champion, Winston Churchill. In the scenario in which he was compelled to resign, it was important Halifax and Churchill carry the government forward with him in support. This appeared to be the sentiment conveyed in his letter to sister, Hilda, on 4 May.

The degree of common purpose between Churchill and Chamberlain and evidence of the former's limited personal aspirations until the very last moment can be seen in other events of 8 and 9 May. They are small matters, generally well known and individually of limited apparent consequence, but taken together and at their face value, they undermine the adversarial context of the Churchill-Chamberlain relationship and point to something quite different. In the evening of the eighth, Harold Macmillan found Churchill in the smoking room of the House, awaiting his turn to speak. Macmillan wished Churchill luck, adding that he hoped Churchill's speech would not be too convincing because "we must have a new Prime Minister, and it must be you." Churchill responded "gruffly that he had signed on for the voyage and would stick to the ship," but Macmillan concluded that he (Churchill) was not really angry with him.[63] Immediately after his robust defense of the government, Churchill alone was invited to the chambers of a despondent Chamberlain, who, thereafter, discussed at length the future prospects of the government. Churchill has recorded, "Aroused by the antagonisms of the debate, and being sure of my own past record on the issues at stake, I was strongly disposed to fight on." He told Chamberlain: "This has been a damaging debate, but you have a good majority. Do not take the matter grievously to heart. You have a better case about Norway than it has been possible to convey to the House. Strengthen your Government from every quarter, and let us go on until our majority deserts us."[64]

Churchill's recollections indicate that even in the evening of 8 May, and in contrast to Chamberlain, he considered the harm done to the government was not terminal. Some historians have seen these words merely as a good man consoling the defeated; others are more alert to the extraordinary qualities of the moment.[65] One of the two men most likely to gain advantage from Chamberlain's resignation was encouraging him to press on. Churchill's recounting of events must be treated with caution, especially because he often got things terribly wrong in the retelling, but there is considerable reason to accept that he gave Chamberlain encouragement to carry on as prime minister and that he was earnest in doing so.[66] As intimated, albeit obliquely, in *The Gathering Storm*, it is probable Churchill's sentiments were driven by the rough handling he and the government had received from Labour. Given the clarion call for a national government and the probability of Labour's refusal to participate as long as Chamberlain was prime minister, Chamberlain had concluded that he must resign. Churchill was not, initially, as easily persuaded of the need for Labour's participation in a new government, and he thought Chamberlain could and should remain leader.

On the issue of Labour and Churchill's reluctance to have them in a government—a sentiment that apparently overrode any aspirations or expectations he might have had for the premiership—it is desirable to return to Lord Camrose's records considered earlier and note the nature of the government Churchill indicated he would have formed or, at least, the government he thought Chamberlain ought to. No Labour member is mentioned. We can also note Camrose's rather strange observation that Churchill feared Liberal and Conservative criticism; again, there is no mention of Labour. Churchill's disregard, and even dislike, for Labour is corroborated by comments made to Chamberlain by John Simon at this time: "Winston had taken the view that Labour had nothing to contribute, the way to broaden the Government was to bring in a selection of . . . rebels."[67]

The conclusion to be drawn is, rather than having any sense of his own destiny, Churchill was, at least in the evening of 8 May, encouraging Chamberlain to bring in the Conservative critics and possibly Sinclair but leave out the Labour Party in a new Chamberlain government. Evidently, Churchill was against the idea of a genuine national government at this point, for he was offering Chamberlain counsel against something Chamberlain himself believed necessary. Churchill reinforces the extent to which he believed he was in the same boat as Chamberlain with his description in *The Gathering Storm* of why Chamberlain thought him unsuited to take over the reins of power. Chamberlain had apparently seen and heard enough during and after the debate to wonder at Churchill's capacity to work with Labour and to wonder at Labour's willingness to work with Churchill. When he subsequently put forward Halifax as the better man to form a government and replace him, Churchill believed Chamberlain had in mind the debate during which Churchill was in "such heated controversy with the Labour Party." Chamberlain had expressed concern Churchill might have difficulty "obtaining their adherence."[68] No doubt, in making his recommendation,

Chamberlain also had in mind his extensive discussion with Churchill in the evening of 8 May. Here is further evidence to explain Churchill's apparent blindness toward, or indifference to, his destiny and the sincerity of his support for Chamberlain. In the immediate aftermath of the debate, he apprehended that Labour would make its participation in a national government conditional on the exclusion, not only of Chamberlain, but of himself.

It seems probable, therefore, in the evening of 8 May, while Chamberlain had concluded he must put national unity before all else, Churchill had again weighed his future and concluded he was better remaining with the man with whom he now had a positive working relationship and who was disposed to increase his control over the military side of the war. That Chamberlain began exploring survival as prime minister as early as his meeting with the king near midnight in the evening of 8 May—and certainly by the following morning—only to be described as "limpet-like" by Brendan Bracken is, remarkably, best explained by Churchill's encouragement to soldier on. Churchill's support of Chamberlain might have been a complete lack of self-interest; more likely self-interest was a primary motivation. What is almost certain, however, is that his encouragement of Chamberlain was genuine. There were no guarantees at all in the evening of 8 May that Churchill would be better off if Chamberlain resigned, and there was little or no prospect Churchill would become prime minister if Chamberlain did.

As far as Chamberlain's "limpet-like" desire to remain prime minister, there is evidence that David Margesson, the Conservative Party whip, spent some of the morning canvassing a new Chamberlain government—perhaps along the lines suggested by Churchill—but most of Chamberlain's day was spent determining who should best replace him as leader in a national government, if this were required.

Prime Minister Churchill

The absence of the "limpet-like" Chamberlain and the "man of destiny" Churchill in the final days of Chamberlain's premiership can also be noted in the way it was decided that Churchill, rather than Halifax, would replace Chamberlain as prime minister. The emphasis of writing is typically on Chamberlain's determination to see Halifax as prime minister rather than

Churchill; assumptions of animosity and dislike are not far behind. However, although evidence supports the idea of Chamberlain's preference, it does not support this motivation. While it is probable Chamberlain preferred Halifax, there is little direct evidence to show this was a determined preference. It must not be forgotten that in any likely scenario, Chamberlain expected Churchill would have a major role. Save the uncertainty surrounding Labour and a national government, Churchill would make a significant contribution to fighting the war.

On 9 May events seemed to have unfolded in the following manner. Churchill rang Anthony Eden around 9:30 a.m. and asked to see him as soon as possible. While shaving, and with Eden present, Churchill "rehearsed the events of the previous evening." Eden recorded that Churchill thought Chamberlain "would not be able to bring in Labour and that a national government must be formed."

While Churchill had now apparently turned this corner, the party whips had not, and they were attempting to cobble together support for changes that did not include Labour. This was interpreted to be limpet Chamberlain desperately clinging to power, but it is entirely possible the whips' activities—and possibly some limited activity from Chamberlain himself—had been prompted by the latter's discussion with Churchill the night before.

Later in the morning, Churchill had a brief conversation with Lord Beaverbrook who, when he asked Churchill if he would serve under Halifax, was disappointed to be told he "would serve under any Minister capable of prosecuting the war."[69] This was an unsurprising response from a man who was not yet fully alive to his prospects. There matters stood for Churchill as he entered the morning's War Cabinet meeting.

In the early afternoon and post-cabinet, Eden lunched with Churchill and Kingsley Wood. Here Eden claimed he was told that "Neville had decided to go."[70] Churchill stated things differently and, in this instance, almost certainly more accurately in *The Gathering Storm* when he recorded, "Mr Chamberlain was resolved upon the formation of a National Government and, if he could not be Head, he would give way to anyone commanding his confidence who could." Churchill claimed it was during this discussion with Eden and Wood that he, for the first time, considered, "I might well be called upon to take the lead."[71] Also during this meeting, Wood advised Churchill to remain silent if Chamberlain asked if he would serve under Halifax. Eden agreed with this advice.[72]

Around the time of Churchill's discussions with Eden earlier in the morning, Halifax met with Chamberlain. The latter thought it "essential to restore confidence in the Government," and this could be achieved only by having "all Parties in."[73] Chamberlain noted that Churchill had been doubtful as to this necessity but Halifax thought it essential. They agreed the likelihood of Labour serving under Chamberlain was negligible. Chamberlain thought, therefore, that his successor was clearly Churchill or Halifax, but for the second time in two days, Halifax told him that he did not wish to be prime minister. With the uncertainty surrounding Labour's attitude to Churchill, Chamberlain might have wondered who would lead this new national government, if such came to pass.

For the three great players, the middle of the day was filled by the War Cabinet meeting. After it had concluded, and while Churchill lunched with Eden and Wood, Chamberlain had private discussions with several colleagues—most notably John Simon—with the primary purpose of informing them of his intentions. Simon offered to resign if this would help Chamberlain retain the premiership, but the latter considered all such things too late.

At 4:30 p.m. Chamberlain, Churchill, Halifax, and Margesson met at Downing Street. Here Chamberlain stressed the importance of national unity and the need to bring the two opposition parties into the government. Evidently, if he had seriously contemplated the possibility of a reformed government along the lines proposed by Churchill (or his whips), he no longer did; Halifax recorded that Margesson believed a national government was essential and could not be achieved under Chamberlain. Discussion turned to a successor, and Chamberlain indicated Halifax had been mentioned as most acceptable to the various parties. Halifax responded by explaining again why he did not want the position; he would be a mere cipher, and he thought Churchill the better choice. Churchill "did *not* demur. He was very kind and polite but showed that he thought this [the] right solution."[74] Margesson added strength to Churchill's position when he indicated "feeling in the House had been veering towards him." Halifax recorded in his diary that Chamberlain "reluctantly" and "Winston evidently with much less reluctance, finished by accepting my view. So there we left if for the moment, Winston and I having a cup of tea in the garden while the PM kept some other appointment."[75]

Chamberlain's other appointment was with Lord Camrose, and its purpose appears to have been to explain to Camrose what had just taken place and the approach Chamberlain would take in his meeting with Attlee and Greenwood. Camrose's detailed notes of this discussion are eminently reliable and a valuable insight into these events. They clear up an error perpetrated by Cadogan in his diary where he concluded from his discussion with Halifax that the succession was decided after the meeting with Attlee and Greenwood; this had been decided before this meeting, barring, of course, any surprises from Labour. If the Labour executive rejected him, Chamberlain would resign and put forward Churchill to the king or, at least, endorse him if he were asked. Churchill had accepted this proposal on the condition that Chamberlain remained the leader of the party and the House and stayed to assist him.

Of his meeting with Attlee and Greenwood, Camrose recorded Chamberlain explaining that he intended, in the first instance, to place the issue of his leadership to one side. He would inform them of his intention to "broaden the Government" and "stress the necessity of unity at the present time." To this end, Halifax and Churchill "would both point out the danger to the country of any serious differences which might affect the national effort." Chamberlain anticipated Attlee and Greenwood would say that "in no circumstances would they serve under him," but he would ask they secure confirmation of this at the following day's Executive Committee meeting.[76]

As Camrose departed his meeting with Chamberlain sometime around 6:30 p.m., he passed Attlee and Greenwood on the way to theirs. In conformity with his plan, Chamberlain's opening comments were followed by a speech from Churchill supporting stability and including a "glowing summary of Chamberlain's virtues as leader." Attlee's recollection was that Churchill was sincere, focused on the war rather than the leadership issue, and perhaps more than a little aware of his own precarious situation post-Norway: "Winston spoke up and said we should come in under Chamberlain. That was understandable; in any case, Winston had Norway in his back. And he cared more about getting a government that could win the war than about who was to be prime minister. Was quite sincere." This, however, was as far as Chamberlain's strategy was permitted to go. Attlee recorded that Halifax said nothing.[77] Chamberlain's decision to assume his personal leadership of a national government remained a possibility did not prove a success. Attlee and Greenwood found it difficult to understand his attitude. Chamberlain's own explanation for this approach, often ridiculed but plausible and reasonable, was that he would need to satisfy his supporters the effort had been made to retain the leadership.[78]

After the meeting Churchill dined with Eden, who recorded, "[Churchill] thought it plain NC would advise the King to send for him. Edward did not wish to succeed. Parliamentary position too difficult." Of importance, for it reinforces the integrity of Camrose's notes, is Eden's comment, "W had made it plain he hoped NC would stay, would lead the House of Commons and continue as Leader of the party. W would be Minister of Defense as well as PM."[79]

There were two final elements in the story of Churchill's succession to the premiership. The first was the decision made by Chamberlain early in the morning of 10 May to postpone the transition to a national government in view of the German attack in the West. This decision became known by some as early as 9 a.m. (after the 8 a.m. emergency War Cabinet). Chamberlain had phoned Attlee and Greenwood before they departed for their conference, informed them, and asked for a statement of support for the present government. Although all sorts of claims have been made to the contrary, the men appear to have accepted his decision without rancor. There was really little else they could have done. Chamberlain was rescinding, temporarily and at a moment of great crisis, his proposal for a national government, a matter in which the Labour Party had no direct say. The question of whether Labour would, subsequently, join a new government led by Chamberlain or someone else could still be answered later in the day at Bournemouth. The two issues were separate. The statement provided by Attlee, while calculatedly obscure in places, is readily interpreted as meeting Chamberlain's needs: "The Labour Party, in view of the latest series of abominable aggression by Hitler, while firmly convinced that drastic reconstruction of the Government is vital and urgent in order to win the war, reaffirms its determination to do its utmost to achieve victory. It calls on all its members to devote all their energies to this end."[80]

Chamberlain's proposal was widely known by late morning. Some thought it made sense, given the circumstances. Simon was shocked to hear Churchill believed a change of government should go ahead at such a dangerous time. Chamberlain's secretary, Dunglass, set about searching for various members of the Conservative opposition to explain the proposal and found Nicolson at lunch with other members of Salisbury's group. Dunglass reaffirmed the reconstruction but argued for delay: "We must have a triumvirate of Chamberlain, Churchill and Halifax to carry us over these first anxious hours. Sam Hoare, for instance, must be at his desk night and day for the next 36 hours, and it would be quite impossible to replace him by another Minister."[81]

Although a long-term critic of Chamberlain, Nicolson thought there was "some sense" to this and considered the Labour Party statement, which was heard on the wireless at that moment, "quite helpful" because it called for national unity and suggested "the political controversy is suspended for the moment." The idea of Labour suspending its demands in the name of national unity made sufficient sense to Nicolson for him to be surprised later in the day when he learned of Chamberlain's resignation: "I am puzzled by this for a moment, and then realise that he has resigned."[82]

Others, among them Churchill, Hankey, Wood, and Eden, considered Chamberlain's decision unwise; a national government was almost certain to develop from the Labour Party conference that afternoon, whether with Chamberlain at its head or not; it was desirable this transition occur as quickly as possible once this support was given. Eden worried that "conditions for change might become more rather than less difficult." Furthermore, as far as Chamberlain was concerned, he thought there was "the risk to personal position if appearance of clinging on were given."[83] His most severe critics, Amery among them, were far less charitable, gave Chamberlain no concession for the circumstances of the time, and assumed he was merely using these to maintain his grip on power.[84]

Eden recorded that after the 11:30 War Cabinet, the second of the day, Chamberlain told those gathered of the succession discussion he, Churchill, and Halifax had been involved in the previous evening. This was surely a strange thing to do if, as is often accepted, he was set on retaining power. He added the "new attack must cause hold-up," but this was "only temporary." He went on to explain he had informed Attlee of this, and he had accepted. Further he had asked him to put out a notice of support of government pro tem.[85]

Such was Chamberlain's view around 1 p.m. on 10 May. By the time of the third War Cabinet meeting of that day, Chamberlain had changed his mind. Upon receiving the news from Bournemouth, he indicated his intention to tender his resignation and said that it would be assumed that all others had done so. There was no reference to his earlier plan. While it is typically assumed that news from the Labour conference had decided Chamberlain against suspending the transition, there is no evidence to support this.[86] Churchill recorded in *The Gathering Storm* that Kingsley Wood had persuaded him to reconsider his decision sometime in the morning. While Wood might have counseled Chamberlain, the claim this occurred in the morning is evidently untrue.

The import of the foregoing is the extent to which it fails to support or reinforce much of the existing historical analysis. There is little to suggest Chamberlain was acting with other than the best motives. It was eminently reasonable for him to conclude that the circumstances demanded his plans for a new administration be postponed. No doubt this view was firmly bedded in his conviction that a Churchill-Chamberlain-Halifax triumvirate with him at the helm was better than any immediate alternative, but at worst this was hubris at work and not ambition. It is extremely difficult to square this vision of Chamberlain, which goes hand in hand with the combative view of the Churchill-Chamberlain relationship, with his declaration less than a week later that he "was thankful that the primary responsibility is off my shoulders."[87] He was fully aware that Churchill was much more suited to carrying such a burden. Similarly, it is almost impossible to find any sign of acrimony toward Churchill by Chamberlain during these difficult days or at any time after his resignation. Rather, quite the opposite is found. Chamberlain was strongly supportive of Churchill and subsequently did his best to build bridges between him and the Chamberlainites. Churchill too did his best to protect Chamberlain from Liberal and Labour Party members determined to see the last of him. Each continued to afford strong support to the other.

Churchill's premiership had one final hurdle to overcome: the king of England. For all the assumptions about Chamberlain and Churchill, the former made no effort to guide the king in his choice. He informed him of his intention to resign; the king asked of Halifax and was told he wished not to lead. It was the king who concluded the only other possibility was Churchill, and Chamberlain concurred.

Thus did Churchill become prime minister. The two-day debate of 7 and 8 May had proved decisive, although arguably only because Chamberlain had decided to make it so. A change of government had taken place at the moment of great threat. Change had been demanded by the House, and Chamberlain had acceded to it; how now was Churchill to deliver what was expected? Certainly, great changes occurred almost immediately, but Hitler's invasion made these inevitable in any circumstance. On the core issue of air policy—the cause of repeated criticism of Chamberlain—Churchill hesitated for as long as he was able before unleashing this weapon to very modest effect. Other policy issues that had for so long bothered the government's critics were resolved in an instant. There was no longer a demand for proactivity and seizing the initiative; all was now a matter of survival. For some time to come, Churchill was required to be reactive and not proactive. After the fall of France, the war was fought under conditions very much to Britain's advantage—in the air over Britain—where its fighter force could inflict great harm—and it was here that Churchill's reputation was forged.

Almost immediately, Churchill formed a national government that largely satisfied the critics—and that included many of them—but that, nevertheless, was not entirely of the small cabinet concept they had pressed on Chamberlain. As to the pace of rearmament, this certainly quickened, but to what extent was this Churchill and to what extent circumstance? To what extent also was this buildup made possible by the efforts of the previous nine months, which continue to be underrated? To what extent was the survival of Britain over the next several months a result of Chamberlain's focus on airpower?

None of these questions are posed, or these observations made, to diminish the brilliance of Churchill or his subsequent contribution; one can speculate still—with some concern—as to what might have happened at the end of May 1940, amid the evacuations from Dunkirk, with Chamberlain or Halifax still at the helm and not Churchill. However, even here the evidence is that Churchill and Chamberlain at least were of similar mind. Instead, these questions are posed because they invite and apply balance and the much-maligned middle ground to times and events that, although thoroughly explored, have yet to escape a dominating historical partisanship.

CONCLUSION

In September 1939, when Churchill returned from the political wilderness to resume a role as first lord of the Admiralty—a role he had lost twenty-four years earlier after the Dardanelles debacle—he had much to prove. His political career to this point had been a mixture of success and failure, but the latter had always been more visible. It was accepted he had a brilliant mind but poor judgment, and this had limited his rise through the political ranks. In the years before the outbreak of World War II, the foresight he had shown regarding Hitler and repeated vindication of his condemnation of appeasement had helped raise his stocks and ensured an invitation to join the War Cabinet on 3 September, two days after Germany invaded Poland. Nevertheless, for his party and for his prime minister, doubts remained as to the value he could bring to the government. Churchill had no doubts about the contribution he could, and would, make in fighting this new war. The task ahead was for Churchill to justify the opportunity given him and to prove his doubters wrong.

This study has examined how effectively Churchill used his position as first lord of the Admiralty and member of the War Cabinet to take the war to Germany and has concluded he met neither the negative expectations of his detractors nor the great hopes of his more ardent supporters. He showed himself to be neither the savior of the British war effort, as some had hoped, nor the disaster that others had expected. His performance was decidedly mixed. He brought enormous energy to his dual roles, but it was often not well directed, and this diminished the value of his contribution. He had a well-formed and, in many respects, sound strategic vision, but he had great difficulty in squaring aspiration and practicability. Overall, the Phoney War was not a period in which Churchill distinguished himself as a warlord or, indeed, as a man with superior insight or strategic vision. This was not for want of brilliance; Churchill could be eminently wise and insightful. Rather, it was because the glimpses of potential were so often tarnished by excess and idiosyncrasy and undermined by abundant examples of poor judgment and erratic and inconsistent argumentation.

In studying Churchill and this period, one must work hard to sift the good Churchill had to offer from the bad, and there is insufficient evidence to show he was capable of doing this himself. An important objective of this study was to understand why Churchill was not the success he wished himself to be before serendipity cast him into a role in which he was a preeminent success. As with all parts of this work, the answer was a mixture of influences and factors that pointed to no single explanation but that held Churchill as accountable for his shortcomings as it did the extraneous. The conclusions drawn were many of Churchill's initiatives were poorly conceived, and he was often a poor and ineffective advocate for his offensive plans; the decision-making structure was flawed and not conducive to the aggressive prosecution of the war he sought; Chamberlain, although always determined to contain Churchill's excesses, was much less the obstruction to Churchill's plans and schemes than is supposed; too often assumptions about Churchill's resistance to War Cabinet strategy are inconsistent with his real views on important issues; much of Churchill's frustration and folly, as deeply intermixed as they were, was an unavoidable result of the war he and the War Cabinet sought to fight; and finally—and intimately linked to the former—the frustrations Churchill faced were very much, as Halifax noted, a product of the time. This was not a time in which Churchill was ever likely to shine. Rather, it was a period when frustration rather than fulfillment was the likely order of the day, and when frustrated Churchill was at his most unwise and impulsive.

One of the great ironies of the Phoney War was that although often deeply frustrated by the inactivity that characterized the period, Churchill was a major contributor to the wider political frustration that eventually provided him the greatest opportunity of his life. He agreed with government policy regarding air bombing and was among the most reluctant in the War Cabinet to impose greater aggression on the French; yet this was not generally known by those who demanded greater proactivity and who were instrumental in Chamberlain's removal. The truth was that although more animated than many of his colleagues to take the war to the Germans, Churchill was more cautious than he or his reputation have admitted and the Chamberlain government very much less supine. Nevertheless, having once been identified as the most proactive member of the War Cabinet, he was always destined to reap the greatest benefit from the perception the government could and should do more.

It is difficult to see just what Churchill might have done differently and more successfully than Chamberlain. He might have made things very much worse. Churchill's vigor and aggression were admirable qualities; his questionable judgment, his recklessness, his inconsistent and erratic thinking were not. The judgment of history should more readily acknowledge that where Churchill and Chamberlain differed on matters of caution and aggression during the Phoney War, the wiser course is not easily identified. Moreover, all assessments of Chamberlain's inaction must recognize the challenges presented by the Anglo-French alliance.

Rather than viewing Churchill's belated ascendancy to the premiership as good fortune delayed and Chamberlain's maintenance of this position until 10 May as a dead hand too late removed, there is much to be said for the notion that each was, in many respects, the best man for their time. It is certainly difficult to imagine Chamberlain being the war leader that Churchill was after May 1940. It is as difficult to imagine Churchill negotiating the Phoney War period more successfully than Chamberlain; Churchill was, after all, complicit in some of the greatest failures of the Chamberlain period, and he needed to be deflected from action that might readily have added to this list.

When Churchill became prime minister, he continued to be the complicated mix of strengths and failings that he had been during the first nine months of war, but the circumstances now fitted his strengths much more closely. The events of May 1940 meant that he was freed from the frustrating politico-military straitjacket of the Phoney War that had confounded him as much as it had his predecessor: his path was clearer, his task was simpler, if much more formidable. The man finally met the moment, and this gave him his finest hour.

Notes

Introduction

1. Cosgrave, *Churchill at War.*
2. For a less polarized view of these issues, see Smart, *British Strategy.*
3. An example of the view that Chamberlain maintained the same strategic posture throughout the Phoney War period can be found in Self, *Neville Chamberlain,* 394–98.
4. The term "Finnish option" has been coined by this writer for the purpose of this study.
5. The primary and most influential advocate of this view has been Stephen Roskill. See in particular, Roskill, *Churchill and the Admirals,* 94–95, Appendix: An Historical Controversy.
6. For Churchill's contemporary criticisms of the decision-making process, see Churchill to Halifax, 15 January 1940, FO 800/328, British National Archives (BNA) (also in Gilbert, *At the Admiralty,* 642); Churchill to Halifax, 14 March 1940, FO 800/328, BNA (also in Gilbert, *At the Admiralty,* 883). For the views he expressed after the war, see Churchill, *Gathering Storm,* 586, 641.
7. Gretton, *Former Naval Person*; Lamb, *Churchill as War Leader,* 24; Churchill to Phillips, 28 September 1939, ADM 205/2, BNA.

Chapter One. U-Boats and the Protection of Trade

1. For assessments of Churchill's attitude to convoy and the influence of his offensive minded-ness, see Marder, *From the Dardanelles,* 119–20; Gretton, *Former Naval Person,* 264–65; Brodhurst, *Churchill's Anchor,* 127–28; Hough, *Former Naval Person,* 134–35; Terraine, *Business in Great Waters,* 244–45; Roskill, *Churchill and the Admirals,* 90; D'Este, *Warlord,* 388–90, 396.
2. "Protection of Shipping at Sea," 1939, 69, ADM 239/40, BNA.
3. "Protection of Shipping," 69–70.
4. "Protection of Shipping," chap. 4.
5. "Protection of Shipping," pt. 2.
6. "Proposal by Commander-in-Chief Western Approaches to Form Anti-submarine Striking Force," 23 September 1939, and comments by Phillips, 25 September 1939, ADM 199/124, BNA. Phillips' comments reaffirmed the assessment made by Vice Admiral Thomas (Hugh) Binney's committee a fortnight before. Gretton has noted that despite Binney's recommenda-tion, "no guidance . . . was sent to the Commanders-in-Chief" about the priority to be given to escort over offensive patrolling. At least regarding the most important commander in chief in the anti-U-boat war, this is clearly incorrect. See Gretton, *Former Naval Person,* 265. This recommendation challenges the claim that Pound was a strong advocate of offensive patrolling. For example, see Marder, *From the Dardanelles,* 119, 121; Terraine, *Business in Great Waters,* 245.

7. ADM 199/124. At this time convoys were oftentimes accompanied by two escorts only.

8. Churchill, notes of a meeting, 4 September 1939, ADM 205/2, BNA.

9. Churchill, speech, House of Commons, 26 September 1939, in Gilbert, *At the Admiralty*, 154–59.

10. Churchill, "Memorandum on Sea-Power, 1939," 27 March 1939, in Gilbert, *Coming of War*, 1414.

11. Churchill, speech to the House of Commons, 26 September 1939, in Gilbert, *Coming of War*, 155.

12. Churchill, "U-Boat Warfare," speech, 26 September 1939, in Gilbert, *At the Admiralty*, 154–59.

13. Churchill, oral answers, 352 Parl. Deb. H.C. (5th ser.) (1939) cols. 686–90 (also in Gilbert, *At the Admiralty*, 256).

14. This is the position taken by the director of naval intelligence (DNI), Admiral Godfrey, in his postwar memoirs and has been accepted by such historians as Beesly, *Very Special Intelligence*, and McLachlan, *Room 39*. These men, like Godfrey, were wartime intelligence specialists. This is important for the insight they offer into the intelligence world. However, there is enough that is incorrect in their recollections to suggest they knew less of Churchill's thinking and motivation than they thought they did.

15. Admiral John Henry Godfrey (1888–1971) was DNI from 1939 to 1942. Captain (later Rear Admiral) Douglas Adams Bugden (1889–?) held the position of director of the Anti-Submarine Warfare Division (DA/SWD) from 2 October to 15 November. Biographical details for Budgen are scarce.

16. Churchill, speech to the House of Commons, 26 September 1939, in Gilbert, *Coming of War*, 155.

17. *Monthly Anti-submarine Reports*, 1939–40, ADM 199/2057, BNA. These statistics are found in the September edition of the *Monthly Anti-submarine Report*, which was probably printed and circulated early to mid-October 1939.

18. This was in addition to the two U-boats actually destroyed. The Germans had eighteen U-boats in the Western Approaches at the start of war. The Admiralty believed the figure closer to five or six at any one time.

19. uboat.net. This website includes details drawn from German archives and other sources for every U-boat. Remarkably, there is a poor correlation between the attacks recorded by the U-boats and those A/SWD believed to have caused damage. The figure of thirty-five does not include attacks that resulted in the destruction of the U-boat.

20. "Enquiry into Assessment of U-Boat Losses," 1940, ADM 199/138, BNA. Hereafter cited as Dreyer inquiry.

21. Churchill to DA/SWD, 1 November 1939, Char 19/3, Churchill Archive Centre (also in Gilbert, *At the Admiralty*, 321).

22. "Visit of Dominion Ministers: Review of Strategic Situation," 28 October 1939, CAB 66/3/3, BNA. It was also mentioned that twelve had been damaged and six of these seriously.

23. During the Dreyer Committee investigations in the latter half of 1940, Captain Talbot expressed this conviction while being asked about U-boat losses (ADM 199/138). Talbot also noted that during his time as flotilla captain, his flotilla was attributed with

one known, three probables, and one damaged. He said that in April 1940 (undoubt-edly because of the information gained from U-49), he withdrew most of these, but he expressed the conviction that three of the probably sunk were certainly seriously damaged but made their way back to port. It is certain he was wrong.

24. CAB 65/56, BNA. It is likely this was the Danish-sourced intelligence discussed later in the chapter. Clearly, Churchill was taking the intelligence seriously.

25. Beesly, *Very Special Intelligence*, 126.

26. Testimony by Captain Talbot, in Dreyer inquiry, 43.

27. U-49 was sunk off the coast of Norway. Documents recovered from the vessel provided extensive details of all German U-boats in the Norwegian campaign.

28. Dreyer inquiry, folio 7.

29. These views are from Churchill's speech to the House of Commons, 6 December 1939. See 355 Parl. Deb. H.C. (5th ser.) (1939) cols. 689–96 (also in Gilbert, *At the Admiralty*, 469–75).

30. Early in the war NID supplied a projection of U-boat construction that proved very inaccurate. Many fewer U-boats were under construction at the start of the war than was estimated, and existing construction capacity was also overstated.

31. Dreyer inquiry, folio 7.

32. Godfrey was concerned about the opposite possibility: that an overestimation of U-boat kills might lead to a relaxation of effort. For this reason he was critical of what he considered was Churchill's deliberate exaggeration.

33. Dreyer inquiry.

34. If Lindemann did not understand the way U-boats operated, Churchill, at least, did. See his speech to the House of Commons, 27 February 1940, in 357 Parl. Deb. H.C. (5th ser.) (1940) cols. 1923–36 (also in Gilbert, *At the Admiralty*, 809).

35. Lindemann's ebb-and-flow theory of U-boat numbers was not without merit. Early in the war Doenitz declared that he would follow a procedure by which he could, at intervals, place larger numbers of U-boats in the Western Approaches because this conformed with his wolf-pack aspirations. For one reason or another—losses, breakdowns, wear and tear on his limited craft, and the need to maintain a presence at all times—this aspiration was rarely met during the period under consideration here.

36. Pound's view at this time varied only slightly from Churchill's. He suspected fewer U-boats had been sunk than Churchill did; however, the explanation of "false contacts" was only one of five possibilities. Among others he nominated were incorrect placement of depth-charge patterns and depth charges sent to the wrong depth. See Pound to Forbes, 15 September 1939, ADM 205/3, BNA. It is interesting to note John Keegan's misinterpretation of these times: "The difficulties of the procedure, akin to those of precision bombing by aircraft on land, resulted in a low ratio of sinkings to attacks throughout 1939–40." See Keegan, *Price of Admiralty*, 238.

37. AVAR Papers, Churchill Archive Centre.

38. Churchill's first order of business upon receiving the Dreyer report was to inquire into improvements being made to the depth charge. There is little doubt that killing U-boats was problematic at this point in the war, but this was not the reason for the vast difference between (assumed) attacks and kills.

39. It seems likely that as the war progressed, both U-boat detection and U-boat killing became appreciably more accurate and successful. In other words there were many fewer false attacks on U-boats, and when U-boats were attacked, they were much more likely to be sunk.

40. To these factors, we can add the problems the Germans were facing with their torpedoes. On at least one occasion when a convoy was found, torpedo failure saved the convoy considerable harm.

41. I have not found any assessment of the value of offensive patrolling in conjunction with a successful convoy system as existed during the Phoney War. There appears to have been no study of the advantages patrolling offered to the protection of trade—whether or not U-boats were sunk or seen by patrolling vessels—if the U-boats themselves sighted a patrol vessel and then reacted to it.

42. Llewellyn-Jones, *Royal Navy*, 18.

43. The typical criticism of Churchill on this matter claims that the War Cabinet recommended the operations be discontinued and not resumed. There is no evidence of this. Rather, the most likely reason they were discontinued was that the exceptional need of September 1939 had disappeared. Another reason might have been that all future search missions would have required at least seven destroyers, with four always acting as a screen.

44. Churchill to Pound, Admiral Phillips, and others, 9 November 1939; Churchill to Pound, Phillips, and Sir Archibald Carter, 20 November 1939, both in ADM 205/2, BNA.

45. War Cabinet Meeting, Minutes, 9 November 1939, CAB 65/2, BNA.

46. Churchill to Pound, Phillips, and others, 9 November 1939.

47. There were, of course, occasions when Churchill expressed concerns some ships were not being convoyed when he thought they should be. See Churchill to Pound and others, 15 October 1939, Char 19/3.

48. "Conclusions of a Meeting in the First Lord's Room to Consider How to Reduce the Slowing Down of Import and Export Trade Caused by War," 9 November 1939, ADM 205/4, BNA. When Churchill summarized for the War Cabinet the idea of releasing ships of a certain size from convoy on the east coast, he said that permission was granted for ships up to 2,000 tons. This apparently was already occurring. It is not clear, therefore, if any further relaxation actually took place. See War Cabinet Meeting, Minutes, 10 November 1939, CAB 65/2, BNA.

49. "Conclusions of a Meeting," 9 November 1939.

50. Vice Admiral Kenneth Dewar's papers indicate the question of the number of ships sunk during World War I while sailing over fifteen knots was referred to the Admiralty Historical Section either before the war or in September 1939. No evidence was found as to the conclusions drawn or as to if an investigation was undertaken. See DEW 11-12, Caird Library and Archives.

51. Schofield, "Defeat of the U-boats," 121. For a summary of issues surrounding the convoy–independent sailing debate, see Grove, *Defeat of the Enemy*, app. 6.

52. The mining threat gave a significant boost to the notion of offensive patrolling because U-boats need not go anywhere near a convoy to cause serious harm to shipping. Escorts were, therefore, seen as little help in this situation.

53. Grove, *Defeat of the Enemy*, x.

54. "Steps to Be Taken to Meet the Enemy Magnetic Mine," n.d. (20 November 1939?), ADM 205/4, BNA.

55. "Steps to Be Taken."

56. ADM 199/124.

57. Talbot, "Review of Methods of Dealing with the U-Boat Menace," March 1940, ADM 1/10468, BNA.

58. Draft Construction Programme, Section F, 9 January 1940, ADM 205/5, BNA.

59. Andrew Lambert has argued, correctly, that Churchill should not be held responsible for not anticipating the consequences of France's defeat on the naval war. German bases on the French west coast allowed U-boats to operate much farther into the Atlantic, and this transformed the U-boat war. The escorts being built were not suited to the broader Atlantic conditions. Nonetheless, in building large numbers of corvettes and not doing enough to construct larger escorts, the Admiralty was always taking a calculated gamble as to future needs. Even in 1939 there was evidence the U-boats would operate farther afield (e.g., their emphasis on the Type VII design). Churchill and the Admiralty were gambling that a policy of containment would work. However, this was premised on a misplaced faith in defensive minefields (except in limited areas such as the Channel) and the uncertain efficacy of offensive patrolling, neither of which proved a great success. Further, although Churchill is closely linked to the "cheap and nasties" of the whale-catcher design (corvettes), which are often seen as the salvation of British trade protection, his own preference was for a vessel some three hundred tons lighter. It is unlikely these vessels could have been adapted to the role of escort in the wide Atlantic, something the corvettes were barely able to do.

60. Char 19/4, Churchill Archive Centre. Churchill submitted his memorandum "The Northern Barrage" to the War Cabinet on 19 November. In the previous three days, nine vessels had succumbed to the magnetic mine.

61. Churchill, "Northern Barrage," notes, 19 November 1939, in Gilbert, *At the Admiralty*, 283–387 (also in Char 19/4). To support his arguments in favor of the barrage, Churchill referred to the loss of some six U-boats in a short space of time in the northern barrage of World War I. Three others were said to have been damaged. That more were not harmed, he attributed to the fact that "American antennae mines laid . . . were set to explode outside 'killing' range."

62. Churchill, speech, 9 December 1939, 355 Parl. Deb. (5th ser.) (1939) cols. 689–96 (also in Gilbert, *At the Admiralty*, 472).

63. For the best summary of the value of convoy in the antimine campaign, see Grove, *Defeat of the Enemy*, chaps. 23, 24.

64. One reason for the declining interest in these operations is that the Germans had no way of knowing how successful their mine-laying operations had been.

Chapter Two. Catherine

1. Clews, *Churchill's Dilemma*, 310.

2. Winston S. Churchill, "Memorandum on Sea-Power, 1939," 27 March 1939, Churchill Papers, 4/96, Churchill Archive Centre (also in Gilbert, *Coming of War*, 1415); CHT 6/4-5, Caird Library and Archives.

3. Churchill, "Memorandum on Sea-Power."

4. Churchill, "Memorandum on Sea-Power." In providing feedback on his memorandum, Desmond Morton asked, "Apart from Singapore, what after all, are our interests and possessions in the Yellow Sea." Desmond Morton to Churchill, 27 March 1939, in Gilbert, *Coming of War*, 1417. It is reasonable to assume that Churchill was expressing a willingness to surrender Hong Kong but not Singapore.

5. Churchill, "Memorandum on Sea-Power," 1414.

6. Churchill, "Memorandum on Sea-Power."

7. Churchill, "Memorandum on Sea-Power." In the copy of this memorandum forwarded to Prime Minister Chamberlain, Churchill added significantly, although in afterthought: "However by that time the entry would probably be fortified, and Denmark in German hands. Therefore the whole idea is purely hypothetical as well as remote."

8. "Notes by Lord Chatfield," 29 March 1939, CHT 6/4-5, Caird Library and Archives.

9. Churchill, "Memorandum Catherine," 11 September 1939, ADM 205/4, BNA. The R class, or *Revenge* class (also referred to as *Royal Sovereign* class), was made up of HMS *Revenge*, HMS *Resolution*, HMS *Royal Oak*, HMS *Royal Sovereign*, and HMS *Ramilles*. They had received little or no reconstruction during the interwar period because most attention was given to the reconstruction of the Queen Elizabeth class.

10. Churchill, "Memorandum Catherine."

11. Churchill, "Memorandum Catherine."

12. Churchill, "Notes on the General Situation," cabinet paper, 25 September 1939, CAB 66/2/2, BNA (also in Gilbert, *At the Admiralty*, 147–49; Churchill Papers, 20/15). Churchill viewed the Russian occupation of eastern Poland in mid-September strictly as a matter of self-interest.

13. The expression "cigar-butt" is from Barnett, *Engage the Enemy*, 93.

14. Director of Plans, "Plan C," 12 September 1939, ADM 116/6289, BNA.

15. Although it is unlikely Danckwerts had seen Churchill's Catherine memo, it is probable Churchill had proposed the R-class battleships in his first discussion with naval staff. This would explain why Danckwerts addressed the issue of the Rs in his appreciation.

16. An early spring entry into the Baltic would take advantage of longer nights. Danckwerts nominated a substantial fleet: the three modernized capital ships (*Warspite, Valiant,* and *Renown*), one modern cruiser squadron with maximum antiaircraft protection, two flotillas of modern large destroyers, one fast minesweeping flotilla, and two antiaircraft cruisers. The force would have to be self-supporting for four months.

17. DCNS Phillips, "Plan C," 14 September 1939, ADM 116/6289, BNA.

18. Phillips doubted Danckwerts' suggestion that the operation would face a threat from fourteen hundred aircraft, but nevertheless, he clearly saw aircraft as a major threat.

19. "Plan C. Part II: Operations in the Baltic," ADM 116/6289, BNA.

20. A distinction should be made between Catherine and the 1915 plans of Churchill and Wilson. Catherine had more in common with the Baltic plans proposed by Lord Fisher in the first decade of the twentieth century. The key point here, however, is that in both wars Churchill established an ad hoc committee to develop these ideas rather than using the existing planning structure.

21. Churchill to Pound, 19 September 1939, ADM 199/1939, BNA.

22. Pound to Churchill, 20 September 1939, ADM 199/1939, BNA. Presumably he meant that Germany could access Russian ore. It was subsequently contended that this was unlikely the case in the short term.

23. Pound to Churchill, 20 September 1939.

24. Churchill to Admiral Forbes, 15 September 1939; Pound to Admiral Holland, 25 October 1939, both in ADM 205/3, BNA.

25. Churchill to Pound, 20 September 1939, ADM 205/4, BNA (also in Gilbert, *At the Admiralty*, 127).

26. Cork's report was submitted on 26 September under the heading "Catherine." ADM 205/4, BNA.

27. Cork emphasized his was a military study that did not consider the political issues or the consequence of withdrawing ships from service "under existing conditions." Cork, "Catherine," memorandum, 26 September 1939, ADM 205/4, BNA.

28. Cork, "Catherine." Cork settled on *Warspite*, *Valiant*, and *Malaya*, all reconstructed battleships of the Queen Elizabeth class.

29. Cork, "The Entry: Co-operation of Other Forces," memorandum, n.d., ADM 199/1928, BNA. Cork was keen to include French forces in the operation, but Churchill would not allow this. The Spitfires mentioned in Cork's plan were intended to offer temporary cover to the fleet in stages and then fly on to Sweden. It is not clear how many of these craft he expected to remain there. This suggestion, however, indicates that Cork assumed an understanding with Sweden over Catherine before the operation began.

30. These were Chamberlain, Halifax, Chatfield, and Simon, the latter of whom had to agree to the funding of the project.

31. Churchill, "Memorandum on Sea-Power."

32. Churchill, "A Note on the War in 1940," memorandum, 25 December 1939, Char 19/3.

33. Churchill, "A Note on the War in 1940," memorandum, 25 December 1939, Char 19/3.

34. During the Phoney War, several difficult political episodes arose with the Japanese. Churchill was uncharacteristically accommodating in meeting the Japanese requests. He was fully alive to the need to not antagonize Japan and to give a level of support to the more moderate elements in the government.

35. Of course, Chamberlain, Halifax, and Simon apart, no one was officially aware of the Catherine plan outside the Admiralty.

36. Cork to the First Lord, First Sea Lord, Controller, Fourth Sea Lord, and DCNS, memorandum, 17 November 1939, ADM 1/205/4, BNA.

37. In early October, for example, he emphasized the importance of a spring start by declaring that "for an operation such as this SURPRISE IS EVERYTHING; the expedition is doomed to failure unless surprise is at least partial achieved." See Cork, untitled paper, 10 October 1939, ADM 199/1928, BNA.

38. The UP weapon was Churchill's and Lindemann's pet solution to the air problem. It would never prove efficacious.

39. Pound to Churchill, memorandum, 3 December 1939, ADM 199/1928, BNA.

40. Cork to First Lord, 5 December 1939; Churchill's comments, 11 December 1939, both in ADM 199/1929, BNA.

41. War Cabinet Meeting, Conclusions, 8 December 1939, 11:30 a.m., CAB 65/2/42, BNA.

42. War Cabinet Meeting, Conclusions. On 6 December Churchill drew the War Cabinet's attention to the "great importance from the point of view of naval strategy of continuing our present satisfactory relations with Italy." Churchill, 6 December 1939, 11:30 a.m., CAB 65/2, BNA.

43. Churchill to Pound, Phillips, and Carter, 11 December 1939, ADM 199/1928, BNA.

44. Pound to Churchill, 25 December 1939, ADM 199/1929, BNA.

45. Churchill, "Note on the War."

46. Churchill, "Note on the War."

47. Coincidentally, like Pound, Churchill considered that, if Catherine was not possible, submarines (and mines) could be used instead to interdict or do serious harm to a German invasion, which he assumed would be an inevitable response to the Allied occupation of the ore fields.

48. Churchill to Cork, 29 December 1939, ADM 205/4, BNA. The quotation is from Churchill's Christmas Day letter. Although he had acknowledged the air threat and claimed it was a problem that he "in no wise underrate[d]," his hypotheticals tended to do just that.

49. The other hypotheticals in Churchill's 29 December letter were that Allies could occupy in strong force the ore field and hold the port of Lulea and could also have the port of Gavle; that supplies of all kinds, including oil, can pass across Norway and Sweden to ports in the Gulf of Bothnia; that adequate aviation was available to protect Lulea and the northern part of the Gulf of Bothnia from a German counterstroke; and that Finland still maintained its independence and that the country was not an effective base for Russian or German aircraft.

50. To accommodate Pound's and his own concerns over the number of destroyers (three flotillas) proposed for the operation, Churchill had asked Cork if two would be sufficient.

51. Pound to Churchill, 31 December 1939, ADM 205/4, BNA (also in Gilbert, *At the Admiralty*, 589–91). On the same day he received Pound's reply to his hypotheticals, Churchill received the COS assessment titled "Military Implications of a Policy Aimed at Stopping the Export of Swedish Ore to Germany." Pound referred to this in his correspondence (COS Report, 31 December 1939, CAB 66/4/29, BNA). Churchill was mortified that this report had dismissed a naval solution (Catherine) to the northern strategy at a time when he still believed the matter was under discussion. Churchill's response to the COS reports was published as "Swedish Iron Ore," War Paper (WP) 3, 31 December 1939, CAB 66/4/33, BNA.

52. He argued, for example, that any Russian air bases used by the Germans, if Finland was not occupied, would be too distant to be of use; the railway was not likely to be taken up by supplying a large force before April or May, and this would afford time to accumulate oil supplies in Sweden; more than three squadrons of aircraft could be maintained in the "wide expanses of Norway."

53. Churchill to Pound, 1 January 1940, ADM 205/4, BNA (also in Gilbert, *At the Admiralty*, 592–93).

54. First Sea Lord Pound to Churchill, 10 January 1940, ADM 199/1928, BNA.

55. Churchill to Admiral Pound, 15 January 1940, ADM 199/1928, BNA.

56. Several authors have commended Churchill for his visionary strategy: David Reynolds, "Churchill in 1940: The Worst and Finest Hour," in Blake and Louis, *Churchill*, 245; and Ben-Moshe, *Churchill*, 119–20. They are too kind.

Chapter Three. New Construction and Churchill's Inshore Squadron

1. In late July 1939 a meeting chaired by the Admiralty controller addressed the matter of battleship construction. It was proposed to advance the five KGV-class battleships and give the four battleships of the subsequent two programs a low priority for the first few months of war. Churchill's fall 1939 proposal, however, was evidently viewed as a step too far.

2. This recommendation was made on 11 September. Churchill first made known his intention to focus on short-term construction on 6 September, when he rejected the Admiralty's proposal for the additional construction of new cruisers, "which cannot be finished for at least two years, even under war conditions." However, he approved all proposals for smaller vessels, "as it all bears on U-boat hunting and ought to be ready within the year." He noted that this matter could be reviewed during the next three months. See Churchill to Pound, Phillips, and others, minute, 11 September 1939, ADM 205/2, BNA (also in Gilbert, *At the Admiralty*, 38).

3. Churchill to Chamberlain, 10 September 1939, Chamberlain Papers.

4. Churchill to Rear Admiral Hood, 8 August 1914, ADM 1/8388, BNA (also in Gilbert, *At the Admiralty*, 21–22).

5. Churchill to Chamberlain, 18 September 1939, Chamberlain Papers.

6. "Suspension of Work on Capital Ships Not Completing before the End of 1941 (ie. Beatty and 16 Inch Gunned Ships)," n.d. (September 1939?), ADM 205/2, BNA. This paper was part of a preliminary assessment provided by naval staff before the meeting and in response to Churchill's 11 September minute to Pound and others (also found in ADM 205/2).

7. Untitled paper, circulated 22 September 1939, ADM 205/2, BNA.

8. Admiralty Board Meeting, Minutes and attendant documents, 28 September 1939; Controller, "New Construction Program: Review in Light of War Conditions," 27 September 1939, both in ADM 167/105, BNA.

9. Tooze, *Wages of Destruction*, 338.

10. Churchill to Pound and others, "New Construction," minute, 8 October 1939, ADM 205/2 (also in Gilbert, *At the Admiralty*, 223–24). Churchill got his way.

11. Churchill to Pound and others, 18 September 1939, Char 19/3 (also in Gilbert, *At the Admiralty*, 113–14).

12. Churchill to Pound and others, 21 September 1939, ADM 199/1928, BNA (also in Gilbert, *At the Admiralty*, 136–37).

13. Churchill to Pound, 1 October 1939, ADM 205/2, BNA (also in Gilbert, *At the Admiralty*, 276).

14. His first efforts at building an inshore squadron revolved around some bulged cruisers and a force of big-gunned monitors. By 1917 he was thinking of bulged battleships of the combined British and American fleets.

15. "Naval Policy 1917," memorandum, 7 July 1917, Char 8/104, Churchill Archive Centre.

16. Churchill made this clear to his naval staff many times. He also explained this view at length to the House of Commons during his naval estimates speech of 27 February 1940. See Churchill, speech to House of Commons, 27 February 1940, 357 Parl. Deb. H.C. (5th ser.) (1940) cols. 1923–36 (also in Gilbert, *At the Admiralty*, 812–13).

17. The expression comes from Barnett, *Engage the Enemy*. For similar assessments, see Gretton, *Former Naval Person*, 248; Marder, *From the Dardanelles*, 55; Hough, *Former Naval Person*, 131–32, 141, 145; Lamb, *Churchill as War Leader*, 24.

18. First Lord Personal Minute 55, 11 December 1939, ADM 199/1928, BNA (also in Gilbert, *At the Admiralty*, 496–97).

19. This issue has been developed in Lambert, "Seapower 1939–1940."

20. On 24 October Churchill wrote to Fraser, "These are ships to fight *Scharnhorst* and *Gneisenau* in North Sea or perhaps against Italy in the Mediterranean. They have no other purpose." Char 19/3 (also in Gilbert, *At the Admiralty*, 288).

21. Pound to Churchill, 22 October 1939, ADM 205/3, BNA. By coincidence it had fallen to Pound in 1917 to respond to Churchill's request for an inshore squadron. He showed some interest in the project, although this might have been Pound the diplomat at work. See "Mr Churchill's Proposals," memorandum, n.d., DUPO 5/2, Churchill Archive Centre.

22. Particular attention was given to the *Queen Elizabeth*, primarily because there were still nine months left in the current refit. Pound contended that if additional work was done to this ship, similar work should be considered for her sister ships, *Valiant* and *Warspite*. By 11 November it had been concluded for a variety of tactical and strategic reasons that "the proposed re-bulging of the three WARSPITES is not considered worth the sacrifice entailed." See "Effect of Re-bulging and Re-arming the Three Warspite," memorandum, 11 November 1939, ADM 205/3, BNA.

23. Meeting in First Lord's Room, Minutes, 8 November 1939, ADM 205/3, BNA.

24. It was anticipated that *Lion* and *Temeraire* would be completed in March and September 1944 and *Conquerer* and *Thunderer* would be completed in January and June 1945. It was anticipated HMS *Vanguard* would be completed in December 1943.

25. Churchill to Simon, 21 January 1940, ADM 205/5, BNA.

26. The rather vague time frame for this war appeared to have been extended to late 1943 as a result of Churchill's support for *Vanguard*.

27. Danckwerts, DP, "War Construction Program: Amendment," memorandum, 10 January 1940, ADM 205/5, BNA.

28. Churchill, "Draft Submission for the 1940/41 Construction Program," 1 February 1940, ADM 205/5, BNA.

29. Churchill, "Draft Submission," 1 February 1940. Churchill's proposals would achieve substantial savings, but these savings would be enhanced by not adding any new carriers. Additionally, he argued that the battle cruisers would prove a satisfactory substitute for several of the 8-inch-gunned cruisers proposed. Other reductions were consistent with many of the sea lords' recommendations.

30. Churchill to Pound, 15 January 1940, ADM 199/1928, BNA.

31. Phillips, untitled paper, 2 February 1940, ADM 205/5, BNA. "In the late war it will be recollected that not only did we go on and complete the battleships then building, i.e. five Queen Elizabeths, five Royal Sovereigns, and three foreign ships taken over, but in 1915 we laid down five battle cruiser type ships (*Renown, Repulse, Courageous, Glorious, Furious*) and in 1917 we laid down the Hoods."

32. Fraser to Pound, 2 February 1940, ADM 205/5, BNA.

33. Unnumbered WP, "Naval Program 1940–41," 11 February 1940, Char 19/6, Churchill Archive Centre.

34. Churchill defended this proposal by referencing the need for a fast ship to deal with "the super-pocket-battleships [German?] and the heavy 12 inch gunned cruisers now being built by Japan," a sign perhaps that he was already thinking about trade protection in a war with Japan rather than about a large fleet for Singapore.

35. Churchill to Pound, Carter, and Fraser, 7 February 1940, Char 19/6 (also in Gilbert, *At the Admiralty*, 724).

36. "Naval Program 1940–41," WP (40) 53, n.d., CAB 66/5/33, BNA. Also changed from the mid-February proposal was the dropping of two Fiji-class cruisers, ten whalers, and significantly, twelve escort destroyers. The number of escort destroyers had been sixty-six in Churchill's 1 February proposal, eighty-two in the mid-February proposal, and seventy in the final submission.

37. Churchill to Pound, memorandum, 23 March 1940, Char 19/6.

38. It is likely Churchill placed great store in the bulging of his battleships to protect against the torpedo, but these improvements had not kept pace with the warheads of modern torpedoes.

39. Churchill to Pound, 23 March 1940. Yet it has been written that "nowhere on land or at sea did there appear to be a revisionist-realist like Herbert Richmond who recognised the deadly dangers from shore-based aircraft to a fleet with inadequate air cover and inadequate air power to strike back effectively." Hough, *Former Naval Person*, 141.

40. On 23 March 1940, Churchill wrote to Pound that the UP weapons "may even before this year is out furnish HM Ships with the means of inflicting losses of an effectual deterring character upon hostile aircraft." Churchill to Pound, 23 March 1940. For evidence of his anxiety over his ships' antiaircraft defenses, see Churchill to Pound and Phillips, minute, 27 September 1939, ADM 205/2, BNA; Churchill to Pound, Phillips, Fraser, and Carter, 17 March 1940, Char 19/6.

41. Neither Germany nor Italy had carriers. Churchill (like Chatfield) considered the torpedo plane threat more formidable than the dive-bomber and was relieved that the Germans had chosen not to develop, or at least use, such a weapon to this point in the war. See War Cabinet Meeting, March 1940, CAB 65/6, BNA.

42. Churchill to Pound, 12 January 1940, Char 19/6.

43. Churchill to Pound, 12 January 1940.

44. Churchill to Pound, 12 January 1940. As the minute points out, Churchill had already organized the formation of two land-based FAA squadrons for the Orkneys to protect Scapa and surrounds. This was an additional initiative.

45. C. in C. Home Fleet to Vice Admiral Commanding Orkneys, 6 January 1940, ADM 1/10737, BNA.

46. Keyes to Churchill, 12 February 1940, ADM 205/6, BNA.

47. Churchill to Royle, 26 February 1940, Char 19/6 (also in Gilbert, *At the Admiralty*, 804).

48. Churchill to Royle, 20 February 1940, Char 19/6.

49. Churchill to Pound, 11 March 1940, Char 19/6. In a typically quixotic moment, Churchill suggested that, as part of their new role, a carrier or two might sit permanently offshore

along the flight path of German bombers so that their force of fighters might more effectively attack the enemy before they reached the fleet base. Pound would subsequently point out that such a proposal would likely make the carriers themselves the object of air attack.

50. Churchill to Pound, 11 March 1940.

51. Churchill was somewhat mercurial in his attitude to the FAA. Around the time he was expressing these opinions and curtailing the function of his carrier forces, a brief panic occurred over the completion date of *Bismarck*. In the absence of any KGVs, Churchill worried that it would be impossible to catch and kill this ship with the battleships in hand. He, therefore, immediately looked to a carrier and battleship combination to deal with this threat, although he was not enthusiastic about the prospect. Like most naval personnel of this time (except for those in the Naval Air Arm itself), Churchill accepted the capacity of FAA aircraft to slow large ships of war but doubted their capacity to sink them. This, he continued to believe, was best done by another battleship.

52. *Vanguard* was launched before Japan's defeat but took no part in the war. None of the four *Lion*-class battleships were ever completed.

Chapter Four. Fighting the War

1. Chamberlain to Hilda, 15 April 1939, in *Chamberlain Diary Letters*. All letters from this source are dated, and they appear in the book chronologically.

2. Chamberlain to Hilda, 15 April 1939. In this letter to Hilda he wondered if Churchill would "help or hinder in Cabinet or in Council" or if he would "wear me out resisting rash suggestions." In a letter to Ida, he wrote that "if there was any possibility of easing the tensions and getting back to normal relations with the dictators," he would not risk having Churchill join the cabinet, but he also admitted that "the nearer we get to war the better his chances and vice versa." Chamberlain to Ida, 23 April 1939, *Chamberlain Diary Letters*.

3. War Cabinet, "Report by the Land Forces Committee," 8 September 1939, CAB 66/1/14, BNA.

4. "Report of the Land Forces Committee," 10 September 1939, CAB 66/1/21, BNA. It was hoped this would consist of a thirty-two-division British Army, fourteen divisions from the Dominions, four divisions from India, and five divisions for assistance to allies.

5. War Cabinet, Land Forces Committee minutes, 7 September 1939, CAB 92/111, BNA (also in Gilbert, *At the Admiralty*, 43–45). Churchill sought to have twenty divisions within six months and forty divisions within twelve months, with a grand total of some fifty to sixty divisions.

6. Churchill to Chamberlain, 10 September 1939, Chamberlain Papers (also in Gilbert, *At the Admiralty*, 60–65).

7. Churchill to Chamberlain, 18 September 1939, Chamberlain Papers (also in Gilbert, *At the Admiralty*, 111).

8. For a summary of Lindemann's brief, see Churchill to Carter, 9 October 1939, Char 19/3 (also in Gilbert, *At the Admiralty*, 227–28).

9. See Churchill's untitled War Cabinet paper, 8 February 1940, 39, CAB 65/5, BNA (also in Gilbert, *At the Admiralty*, 727–30). It is probable Churchill's comparisons, and the

assumptions behind them, were of little relevance to Britain's capacity to meet the targets he sought. According to Hancock and Gowing, *British War Economy*, 242, to meet a target of fifty-five divisions in two years, "the British war economy would have to achieve in two years of war an expansion three times as great as that which was achieved in the four years of 1914–1918."

10. Churchill argued that the estimated gap of £390 million between income and expenditure in the first year of the war was "inexcusable" and that it would fall nearer £150 million. The figure for 1939 would prove to be over £400 million, and the figure for 1940, over £700 million. Stamps' estimates appear to have been from September 1939 to September 1940. The estimates given here and sourced from the chart on external trade in Central Statistical Office, *Statistical Digest of the War*, 162–63, were from March 1939 to March 1940. Churchill's (and Lindemann's) concerns were addressed at the War Cabinet on 13 February, when it was explained that several of the first lord's concerns were based on misunderstanding and miscalculation. See CAB 65/4/40, BNA.

11. CAB 66/1/41, BNA.

12. Churchill's assessment undoubtedly had much to do with the fact the navy had many fewer capital ships. At the end of World War II, the Royal Navy employed over 800,000 personnel. During World War I the figure was approximately half this figure. See Central Statistical Office, *Statistical Digest of the War*, 9. The strength of the navy in June 1945 was 783,000 plus 72,000 Women's Royal Naval Auxiliary Service. According to the first lord's Explanation of the Naval Estimates for 1919–1920, the size of the Royal Navy at the armistice, including the Royal Naval Division, was 415,162.

13. Lord Privy Seal, "The Extent to Which Shipping Considerations Call for a Review of Our Import Program," 23 February 1940, CAB 66/5/44, BNA.

14. Churchill, "Note on the Lord Privy Seal's Memorandum," 29 February 1940, CAB 66/6, BNA.

15. See Churchill, "Navy Estimates, 1940; Navy Supplementary Estimate, 1939, Mr Churchill's Statement," speech to the House of Commons, 27 February 1940, 357 Parl. Deb. H.C. (5th ser.) (1940) cols. 1923–36 (also in Gilbert, *At the Admiralty*, 815–16).

16. See Churchill, "Note on the Lord Privy Seal's Memorandum."

17. Behrens, *Merchant Shipping*, 51n. 5.

18. "Imports into the United Kingdom," in Central Statistical Office, *Statistical Digest of the War*, 198, table 161. This figure was achieved because British shipping was operating more efficiently than it had at any time before the war.

19. The caution to be found in the lord privy seal's document was, of course, entirely justified by the drop of imports in the next several years of war.

20. Paper dated 1 February 1940, H 107/3, Lindemann Papers. For Churchill's comments to the War Cabinet, see War Cabinet Meeting, Minutes, 13 February 1940, CAB 65/5/40, BNA.

21. War Cabinet Meeting, Minutes, 13 February 1940.

22. For example, see Churchill speech, 27 January 1940, in Gilbert, *At the Admiralty*, 695. As for delicacy, see correspondence with Geoffrey Shakespeare, 11 March and 22 March 1940, in Gilbert, *At the Admiralty*, 865, 910.

23. Churchill War Paper, 8 February 1940, CAB 66/5, BNA (also in Gilbert, *At the Admiralty*, 730).

24. French, *Raising Churchill's Army*, 185.

25. Jackson, *Fall of France*, 59. For a comment on Churchill's preoccupation with raw numbers rather than the "military utility of plans," see Alexander, "Fighting to the Last Frenchman?" 243.

26. One of the earliest tasks set for Lindemann and his statistical unit was not a naval matter but the matter of aircraft delivery. See F88–F108, Lindemann Papers.

27. Churchill, War Cabinet Paper 39/40, War Cabinet Meeting, 13 February 1940, CAB 66/5/40, BNA. At this meeting Churchill expressed the view he "would rather more men in the line with smaller scales of equipment than smaller forces with an ideal scale."

28. Evidence suggests Churchill's desire to send men to France as quickly as possible was not welcomed by the BEF itself. See, for example, entries for 26 and 28 November, in Alanbrooke, *War Diaries*, 20.

29. MCC meeting, 18 March 1940, CAB 83/3, BNA.

30. Throughout the war Britain established many formations, indeed many more than the fifty-five divisions Churchill strived for. However, these formations never existed at the same time, many were disbanded as others were established, and many more were understrength and inadequately equipped. For a study of these issues, see French, *Raising Churchill's Army*, chap. 6.

31. French, *Raising Churchill's Army*, 186.

32. Appendix A: Minute, Prime Minister to Minister of Aircraft Production, 24 May 1940, in Churchill, *Their Finest Hour*, 635–44.

33. See Churchill to Admiral Pound and others, 18 September 1939, Char 19/3.

34. For Ironside's comments on this issue but also Churchill's unrealistic expectation for the growth of the army, see the diary entry for 24 October, in Ironside, *Ironside Diaries*, 134.

35. Churchill to Wood, 30 October 1939, AIR 19/20, BNA. Wood replied suggesting that such an order should await "a little more practical experience." Wood to Churchill, 8 November 1939, AIR 19/20, BNA.

36. See Simon to Churchill, "Naval Construction Program 1940/41," 20 January 1940, Papers of the First Sea Lord, ADM 205/5, BNA.

37. PREMIER 1/404, BNA. These words were drafted by Chatfield in his letter to Chamberlain of 19 October and used commonly thereafter.

38. See Roskill, *Hankey*, 3:413; Manchester, *Caged Lion*, 519.

39. Roskill, *Hankey*, 3:413.

40. Stewart, *Burying Caesar*, 385.

41. Addison, *Churchill*, 156.

42. Hankey to his wife, 3 September 1939, in Roskill, *Hankey*, 3:419. In the first months of the war, Hankey was always a member of the ad hoc committees of the service ministers and COS but was not part of the MCC when formed. In April 1940 Hankey took it upon himself to write to Chamberlain and criticize Churchill's influence on operational decisions during the Norwegian campaign.

43. Churchill to Chamberlain, 21 September 1939, Char 19/2 (also in Gilbert, *At the Admiralty*, 132).

44. Chatfield to Chamberlain, 12 October 1939, PREMIER 1/404, BNA.

45. Wilson to Chamberlain, 13 October 1939, PREMIER 1/404.

46. PREMIER 1/104 documents provide extensive details of the discussion that led to the development of the MCC.

47. On several occasions during October, ad hoc ministerial committees, which also included the COS, were established to discuss specified issues. Among the issues considered by these committees was air bombing policy.

48. Churchill, note, 2 January 1940, ADM 116/4471, BNA. In CAB 65/56 Churchill's frustration with Joint Planning Staff (JPS) and COS interference in policy is mentioned on 19 and 21 January. On 21 January Bridges wrote: "The First Lord again demonstrates his extreme susceptibility to any business being transacted by the Chiefs of Staff. He regards their responsibility as in some ways interfering with the due responsibility of Ministers."

49. This was an impediment to action that caused Churchill particular frustration in mid-January. See Churchill to Halifax, 15 January 1940, FO 800/328, BNA.

50. MCC memorandum, CAB 83/1, BNA.

51. Ironside's view was that the prime minister was "forced to sit on the Committee himself to prevent Winston from running off the rails." See 25 April 1940 entry, in Ironside, *Ironside Diaries*, 282.

52. For John Colville's partisan view, see 17 April 1940 entry, in *Fringes of Power*, 119. For Chamberlain's confident assessment of his skills as chairman, see Chamberlain to Hilda, 20 April 1940, in *Chamberlain Diary Letters*.

53. Chamberlain to Hilda, 20 April 1940.

54. Further Notes on Meeting, 15 January 1940, CAB 65/56, BNA.

55. MCC Meeting, Minutes, 20 December 1939, CAB 83/1; War Cabinet Meeting, Minutes, 22 December 1939, CAB 65/4/29, BNA.

56. In an interview with W. P. Crozier, Samuel Hoare said that Churchill had been offered Chatfield's job without portfolio but had chosen to stay at the Admiralty. See Crozier, *Off the Record*, 159.

57. Churchill to Chamberlain, 1 April 1940, Chamberlain Papers (also in Gilbert, *At the Admiralty*, 948).

58. Charmley, *Churchill*, 381. He sees the promotion as a "tactical success."

59. Chamberlain, remarks to Lord Camrose, in Gilbert, *At the Admiralty*, 968. In a letter to his sister Hilda, Chamberlain related an incident in which Churchill pressed a course of action that neither Chamberlain nor the COS supported. Chamberlain noted that he decided to leave the decision to Churchill: "Thus the responsibility was laid squarely on his shoulders and as I expected he wouldn't take it." It was likely incidents such as these that were, at least in part, behind Chamberlain's decision to appoint Churchill chairman. More accountability would make Churchill more responsible. See Chamberlain to Hilda, 4 May 1940, *Chamberlain Diary Letters*.

60. Churchill, *Gathering Storm*, 463.

61. Churchill to Chamberlain, unsent letter, 24 April 1940, Char 19/2.

62. Chamberlain to Hilda, 4 May 1940.

63. Chamberlain to Ida, 27 April 1940, *Chamberlain Diary Letters*.

64. "Draft of Defense Organisation," WP 9 (40) 120, 30 April 1940, PREMIER 1/404.

65. 18 May 1940 entry, in Colville, *Fringes of Power*, 157.

66. Chamberlain to Hilda, 17 May 1940, *Chamberlain Diary Letters*.

67. G. D. A. MacDougall, "The Prime Minister's Statistical Section," in Chester, *Lessons of the British*, 61. MacDougall noted that the breadth of the responsibilities, especially in the early period of Churchill's statistical section, resulted in some "amateurish dabbling."

68. For an interesting comment on this particular challenge, see Fort, *Prof*, 190.

69. For a less critical view of Lindemann's contribution see Fort, *Prof* chap. 10.

Chapter Five. "Don't Hurt Them, Dear!"

1. The expression "taking the gloves off" was used routinely in War Cabinet discussion. It referred to the application of unrestricted aerial warfare save for the deliberate bombing of civilians or targets that were neither military nor industrial in nature.

2. For examples, see Manchester, *Caged Lion*, 584–85; Prior, "Half Hearted War," in *When Britain Saved.*

3. War Cabinet, 3 September 1939, CAB 66/1/19, BNA.

4. This principle was established in July 1939 (see War Cabinet, Confidential Annex, 11 September 1939, CAB 65/1/19, BNA). Also note the views of Gamelin explained in War Cabinet Meeting, Confidential Annex, 5 September 1939, CAB 65/3/1, BNA.

5. At the 4 September War Cabinet meeting, it was concluded that Gamelin should be reassured the French would receive air support for coordinated military operations but that Britain did not intend to "undertake sporadic bombing which would lead to no permanent military result, but would cause unnecessary loss of aircraft." See War Cabinet Meeting, Conclusions, 4 September 1939, CAB 65/1/2, BNA.

6. War Cabinet Meeting, Confidential Annex, 5 September 1939.

7. War Cabinet Meeting, Conclusion, 3 September 1939, CAB 65/1/1, BNA.

8. During the subsequent staff talks Gamelin explained, "The French Air Force was barely equipped, had no air plan other than limited operations in cooperation with the general plan of the French Army." War Cabinet Meeting, Conclusions, Minute 1, 5 September 1939, CAB 65/3/1, BNA.

9. War Cabinet Meeting, Conclusions, 4 September 1939, CAB 65/1/2, BNA.

10. War Cabinet Meeting, Confidential Annex, 5 September 1939.

11. Newall was not convinced that *Athenia* represented a deliberate German policy. He was correct. See War Cabinet Meeting, Confidential Annex, 5 September 1939.

12. War Cabinet Meeting, Confidential Annex, 5 September 1939.

13. "British Air Action: Possible Extension of Scope," Minute 14, CAB 65/3/2, BNA.

14. War Cabinet Meeting, "Air Policy," Confidential Annex, Minute 6, 11 September 1939, CAB 65/3/4. Subsequently, some doubt emerged over whether the Germans had in fact begun unrestricted aerial warfare in Poland. The COS recommended that the United States be asked to establish the true state of affairs in Poland. "Report by Chiefs of Staff Committee on German Observance of International Law," WP 26, 13 September 1939, CAB 66/1/26. In due course the COS accepted that international law had been breached, but this was not used as grounds for escalating the air war. The inclination of the War Cabinet was to wait for the Germans to do this in the West, but in the end the matter became somewhat irrelevant. Policy was guided more by the consequences of retaliation.

15. Confidential Annex, 11 September 1939, CAB 66/1/19.

16. Churchill to Chamberlain, "Bombing Policy," 10 September 1939, Chamberlain Papers (also in Gilbert, *At the Admiralty*, 60).

17. For COS comments on Roosevelt's statement, see COS, "Air Policy," 11 September 1939, CAB 66/1/19, BNA.

18. War Cabinet Meeting, Confidential Annex, 14 September 1939, CAB 65/3/6, BNA. Almost precisely the same view had been presented by the CAS at the 4 September War Cabinet meeting.

19. "Note on the General Situation," 25 September 1939, Char 20/15, Churchill Archive Centre (also in Gilbert, *At the Admiralty*, 149).

20. Broadcast, 12 November 1939, BBC Written Archives Centre (also in Gilbert, *At the Admiralty*, 357–62); Churchill, speech in Manchester, 27 January 1940, in *Into Battle*, 163–69 (also in Gilbert, *At the Admiralty*, 694). The sentiments expressed in these speeches were almost identical.

21. Churchill speech, 27 January 1940.

22. Churchill to Lord Trenchard, 5 January 1940, in Gilbert, *At the Admiralty*, 613.

23. Churchill, *Gathering Storm*, 508.

24. Churchill to Pound and Phillips, 19 November 1939, ADM 205/2, BNA.

25. Churchill to Fraser and Boyd, 19 November 1939, ADM 205/2. At this time Denis William Boyd (1891–1965) was captain of HMS *Vernon*.

26. A meeting was organized with Jefferis on 23 November, and his designs were discussed. Notes on a Meeting, 23 November 1939, ADM 205/2.

27. War Cabinet Meeting, Confidential Annex, 24 November 1939, CAB 65/4/20, BNA. Hankey asked that Churchill consider using the mines in the Danube to interrupt Germany's oil supply from Romania.

28. AIR 19/20, BNA. The paper, titled "Considerations Affecting Air Counter-Measures against the German Attack on British Sea-Borne Trade," was submitted by Collier on 9 December 1939.

29. "Mining the Rhine: The Legal Aspect," 7 December 1939, ADM 116/4239, BNA (also in Gilbert, *At the Admiralty*, 482–85).

30. Churchill to Wood, 9 December 1939, ADM 116/4239.

31. War Cabinet Meeting, 10 December 1939, CAB 65/2/44, BNA. Although recorded as a meeting of the War Cabinet, Churchill, Wood, and Simon were the only ministers present. There is no evidence to show the full War Cabinet subsequently challenged these conclusions.

32. The air force's resistance to attacking Sylt continued to upset Churchill. On 16 January he wrote (but did not send) a letter to Wood that reflected his frustrations over the air force's strict interpretation of air policy. He agreed that Britain's interests were served by not inviting attacks on factories and harbors, and he did not intend to press Wood to attack "German island fortresses or Naval building yards," but he contended that the Germans were not refraining from doing the same to "humanity" and would do so "whenever they judge the action advantageous." He wrote, "Previous provocation is not an indispensable condition to them nor should it be to us." This latter remark represented a change in the views he held in September. Churchill to Wood, 16 January 1940, ADM 116/4239.

33. Churchill, memorandum, 12 December 1939, ADM 116/4239 (also in Gilbert, *At the Admiralty*, 500–502). Among the features of the mines was a mechanism by which the mine would explode before it left German waters. A great deal of effort was being made to make the weapon as targeted as possible.

34. Churchill to Gamelin, 6 March 1940, ADM 116/4239. Recently promoted to rear admiral, John U. P. Fitzgerald (1888–1940) was director of torpedoes and mining until February 1940.

35. Royle to Churchill, n.d., ADM 116/4239.

36. ADM 116/4239. Churchill had mentioned this at a meeting of 23 February 1940, but the point had been noted earlier.

37. Churchill to Gamelin, 16 March 1940, ADM 116/4240, BNA.

38. War Cabinet Meeting, Confidential Annex, 14 October 1939, CAB 65/3/26, BNA.

39. Committee Set Up by the War Cabinet, 18 October 1939, CAB 83/1, BNA.

40. COS, "Air Policy," 11 November 1939, CAB 66/3/18, BNA. For CAS's response to this, see War Cabinet Meeting, 14 November 1939, CAB 66/3/22, BNA.

41. Gamelin to Air Vice Marshal Evill, following meeting with French High Command, 24 October 1939, CAB 66/3/18.

42. These sentiments toward the Low Countries are inconsistent with the claim that Gamelin's strategy, including plans to enter Belgium, and subsequent efforts to assist Holland were driven by his desire to prevent these countries experiencing the same fate as other neutrals at the hands of the dictators. For historians who take this line, see Alexander, "Repercussions of the Breda Variant," 481; Horne, *To Lose a Battle*, 16; and Alexander, *Republic in Danger*, 398.

43. War Cabinet Meeting, Confidential Annex, 7 October 1939, CAB 63/5/21, BNA.

44. COS, "Air Policy: Note by Secretary," 4 November 1939, CAB 80/4, BNA.

45. COS, "Military Implications of a German Invasion of Holland," 2 November 1939, CAB 66/3/8, BNA.

46. War Cabinet Meeting, Confidential Annex, 6 November 1939, CAB 65/4/5, BNA.

47. War Cabinet Meeting, Confidential Annex, 9 November 1939, CAB 65/4/8, BNA.

48. Ironside first heard of this proposal around 7 November. See Meeting of the Chiefs of Staff, 7 November 1939, CAB 79/2, BNA.

49. Nor was the suggestion fully understood by the COS, which on 10 November indicated it did not know why Gamelin had proposed this extension to the Dyle plan. See Minutes of the COS Committee Meeting, 10 November 1939, CAB 79/2.

50. Minutes of the COS Committee Meeting, 10 November 1939.

51. Minutes of the COS Committee Meeting, 10 November 1939.

52. War Cabinet Meeting, Confidential Annex, 9 November 1939, CAB 65/4/8, BNA.

53. COS, "Air Policy," 11 November 1939.

54. Meeting of the COS, 12 November 1939, CAB 79/2, BNA.

55. War Cabinet Meeting, Confidential Annex, 14 November 1939, CAB 65/4/13, BNA.

56. COS, "German Invasion of Holland," 10 November 1939, 117, CAB 80/5, BNA.

57. Anglo-French Liaison, 68th Meeting, 12 November 1939, CAB 80/5.

58. COS, "German Invasion of Holland: Note by the Secretary" (forwarding correspondence from French delegation), 14 November 1939, CAB 80/5.

59. It is interesting to compare this perspective with, for example, Cairns, "Britain and the Fall," 367.

60. SWC Meeting, 17 November 1939, CAB 9/3, BNA.

61. War Cabinet Meeting, 17 November 1939, CAB 65/4, BNA.

62. For early discussion of this issue, see COS, "Intervention in Scandinavia: Plans and Implications," 28 January 1940, CAB 66/5/15, BNA. The report was discussed at the 2 February War Cabinet. This was followed by Chamberlain's inquiry at the SWC on 5 February. Subsequently, discussion occurred at a War Cabinet meeting of 9 February (CAB 65/11/26, BNA), this time pertaining to an attack on Oslo. COS, "Protection of Oslo against Air Attack," 14 February 1940, CAB 66/5/35, BNA; War Cabinet, Confidential Annex, 14 February 1940, CAB 65/11/30, BNA. The COS revisited the question for the final time on 2 March, and this led to the discussion during the 3 March War Cabinet meeting.

63. Minutes of Supreme War Council, 5 February 1940, CAB 99/3, BNA.

64. COS, "Scandinavia—Assurance against Air Attack," memorandum, 2 March 1940; War Cabinet Meeting, Confidential Annex, 4 March 1940, both in CAB 65/11, BNA.

65. War Cabinet Meeting, Confidential Annex, 4 March 1940.

66. Meeting of the Supreme War Council, 28 March 1940, CAB 99/3.

67. See, for example, Churchill, "Royal Marine," memorandum for the MCC, 7 April 1940, CAB 83/5, BNA. For other motivation, see Proceedings of MCC, 8 April 1940, CAB 83/3, BNA.

68. Churchill, "Royal Marine."

69. COS, "German Invasion of Holland: Allied Policy," Minutes of Meeting, 7 April 1940, CAB 79/3, BNA.

70. Meeting of Supreme War Council, 9 April 1940, CAB 99/3.

71. War Cabinet, "Western Front," Confidential Annex, 12 April 1940, CAB 65/12/22, BNA.

72. War Cabinet, "Air Policy If Holland Is Invaded," Confidential Annex, 12 April 1940, CAB 65/12/22.

73. War Cabinet, "Air Policy If Holland Is Invaded."

74. War Cabinet, Confidential Annex, 14 April 1940, CAB 65/12/24, BNA.

75. COS, "Air Action to Be Taken in the Event of a German Invasion of Low Countries," WP (40) 132, 19 April 1940, CAB 66/7/12, BNA.

76. COS, "Air Action to Be Taken."

77. War Cabinet, Confidential Annex, 21 April 1940, CAB 65/12, BNA.

78. SWC Meeting, 23 April 1940, CAB 93/3, BNA.

79. In reality, this concession was not significant. The Germans invaded Belgium and Holland simultaneously, and the Belgians did not hesitate to call in the Allied armies, so the possibilities that might have arisen, and that had caused considerable angst over many months, did not.

80. Minute 1, 7 May 1940, CAB 65/13, BNA.

81. War Cabinet Meeting, Confidential Annex, 8 May 1940, CAB 65/13.

82. War Cabinet Meeting, Confidential Annex, 10 May 1940, CAB 65/13.

83. War Cabinet Meeting, Confidential Annex, 10 May 1940.

84. War Cabinet Meeting, Confidential Annex, 10 May 1940. During the night of 10–11 May, a small force of heavy bombers attacked München-Gladbach. Presumably this was an attack on marshaling yards deemed to be actively used by German forces. München-Gladbach is west of the Rhine.

85. War Cabinet Meeting, Confidential Annex, 12 May 1940, CAB 65/12/22.

86. War Cabinet Meeting, Confidential Annex, 13 May 1940, CAB 65/13.

87. Churchill, *Gathering Storm*, 574. Of some interest and importance, Churchill used the expression "Don't be unkind to the enemy" to condemn the French. This was very similar to the expression "Don't hurt them, dear," which Churchill used to criticize Malkin's pedantic rejection of Royal Marine. Churchill ignores this similarity in *The Gathering Storm*. Despite this, he claimed that the rejection of Royal Marine was "a method of refusal which I had never met before or since."

88. Reynolds, *In Command of History*, 165–66. This study shares Reynolds' view of Churchill's tendentious assessment of Allied strategy on the western front but not his assessment of French motivation regarding the Dyle plan.

Chapter Six. Lines of Least Resistance

1. Royal Marine was, of course, Churchill's other initiative, but it was rarely discussed within the War Cabinet after it had received conditional support in December.

2. Churchill to Halifax, 15 January 1940, FO 800/328, BNA (also in Gilbert, *At the Admiralty*, 642).

3. Churchill to Halifax, 14 March 1940, FO 800/328 (also in Gilbert, *At the Admiralty*, 883).

4. Halifax to Churchill, 13 January 1940, Char 19/2 (also in Gilbert, *At the Admiralty*, 638).

5. Halifax to Churchill, 15 March 1940, FO 800/328 (also in Gilbert, *At the Admiralty*, 884).

6. For an existing view of Churchill's criticism, see Dilks, "Great Britain and Scandinavia," 29–51.

7. D'Este, *Warlord*, 410; Lamb, *Churchill as War Leader*, 27; Imlay, "Reassessment of Anglo-French," 361.

8. Chamberlain to Ida, 8 October 1939, in *Chamberlain Diary Letters*.

9. Churchill to Godfrey and Mansergh, 21 November 1939, Char 19/3 (also in Gilbert, *At the Admiralty*, 404). For his comments on priority given to the charter agreement, see also Churchill to Pound, Phillips, and others, 27 November 1939, Char 19/3 (also in Gilbert, *At the Admiralty*, 432).

10. "Germany: Supplies of Swedish Iron Ore," memorandum, 27 November 1939, "Scandinavian Affairs: Tactical and Strategical Policy to Be Adopted" file, ADM 116/4471. The memorandum contended that so little ore had been received in Germany since the outbreak of the war that if the winter supply could also be cut, the reduced amount available to the Germans might not be sufficient to "stave off a crisis" even with the reopening of Lulea in May. It is not clear that historians are aware of this memo. Munch-Petersen, *Strategy of Phoney War*, for example, makes no mention of it and refers only to the subsequent MEW assessment.

11. The issue of Germany and its iron ore needs has been a matter of much debate. However, for an emphatic assessment of the degree to which German military production was independent of Swedish ore, especially in the short term, see Jorg-Johannes, "Sweden's Iron Ore," 139–47.

12. For views on these matters and for another important assessment of Swedish ore and Germany, see Fritz, "Swedish Iron Ore," 133–44.

13. Munch-Petersen, *Strategy of Phoney War,* 77, cites comments by MEW staff member Harry Sporborg that indicated the MEW was not backward in providing the maximum gloss on their proposals. In submitting the 10 December report on the same subject, Sporborg informed Desmond Moreton, principal assistant secretary of MEW, that he had given as much emphasis as possible to the positive effects of their proposals to help overcome the objections of other departments such as Supply and Trade.

14. Churchill to Pound, Phillips, and others, 27 November 1939.

15. Churchill to Pound, Phillips, and others, 27 November 1939. However, because the Allies themselves were unprepared to acknowledge the four-mile limit, this issue was not pressed.

16. War Cabinet Meeting, Conclusions, 30 November 1939, CAB 65/2/33, BNA.

17. War Cabinet Meeting, Minutes, 11 December 1939, CAB 65/2/45, BNA.

18. War Cabinet Meeting, Minutes, 3 January 1940, CAB 5/11/2, BNA. The degree to which the MEW eventually pulled the rug from under Churchill's feet is illustrated by the minister of economic warfare's comments to the War Cabinet on 3 January, when he declared, "The game would only be worth the candle if we succeeded in stopping of all the ore supplies from the North Swedish mines."

19. When next discussed the proposal met with the usual resistance for the usual reasons: its potential impact on neutral opinion, the risks surrounding the Norwegian charter agreement, the loss to Britain of its own supply of Scandinavian material, and so on.

20. Churchill, War Cabinet Paper, 16 December 1939, CAB 66/4, BNA.

21. Halifax, "The German Iron Ore Traffic," WP 168, 20 December 1939, CAB 66/4/18, BNA.

22. COS Report, 20 December 1939, CAB 83/2; also CAB 66/4/19, both in BNA.

23. CAB 66/4/19.

24. An attraction of the Finnish option for the War Cabinet was that it would deflect the French from their evident keenness for action in the Mediterranean. The British COS remained unequivocal in arguing that unless and until Italian neutrality was assured, operations in the Mediterranean should be avoided.

25. War Cabinet Meeting, Confidential Annex, 22 December 1939, CAB 65/4/29, BNA.

26. Of the discussions around this time, Lamb (*Churchill as War Leader,* 29) has argued that Churchill was unsuccessful in his initiating action because "Chamberlain and his pre-war appeasement colleagues were opposed to anything which might escalate the cold war into a shooting war." However, Chamberlain's actions often do not fit this mold. For an insightful perspective on such issues, see Smart, *British Strategy,* 137–40.

27. See comments by Chatfield and Dalton, War Cabinet Meeting, Confidential Annex, 22 December 1939, CAB 65/4/29.

28. War Cabinet Meeting, Confidential Annex, 27 December 1939, CAB 65/4/30, BNA.

29. War Cabinet Meeting, Confidential Annex, 27 December 1939.

30. War Cabinet Meeting, Confidential Annex, 27 December 1939.

31. These were COS, "Military Implications of a Policy Aimed at Stopping the Export of Iron Ore to Germany," WP (39) 179, 31 December 1939, CAB 66/4/29; and COS, "Stoppage

of the Export of Iron Ore to Germany: Balance of Advantage of the Minor and Major Projects," WP (39) 140, 31 December 1939, CAB 66/4/30, both in BNA.

32. Churchill, "Swedish Iron Ore," 31 December 1939, CAB 66/4, BNA (also in Gilbert, *At the Admiralty*, 387–88).

33. War Cabinet Meeting, Confidential Annex, 3 January 1940, CAB 65/11/2, BNA.

34. War Cabinet Meeting, Confidential Annex, 9 January 1940, CAB 65/11/7, BNA.

35. War Cabinet Meeting, Confidential Annex, 13 January 1940, CAB 65/11/10, BNA.

36. War Cabinet Meeting, Confidential Annex, 10 January 1940, CAB 65/11/8, BNA.

37. In late February Churchill used the *Altmark* incident to resurrect his Narvik plan. The issue was explored, but Chamberlain declined. A number of reasons were given, including ongoing efforts to secure a charter agreement with Norway, the need not to alienate Sweden, and the danger that the Narvik operation could compromise efforts to help Finland. The Dominion ambassadors again spoke out against it. See Notes of a Meeting Submitted to Chamberlain by Eden, 28 February 1940, PREMIER 1/408, BNA.

38. War Cabinet Meeting, Confidential Annex, 2 February 1940, CAB 65/11/23, BNA.

39. War Cabinet Meeting, Confidential Annex, 8 March 1940, CAB 65/12/8, BNA. Churchill was absent from this meeting, and his message was conveyed to the War Cabinet by Pound.

40. War Cabinet Meeting, Confidential Annex, 11 March 1940, CAB 65/12/10, BNA.

41. Naval Staff, "Effect of the Russo-Finnish Treaty on Our Naval Situation," memorandum, 14 March 1940, CAB 66/6/26, BNA; War Cabinet Meeting, Confidential Annex, 14 March 1940, CAB 65/12/12, BNA.

42. See War Cabinet Meeting, Confidential Annex, 14 March 1940.

43. "French Government's Views on the Future Conduct of the War," 25 May 1940, CAB 66/6/39, BNA.

44. War Cabinet Meeting, Conclusions, 26 April 1940, CAB 65/6/21, BNA.

45. SWC, 28 March 1940, CAB 69/3, BNA.

46. War Cabinet Meeting, Conclusions, 1 April 1940, CAB 65/6/23, BNA.

47. Hankey, "The Grand Strategy of the Allies," Note by the Minister Without Portfolio, 23 March 1940, CAB 66/6/33, BNA. Hankey had begun this on 19 March and amended it on 23 March. See also Halifax, "South-Eastern Europe," memorandum, 26 March 1940, CAB 66/4/40, BNA; COS, "Certain Aspects of the Present Situation," memorandum, 26 March 1940, CAB 66/4/41, BNA.

Chapter Seven. Norway, Part 1

1. Phillips to First Lord, 28 March 1940, ADM 116/4471, BNA. Phillips' letter was prompted by an NID minute concerning a German request for cessation of ore deliveries to Narvik on 26 March and other intelligence received on 27 March regarding German movements.

2. War Cabinet Meeting, Minutes, 29 March 1940, CAB 65/12/14, BNA.

3. COS, "Certain Operations in Territorial Waters," 31 March 1940, CAB 66/6/45, BNA.

4. "Machinery for Setting in Motion R4," 4 April 1940, CAB 66/7/2, BNA.

5. "Machinery for Setting in Motion R4," 4 April 1940.

6. War Cabinet Meeting, Confidential Annex, 3 April 1940, CAB 65/12/15, BNA.

7. Minutes of the Chiefs of Staff Committee, 4 April 1940, CAB 79/85, BNA.

8. Ralph Edwards, excerpts from diary, 4 April 1940, Rosk 4/75, Churchill Archive Centre. This was an elaboration on his original diary.

9. Ralph Edwards, original diary, 6 April 1940, Redw 1/1, Churchill Archive Centre.

10. Haarr, *German Invasion of Norway*, 49.

11. Redw 2/19, Churchill Archive Centre. A copy in the Roskill Papers indicated that the telegram with the additional information was generated by NID but was approved by Phillips. Phillips' approval is somewhat surprising given his comments to Churchill at the end of March regarding German activities.

12. Churchill, speech to House of Commons, 11 April 1940, Parl. Deb. H.C. (5th ser.) (1940) cols. 733–49 (also in Gilbert, *At the Admiralty*, 1014).

13. War Cabinet Minutes, 9 April, 12 noon, CAB 65/9, BNA.

14. During the war Edwards wrote his thoughts and description of events in a contemporary, rough diary. Subsequently, and periodically (although how long after the events themselves is unclear), he built on these diary entries with additional information and detail. The Churchill Archive Centre at Churchill College, Cambridge, now hold Edwards' contemporary diary. Additionally, however, the Roskill Papers (also in the Churchill Archive Centre) contain copies of at least two versions of expanded diary entries for the period of the Norwegian campaign. These include two or three pages in Roskill's challenging handwriting detailing the events of 7–10 April; these pages are titled "Transcript of RAB Edwards' Contemporary Notes on Norway." The pages provide additional insight into these vital days but generally corroborate the diaries and subsequent elaborations found elsewhere. The title given these pages, plus evidence of interpolation from Roskill (via bracketed questions and comments), suggests that Roskill was transcribing original handwritten notes supplied to him by Edwards and was having trouble deciphering the writing. The notes themselves appear to have been wartime expansions of the original diary entries. Cumulatively, the various versions of Edwards' diaries represent a valuable—indeed, vital—source. However, they must be treated with caution. On several occasions Edwards has made careless, sometimes inexplicably obvious, errors regarding dates and events, and it is probable that as far as the matters discussed here are concerned, they have contributed to an inaccurate historical record.

15. The original is to be found in Redw 2/19. The other versions are to be found in Rosk 4/75.

16. Chris Bell, in his book *Churchill and Sea Power*, has taken important steps toward correcting this assessment, but there is more to be said. Bell's criticism of Roskill's misuse of Edwards' diaries is justified. It is difficult to understand how Roskill drew the conclusions he did from the Edwards' diary notes in his possession. More than this misuse of Edwards' diary, Roskill's first volume of his official history, *War at Sea*, made two other unfortunate contributions to the view that the Admiralty was focused almost entirely on the breakout of capital ships. Roskill's description of the relevant events in *War at Sea* makes almost no mention of the movements of CS2 during 7–8 April (see chapter 9 of the volume). As will be understood from the following, the instructions given to the commander of CS2, and the initiatives of the commander himself, indicate that Forbes took precautions against a threat to Norway much earlier than Roskill contended. Roskill is also in error in believing that Forbes was not aware

of the movement of the German ships until the late morning of seventh. The view that the sighting information from Coastal Command aircraft was delayed two and a half hours is generally accepted, but this is incorrect. It is certain that Forbes knew of this threat at the same time as CS2 and his destroyer flotilla (8:48 a.m.). For the latter, see "Home Fleet Destroyer Command Diaries," 7 April, ADM 199/427, BNA. Forbes delayed reacting to the information pending news of an air attack, but he may have had other reasons for doing so. Roskill's erroneous deductions in his official history also extended to his mistiming of the disembarkation orders for R4.

17. Rhys-Jones, *Churchill and the Norwegian Campaign*, 33; Reynolds, *In Command of History*, 123; and Barnett, *Engage the Enemy*, 109, are examples of this view.

18. Admiral Binney, "Committee for Investigation of War Problems," 6 October 1939, ADM 205/1, BNA.

19. Pound to Forbes, 6 September 1939, ADM 205/3, BNA.

20. Edwards diary (copy), 7 April 1940, Rosk 4/75.

21. Edwards diary (copy). It might be asked here to whom Pound and Phillips were making these recommendations. The obvious answer is Churchill. The point here is that Churchill was being consulted but conforming, sometimes reluctantly, to the recommendation of his staff.

22. Edwards diary (copy).

23. "Transcript of RAB Edwards' Contemporary Notes."

24. Roskill's writing on the timing is a little obscure. In his official history, *War at Sea*, 1:161–62, he contends the instructions were given on the evening of 7 April by Pound. In his book *Churchill and the Admirals*, he is vague and does not pinpoint the decision to the evening of the seventh. His notes beside some of Edwards' diary entries indicate he believed the decision was made on the evening of the seventh. See Rosk 4/75. Some recent studies pinpoint the key decisions to 8 April, but primarily because their focus is elsewhere, they do not address the extent to which this complicates traditional views of these events.

25. R4 guidelines placed the decision for the implementation and timing of the operation with the navy. It is moot, therefore, if disembarkation of the soldiers was something that really required the prior approval of the War Cabinet; in any event it seems highly unlikely the War Cabinet would have challenged the decision.

26. Both, however, contributed to the neutralization of the available military forces.

27. Admiralty telegrams are numbered by the hour/the day. The Admiralty telegrams, bearings, times, and locations cited in this chapter have been sourced primarily, although not exclusively, from Home Fleet War Diary, "The Conjunct Expedition to Norway," Battle Summary No. 17, n.d. (1942?), ADM 1/12467; the war diaries of CS1, CS2, and the First Battlecruiser Squadron (BC1), http://naval-history.net/xDKWarDiaries-Contents .htm; and several prior histories, in particular the extensive work of Geirr Haarr.

28. Home Fleet diaries, 7 April 1940, ADM 199/361, BNA.

29. ADM 199/2202, BNA.

30. ADM 199/2202.

31. The failed bombing attack had occurred several hours before, but the aircraft involved maintained radio silence until they returned.

32. By the time Forbes set off with the Home Fleet in the late evening of the seventh, this sighting, perhaps as a result of study of photographs taken by the aircraft, had grown to one battle cruiser, one pocket battleship, three cruisers, and about twelve destroyers.

33. ADM 199/2202. The telegram was sent by Pound at 6:08 p.m. Edwards (DOD [H]) rang through the same message at about 6:30 p.m.

34. The decision regarding *Sheffield* is referred to in the Home Fleet diary, but the Tribals are not mentioned. There is no doubt, however, that these went north with Forbes, as did *Sheffield*, which was, in fact, instructed to precede the Home Fleet in its movements north.

35. Edwards diary (copy), 7 April 1940, Rosk 4/75.

36. "War Diary of First Cruiser Squadron," n.d., ADM 199/388, BNA.

37. The 746th Infantry Brigade disembarked at 1 p.m., and HMS *York* and HMS *Berwick* put to sea at 1:15 p.m. The 148th Infantry Brigade disembarked from HMS *Glascow* and HMS *Devonshire* at 12:30 p.m. Several of the ships in the Clyde were directed to Scapa.

38. Rosk 4/75. Inexplicably, Roskill claimed the order to disembark was given by Churchill. This was based on his correspondence with General Sir Ian Jacob, who was military assistant secretary to the War Cabinet, 1939–46. Jacob had written to Roskill relating what Churchill had said in the War Cabinet meeting at 11:30 a.m., 8 April. Jacob described a "sheepish" look on Churchill's face when he related the disembarkation of R4 forces, and Roskill was sufficiently impressed by this to categorically conclude that the decision was made by Churchill. See *Churchill and the Admirals*, 98–99.

39. In a postwar letter to Roskill, Forbes speculated as much when he wrote, "I think that by 1100/8 the Admiralty must have made up their minds that all the Germans intended to do was send an expedition to Narvik and nothing else." See Forbes to Roskill, 30 July 1949, Rosk 4/76.

40. 8 April 1940 entry, in Ironside, *Ironside Diaries*, 248.

41. The Admiralty instructed CS1 and a French force to go north unless, and until, directed by Forbes. It is probable the Admiralty wished this force to join the search for the battle cruisers. Subsequently, Forbes directed this force to join CS2 farther east, suggesting different priorities. See Home Fleet Diaries, 8 April 1940, ADM 199/361.

42. The D2 destroyers were *Hardy, Hotspur, Havock, Hunter,* and *Hostile.* The D20 destroyers were *Esk, Impulsive, Icarus,* and *Ivanhoe.*

43. Haarr, *German Invasion of Norway*, 105, notes that this episode has "never been adequately explained."

44. D20, the force that laid the mines, was just to the west of the fjord when instructed to join *Renown.* The destroyers were on their way to join *Teviot Bank*, an auxiliary minelayer, and other mine-laying destroyers at N 65°, E 2°. The minefield in the fjord was to be guarded by *Renown*, its screening destroyers (now, after a series of mishaps, reduced to *Greyhound*), and the destroyers of D2, destined to fight the first battle of Narvik.

45. Barnett, *Engage the Enemy*, 110, for example, directly attributes this decision to Churchill and Pound ("as inseparable in naval command as Rodgers and Hammerstein in music").

46. The Home Fleet War Diary shows that at 10 a.m., 8 April, Forbes messaged to his forces the disposition of supporting forces about the North Sea. He placed *Renown* in the Vestfjord alongside the destroyers of the mining force. By this time *Renown* had long set off to assist *Glowworm.*

47. There is no evidence of any communication regarding his movement south toward *Glowworm* to be found in the Home Fleet War Diary or the Battle Cruiser Squadron Diary, ADM 199/379, BNA.

48. Ironically, the direction taken by D20 to meet its rendezvous with *Teviot Bank* placed it, for a time, much closer to *Renown* on its way to *Glowworm* than it would have been in the Vestfjord itself.

49. War Cabinet Meeting, Minutes, 11:30 a.m., 8 April 1940, CAB 65/6, BNA.

50. All the maps produced on the Norwegian campaign show the encounter to the northwest of Trondheim, as per *Glowworm*'s signal, but this location itself suggests Haarr's is correct. There does not appear to have been any reason for *Hipper* or its destroyers to be very far north of Trondheim, let alone, as Haarr suggests, still in the company of Lutjen's force at this time. If *Glowworm*'s coordinates (which place it north of Trondheim) were correct and so was *Hipper*'s southward movement to attack *Glowworm*, this would mean that *Hipper* had moved from a position even farther north to attack *Glowworm*. This would have placed *Hipper* farther north of Trondheim than would make sense. More than this, Haarr records that after its battle with *Glowworm*, *Hipper* traveled northward to establish its position off the Haltern Lighthouse, just to the north of Trondheim fjord. All this points to contact between *Hipper* and *Glowworm* just south of Trondheim.

51. Some within the Admiralty initially considered it possible its objective was the northern patrol. Edwards diary notes, 8 April 1940, Rosk 4/75.

52. Forbes might also have been confused by the progress of this force that the various pieces of information suggested: a mad rush northward during the night to the point where it met *Glowworm*, a retreat to the southward, a lingering about Trondheim, and finally, of course, the westward movement. But as contended, this surely might also have pointed to a threat to Trondheim.

53. The Admiralty would have had to consider that given the preparation evident in the German moves, U-boats would have been placed strategically near all their objectives. This would not have encouraged the transportation of soldiers.

54. Haarr, *German Invasion of Norway*, 108–9.

Chapter Eight. Norway, Part 2

1. For example, see Barnett, *Engage the Enemy*, 120.

2. Roskill, *Churchill and the Admirals*, 100–102; Barnett, *Engage the Enemy*, 113–17. Barnett oftentimes used Roskill as his source.

3. CS2 was given the responsibility of guarding the southern entrance to Bergen. It set off to do this with the French squadron in support. Having spent the previous twenty-five hours in search of the other cruisers and the Home Fleet, the squadron had completed what amounted to a full circle (and one or two repeat journeys) and soon found itself close to where it had been at 6:05 the previous evening. It had achieved nothing. Had it remained where it had been the previous evening, the story of Bergen might have been different.

4. Barnett asserts that Forbes wished Layton to proceed with the operation, despite knowledge of the additional cruisers in Bergen. The Home Fleet War Diary does not indicate that any message regarding a second cruiser (let alone a third) was received by Forbes. As far as Layton was concerned, the Conjunct History indicates he was warned only of

a second cruiser. There is little reason to believe Forbes would have proceeded with the operation had he known of these ships, especially following the air attack on his fleet and given his concerns about German control of the Bergen forts. The Bergen force, then apparently returning to fleet after having received instructions, was attacked and lost destroyer *Gurkha*. Following this attack Forbes proposed the southern regions be left to British submarines and airpower. He conformed to the Admiralty requests to have Layton patrol off Bergen but instructed him to break this off around 4:00 a.m., presumably to give him time to avoid further air attack. This opened the gates for the escape of *Köln*, still hidden near Bergen.

5. Home Fleet War Diary, "Conjunct Expedition to Norway."

6. "First Lord's Updates: Daily Operation Report for First Lord," No. 219, 9 April 1940, 7:30 a.m., to 10 April 1940, 7:30 a.m., ADM 199/1940, BNA. This mentions only Forbes' plans to send two cruisers and six destroyers. Also, E. A. Seal, "Notes for Vice Admiral Sir Ralph Edwards," n.d., Rosk 4/75. Seal speculated that the order was given because the force being sent was not sufficiently strong, although he quotes the full force sent to Bergen and not the one originally proposed. Perhaps, most important are the expanded notes taken by Ralph Edwards (Rosk 4/75), which criticize Forbes for using a small force instead of the larger force Forbes proposed to use. This, of course, is the opposite of what happened and is a sign of just how confusing things were during these days.

7. Seal, "Notes for Vice Admiral."

8. Barnett, in *Engage the Enemy*, 121, claims that Churchill only belatedly "stumbled on the strategic truth" that "the Trondheim area . . . was the key to control of the whole country to the northwards, including Narvik." There was little consensus on this at the time, however. The COS thought Trondheim the best "military" and Bergen the best "political" objective. See COS, Conclusions, 9 April 1940, 11 a.m., CAB 79/3, BNA. For Pound's initial recommendation—Bergen—see an undated note probably written on 9 April on "Scandinavian Affairs," ADM 116/4471, BNA. In his private diary Ralph Edwards recorded his preference for a "quick dart at Trondheim which is much more the key to the situation than Bergen." See Edwards diary (copy), 9 April 1940.

9. War Cabinet Meeting, Confidential Annex, 10 April 1940, CAB 65/12/19, BNA. Churchill shared Chamberlain's views on this. It was Ironside who first nominated Narvik for priority.

10. See COS Meeting, Minutes, 10 April 1940, CAB 79/3, BNA.

11. Churchill to Pound, ADM 116/4471 (also in Gilbert, *At the Admiralty*, 1000–1001).

12. For examples of this view, see Barnett, *Engage the Enemy*, 120. Barnett writes that there was confusion over priorities "not least . . . because the mind of the First Lord . . . was puffed this way and that by the shifting breeze of opportunity." Also Lamb, *Churchill as War Leader*, 36–37; and Rhys-Jones, *Churchill and the Norwegian Campaign*, 198. Rhys-Jones is particularly hard on Churchill regarding Trondheim.

13. See Bell, *Churchill and Sea Power*, 333.

14. Home Fleet War Diary, "Conjunct Expedition to Norway," chap. 7. CAS Newall had broached the idea of preparation for action against Bergen or Trondheim at the MCC meeting earlier in the afternoon. Churchill had given code name Maurice for this operation but had made clear that no action should take place until it was known what would be required to secure Narvik. Meeting of MCC, 11 April 1940, CAB 83/3, BNA.

15. Reference is made to the "heat" of these discussions in both Ironside's and Edwards' diaries. This meeting has sometimes been confused with another on the morning of 14 April (more on this later). See, for example, Roskill, *Churchill and the Admirals*, 102 fn. It is likely that in his postwar recollections Ironside (as MacLeod in his) also confused the two meetings.

16. It is probable that Churchill intended to replace the diverted force with a second force destined to go to Namsos some days later. The diversion would prove a blessing, despite causing some issues with equipment loss and misplacement. There was congestion and confusion enough with the arrival of the single brigade.

17. Churchill to Chamberlain and Halifax, 11 April 1940, PREMIER 1/419, BNA.

18. War Cabinet Meeting, Confidential Annex, 13 April 1940, CAB 65/12/21, BNA.

19. "Notes by the Chairman of the Military Co-ordination Committee for the Joint Planning Staff," 12 April 1940, PREMIER 1/419.

20. War Cabinet Meeting, Confidential Annex, Minute 5, 13 April 1940, CAB 65/12/22, BNA.

21. MCC Meeting, Minutes, 12 April 1940, 5:30 p.m., CAB 83/3; "Notes by the Chairman," 12 April 1940.

22. In "Notes by the Chairman," 12 April 1940, Churchill mentioned a discussion was supposed to take place in the evening of the twelfth with the secretary of state for war and CIGS. Ironside's diary makes no mention of the meeting or its conclusions.

23. Ironside had his discussion with Churchill on the evening of the twelfth. He wrote that according to Churchill's chat, action at Trondheim would be a "diversion," and he (Ironside) was worried that the War Cabinet saw it as the "main operation . . . because of a wire that has come in from the Military Attache at Stockholm." As a result of this meeting with Churchill, Ironside sent word to Mackesy to "curtail his wings after taking Narvik and to Carton de Wiart to open his wings a bit at Namsos." 13 April 1940 entry, in Ironside, *Ironside Diaries*, 255.

24. Churchill to Stanley, 13 April 1940, Char 19/2.

25. To limit the risk of these landings, Churchill asked if the forces available might be "stiffened by one or two regular regiments of mechanised cavalry." Unhelpfully, Ironside declined to offer such a force and recommended only a few bren carriers be sent.

26. War Cabinet Meeting, Minutes, 13 April 1940, 11:30 a.m., CAB 65/12/23, BNA.

27. War Cabinet Meeting, Minutes, 13 April 1940, 11:30 a.m.

28. It was considered desirable to explain that the Allied forces had no intention of advancing toward the Swedish border, something that was now the case. The point was to alleviate Scandinavian concerns that Narvik was only about Swedish ore and to indicate that the substantial forces destined for Narvik would, upon its capture, be immediately used elsewhere.

29. MCC Meeting, Minutes, 13 April 1940, 5 p.m., CAB 83/3.

30. 14 April 1940 entry, in Ironside, *Ironside Diaries*.

31. This outline was put to the French minister of defense by Churchill that day.

32. 13 April 1940 entry, in Cadogan, *Diaries of Sir Alexander*, 270.

33. War Cabinet Meeting, 14 April 1940, CAB 65/12/24, BNA (also in Gilbert, *At the Admiralty*, 1059).

34. It was always recognized that the diversion would cause problems—much discussed by historians. The diverted force would temporarily be without a brigadier, and he would be without appropriate maps. But after discussion in the MCC and COS meetings, it was thought these problems could be overcome, and preparations were made to proceed.

35. MCC Meeting, Minutes, 13 April 1940, 10:30 p.m., CAB 83/3.

36. Ironside, *Ironside Diaries*, 255. For examples of how this meeting has been interpreted see Rhys-Jones, *Churchill and the Norwegian Campaign*, 75; Lamb, *Churchill as War Leader*, 37; Kersaudy, *Norway: 1940*, 97. For an alternative view, see Bell, *Churchill and Sea Power*, 331–32.

37. This was the meeting at which Churchill had first broached the idea of diverting some of the forces for Narvik to Namsos. Together, these meetings have caused much confusion to historians, including Roskill. Roskill assumed, for example, that only one meeting of this nature took place, but the first and not the second.

38. Ironside, *Ironside Diaries*, 255–56. It is my contention that all the entries made under the heading of 13 April were actually diary entries made on 14 April. The entries made under 13 April were details of events of 14 April or reflections on the day before. This makes highly problematic much of the post facto elaboration (bottom of page 256 to end of 259), which appears to be Ironside's postwar musings and MacLeod's erroneous commentary. Cumulatively, these pages present conflicting versions of the same events. Further, it is, as noted earlier, my belief that this writing includes a mixture of discussion that occurred at the first meeting with Churchill in the late evening of 11–12 April described earlier in this chapter. There is reference here to Ironside losing his temper at this meeting. We know he did so in the meeting of 11–12 April, but there is no evidence of "heat" in response to the proposal Churchill put to Ironside early in the morning of the 14 April. Ironside's diary entries indicate he accepted with equanimity the need to divert forces to Namsos. It is probable he did not like the change in strategy but, like Churchill, accepted there was no choice.

39. MCC Meeting, Minutes, 14 April 1940, CAB 83/3.

40. Ironside, *Ironside Diaries*, 260.

41. 14 April 1940 entry, in Cadogan, *Diaries of Sir Alexander*, 270.

42. Also see the views of Bell, *Churchill and Sea Power*, chap. 6, esp. 187–94.

43. COS Meeting, Confidential Annex, 16 April 1940, CAB 79/85, BNA.

44. Ironside, *Ironside Diaries*, 262–63.

45. Churchill to Forbes, 17 April 1940, ADM 199/1929, BNA. Churchill and Ironside were writing of different days, but nevertheless, they were clearly taking heart that so little had been achieved by the German air attacks to foil the landings.

46. War Cabinet Meeting, Confidential Annex, 15 April 1940, CAB 65/12/25, BNA.

47. Sir Edward Bridges, Recollection, 25 April 1940, PREMIER 1/404, BNA (also in Gilbert, *At the Admiralty*, 1071–72).

48. All the foregoing is drawn from Bridges' recollection, 25 April 1940.

49. War Cabinet Meeting, Confidential Annex, 15 April 1940, CAB 65/12/25, BNA. After the MCC meeting of that day, Churchill recommended most strongly that "the force to be landed [at Trondheim] should not be less than 7000 or 8000 men composed of the best fighting men available." See MCC Meeting, Note by the Chairman, 16 April 1940,

ADM 199/1929, BNA (also in Gilbert, *At the Admiralty*, 1076–77). Ironside was intending to use far fewer. War Cabinet Meeting, Confidential Annex, 15 April 1940, CAB 65/12, BNA.

50. MCC Meeting, Note by the Chairman, 16 April 1940.

51. The MCC meeting of 14 April considered the question, What would happen at Narvik if the forces sent there were not able to do the job? The COS said the forces could then be reinforced by the Chasseurs. Presumably this replied to the second echelon to follow the first.

52. See, for example, Roskill, *Churchill and the Admirals*, 106.

53. John Colville was instructed by Chamberlain to organize an early morning MCC meeting the following day. He recorded in his diary, "I gather our forces at Narvik under Lord Cork are rather loth to make an attack because of the snow, but Winston feels that a long delay would be disastrous both for military and psychological reasons." See 16 April 1940 entry, in Colville, *Fringes of Power*, 119. There was no doubt Churchill was worried that delay would give the Germans time to consolidate. However, it is also evident he hoped to use the Narvik forces later at Trondheim, although how he imagined this is difficult to understand.

54. Nevertheless, Churchill's use of *Gathering Storm* to attribute the failure at Narvik to Mackesy's dilatoriness, while ignoring his own contribution, is demanding of special censure.

55. Roskill attempts to score off A. J. Marder in their long-running dispute by referencing this telegram in his book *Churchill and the Admirals*, 292. He notes that it was the first private and personal telegram sent to Cork and Mackesy by Churchill. He appears not to have been aware of the considerable vetting of the communication.

56. COS Meeting, 18 April 1940, CAB 78/95, BNA. The COS, presumably at the behest of Ironside, recommended he be told to act on AT 1350/17, as recommended by Churchill. For a copy of the telegram, see MCC Meeting, minutes, 18 April 1940, CAB 83/3.

57. 18 April 1940 entry, in Ironside, *Ironside Diaries*, 268. These observations are not intended to pass judgment on Mackesy's inertia. Rather, they are intended to show that Churchill was not alone in the unfortunate behavior he displayed.

58. Wilson, note, 25 April 1940, PREMIER 1/404 (also in Gilbert, *At the Admiralty*, 1073). For a copy of a letter written by Hankey to Chamberlain on 17 April 1940, see CAB 63/160. For Colville's view of these events, see 17 April 1940 entry, in Colville, *Fringes of Power*, 119 (also in Gilbert, *At the Admiralty*, 1086).

59. War Cabinet Meeting, Confidential Annex, 17 April 1940, CAB 65/12/26, BNA.

60. The request for a review of Hammer appears not to have come from the War Office. Ironside recorded in his diary that he received a note at 1 p.m., 19 April 1940, for a COS meeting at 2 p.m. to discuss the matter. Ironside, *Ironside Diaries*, 269.

61. COS Meeting, Minutes, 19 April 1940, 2 p.m., CAB 79/3, BNA.

62. COS Meeting, Confidential Annex, 19 April 1940, CAB 79/85; Phillips, untitled memorandum, 25 April 1940, ADM 199/129, BNA. In his memorandum Phillips suggests this was one of the most important influences in making the move away from Hammer. Curiously, he makes no reference to the naval risks of the operation, which are most commonly identified as the main reasons for the switch.

63. MCC Meeting, Minutes, 19 April 1940, CAB 83/3. Colville recorded that another reason for the move away from Hammer was the "dangerously truthful prognostications in the press." 22 April 1940 entry, in Colville, *Fringes of Power*, 120.

64. Churchill, *Gathering Storm*, 628–29, invites the conclusion that had Hammer gone ahead, it would have succeeded, and all would have been well, and that it did not go ahead was not of Churchill's making.

65. This includes copies of Churchill's notes, "Operations in Norway," 19 April 1940; and COS, "Aide de Memoire," 19 April 1940, both in CAB 66/7/13, BNA.

66. Although other battleships could have been called on, Cork preferred *Warspite* because of its secondary armament, which he believed offered much greater value in bombardment operations. It is interesting to note that Pound had argued at the 19 April MCC meeting that Cork had sufficient firepower to do without *Warspite*, and it was decided that Cork's operation could go ahead without it. The committee concluded that Operation Maurice should take precedence over Rupert (the landings at Narvik) and that there must be no interference with the forces allocated to it by the Admiralty. Evidently, Pound had a significant and rapid change of heart at some point after the 11:30 a.m. meeting regarding Rupert and Maurice. See MCC Meeting, Minutes, 19 April 1940, CAB 83/3.

67. Churchill sent a telegram to Cork at 7:26 p.m. on 19 April. The idea had, however, first been proposed in Pound's presentation to the COS.

68. MCC Meeting, 19 April 1940, CAB 83/3.

69. Churchill, "Operation Rupert," 20 April 1940, CAB 83/5, BNA.

70. War Cabinet Meeting, Confidential Annex, 20 April 1940, CAB 65/12/29, BNA.

71. War Cabinet Meeting, Confidential Annex, 20 April 1940.

72. W.O., "Aide de Memoire for Chamberlain," 21 April 1940, ADM 116/4471.

73. MCC Meeting, 19 April 1940, 10 p.m., CAB 83/3.

74. Ismay, "The Scandinavian Campaign, General Conception," 21 April 1940, CAB 83/3.

75. COS Meeting, Minutes, 23 April 1940, CAB 79/85.

76. COS Meeting, Minutes, 22 April 1940; COS Meeting, Minutes, 23 April 1940, both in CAB 79/3, BNA; Phillips, untitled memorandum, 25 April 1940.

77. Supreme War Council, Minutes, 22 April 1940, CAB 99/3, BNA.

78. Barnett, *Engage the Enemy*, 130, is a keen supporter of the view of the whimsical nature of Churchill's decision making and has Churchill "peddling" the new version of Hammer.

79. General Hugh Massy was conceiving a plan that involved a small landing inside the Trondheim Fjord supported by the navy. Pound balked at the prospect and asked to be "assured that the object of the operation was clearly recognised and worthwhile." COS Meeting, Minutes, 24 April 1940, 10 a.m., CAB 79/85.

80. COS Meeting, Minutes, 25 April 1940, 9 p.m., CAB 79/85.

81. Rhys-Jones, *Churchill and the Norwegian Campaign*, 121, cites Ironside on this, but I can find no evidence in Ironside's diary to support the claim.

82. Churchill to Chamberlain and Halifax, 11 April 1940, PREMIER 1/419.

83. MCC Meeting, Minutes, 24 April 1940, CAB 83/3.

84. Barnett, *Engage the Enemy*, 120.

85. He has also been criticized for not focusing on and persisting with Narvik. See, for example, Lamb, *Churchill as War Leader*, 37.

86. SWC Meeting, 26 April 1940, CAB 99/3.
87. War Cabinet Meeting, Confidential Annex, 29 April 1940, CAB 65/12/38, BNA. This view was not Chamberlain's alone. See MCC Meeting, Minutes, 26 April 1940, CAB 83/3.
88. This, of course, is why historians are critical of the decision to focus on Narvik over Trondheim.
89. War Cabinet Meeting, Confidential Annex, 26 April 1940, CAB 65/12/35, BNA.
90. Hankey, "Scandinavia," memorandum, 25 April 1940, ADM 116/4471.
91. MCC Meeting, Minutes, 26 April 1940.
92. In a memorandum of 27 April, Phillips proposed that once Narvik was captured, the Swedes be told the Allies intended to press on to Gallivare and Lulea whether they liked it or not. He believed the Germans would occupy Lulea as soon as the ice melted. See ADM 116/4471.
93. War Cabinet Meeting, Confidential Annex, 26 April 1940, CAB 65/12/35.
94. Dalton to Churchill, 31 May 1940, ADM 116/4471.
95. In May the idea appeared to develop that ore and timber might come through Kirkenes even farther north. So it is not entirely clear that it was expected Narvik would operate as a port so much as an outpost protecting Kirkenes.
96. Churchill had presented an idea of sending bombers from carriers off Narvik to bomb Gallivare and Lulea. The secretary of state for air questioned the efficacy of this and suggested that an air presence at Narvik itself was desirable. Churchill was, therefore, not alone in the propagation of this particular nonsense.
97. To the last there were those other than Churchill who would weigh the advantages and disadvantages of remaining in northern Norway in equal measure when the scales were surely on the debit side. See Alexander to Churchill, memorandum, 20 May 1940, ADM 116/4471. Pound maintained a more detached view, focused on the impact the continuing conflict would have on the navy, and recommended an immediate evacuation. See Pound to First Lord, 26 May 1940, ADM 116/4471.
98. JPS, "Military Implications of a Complete Withdrawal from Norway," CAB 80/11, BNA.
99. War Cabinet Meeting, Minutes, 20 May 1940, CAB 69/1, BNA.

Chapter 9. First Lord to Prime Minister

1. The reference to Chamberlain behaving "limpet-like" in his efforts to retain the leadership was made by close associate and adviser, Brendan Bracken.
2. Another view of the Churchill-Chamberlain relationship before the latter's resignation was presented by Lawlor, *Churchill and the Politics of War*, 98–99. Lawlor argued Churchill's scrupulous loyalty toward Chamberlain before and after the latter was ousted was because he wished not to alienate the core Conservatives essential to his own leadership prospects. She maintains that Churchill neither helped Chamberlain's opponents nor took any action to keep Chamberlain in government. This chapter accepts the first assertion but will challenge the second.
3. Chamberlain to Hilda, 4 May 1940, in *Chamberlain Diary Letters*.
4. Witherell, "Lord Salisbury's 'Watching Committee,'" 1154.
5. See, for example, 4 April 1940 entry, in Amery, *Empire at Bay*, 585.
6. 360 Parl. Deb. H.C. (5th ser.) (1940) cols. 1484–96 (comments of Richard Law).

7. 358 Parl. Deb. (5th ser.) (1940) col. 1866.

8. 358 Parl. Deb. (5th ser.) (1940) col. 1860.

9. See Amery's assessment, 14 March 1940, in *Empire at Bay*, 584.

10. 358 Parl. Deb. (5th ser.) (1940) col. 1881.

11. 358 Parl. Deb. (5th ser.) (1940) cols. 1911–12.

12. 358 Parl. Deb. (5th ser.) (1940) col. 1951.

13. See 3 April 1940 entry, in Amery, *Empire at Bay*, 585.

14. 359 Parl. Deb. (5th ser.) (1940) cols. 508, 510.

15. Shakespeare, *Six Minutes in May*, 214.

16. It was not likely this censure would have come from Sinclair, who was a good friend of Churchill's.

17. 359 Parl. Deb. (5th ser.) (1940) cols. 753, 754.

18. 359 Parl. Deb. (5th ser.) (1940) col. 756.

19. See also comments by Robert Boothby and Labour MP Robert Craigmyle Morrison in 359 Parl. Deb. (5th ser.) (1940) col. 759.

20. The "duds" comment was made by Nancy Witcher Langhorne Astor, Viscountess Astor, Conservative MP. The "likes and dislikes" comment was made by Eleanor Florence Rathbone, British Independent MP.

21. Lord Salisbury, memorandum on his interview with the Prime Minister, S(4)WC7/20, Hatfield House Archive Center.

22. Lord Salisbury memorandum.

23. Salisbury, memorandum on his interview with Churchill on his appointment as coordinating minister, 20 April 1940, S(4)WC8/37, Hatfield House; also 23 April 1940 entry in Nicolson, *Harold Nicolson Diaries*.

24. Salisbury to Churchill, 24 April 1940, S(4)WC 8/44, Hatfield House.

25. The committee's hopefulness may have been influenced by Salisbury's discussion with Churchill on 19 April. Churchill had been upbeat and had contended that there would be "no reverse" in Norway but that there would no "decisive result" before the end of summer. It is most unlikely Churchill would have been as hopeful a day or two later. Salisbury, memorandum on his interview with Churchill, 20 April 1940.

26. Chamberlain to Ida, 27 April 1940, in *Chamberlain Diary Letters*. Churchill had expressed these sentiments to Salisbury on 19 April, although it is not clear if these were to complaints to which Chamberlain referred.

27. Chamberlain to Ida, 27 April 1940. For a different assessment of these discussions between Churchill and Chamberlain, see Shakespeare, *Six Minutes in May*, 135–37 (also relevant, 186–87). Shakespeare's assessment does not mention the Salisbury correspondence. Elsewhere he has Churchill writing his unsent letter after his meeting with Chamberlain and not before. Also, he assumes the meeting between Churchill and Chamberlain did not go well whereas Chamberlain's subsequent correspondence with his sister indicates the discussion went very well. That decisions were made during this meeting to give Churchill more power is also reinforced by the fact that the following day Chamberlain spent time drafting an outline of Churchill's new powers. For all these reasons, I am not persuaded by Shakespeare's version of events and the conclusions he draws from it.

28. For evidence of discontent with air policy, see extracts from Lord Cranborne to Salisbury, 18 April 1940, S(4)WC1/119, Hatfield House; Salisbury to Cranborne, 17 April 1940, S(4) WC8/25, Hatfield House.

29. By an interesting coincidence Churchill wrote a brief note to Chamberlain on 24 April that read, somewhat obscurely, "If the combination of secondary difficulties becomes unduly exhausting, strike with Air Force at vital key points in Germany." Gilbert, *At the Admiralty*, 1129. There is no guidance as to the source or location of the "secondary difficulties." This writer is again struck by the fact that at this significant juncture, Churchill appears to be encouraging Chamberlain to consider action he is aware would take the heat out of much of the criticism that threatened his government.

30. The following summary of the discussion with Halifax is based on Salisbury, "Conduct of the War," memorandum, 29 April 1940, S(4)WC1/163–168, Hatfield House.

31. Salisbury, "Conduct of the War."

32. Bracken had rushed to inform Amery and his supporters during a dinner the evening of 1 May. (See Gilbert, *At the Admiralty*, 590.)

33. Addison, *Road to 1945*, chap. 3, views this episode differently. Addison suggests that Chamberlain drew attention to Churchill's promotion during the debate to give the impression that Churchill had held this role during the debacle of Norway and that, therefore, Churchill was responsible for much of what had occurred. I believe Chamberlain wished to achieve quite a different effect: to demonstrate he had been listening to those seeking greater influence for Churchill.

34. Meeting with Churchill, 1 May 1940, 5 p.m., in Crozier, *Off the Record*, 167–70.

35. Camrose's diary, 3 May 1940 entry, in Gilbert, *At the Admiralty*, 1190.

36. Camrose's diary, 3 May 1940.

37. Camrose's diary, 3 May 1940.

38. Churchill to Cork, telegram, 4 May 1940, ADM 199/1929, BNA. Churchill had sent a similarly urgent telegram the day before. This is not to suggest that Churchill was anxious about Narvik for political reasons alone. He feared that if there were delay in its capture, the Germans might reinforce via Sweden with the melting of the ice in the Gulf of Bothnia.

39. 3 May 1940 entry, in Colville, *Fringes of Power*, 134. The comments recorded were those of Portal.

40. 1 May 1940 entry, in Nicolson, *Harold Nicolson Diaries*.

41. The term "debunking" was used by Reith in his diary entry of 1 May. See Reith, *Reith Diaries*, 249.

42. 1 May 1940 entry, in Reith, *Reith Diaries*, 249 (also in Gilbert, *At the Admiralty*, 1176); 1 May 1940 entry, in Channon, *Chips*, 244 (also in Gilbert, *At the Admiralty*, 1182).

43. Gilbert, 1136.

44. 3 May 1940 entry, in Colville, *Fringes of Power*. Some of Chamberlain's supporters shared his view of Churchill: "Lord Portal's intelligence was that Winston himself was being loyal to the PM."

45. Chamberlain to Hilda, 4 May 1940, in *Chamberlain Diary Letters*.

46. Watching Committee member Lord Davies wrote to Churchill on 2 May warning, "Some of your colleagues will doubtless try and shift the responsibility on to your shoulders, without conferring upon you the necessary powers and authority. If anything goes wrong,

you will be blamed." Char 2/393, Churchill Archive Centre (also in Gilbert, *At the Admiralty*, 1185–86).

47. War Cabinet, Confidential Annex, 30 April 1940, CAB 65/4, BNA.

48. 29 April 1940 entry, in Amery, *Empire at Bay*, 589.

49. 29 April 1940 entry, in Amery, *Empire at Bay*. Keyes said something similar to Harold Nicolson the following day, although he apparently spoke more broadly in terms of the Admiralty Board. This was a more accurate assessment. 30 April 1940 entry, in Nicolson, *Harold Nicolson Diaries*.

50. 30 April 1940 entry, in Amery, *Empire at Bay*, 590.

51. 30 April 1940 entry, in Amery, *Empire at Bay*.

52. 3 May 1940 entry, in Amery, *Empire at Bay*, 592.

53. A day later (3 May) Amery recorded, "Our non-bombing of Germany also greatly upset the Swedes' confidence in us." 3 May 1940 entry in Amery, *Empire at Bay*.

54. 2 May 1940 entry, in Amery, *Empire at Bay*, 591.

55. 4 May 1940 entry, in Nicolson, *Harold Nicolson Diaries*.

56. Another, more recent explanation for Labour's call for a division is intelligence received by Attlee during the morning of 8 May outlining a long list of supply failures experienced by the forces in Norway. These were addressed at some length by Herbert Morrison during his speech. See Corfield, "Why Chamberlain Really Fell."

57. Curiously, Chamberlain described it otherwise. He expected the debate to be primarily about Norway but believed "it was recognized that the Government had a pretty good case there, and no doubt that impression must have been greatly strengthened by the events which have occurred since on the Continent." It is interesting that, despite these comments to his sister, he had always intended to address issues beyond Norway. Chamberlain to Ida, 11 May 1940, in *Chamberlain Diary Letters*.

58. Chamberlain was aware that the government was exposed on the issue of unpreparedness, and he had raised this within the War Cabinet on 2 May.

59. 360 Parl. Deb. H.C. (5th ser.) (1940) cols. 1073–1196.

60. 360 Parl. Deb. H.C. (5th ser.) (1940) cols. 1073–1196.

61. 360 Parl. Deb. H.C. (5th ser.) (1940) cols. 1073–1196.

62. 360 Parl. Deb. H.C. (5th ser.) (1940) col. 1439.

63. Macmillan, *Blast of War*, 74.

64. Churchill, *Gathering Storm*, 561.

65. For an example of the latter, see Smart, "Four Days in May," 215–43.

66. See, for example, Birkenhead, *Halifax*, 453–54; also Gilbert, *At the Admiralty*, 1257; Macmillan, *Blast of War*, 75.

67. See Smart, "Four Days in May," n114.

68. Churchill, *Gathering Storm*, 663.

69. Taylor, *Beaverbrook*, 409; also Gilbert, *At the Admiralty*, 1255.

70. Eden, *Reckoning*, 96.

71. Churchill, *Gathering Storm*, 522.

72. We are told that Brendan Bracken made a similar request of Churchill at some point during the day.

73. Birkenhead, *Halifax*, 453–54 (also in Gilbert, *At the Admiralty*, 1257–58).

74. Cadogan, *Diaries of Sir Alexander*, 280. (In Birkenhead, *Halifax*, it is recorded, "Winston, with suitable expressions of regard and humility, said he could not but feel the force of what I had said.")

75. Birkenhead, *Halifax*, 454.

76. Gilbert, *At the Admiralty*, 1260–61.

77. Harris, *Attlee*, 174.

78. Chamberlain to Ida, 11 May 1940, in *Chamberlain Diary Letters*.

79. Eden, *Reckoning*, 97.

80. Harris, *Attlee*, 174.

81. 10 May 1940 entry in Nicolson, *Harold Nicolson Diaries*.

82. Eden, *Reckoning*, 97

83. Eden. Churchill claimed that Kingsley Wood had persuaded Chamberlain on the morning of 10 May not to stay on as prime minister. Churchill, *Gathering Storm*, 523. This is inconsistent with other recollections, including Eden's.

84. 10 May 1940 entry, in Amery, *Empire at Bay*, 613.

85. Eden, *Reckoning*, 97

86. For an important example of this, see Jefferys, "May 1940," 375.

87. Chamberlain to Hilda, 17 May 1940, in *Chamberlain Diary Letters*.

Bibliography

Primary Sources

BBC Written Archive Centre, Reading, UK.

British National Archives, Kew.

Caird Library and Archives, National Maritime Museum, Greenwich, UK.

Chamberlain, Neville. Papers. Cadbury Research Library, University of Birmingham.

Churchill Archive Centre, Churchill College, Cambridge.

Lindemann, Frederick Alexander, C.H., F.R.S., Viscount Cherwell of Oxford. Papers. Nuffield College Archives, University of Oxford.

Articles

Alexander, Don W. "Repercussions of the Breda Variant." *French Historical Studies* 8, no. 3 (Spring 1974): 459–88.

Alexander, Martin S. "'Fighting to the Last Frenchman?' Reflections on the BEF Deployment to France and the Strains in the Franco-British Alliance, 1939–40." *Historical Reflections / Réflexions Historiques* 22, no. 1 (1996): 235–62.

Ball, Stuart. "Churchill and the Conservative Party." *Transactions of the Royal Historical Society* 2 (2001): 307–30.

Barclay, Glen St. J. "Diversion in the East: The Western Allies, Scandinavia, and Russia, November 1939–April 1940." *Historian* 41, no. 3 (1979): 483–98.

Beaumont, Roger. "The Bomber Offensive as a Second Front." *Journal of Contemporary History* 22, no. 1 (1987): 3–19.

Bédarida, François. "France, Britain and the Nordic Countries." *Scandinavian Journal of History* 2, no. 1–4 (1977): 7–27.

Best, Antony. "'This Probably Over-Valued Military Power': British Intelligence and Whitehall's Perception of Japan, 1939–41." *Intelligence and National Security* 12, no. 3 (1997): 67–94.

Bond, Brian. "The Calm before the Storm: Britain and the 'Phoney War' 1939–40." *RUSI Journal* 135, no. 1 (1990): 61–67.

Cairns, John C. "Britain and the Fall of France: A Study in Allied Disunity." *Journal of Modern History* 27, no. 4 (December 1955): 365–409.

———. "Reflections on France, Britain and the Winter War Prodrome, 1939–40." *Historical Reflections / Réflexions Historiques* 22, no. 1 (1996): 211–34.

Claasen, Adam. "Blood and Iron, and Der Geist Des Atlantiks: Assessing Hitler's Decision to Invade Norway." *Journal of Strategic Studies* 20, no. 3 (1997): 71–96.

Cliadakis, Harry. "Neutrality and War in Italian Policy 1939–40." *Journal of Contemporary History* 9, no. 3 (1974): 171–90.

Connelly, M. "The British People, the Press and the Strategic Air Campaign against Germany, 1939–45." *Contemporary British History* 16, no. 2 (2002): 39–48.

Corfield, Tony. "Why Chamberlain Really Fell. (British Leader Neville Chamberlain in 1940)." *History Today* 46, no. 12 (1996): 22.

Corum, James S. "The German Campaign in Norway 1940 as a Joint Operation." *Journal of Strategic Studies* 21, no. 4 (1998): 50–77.

———. "Uncharted Waters: Information in the First Modern Joint Campaign—Norway 1940." *Journal of Strategic Studies* 27, no. 2 (2004): 345–69.

Dilks, David. "Great Britain and Scandinavia in the 'Phoney War.'" *Scandinavian Journal of History* 2, no. 1 (1977): 29–51.

———. "The Twilight War and the Fall of France: Chamberlain and Churchill in 1940." *Transactions of the Royal Historical Society* 28, (1978): 61–86.

Dutton, D. J. "Power Brokers or Just 'Glamour Boys'? The Eden Group, September 1939–May 1940." *English Historical Review* 118, no. 476 (2003): 412–24.

Fair, John D. "The Norwegian Campaign and Winston Churchill's Rise to Power in 1940: A Study of Perception and Attribution." *International History Review* 9, no. 3 (1987): 410–37.

Faulkner, Marcus. "The Kriegsmarine, Signals Intelligence and the Development of the B-Dienst before the Second World War." *Intelligence and National Security* 25, no. 4 (2010): 521–46.

Ford, Douglas. "Planning for an Unpredictable War: British Intelligence Assessments and the War against Japan, 1937–45." *Journal of Strategic Studies* 27, no. 1 (2004): 136–67.

Fritz, Martin. "Swedish Iron Ore and German Steel 1939–40." *Scandinavian Economic History Review* 21, no. 2 (1973): 133–44.

Gordon, Andrew. "The Admiralty and Imperial Overstretch, 1902–1941." *Journal of Strategic Studies* 17, no. 1 (1994): 63–85.

Gordon, G. A. H. *British Seapower and Procurement between the Wars: A Reappraisal of Rearmament.* Basingstoke, UK: Macmillan, 1987.

Gowing, Margaret. "The Organisation of Manpower in Britain during the Second World War." *Journal of Contemporary History* 7, no. 1 (1972): 147–67.

Grenfell, Russell. "This Question of Superior Orders." *RUSI Journal* 96, no. 582 (1951): 263–66.

Imlay, Talbot. "Allied Economic Intelligence and Strategy during the 'Phoney War.'" *Intelligence and National Security* 13, no. 4 (1998): 107–32.

———. "From Villain to Partner: British Labour Party Leaders, France and International Policy during the Phoney War, 1939–40." *Journal of Contemporary History* 38, no. 4 (2003): 579–96.

———. "A Reassessment of Anglo-French Strategy during the Phony War, 1939–1940." *English Historical Review* 119, no. 481 (2004): 333–72.

Jefferys, Kevin. "May 1940: The Downfall of Neville Chamberlain." *Parliamentary History* 10, no. 2 (1991): 363–78.

Johnson, D. W. J. "Britain and France in 1940." *Transactions of the Royal Historical Society* 22 (1972): 141–57.

Jorg-Johannes, Jager. "Sweden's Iron Ore Exports to Germany, 1933–1944: A Reply to Rolf Karlbom's Article on the Same Subject." *Scandinavia Economic History Review* 15, no. 1–2 (1967): 139–47.

Karlbom, Rolf. "Sweden's Iron Ore Exports to Germany, 1933–1944." *Scandinavian Economic History Review* 13, no. 1 (1965): 65–93.

———. "Swedish Iron Ore Exports to Germany, 1933–1944: A Reply." *Scandinavian Economic History Review* 16, no. 2 (1968): 171–75.

Kelly, Bernard. "Drifting Towards War: The British Chiefs of Staff, the USSR and the Winter War, November 1939–March 1940." *Contemporary British History* 23, no. 3 (2009): 267–91.

Koch, H. W. "The Strategic Air Offensive Against Germany: The Early Phase, May–September 1940." *Historical Journal* 34, no. 1 (1991): 117–41.

Lambert, Andrew. "Seapower 1939–1940: Churchill and the Strategic Origins of the Battle of the Atlantic." *Journal of Strategic Studies* 17, no. 1 (1994): 86–108.

Levy, James. "Lost Leader: Admiral of the Fleet Sir Charles Forbes and the Second World War." *Mariner's Mirror* 88, no. 2 (2002): 186–95.

Maiolo, Joseph A. "The Knockout Blow against the Import System: Admiralty Expectations of Nazi Germany's Naval Strategy, 1934–9." *Historical Research* 72, no. 178 (1999): 202–28.

Maurer, John. "'Winston Has Gone Mad': Churchill, the British Admiralty, and the Rise of Japanese Naval Power." *Journal of Strategic Studies* 35, no. 6 (2012): 775–97.

McGucken, William. "The Royal Society and the Genesis of the Scientific Advisory Committee to Britain's War Cabinet, 1939–1940." *Notes and Records of the Royal Society of London* 33, no. 1 (1978): 87–115.

Parker, R. A. C. "Britain, France and Scandinavia, 1939–40." *History* 61, no. 203 (1976): 369–87.

Paschall, Rod. "Scandinavian Twist: Churchill's Fiasco in Norway in 1940." *MHQ: The Quarterly Journal of Military History* 23, no. 2 (2011): 26.

Rentola, Kimmo. "Intelligence and Stalin's Two Crucial Decisions in the Winter War, 1939–40." *International History Review* 35, no. 5 (2013): 1089–1112.

Richardson, Michael W. "Forcible Entry and the German Invasion of Norway, 1940." Master's thesis, U.S. Army Command and General Staff College, 2001.

Riste, Olav. "Intelligence and the 'Mindset': The German Invasion of Norway in 1940." *Intelligence and National Security* 22, no. 4 (2007): 521–36.

Ritchie, Sebastian. "The Price of Air Power: Technological Change, Industrial Policy, and Military Aircraft Contracts in the Era of British Rearmament, 1935–39." *Business History Review* 71, no. 1 (1997): 82–111.

Rolfe, Sidney E. "Manpower Allocation in Great Britain during World War II." *Industrial and Labor Relations Review* 5, no. 2 (1952): 173–94.

Roskill, S. W. "Marder, Churchill and the Admiralty 1939–42." *RUSI Journal* 117, no. 669 (1972): 49–53.

———. "The Ten Year Rule—The Historical Facts." *RUSI Journal* 117, no. 665 (1972): 69–71.

Roskill, S. W., and Napier Crookenden. "Lord Hankey—The Creation of the Machinery of Government." *RUSI Journal* 120, no. 3 (1975): 10–18.

Rossi, John. "Churchill and the Revisionist Historians." *Contemporary Review* 280, no. 1634 (2002): 162.

Salmon, Patrick. "Churchill, the Admiralty and the Narvik Traffic, September–November 1939." *Scandinavian Journal of History* 4, no. 1 (1979): 305–26.

Schofield, B. B. "The Defeat of the U-boats During World War Two." *Journal of Contemporary History* 16, no. 1 (January 1981): 121.

Skålnes, Lars S. "Grand Strategy and Foreign Economic Policy: British Grand Strategy in the 1930s." *World Politics* 50, no. 4 (1998): 582–616.

Skodvin, Magne. "Norwegian Neutrality and the Question of Credibility." *Scandinavian Journal of History* 2, no. 1–4 (1977): 123–45.

Smart, Nick. "Four Days in May: The Norway Debate and the Downfall of Neville Chamberlain." *Parliamentary History* 17, no. 2 (1998): 215–43.

Wark, Wesley. "In Search of a Suitable Japan: British Naval Intelligence in the Pacific before the Second World War." *Intelligence and National Security* 1, no. 2 (1986): 189–211.

———. "Something Very Stern: British Political Intelligence, Moralism and Grand Strategy in 1939." *Intelligence and National Security* 5, no. 1 (1990): 150–70.

Witherell, Larry. "Lord Salisbury's 'Watching Committee' and the Fall of Neville Chamberlain, May 1940." *English Historical Review* 116, no. 469 (November 2001): 1134–66.

Zeitlin, Jonathan. "Flexibility and Mass Production at War: Aircraft Manufacture in Britain, the United States, and Germany, 1939–1945." *Technology and Culture* 36, no. 1 (1995): 46–79.

Books

Addison, Paul. *Churchill: The Unexpected Hero.* New York: Oxford University Press, 2006.

———. *The Road to 1945: British Politics and the Second World War.* London: Pimlico, 1994.

Alanbrooke, Lord. *War Diaries 1939–1940: Field Marshal Lord Alanbrooke.* Edited by Alex Danchev and Daniel Todman. London: Phoenix, 2002.

Alexander, Martin S. *The Republic in Danger: General Maurice Gamelin and the Politics of French Defence, 1933–1940.* Cambridge: Cambridge University Press, 1992.

Amery, Leo. *The Empire at Bay: The Leo Amery Diaries 1929–1945.* Edited by John Barnes and David Nicholson. London: Hutchinson, 1988.

Barnett, Correlli. *Engage the Enemy More Closely: The Royal Navy in the Second World War.* New York: Norton, 1991.

Beesly, Patrick. *Very Special Intelligence: The Story of the Admiralty's Operational Intelligence Centre 1939–1945.* London: Hamish Hamilton, 1977.

Behrens, C. B. A. *Merchant Shipping and the Demands of War.* London: HMSO, 1978.

Bell, Christopher M. *Churchill and Sea Power.* Oxford: Oxford University Press, 2013.

———. *The Royal Navy, Seapower and Strategy between the Wars.* Stanford, CA: Stanford University Press, 2000.

Bennett, G. H. *Survivors: British Merchant Seamen in the Second World War.* London: Hambledon Continuum, 2007.

Ben-Moshe, Tuvia. *Churchill: Strategy and History.* Boulder, CO: Lynne Rienner, 1992.

Best, Geoffrey. *Churchill and War.* London: Hambledon and London, 2005.

Birkenhead, Frederick Winston Furneaux Smith, Earl of. *Halifax: The Life of Lord Halifax.* London: Hamilton, 1965.

Blair, Clay. *The Hunters 1939–1942.* Vol. 1 of *Hitler's U-Boat War.* London: Weidenfeld and Nicolson, 2011.

Blake, Robert, and William R. Louis, eds. *Churchill: A Major New Assessment of His Life in Peace and War.* Oxford: Oxford University Press, 1993.

Blatt, Joel. *The French Defeat of 1940: Reassessments.* Providence, RI: Berghahn Books, 1998.

Bond, Brian. *Britain, France and Belgium 1939–1940.* 2nd ed. London: Brassey's, 1990.

Brodhurst, Robin. *Churchill's Anchor: Admiral of the Fleet Sir Dudley Pound.* Barnsley, UK: Leo Cooper, 2000.

Cadogan, Alexander. *The Diaries of Sir Alexander Cadogan, O.M., 1938–1945.* Edited by David Dilks. London: Cassell, 1971.

Central Statistical Office. *Statistical Digest of the War.* Rev. ed. London: HMSO, 1975.

Chalmers, W. S. *Max Horton and the Western Approaches.* London: Hodder and Stoughton, 1954.

Chamberlain, Neville. *The Neville Chamberlain Diary Letters.* Edited by Robert C. Self. Burlington, VT: Ashgate, 2000.

Channon, Henry. *Chips: The Diaries of Sir Henry Channon.* Edited by Robert Rhodes James. London: Weidenfeld and Nicolson, 1967.

Charmley, John. *Churchill: The End of Glory: A Political Biography.* London: Hodder and Stoughton, 1993.

Chester, D. N., ed. *Lessons of the British War Economy.* Westport, CT: Greenwood Press, 1972.

Churchill, Winston. *The Gathering Storm.* Vol. 1 of *The Second World War.* London: Cassell, 1948.

———. *Into Battle: The Speeches of Winston Churchill.* London: Cassell, 1941.

———. *Their Finest Hour.* Vol. 2 of *The Second World War.* London: Cassell, 1948.

Clews, Graham. *Churchill's Dilemma: The Real Story behind the Origins of the 1915 Dardanelles Campaign.* Santa Barbara, CA: Praeger, 2010.

Colville, John. *The Fringes of Power: Downing Street Diaries, 1939–1955.* New York: Norton, 1985.

Connelly, Mark. *Reaching for the Stars: A New History of Bomber Command in World War II.* London: I. B. Tauris, 2001.

Cosgrave, Patrick. *Churchill at War.* London: Collins, 1974.

Creswell, John. *Sea Warfare, 1939–1945: A Short History.* London: Longmans, Green, 1950.

Crozier, W. P. *Off the Record.* London: Hutchinson, 1973.

Cruickshank, Charles. *SOE in Scandinavia.* New York: Oxford University Press, 1986.

Dean, Maurice. *The Royal Air Force and the Two World Wars.* London: Cassell, 1979.

Derry, D. K. *The Campaign in Norway.* London: HMSO, 1952.

D'Este, Carlo, *Warlord: A Life of Churchill at War.* New York: Harper, 2008.

Dilks, David. *Neville Chamberlain.* New York: Cambridge University Press, 1984.

Dixs, Anthony. *The Norway Campaign and the Rise of Churchill 1940.* Barnsley, UK: Pen and Sword, 2014.

Eden, Anthony. *The Reckoning: The Eden Memoirs.* London: Cassell, 1965.

Fort, Adrian. *Prof: The Life of Frederick Lindemann.* London: Jonathan Cape, 2003.

Foynes, J. P. *The Battle of the East Coast (1939–1945).* Self-published, 1994.

Franks, Norman L. R. *U-Boat versus Aircraft.* Edited by Eric Zimmerman. London: Grub Street, 1998.

French, David. *Raising Churchill's Army: The British Army and the War against Germany, 1919–1945.* New York: Oxford University Press, 2000.

Fritz, Martin. *German Steel and Swedish Iron Ore, 1939–1945.* Göteborg, Sweden: Institute of Economic History of Gothenburg University, 1974.

Gates, Eleanor M. *End of the Affair: The Collapse of the Anglo-French Alliance, 1939–40.* London: George Allen and Unwin, 1981.

Gerrard, Craig. *The Foreign Office and Finland, 1938–1940: Diplomatic Sideshow.* London: Frank Cass, 2005.

Gibbs, N. H., J. R. M. Butler, J. M. A. Gwyer, John Ehrman, and Michael Howard. *Grand Strategy.* London: HMSO, 1956.

Gilbert, Martin, ed. *At the Admiralty, September 1939–May 1940.* Vol. 1 of *The Churchill War Papers.* New York: Norton, 1993.

———. *Churchill: A Life.* London: Pimlico, 2000.

———. *The Coming of War, 1936–1939.* Vol. 13 of *The Churchill Documents.* London: Heinemann, 1982.

———. *Finest Hour: Winston S. Churchill, 1939–1941.* London: Minerva, 1989.

———. *Never Surrender, May 1940–December 1940.* Vol. 2 of *The Churchill War Papers.* New York: Norton, 1995.

Gordon, G. A. H. *British Seapower and Procurement between the Wars: A Reappraisal of Rearmament.* Basingstoke, UK: Macmillan, 1987.

Gretton, Peter. *Convoy Escort Commander.* London: Cassell, 1964.

———. *Former Naval Person: Winston Churchill and the Royal Navy.* London: Cassell, 1968.

Grove, Eric, ed. *The Defeat of the Enemy Attack upon Shipping, 1939–1945.* Rev. ed. London: Routledge, 1997.

Gunsburg, Jeffery A. *Divided and Conquered: The French High Command and the Defeat of the West, 1940.* Westport, CT: Greenwood Press, 1979.

Haarr, Geirr H. *The Battle for Norway, April–June 1940.* Annapolis, MD: Naval Institute Press, 2010.

———. *The Gathering Storm: The Naval War in Northern Europe, September 1939–April 1940.* Barnsley, UK: Seaforth Publishing, 2013.

———. *The German Invasion of Norway: April 1940.* Annapolis, MD: Naval Institute Press, 2009.

Hague, Arnold. *The Allied Convoy System 1939–1945: Its Organization, Defense and Operation.* London: Chatham, 2000.

Hamer, David J. *Bombers versus Battleships: The Struggle between Ships and Aircraft for the Control of the Surface of the Sea.* St. Leonards, NSW: Allen and Unwin, 1998.

Hancock, W. K., and M. M. Gowing, ed. *British War Economy.* London: HMSO, 1949.

Harris, Kenneth. *Attlee.* London: Weidenfeld and Nicolson, 1982.

Harvey, Maurice. *Scandinavian Misadventure.* Tunbridge Wells, UK: Spellmount, 1990.

Haslop, Dennis. *Britain, Germany and the Battle of the Atlantic: A Comparative Study.* London: Bloomsbury Academic, 2013.

Hastings, Max. *Bomber Command.* London: Pan, 1999.

Hinsley, F. H. *British Intelligence in the Second World War.* Vol. 1. London: HMSO, 1993.

Holmes, Richard. *In the Footsteps of Churchill: A Study in Character.* New York: Basic Books, 2005.

Horne, Alistair. *To Lose a Battle: France 1940.* London: Penguin, 1988.

Hough, Richard. *Former Naval Person: Churchill and the Wars at Sea.* London: Weidenfeld and Nicolson, 1985.

———. *The Longest Battle: The War at Sea, 1939–45.* London: Cassell, 2003.

Imlay, Talbot C. *Facing the Second World War: Strategy, Politics, and Economics in Britain and France, 1938–1940.* Oxford: Oxford University Press, 2003.

Ironside, Edmund. *The Ironside Diaries, 1937–1940.* Edited by Roderick Macleod and Denis Kelly. London: Constable, 1962.

Ismay, Hastings Lionel. *The Memoirs of General the Lord Ismay.* London: Heinemann, 1960.

Jackson, Julian. *The Fall of France: The Nazi Invasion of 1940.* New York: Oxford University Press, 2003.

Jenkins, Roy. *Churchill.* London: Macmillan, 2001.

Keegan, John. *The Price of Admiralty: The Evolution of Naval Warfare.* New York: Viking, 1988.

Kersaudy, Francois. *Norway, 1940.* New York: St. Martin's Press, 1991.

Lamb, Richard. *Churchill as War Leader: Right or Wrong?* London: Bloomsbury, 1991.

Lawlor, Sheila. *Churchill and the Politics of War, 1940–1941.* New York: Cambridge University Press, 1994.

Levy, James P. *The Royal Navy's Home Fleet in World War II.* Basingstoke, UK: Palgrave Macmillan, 2003.

Llewellyn-Jones, Malcolm. *The Royal Navy and Anti-Submarine Warfare, 1917–49.* New York: Routledge, 2006.

Lukacs, John. *The Last European War, September 1939–December 1941.* New Haven: Yale University Press, 1976.

Lunde, Henrik O. *Hitler's Preemptive War: The Battle for Norway, 1940.* Havertown, PA: Casemate, 2009.

Macintyre, Donald. *U-Boat Killer.* London: Seeley Service, 1976.

Macmillan, Harold. *Blast of War.* London: Macmillan, 1967.

———. *Winds of Change 1914–1939.* London: Macmillan, 1966.

Manchester, William. *The Caged Lion: Winston Spencer Churchill, 1932–1940.* London: Cardinal, 1989.

Marder, Arthur J. *From the Dardanelles to Oran: Studies of the Royal Navy in War and Peace, 1915–1940.* London: Oxford University Press, 1974.

———. *Winston Is Back: Churchill at the Admiralty, 1939–40.* London: Longman, 1972.

Maurer, John H., ed. *Churchill and Strategic Dilemmas before the World Wars: Essays in Honour of Michael I. Handel.* London: Frank Cass, 2003.

McLachlan, Donald. *Room 39: Naval Intelligence in Action 1939–45.* London: Weidenfeld and Nicolson, 1968.

Ministry of Labour and National Service. *Manpower: The Story of Britain's Mobilization for War.* London: HMSO, 1944.

Moulton, J. L. *A Study of Warfare in Three Dimensions: The Norwegian Campaign of 1940.* Athens: Ohio University Press, 1968.

Munch-Petersen, Thomas. *The Strategy of Phoney War: Britain, Sweden, and the Iron Ore Question, 1939–1940.* Stockholm: Militarhistoriska Forlaget, 1981.

Naval Staff. *Mediterranean.* Vol. 1, *September 1939–October 1940.* London: Historical Section, Admiralty, 1952.

———. *Naval Operations of the Campaign in Norway, April–June 1940.* London: Historical Section, Admiralty, 1951.

Nevakivi, Jukka. *The Appeal That Was Never Made: The Allies, Scandinavia and the Finnish Winter War, 1939–1940.* London: C. Hurst, 1976.

Nicolson, Harold. *Harold Nicolson Diaries and Letters 1939–1945.* Edited by Nigel Nicolson. London: Collins, 1967.

Overy, R. J. *The Air War 1939–1945.* London: Europa, 1980.

———. *The Bombing War: Europe 1939–1945.* London: Allen Lane, 2013.

Padfield, Peter. *War Beneath the Sea: Submarine Conflict 1939–1945.* London: BCA, 1995.

Peden, G. C. *British Rearmament and the Treasury, 1932–1939.* Edinburgh: Scottish Academic Press, 1979.

Postan, M. M. *British War Production.* London: HMSO, 1975.

Price, Christopher. *Britain, America, and Rearmament in the 1930s: The Cost of Failure.* Houndmills, UK: Palgrave, 2001.

Prior, Robin. *Churchill's World Crisis as History.* London: Croom Helm, 1983.

———. *When Britain Saved the West: The Story of 1940.* New Haven: Yale University Press, 2015.

Ray, John. *The Battle of Britain: New Perspectives: Behind the Scenes of the Great Air War.* London: Arms and Armour, 1994.

Reith, John. *The Reith Diaries.* Edited by Charles Stuart. London: Collins, 1975.

Reynolds, David. *In Command of History: Churchill Fighting and Writing the Second World War.* New York: Basic Books, 2007.

Rhys-Jones, Graham. *Churchill and the Norwegian Campaign.* South Yorkshire, UK: Pen & Sword, 2018.

Ritchie, Sebastian. *Industry and Air Power: The Expansion of British Aircraft Production, 1935–41.* London: Frank Cass, 1997.

Roberts, Andres. *The Holy Fox: A Biography of Lord Halifax.* London: Weidenfeld and Nicolson, 1991.

Rohwer, Jurgen. *Chronology of the War at Sea, 1939–1945.* Edited by Gerhard Hummelchen. New York: Arco, 1973.

Roskill, Stephen. *Churchill and the Admirals.* London: Collins, 1977.

———. *Hankey: Man of Secrets.* Vol. 3. London: Collins, 1974.

———. *The War at Sea, 1939–1945.* Vol. 1. London: HMSO, 1954.

Salmon, Patrick, ed. *Britain and Norway in the Second World War.* London: HMSO, 1995.

Self, Robert C. *Neville Chamberlain: A Biography.* Aldershot, UK: Ashgate, 2006.

Shakespeare, Nicholas. *Six Minutes in May: How Churchill Unexpectedly Became Prime Minister.* London: Harvill Secker, 2017. E-book.

Sheffield, G. D., and Geoffrey Till, eds. *The Challenges of High Command: The British Experience.* Basingstoke, UK: Palgrave Macmillan, 2003.

Shores, Christopher F. *Fledgling Eagles.* London: Grub Street, 1991.

Smart, Nick. *British Strategy and Politics during the Phony War: Before the Balloon Went Up.* Westport, CT: Praeger, 2003.

———. *Neville Chamberlain.* London: Routledge, 2010.

Spears, Edward. *Assignment to Catastrophe.* London: Reprint Society, 1956.

Stewart, Graham. *Burying Caesar: Churchill, Chamberlain and the Battle for the Tory Party.* London: Phoenix, 2000.

Taylor, A. J. P. *Beaverbrook*. London: Hamish Hamilton, 1972.

Tennant, Peter. *Touchlines of War*. London: University of Hull Press, 1992.

Terraine, John. *Business in Great Waters: The U-Boat Wars, 1916–1945*. London: Cooper, 1989.

———. *The Right of the Line: The Royal Air Force in the European War, 1939–1945*. London: Hodder and Stoughton, 1985.

Thompson, R. W. *Churchill and Morton: The Quest for Insight in the Correspondence of Major Sir Desmond Morton and the Author*. London: Hodder and Stoughton, 1976.

Todman, Daniel. *Britain's War: Into Battle, 1937–1941*. London: Allen Lane, 2016.

Tooze, Adam. *The Wages of Destruction: The Making and Breaking of the German Economy*. London: Penguin, 2000. Penguin e-book.

Webster, Charles, and Noble Frankland. *The Strategic Air Offensive against Germany, 1939–1945*, Vols. 1 and 4. London: HMSO, 1961.

Index

Note: Subentries use WC to refer to Churchill. Maps are indicated by italicized page numbers. Unless otherwise noted, all ships are UK ships.

About the Author

Graham T. Clews is a teacher, now retired. He was born in Perth, Western Australia. He has had a lifetime passion for history and, in particular, military history. In 2008, his first book was published: *Churchill's Dilemma: The Real Story behind the 1915 Dardanelles Campaign*. *Churchill's Phoney War*, his PhD thesis, is his second book.

The Naval Institute Press is the book-publishing arm of the U.S. Naval Institute, a private, nonprofit, membership society for sea service professionals and others who share an interest in naval and maritime affairs. Established in 1873 at the U.S. Naval Academy in Annapolis, Maryland, where its offices remain today, the Naval Institute has members worldwide.

Members of the Naval Institute support the education programs of the society and receive the influential monthly magazine *Proceedings* or the colorful bimonthly magazine *Naval History* and discounts on fine nautical prints and on ship and aircraft photos. They also have access to the transcripts of the Institute's Oral History Program and get discounted admission to any of the Institute-sponsored seminars offered around the country.

The Naval Institute's book-publishing program, begun in 1898 with basic guides to naval practices, has broadened its scope to include books of more general interest. Now the Naval Institute Press publishes about seventy titles each year, ranging from how-to books on boating and navigation to battle histories, biographies, ship and aircraft guides, and novels. Institute members receive significant discounts on the Press' more than eight hundred books in print.

Full-time students are eligible for special half-price membership rates. Life memberships are also available.

For a free catalog describing Naval Institute Press books currently available, and for further information about joining the U.S. Naval Institute, please write to:

Member Services
U.S. Naval Institute
291 Wood Road
Annapolis, MD 21402-5034
Telephone: (800) 233-8764
Fax: (410) 571-1703
Web address: www.usni.org